Turkey in Africa

This book offers a comprehensive and multidisciplinary analysis of Turkey–Africa relations.

Bringing together renowned authors to discuss various dimensions of Turkey's African engagement while casting a critical analysis on the sustainability of Turkey–Africa relations, this book draws upon the rising power literature to examine how Turkish foreign policy has been conceptualized and situated theoretically. Moving from an examination of the economic and military dimensions of Turkey's policy including trade relations, business practices, security cooperation and peacekeeping discourse, it then illuminates the multilateral dimension of Turkey's Africa policy with a focus on soft power instruments of public diplomacy, humanitarian/development assistance, religious activities and airline diplomacy. Overall, it shows how Turkey's African opening can be integrated into its wider interest in gaining global power status and its desire to become a strong regional power.

This book will be of key interest to scholars and students of Turkish foreign policy/politics, African politics, and more broadly to international relations.

Elem Eyrice Tepeciklioğlu is a faculty member at Yasar University, International Law Implementation and Research Center, Turkey.

Ali Onur Tepeciklioğlu is a faculty member at Ege University, Department of International Relations, Turkey.

Routledge Studies in African Politics and International Relations

Series Editor: Daniel C. Bach, Emile Durkheim Centre for Comparative Politics and Sociology, Sciences Po Bordeaux, France.

Political Trust and the Politics of Security Engagement
China and the European Union in Africa
Benjamin Barton

Human Rights and the Judicialisation of African Politics
Peter Brett

The Finances of Regional Organisations in the Global South
Follow the Money
Edited by Ulf Engel and Frank Mattheis

African Foreign Policies
Selecting Signifiers to Explain Agency
Edited by Paul-Henri Bischoff

Regional Economic Communities and Peacebuilding in Africa
Lessons from ECOWAS and IGAD
Edited by Victor Adetula, Redie Bereketeab and Cyril Obi

Spatializing Practices of Regional Organizations during Conflict Intervention
The Politics of ECOWAS and the African Union
Jens Herpolsheimer

Personalist Rule in Africa and Other World Regions
Jeroen J.J. Van den Bosch

Turkey in Africa
A new emerging power?
Edited by Elem Eyrice Tepeciklioğlu and Ali Onur Tepeciklioğlu

For more information about this series please visit: https://www.routledge.com/Routledge-Studies-in-African-Politics-and-International-Relations/book-series/RSAPIR.

Turkey in Africa
A new emerging power?

Edited by
Elem Eyrice Tepeciklioğlu and Ali Onur Tepeciklioğlu

LONDON AND NEW YORK

First published 2022
by Routledge
2 Park Square, Milton Park, Abingdon, Oxon OX14 4RN

and by Routledge
605 Third Avenue, New York, NY 10158

Routledge is an imprint of the Taylor & Francis Group, an informa business

© 2022 selection and editorial matter, Elem Eyrice Tepeciklioğlu and Ali Onur Tepeciklioğlu; individual chapters, the contributors

The right of Elem Eyrice Tepeciklioğlu and Ali Onur Tepeciklioğlu to be identified as the authors of the editorial material, and of the authors for their individual chapters, has been asserted in accordance with sections 77 and 78 of the Copyright, Designs and Patents Act 1988.

All rights reserved. No part of this book may be reprinted or reproduced or utilised in any form or by any electronic, mechanical, or other means, now known or hereafter invented, including photocopying and recording, or in any information storage or retrieval system, without permission in writing from the publishers.

Trademark notice: Product or corporate names may be trademarks or registered trademarks, and are used only for identification and explanation without intent to infringe.

British Library Cataloguing in Publication Data
A catalogue record for this book is available from the British Library

Library of Congress Cataloging-in-Publication Data
Names: Tepeciklioğlu, Elem Eyrice, editor. | Tepeciklioğlu, Ali Onur, editor.
Title: Turkey in Africa : a new emerging power? / edited by Elem Eyrice Tepeciklioğlu and Ali Onur Tepeciklioğlu.
Description: First Edition. | New York : Routledge, 2021. | Series: Routledge Studies on the European Union and global order | Includes bibliographical references and index.
Identifiers: LCCN 2020054813 (print) | LCCN 2020054814 (ebook) | ISBN 9780367502218 (Hardback) | ISBN 9781003049579 (eBook)
Subjects: LCSH: Turkey–Politics and government–21st century. | Turkey–Politics and government–20th century. | Turkey–Foreign relations–Africa. | Humanitarianism–Political aspects–Turkey. | Humanitarian assistance, Turkish–History. | Democracy–Turkey–Religious aspects. | Islam and politics–Turkey. | Turkey–History.
Classification: LCC JQ1805.A7 T868 2021 (print) | LCC JQ1805.A7 (ebook) | DDC 327.56106–dc23
LC record available at https://lccn.loc.gov/2020054813
LC ebook record available at https://lccn.loc.gov/2020054814

ISBN: 978-0-367-50221-8 (hbk)
ISBN: 978-0-367-50345-1 (pbk)
ISBN: 978-1-003-04957-9 (ebk)

Typeset in Times New Roman
by Taylor & Francis Books

To our beloved son, Aras

Contents

List of illustrations   ix
List of contributors   xi
List of abbreviations   xv

Introduction: Contextualizing Turkey's Africa policy   1
ELEM EYRICE TEPECIKLIOĞLU AND ALI ONUR TEPECIKLIOĞLU

PART 1
Historical, theoretical and political foundations of Turkey–Africa relations   17

1 Theorizing Turkey's Africa policy: Turkey as a rising power   19
  ALI ONUR TEPECIKLIOĞLU

2 Ottoman Empire and Africa in the age of colonial expansion: Appreciating the loyalty of African Muslims, debating colonial rupture   38
  MUSTAFA SERDAR PALABIYIK

3 Turkey–Africa relations: A retrospective analysis   56
  NUMAN HAZAR AND ELEM EYRICE TEPECIKLIOĞLU

4 Being "Southern" without being of the Global South: The strange case of Turkey's South–South cooperation in Africa   75
  FEDERICO DONELLI

PART 2
Economic relations and military strategies   91

5 The political economy of Turkey–Africa relations   93
  HÜSEYIN EMRAH KARAOĞUZ AND SELMAN EMRE GÜRBÜZ

6 Interplay between identity and trade in Turkey–Africa relations   109
   SAMIRATOU DIPAMA AND EMEL PARLAR DAL

7 Turkey's military strategy in Africa   127
   BRENDON J. CANNON

8 Turkey and UNPKO in Africa: Reluctant multilateralism   144
   BIRSEN ERDOĞAN

PART 3
Turkey's soft power   165

9 "The voice of the voiceless": Turkey's public diplomacy in Africa   167
   SENEM B. ÇEVIK

10 Turkey's development assistance in Africa in the 2000s: Hybrid humanitarianism in the post-liberal era   182
   GONCA OĞUZ GÖK

11 Turkey's religious diplomacy in Africa   199
   ELEM EYRICE TEPECIKLIOĞLU

12 Turkish Airlines as a source of soft power in Africa   217
   ORÇUN SELÇUK

13 Turkey's diplomatic charm offensive in sub-Saharan Africa: Is Ankara winning the hearts and minds of Africans?   237
   ALEXIS HABIYAREMYE

   Conclusion: Turkey: Just another emerging power in Africa?   257
   ELEM EYRICE TEPECIKLIOĞLU AND ALI ONUR TEPECIKLIOĞLU

   Index   271

Illustrations

Figures

8.1	Turkey as a passive actor	152
8.2	Turkey as a political subject and active agent	158
8.3	Turkey's antagonistic relationship with the West	159
9.1	International students from Africa	174
12.1	Turkish Airlines' number of passengers (2004–2019)	223
12.2	Turkish Airlines' number of passengers by region in 2019	223
12.3	Amount of cargo carried by Turkish Airlines by region in 2019	224
12.4	Amount of cargo carried by Turkish Airlines per million passengers in 2019	224
12.5	Turkey–Africa trade volume (2009–2018)	230
12.6	Turkey–Africa border crossings (2009–2018)	231

Tables

3.1	The list of Turkey's diplomatic missions in sub-Saharan Africa	66
3.2	Presidential and prime ministerial visits to Africa between 2002 and 2020	67
6.1	Turkey–Africa import, export and total trade volume in million USD	113
6.2	Share of Turkey's imports, exports and total trade: Breakdown by region (%)	114
6.3	Share of North and sub-Saharan African countries in Turkey's total exports and imports (%)	116
6.4	Turkey's top six trading partners in Africa, in 2018, in million USD	117
6.5	Sub-Saharan Africa product exports and imports from Turkey in 2018	117
6.6	Main export and import items in Turkey's trade with North Africa	118
6.7	Africa's top five import and export partners in 2018 (%)	122
9.1	Yunus Emre Cultural Centers in Africa	172

x   *List of illustrations*

9.2	Maarif Foundation Schools in Africa	175
9.3	Anadolu Agency in Africa	177
10.1	Ages of humanitarianism vis-à-vis Africa	184
12.1	Turkish Airlines flight destinations by region	225
12.2	Turkey's diplomatic representation in Africa and Turkish Airlines flights	228
13.1	North Africa trust scores for key Turkish foreign policy pillars	250
13.2	Sub-Saharan Africa trust scores for key Turkish foreign policy pillars	251

Contributors

Brendon J. Cannon is assistant professor of International Security at the Institute of International & Civil Security (IICS), Khalifa University, Abu Dhabi, UAE. He earned a PhD in Political Science with an emphasis on International Relations at the University of Utah, USA (2009). His research interests include contextualizing domestic, regional and international relations in eastern Africa, regional security in the Persian Gulf and western Indian Ocean region, Turkey's foreign policy in Africa and the disconnect in discourse between the theories, possession and measurements of hard power and the application thereof. He is the author of multiple articles appearing in *African Security, Terrorism and Political Violence, Defence Studies, Third World Quarterly* and *African Security Review*. brendon.cannon@ku.ac.ae

Senem B. Çevik is a lecturer in the Department of Global and International Studies at University of California, Irvine and University of California, Los Angeles. Her research focuses on strategic communication, nation brands, conflict management, public diplomacy, political communication, humanitarian aid, peacebuilding and global media with an emphasis on Turkey and the Middle East. Dr. Çevik has a co-edited book (with Dr Philip Seib) titled *Turkey's Public Diplomacy* (Palgrave Macmillan, 2015). She is the author of numerous journal articles, book chapters and monographs in both English and Turkish. scevik@uci.edu

Samiratou Dipama is a faculty member in the department of Political Science and International Relations at Tokat Gaziosmanpaşa University. She holds a PhD in EU Politics and International Relations and a master's degree in International Relations from Marmara University (Turkey). She graduated with her bachelor's degree on Law and Political Sciences from University Ouaga2 (Burkina Faso). dipamamis@yahoo.fr

Federico Donelli is a postdoc researcher in International Relations at the University of Genoa, where he teaches History and Politics of the Middle East. His research fields have covered politics and security of the Middle East. Currently he is working on the process of militarization in the Horn

xii List of contributors

of Africa and the growing engagement of the Middle Eastern states in the region. Among his latest works "The Ankara Consensus: The Significance of Turkey's Engagement in Sub-Saharan Africa" in *Global Change, Peace & Security* and "Fluctuating Saudi and Emirati Alignment Behaviours in the Horn of Africa" in *International Spectator*. donellifed@gmail.com

Birsen Erdoğan is a full-time lecturer of International Relations at the Faculty of Law, Maastricht University. She teaches several IR courses at the University College Maastricht. Since 2016, she has been working on discourse analysis and foreign policy. She completed a book on R2P, humanitarian interventions and the Turkish foreign policy discourse (Routledge, 2017). After this book project, she was involved in several projects and coordinating research on the foreign policy discourses of several European countries including Germany and the UK on interventions abroad and the EU–Turkey deal. She is currently working on an article on R2P and its contestations to be published in a special issue of *Global Constitutionalism* and on a book chapter on aid as an instrument to be used in foreign policy. She is also busy editing a book on the Turkish Foreign Policy. She has regularly attended EISA conferences and EWIS workshops acting as convenor and section chair. birsen.erdogan@maastrichtuniversity.nl

Elem Eyrice Tepeciklioğlu is a faculty member at Yasar University, International Law Implementation and Research Center, Turkey. She completed her PhD in 2013 and conducted her post-doctoral studies at the Centre for African Studies, University of Cape Town, South Africa between 2014–2015. Her research interests include but are not limited to African affairs, Turkey–Africa relations and International Relations theory. She has several articles, book chapters and conference papers published in both English and Turkish. She is the author of the recently published book, *Africa in Turkish Foreign Policy: Recent Dynamics, Opportunities and Challenges* (in Turkish). elem.eyrice@yasar.edu.tr

Selman Emre Gürbüz is a PhD candidate at Kadir Has University's International Relations department. He took his undergraduate and graduate degrees from TOBB University of Economics and Technology's International Relations programs. His academic interests cover critical and reflexive approaches in IR, post-colonial studies, critical pedagogy, contemporary political theories, political sociology, historical sociology and international political economy. Recently, he is studying the metatheoretical critics of constructivism in IR within the context of culture and post-colonialism. semregurbuz@gmail.com

Alexis Habiyaremye is an associate professor of economics in the College of Business and Economics of the University of Johannesburg. Before joining the University of Johannesburg, he was a senior research specialist in the inclusive economic development division of the Human Science Research Council. He has previously worked in the departments of

Political Science & International Relations and Economics of Antalya International University. His research interests include the political economy of natural resources, industrial policy and strategic planning, export diversification as well as the economics of innovation and inclusive development. habiyaremye@merit.unu.edu; AHabiyaremye@hsrc.ac.za

Ambassador Numan Hazar (ret.) entered the Ministry of Foreign Affairs, Turkey in 1967. He served in various diplomatic posts abroad: in Ottawa, Canada; in Nicosia, Cyprus; in Washington, DC, USA, in New Delhi, India and in Bonn, Germany. In Ankara, he served at the Office of the President of the Turkish Republic as well as Coordinator for African Affairs, Director General for Bilateral Political Affairs (Ministry of Foreign Affairs). He was Ambassador to Lagos, Nigeria, Ambassador/Permanent Representative to the Council of Europe in Strasbourg and to UNESCO in Paris. He served as Ambassador/Diplomatic Adviser to the Minister of National Defense and later as Chairman of the Inspection Board of the Ministry of Foreign Affairs. He is the author of several books on international relations. His articles on different international issues were published in German, French and English. numan.hazar@gmail.com

Hüseyin Emrah Karaoğuz is an assistant professor at Kadir Has University, International Relations department. His research is mainly on international/comparative political economy and political economy of development. His articles have appeared in *Turkish Studies* and *Journal of Balkan and Near Eastern Studies* among others. emrah.karaoguz@khas.edu.tr

Gonca Oğuz Gök is an associate professor of International Relations at Marmara University, Faculty of Political Science. Her research focuses on Global governance, Norms and Institutions, the UN and Turkish Foreign Policy. She has various publications on these topics. Her most recent book chapter is Oguz Gok G. (2020) "'Humanitarianism' Transformed? Analyzing the Role of Transnational Humanitarian NGOs in Turkish Foreign Policy Toward the Middle East in the 2000s". In: Papuccular H., Kuru D. (eds) *A Transnational Account of Turkish Foreign Policy*. (Middle East Today) Palgrave Macmillan. goncaoguzgok@gmail.com

Mustafa Serdar Palabıyık received his BSc, MSc and PhD degrees from Middle East Technical University, Department of International Relations. Since 2010, he has been working at TOBB University of Economics and Technology, Department of Political Science and International Relations. He has recently studied at the European University Institute in Florence, Italy as a visiting scholar. His main areas of interest include Ottoman diplomatic history and Turkish foreign policy. He has published various books and articles on Ottoman–Turkish diplomatic history with a specific emphasis on entangled histories of Ottoman–European encounters. spalabiyik@etu.edu.tr

xiv List of contributors

Emel Parlar Dal is professor at Marmara University's Department of International Relations. She received her BA from Galatasaray University in 2001, her MA degrees respectively from Paris 1 Panthéon-Sorbonne University (2002) and Paris 3 Nouvelle Sorbonne University (2003). She received her PhD degree on International Relations from Paris 3 Sorbonne Nouvelle University (2009). She is currently the chair holder of a Jean Monnet Project on "EU and Emerging Powers in the Evolving Multilateralism." emelparlar@yahoo.com

Orçun Selçuk is a Visiting Assistant Professor of Political Science at Luther College. He received his PhD in Political Science from Florida International University. He has published articles on populism, polarization, democratization and soft power. He is currently working on a book project on polarizing populism and democratic backsliding in Turkey and Latin America. oselc001@fiu.edu

Ali Onur Tepeciklioğlu is a faculty member at Ege University, Department of International Relations, Turkey. He completed his PhD on International Relations from Middle East Technical University in 2016. He has been a visiting scholar at Aarhus University, Denmark and University of Cape Town, South Africa. His main areas of study include International Relations Theory, the English School and African affairs. He is the author of several articles, book chapters and conference papers on those issues. ali.tepeciklioglu@ege.edu.tr

List of abbreviations

AA	Anadolu Agency
AFAD	Disaster and Emergency Management Presidency
AfDB	African Development Bank
AFRICOM	United States Africa Command
AU	African Union
BAPA	Buenos Aires Plan of Action for Promoting and Implementing Technical Cooperation among Developing Countries
BRICS	Brazil, Russia, India, China, South Africa
CAR	Central African Republic
CGD	Center for Global Development
DAC	The OECD Development Assistance Committee
DEIK	Foreign Economic Relations Board of Turkey/Dis Ekonomik Ilişkiler Kurulu
DLP	Democratic Left Party/Demokratik Sol Parti (DSP)
DP	Democratic Party
EIC	Euro-Asian Islamic Council
EOI	Export-Oriented-Industrialization
EU	European Union
EUCAP Mali	European Union Capacity Building Mission in Mali
EUFOR RCA	European Union Military Operation in the Central African Republic
EUTM Mali	European Union Training Mission in Mali
FDI	Foreign Direct Investment
FLN	Front de Libération Nationale
FTA	Free Trade Agreement
G2P	Government to People
GNA	Government of National Accord
GNP	Gross National Product
GPEDC	Global Partnership for Effective Development Cooperation
GPRA	Gouvernement Provisoire de la République Algérienne
HNGO	Humanitarian Non-Governmental Organization
IBSA	India, Brazil, South Africa Dialogue Forum
IHH	Humanitarian Relief Foundation

IMF	International Monetary Fund
IO	International Organization
ISI	Import–Substitution–Industrialization
JDP	Justice and Development Party/Adalet ve Kalkinma Partisi (AKP)
KYM	Kimse Yok mu Solidarity and Aid Association
LNA	Libyan National Army
MANEM	Manufacture of Military Equipment
MENA	Middle East and North Africa
MIKTA	Mexico, Indonesia, South Korea, Turkey, Australia
MINURCAT	United Nations Mission in the Central African Republic and Chad
MINUSCA	United Nations Multidimensional Integrated Stabilization Mission in the Central African Republic
MINUSMA	United Nations Multidimensional Integrated Stabilization Mission in Mali
MONUC	United Nations Organization Mission in the Democratic Republic of the Congo
MONUSCO	United Nations Organization Stabilization Mission in the Democratic Republic of the Congo
MUSIAD	Independent Industrialists and Businessmen's Association/Mustakil Sanayici ve Is Adamlari Dernegi
NAM	Non-Aligned Movement
NAP	Nationalist Action Party/Milliyetci Hareket Partisi (MHP)
NATO	North Atlantic Treaty Organization
NeST	Network of Southern Think Tanks
NGO	Non-governmental Organization
NIEO	New International Economic Order
OCHA	United Nations Office for the Coordination of Humanitarian Affairs
ODA	Official Development Assistance
OECD	Organisation for Economic Co-operation and Development
OIC	Organization of Islamic Cooperation
ONUCI	United Nations Operation in Côte D'Ivoire
OSCE	Organization of Security and Cooperation in Europe
PCO	Program Coordination Office
PDP	People's Democratic Party/Halklarin Demokratik Partisi (HDP)
RPP	Republican People's Party/Cumhuriyet Halk Partisi (CHP)
SME	Small and Medium-Sized Enterprises
SSA	Sub-Saharan Africa
SSC	South–South Cooperation
TAF	Turkish Armed Forces
TAI	Turkish Aerospace Industries
TBMM	Turkish Parliament
TDV	Turkiye Diyanet Vakfi

List of abbreviations xvii

TET	Technical Cooperation Agreement
TFG	Transitional Federal Government of Somalia
TFP	Turkish Foreign Policy
THY	Turkish Airlines
TIKA	Turkish Cooperation and Coordination Agency
TIS	Turkish–Islamic Synthesis
TMF	Turkish Maarif Foundation/Turkiye Maarif Vakfı (TMV)
TOKI	Housing Development Administration of Turkey
TRT	Turkish Radio and Television
TSKGV	The Turkish Armed Forces Foundation
TUSIAD	Turkish Industry and Business Association/Turk Sanayicileri ve Is Insanlari Dernegi
TUSKON	Turkish Confederation of Businessmen and Industrialists
UAE	United Arab Emirates
UK	United Kingdom
UN	United Nations
UNAMID	United Nations African Union Hybrid Operation in Darfur
UNAMSIL	United Nations Mission in Sierra Leone
UNCTAD	United Nations Conference on Trade and Development
UNDP	United Nations Development Program
UNGA	United Nations General Assembly
UNHCR	United Nations Refugee Agency
UNIFIL	United Nations Interim Force in Lebanon
UNIOSIL	United Nations Integrated Office in Sierra Leone
UNMIL	United Nations Mission in Liberia
UNMIS	United Nations Mission in Sudan
UNMISS	United Nations Mission in South Sudan
UNOCI	United Nations Operation in Côte d'Ivoire
UNOSOM II	United Nations Operation in Somalia II
UNPK	United Nations Peacekeeping
UNPKO	United Nations Peacekeeping Operation
UNSC	United Nations Security Council
UNSOM	United Nations Assistance Mission in Somalia
US/USA	United States of America
WP	Welfare Party/Refah Partisi (RP)
WTO	World Trade Organization
YEE	Yunus Emre Institute
YTB	Presidency For Turks Abroad and Related Communities

Introduction

Contextualizing Turkey's Africa policy

Elem Eyrice Tepeciklioğlu and Ali Onur Tepeciklioğlu

Turkey's opening to Africa started in the late 1990s. Yet, referring to the Ottoman past in Africa, many experts note that Turkey's involvement in the continent is not a new phenomenon (i.e. see: Hazar 2011, 2012; Karaca 2000; Karagul and Arslan 2013; Kavas 2005, 2006; Tandogan 2013; Ucar 2000). Relations between the Ottomans and Africa date back several centuries as the former had a presence particularly in North Africa as well as in the Horn of Africa. The relationship between the Ottoman Empire and those territories that were once subject to the Ottoman rule is not depicted in colonial terms within the utterances of government officials, but instead, there is an overemphasis on the benevolent character of Ottomans in their relations with those peripheral provinces.[1] The official rhetoric suggests that the Ottoman Empire did not embark on a colonial project and even highlights its prevention of colonial expansion especially in northern and eastern parts of the continent.[2] This rigorously created narrative built on a common history and cultural ties does not explain the absence of solid relations with African nations after the establishment of the Turkish Republic until the late 1990s. While it might be true that the Ottomans have a non-colonial record in the continent, so do the other (re)emerging powers rapidly enhancing their role and involvement in Africa including China, Russia, India, Japan and South Korea.

It is also the case that the successor of the Ottoman Empire, the Turkish Republic, showed only a limited interest in developing relations with African countries. Turkish state formation of this period, coupled with other domestic and foreign policy priorities, largely explains this neglect towards Africa. Adopting Western values and institutions, the foreign policymakers of the newly established republic aimed at integrating the country with the Western world while rejecting Turkey's Ottoman past, Islamic identity and cultural proximity to the Eastern world. It is also because of this Western-oriented foreign policy that the young republic distanced itself from non-Western countries. The fact that most African nations were still under colonial rule complicated Turkey's relations with Africa. However, the decolonization period saw a similar policy attitude towards Africa and relations with the continent remained dormant. Unlike Africa's other international partners, particularly China and Russia that provided significant amounts of military, financial and technical assistance to African nationalist movements in their fight with colonialism and racism, Turkey was not an ardent supporter of the anti-colonial rhetoric and African independence struggles. Although Turkey recognized the independence of those African countries, it was mostly after its NATO (North Atlantic Treaty Organization) allies lost their colonies or granted them independence. Yet, Turkey's pro-Western policies and its attitude towards the independence movements unfolding across the continent was to a large extent a product of Cold War dynamics.

Turkey's status in the early years of the Cold War was defined by its membership of NATO and its alliance with the Western bloc. Turkey entered the Western security system in order to counter Soviet threat and to complement its Westernization/modernization efforts. Having established close relations with the United States of America (USA), Turkey benefited from the Marshall Aid Program that boosted its defense capabilities and helped economic recovery. It also joined all Western institutions established after World War II including the Council of Europe, United Nations (UN) and the OEEC (Organization for European Economic Cooperation). Turkey's position towards the decolonization process in Africa was therefore constrained by its concerns about Soviet intentions and its alignment with the West. In the mid-1960s, Turkish efforts to approach African countries to gain their support for its Cyprus cause failed to produce tangible results. Combined with other factors such as the lack of political interest towards the region, financial distress and a fragile democracy scattered by military coups almost every 10 to 20 years, Turkey's engagement with Africa remained limited for a long time.

The 1970s saw the deterioration of relations with the West mainly because of the Cyprus issue and anti-Western sentiments prevalent in Turkish society. Hit by the oil shocks and American arms embargo of the same period, Turkey experienced severe economic depression and started to look for new allies in order to contain its isolation and to overcome the economic repercussions of the oil crisis and US embargo. During this period, Turkish foreign policy (TFP) evolved from a strictly security-oriented understanding to a new approach accepting the importance of the economic dimension. Meanwhile, Turkey was looking again for international support for its Cyprus cause. Having realized that its Western-oriented foreign policy led to its alienation in the developing world, Turkey sought deeper ties with the Third World including African countries. The Turkish foreign ministry designed an opening plan to Africa in order to exploit the opportunities Africa can offer not only as an international partner but also as an attractive market. However, this foreign policy change was not backed with a systematic and consistent approach and therefore could not yield any results. Turkey remained a distant partner for Africa while keeping its pro-Western orientation.

The search for foreign policy alternatives continued in the 1980s and 1990s in conjunction with the country's economic liberalization. Following the end of the Cold War, Turkey approached the Balkans, the Caucasus, Central Asia and Middle East but Africa stayed at the periphery of foreign policy priorities until the late 1990s. The post-Cold War period also saw the resurrection of actors in the international arena including China which was fast to increase its presence in Africa. In the meantime, recent developments in Turkish foreign policy propelled the incumbent government to look for new approaches by extending its influence beyond its regional neighborhood. Without the Soviet threat, Turkey's geopolitical significance to the Western world diminished. Frustrated by its EU membership process and failed in its attempt to create a Turkic community, Turkey started to follow a more assertive and multidimensional foreign policy. This increased foreign policy activism is manifested in the expansion into new areas including Africa and Latin America. The "Action Plan for Opening up to Africa," the background document for developing a systematic Africa policy adopted in 1998, listed detailed measures to forge ties with African countries. The first initiatives for the implementation of the plan began under the auspices of the incumbent coalition government, however, tragic incidents including the 1999 earthquake and the 2000–2001 financial crisis impeded its implementation until the Justice and Development Party (JDP) assumed office in 2002. The JDP inherited the foreign policy activism of the earlier periods and developed it with a heavy emphasis on the use of soft power. Turkey's increasing engagement in Africa should be appreciated in this context.

Before the JDP's coming to power, Turkey showed an interest in Africa only when deteriorating relations with its Western allies compelled the Turkish elites to look for foreign policy alternatives and support for its foreign policy actions, first in the 1960s then in the 1970s and in the late 1990s. Even in those few cases, Turkey was not seeking to establish a long-term partnership with Africa, but instead, its increasing interest in the continent was driven by its short-term and pragmatic considerations. Turkey expected African support especially in cases where relations with its traditional allies were turbulent due to political fallout over particular foreign policy issues and it felt isolated in the international area. Apart from these exceptional moments, Africa was a neglected area for Turkish foreign policy. The new higher priority given to Africa by the JDP also came at a time when relations with Ankara's Western partners weakened due to disagreements over particular foreign policy issues. Turkey's frustrations with US policies in the Middle East and its ambivalent relationship with the European Union (EU) mostly explain its search for new partners. To this end, Ankara also strived to renew old relationships especially with former Ottoman territories. Turkey's recent interest towards Africa is also a part of the JDP government's new foreign policy understanding that assumes a greater international role for Turkey.

Why Africa?

After assuming power in the early 2000s, the JDP embraced the traditional pro-Western foreign policy of the earlier periods with a commitment to the EU membership process. Following the September 11 attacks, Turkey also regained its strategic value for the Western world. It would not be wrong to argue that EU–Turkey relations were at their highest especially during JDP's first period in power (2002–2007). Turkey initiated a series of EU-led reforms and enhanced relations with neighboring Middle East countries in an effort to advance its role in regional and global governance. However, the second term of the JDP government (2007–2011) saw the stagnation of EU–Turkey relations and the slowing down of the reform process. Turkey's rapprochement with its neighbors and increasing relations with distant regions during the same period led many to question if Turkey was breaking away from its Western-dependent foreign policy with an emerging Eastern orientation. This changing nature of Turkish foreign policy was mostly related to disappointment with Turkey's long-standing EU membership process. The shift towards a more balanced foreign policy in search of the diversification of allies was also facilitated by the economic recovery and the stabilization of domestic politics. It was also mostly during the JDP's second term that Turkey started to demonstrate a firm interest in enhancing its presence in Africa. Turkey's global ambitions and regional leadership claims have also grown during this period.

In its search to diversify its foreign policy options and to project its regional power ambitions, Turkey has sought more involvement in regional and global affairs. Turkey's aspiration for power in the global arena has attracted an increased amount of attention in academic circles. As the first chapter will explore in more detail, different theories are employed as a framework to analyze Turkey's new foreign policy orientation and its global aspirations. The book argues, however, that the rising powers literature best reflects Turkey's African engagement. This is not because Turkey's ability matches those of the established powers in the continent but because Turkey, as other rising powers, has advantages in issue-specific areas.

The extant literature studying Turkey's rising power status refers to Turkey's distinct geopolitical position/geostrategic importance, active foreign policy and increasing global aspirations while its democratic credentials and increasing economic performance were once applauded as contributing to its rising power claims. On the other hand, a defining feature of Turkey's status ambitions is its challenge to the current world order, which is perhaps best manifested in President Recep Tayyip Erdogan's widely cited expression, "the world is bigger than five." Turkey's own conception of international order reflects its desire to have a larger influence in international affairs and reform the structure of international organizations, most notably, the UN. Here, Africa provides a space where Turkey can present itself as a humanitarian, caring and donor power and establish new alliances to support its vision of a new world order and to set up its own foreign policy agenda. As Turkey attempts to project its influence beyond its periphery, its call for an equitable world order and restructuring of the UN system finds resonance in African countries that have been long advocating for a more representative global governance.

JDP leadership is now more eager to show Turkey's determination to contribute to global peace and security. Its increasing participation in conflict management and mediation efforts in different contexts together with a heavy investment in soft power capacity and humanitarian involvement even in distant geographies is part of its global ambitions. As Turkey's African engagement boosts its rising power status in various ways, the continent has emerged as a foreign policy priority especially since the second half of the 2000s. This is probably best demonstrated by the increasing number of high-level visits and new embassies across the continent. Turkey has enhanced its diplomatic presence in Africa from 12 to 42 between 2009 and 2020. On the other hand, African embassies in Ankara increased from 10 to 35 in the same period (MFA n.d.). Over the last decade, President Recep Tayyip Erdogan has made over 50 visits to Africa under his tenure first as prime minister and then as president including his visits to Algeria, Senegal and Zambia in early 2020. Hundreds of businessmen accompany the official visits of senior statesmen to African countries. In line with this "diplomatic push," Turkey's bilateral trade with Africa dramatically increased. According to the Turkish Statistical Institute (2020), Turkey's trade volume with African countries was US$3.2 billion before the adoption of the opening plan in the late 1990s while it reached US$21.5 billion in 2019. Although much of this trade concentrates on Northern African countries, trade relations with sub-Saharan Africa (SSA) are also on the rise.

Growing trade relations with African countries is important given that Turkey's interest in the continent is mostly motivated by economic imperatives. Africa provides new opportunities for Turkish firms seeking alternative export markets and investment destinations. Turkey's dependence on energy imports, raising concerns over its energy security and fragile relations with neighboring Middle Eastern countries and Russia, being Turkey's traditional energy partners, explains the recent interest in Africa's energy industry. Yet, Turkey's search for the diversification of economic relations is not a new phenomenon. It can be traced back to the economic liberalization of the 1980s. This period saw the integration of the Turkish economy with world markets and the emergence of a new bourgeoisie that started to explore alternative market opportunities as European markets were already exploited by TUSIAD (Turkish Industry and Business Association), established back in the early 1970s. Defined by many as "Anatolian tigers" or "Islamic capital," this business community was also described as "conservative bourgeoisie" (Atli 2011) or "devout bourgeoisie" (Gumuscu and Sert 2009) that represented a conservative group of Anatolian businessmen. This business community later provided the JDP government's electoral support base, emerged as an important actor in the foreign policymaking process and backed the opening decision to different regions including Africa (Atli 2011, 111–116).

Economic considerations are very influential in shaping Turkey's foreign policy choices, however, relations with African countries are also expected to serve Ankara's short-term foreign policy interests. This includes Turkey's bid for a non-permanent seat at the United Nations Security Council (UNSC). Being one of the largest regional groups in the UN, the voting weight of the African group is now even more important for Turkey in its quest for like-minded allies to cooperate on fundamental foreign policy issues. So, it is hardly a surprise that the honeymoon period in Turkey–Africa relations coincides with Turkey's candidacy endeavors for Security Council membership for the period 2009–2010. When Turkey approached African countries for its UNSC membership, the majority of African countries supported Turkey's position. Turkey later sought to extend its influence in Africa by using this position. For example, in his visit to Tanzania in early 2009, Turkish President Abdullah Gul underlined that most of the issues discussed in the Security Council are related to Africa and pledged Turkey's support for Africa's priorities: "The Turkish Republic will be the spokesman for Africa at the UN. It will support Africa on all of its issues" (Uslu 2009).

In his seminal article published in the same year, Kirisci (2009, 50) asserts that

> Africa is not exactly a part of the world where Turkey has geo-political or geo-strategic interests beyond the short-term interest of mobilizing African support for a non-permanent seat in the Security Council, which Turkey was seeking. Hence, Rosecrance would have probably considered Turkey's interest in Africa by and large a typical manifestation of the rise of the trading state.
>
> (Kirisci 2009, 50)

Yet, Ankara's increasing engagement in Africa is not solely driven by its short-term interests or economic concerns. Turkey's higher ambitions to extend its area of influence steer its Africa policy while increased political and economic interactions with African countries serves its regional and global power projections. As it claims a more prominent role in international platforms, Turkey expects African support for its foreign policy causes.

On the other hand, Turkey's increasing engagement in Africa came at a time when competition in the continent had become ever greater. Africa's ascendance in world politics accompanied by improvements in its growth rate increases the appetite of external powers seeking to expand their roles in the continent. With its young and vibrant population, abundant natural resources, large consumer market, investment opportunities and strategic position, Africa has attracted much attention from both traditional and rising powers. This has contributed to the emergence of a novel narrative of

Africa that presents growing opportunities for foreign actors. Turkey's interest towards the continent is interesting given that it has recently re-emerged as an alternative partner for Africa while its earlier presence in the region dates back to the Ottoman period.

Structure of the book

This volume aims at analyzing Turkey's engagement in the continent through a comprehensive and analytical perspective. In this sense, it discusses Turkish experience in previous Ottoman provinces and asks why Turkey is involved in SSA after nearly a century of neglect, what the Turkish government does to bridge this gap in relations and what it can offer to Africa at large. It also explores how Turkey distinguishes its efforts from other emerging (or re-emerging) powers having diverging intentions in their African involvement. Contributors to this volume critically examine Turkey's foreign policy tools used in the continent including educational activities, scholarship opportunities, humanitarian assistance, development cooperation, trade relations, religious activities and airline diplomacy.

The book is structured into three major parts each comprising four chapters. The first part opens with a theoretically guided chapter on Turkey's relations with Africa. This first chapter by Ali Onur Tepeciklioglu covers recent conceptual and theoretical debates on Turkish foreign policy and locates Turkey's Africa strategy within its general foreign policy framework. It also presents how Turkish foreign policy exhibits the characteristics of a rising power in a number of ways while arguing that Turkey's rising power ambitions most suitably explain its Africa policy. It also elaborates the different ways rising powers deal with Africa, including the role they play in Africa's development, their involvement in the peacebuilding domain or their trade relations with the continent. As such, the chapter both serves as a theoretical background to the entire volume and helps the reader to better understand the main characteristics of Turkey's relationship with the continent.

The second chapter by Mustafa Serdar Palabiyik provides an overview of the Ottoman Empire's direct and indirect rule in Africa and its relations with African territories. In doing so, Palabiyik refers to archival documents as well as late nineteenth and early twentieth-century Ottoman travelogues. The use of primary sources helps us to comprehend Ottoman perceptions of the continent in a volatile period. He notes that Ottoman responses to European colonial penetration were twofold: the strengthening of loose administrative links with Ottoman provinces in the Maghreb through centralization and contacting African Muslims in Saharan and sub-Saharan regions in order to demonstrate the caliphal authority over local Muslim communities and to encourage them to resist Western colonialism. In exploring how this Ottoman past shapes contemporary Turkish foreign policy discourse towards Africa, the chapter reveals the dichotomies and parallels between Ottoman travelers' perception of Africa and the current TFP discourse. It concludes that Ottoman travelers' paradoxical approach to colonialism was not much reflected in contemporary Turkish discourse.

Drawing on the historical and theoretical foundations of Turkey's relations with Africa developed in the first two chapters, the third chapter authored by Elem Eyrice Tepeciklioglu and ambassador (ret.) Numan Hazar, who was assigned by the then Minister of Foreign Affairs, Ismail Cem, to draft the "Action Plan for Opening up to Africa," outlines the evolution of Turkey's Africa relationship starting from the establishment of the Turkish Republic. They discuss how Turkish foreign policy priorities following the establishment of the Republic hindered Turkey's interest in Africa. Having firsthand information on the preparation of the opening plan, Hazar's remarks are particularly insightful in evaluating the major steps that were taken for the implementation of the plan. This chapter goes on to evaluate the motivating factors that guided Ankara's current African involvement and to explore the shifting dynamics of Turkey–Africa relations. Other chapters in the book elaborate the current state of Turkey's African engagement in different areas, so, the focus of the third chapter is the historical overview of Turkey's Africa relationship.

The last few years have seen Turkey increasingly enhance its developmental role in Africa. The tools used in implementing its development and humanitarian projects in the continent employs most of the elements visible in South–South cooperation (SSC) such as non-conditionality, horizontality, respect for sovereignty, non-interference in internal affairs and anti-imperialist narratives. The southern dimension of Turkey's Africa policy is presented by Federico Donelli in Chapter 4. Donelli examines the determinants and the main features of Turkish application of SSC in its Africa policy and reviews how Turkey's economic, political and geographical considerations, in addition to the ideological preferences of the JDP government, are very much connected to the inclination towards the so-called Global South. However, the chapter also highlights that the Turkish model of development assistance occupies a unique position because it adopts the peculiarities of both traditional donors (DAC) and the SSC. Arguing that the Turkish approach places Turkey in a middle position between the North and the Global South, Donelli also notes that Turkey presents itself as provider of an alternative development model that involves trade and investment relations, technology transfer and knowledge sharing.

As discussed before, the economic incentives and business interests of the private sector also guided Turkey's expanding relations with African nations. Similar to Africa's other external partners, Turkey employs a mixture of soft power instruments and trade relations in order to support its strategic interests in the region. For example, its aid activities complement business ventures and provide the basis for its military expansion. Divided into four chapters, the second part of the book focuses on these economic and military aspects of Turkey's Africa policy. For example, Chapter 5 deals with the political economy of Turkey–Africa relations. The existing literature often concentrates on Turkey's search for new markets when discussing the economic imperatives that form the basis for Turkey's Africa strategy. Yet very little has been written on the relationship between business groups and the state when evaluating the factors that underline Turkey's Africa policy. By elaborating the nature of state–business relations, Emrah Karaoguz and Selman Emre Gurbuz trace the economic drivers of Turkey's increasing African involvement to neoliberal restructuring in the 1980s. They note that Turkey's trade-oriented foreign policy and the newly emerging economic actors during this period explain the search for alternative markets. Because Western markets were already penetrated by the secular business circles, this new business class, representing Anatolia's conservative capitalists, pushed up to access new markets in the Middle East and in Africa, regions that were not traditionally targeted by the secular economic elites. As argued by the authors, these conservative businessmen soon played leading roles in shaping the country's foreign economic policy and fostering economic relations with Africa.

Another motivating factor that explains Africa's increasing importance for Turkish businesses is the country's deteriorating relations with its traditional trade partners. Chapter 6 by Samiratou Dipama and Emel Parlar Dal discusses Turkey's trade relations with African countries and notes that Turkish policymakers used trade both as a means to normalize relations with Turkey's immediate neighborhood and to build relations with distant regions including Africa, Latin America and Asia. In assessing the role trade plays in Turkey's Africa policy, Parlar Dal and Dipama use a social constructivist approach to locate Turkey as a newly constructed trading partner of Africa among other developing/emerging countries. They aim at understanding the main patterns and features of the trade–identity nexus in Turkey–Africa relations through the use of statistical data. The chapter argues that Turkey's trade policy towards the continent is part of its changing identity and role in international politics. Trade policies towards Africa would in turn bolster its status as a rising power. Turkey's economic engagement in Africa is dwarfed by Africa's traditional Western partners and it is often smaller than that of other rising powers such as China and India. However, despite existing challenges, the authors maintain, Turkey remains an ambitious actor, which is likely to increase its assertiveness and to consolidate its identity as an emerging trading partner in Africa.

Although Turkey's Africa policy focused mainly on soft power instruments, it recently started to integrate hard power qualities. This includes Turkey's increasingly visible military involvement in different African contexts. For example, in 2017, Turkey opened its largest overseas military facility in Somalia's capital, Mogadishu in order to contribute to the country's post-conflict transformation and state-building process. Some commentators have also taken the recent deal signed between Turkey and Sudan on the renovation of Sudan's strategically located Suakin Island as another attempt at military deployment in the Horn of Africa. On the other hand, Turkey's deep involvement in the Libyan crisis raises concerns of its regional rivals including Saudi Arabia, Egypt and the United Arab Emirates who see it as a sign of Turkey's military ambitions in the region. Turkey's growing military and security interactions with Africa are explored in Chapter 7 by Brendon J. Cannon. Against those arguments that Turkey is emerging as a military actor with an increasing presence especially in the Horn of Africa, Cannon argues that Ankara possesses neither a long-term military strategy towards the continent, nor does it have the hard power capabilities to do so. Instead, Turkey's use of hard power elements in Africa aims at serving its wider foreign policy ambitions. It is also noted that a combination of Turkey's national security and business interests informs its relations and actions in North Africa that lies in Turkey's immediate vicinity. On the other hand, its security interactions in SSA, that is far from its traditional sphere of interest and influence, have generally been ad hoc and opportunistic, exhibiting four basic features: military facilities or bases, peacekeeping, security assistance, and training and arms sales.

Although Ankara's security concerns do not dominate its Africa strategy, it has increased its peacebuilding and peacekeeping initiatives in different African contexts. Still, its participation in UN peacekeeping operations (UNPKO) has been rather limited. Chapter 8 by Birsen Erdogan argues that Turkey's reluctant contribution to the UNPKO is a result of its identity constructions of itself and of others. By taking a post-structuralist position, Erdogan reviews the discursive constructions towards the support (or lack) of UN peacekeeping operations in SSA. For this purpose, the author analyzed the proceedings of debates in the Turkish Parliament on Turkey's contributions to the three UN peacekeeping operations, namely, Somalia, Congo, Mali and Central African Republic (together). Despite being very modest, Turkey's contributions to the UNPKO help to establish a narrative portraying Turkey as a country with no imperialist agenda—as opposed to Africa's traditional partners which are causing these conflicts in Africa. Referring to the literature on the rising powers and their contributions to the UNPKO, Erdogan also discusses how Turkey distinguishes its peacekeeping efforts from those powers as well as Africa's Western partners.

Turkey's African engagement draws on a variety of soft power tools and strategies. The chapters in the third part investigate the multiple dimensions of Turkey's soft power investment in Africa. A detailed analysis of Turkey's public diplomacy efforts in the continent with a special focus on state-based cultural, educational and broadcasting initiatives is the subject of Chapter 9 by Senem Cevik. By examining the efforts of Yunus Emre Institute (YEE) Cultural Centers, Turkish Scholarships of the Presidency for Turks Abroad and Related Communities, Maarif Foundation and Anadolu Agency, Cevik elaborates the extent of Turkey's public diplomacy in Africa. The chapter notes that Turkey's growing interest in Africa overlaps with the institutionalization of public diplomacy within TFP. It also argues that the recent JDP government and Gulenist split shaped Turkey's public diplomacy and hampered its aspirations to be a rising power in Africa. As discussed in the chapter, following the government–Gulen rift that accelerated especially after the failed coup d'état in 2016, Turkey started to invest in building its own public diplomacy infrastructure with a special focus in three areas: educational exchanges, cultural diplomacy and international broadcasting in order to counter the influence of the Gulen network, a former political ally, that was assigned Turkey's public diplomacy efforts.

Turkey's aid activities in Africa, which have substantially increased in recent years, have an increasing role in expressing Turkish soft power. As also discussed in Chapter 5 by Donelli, Turkey seeks to portray itself as an important humanitarian power offering a different development model that is less interest driven. A detailed analysis of Turkish aid to Africa is given by Gonca Oguz Gok in Chapter 10. Through a critical assessment of the rise of humanitarianism as a niche area in TFP, Oguz Gok explores Turkey's development cooperation activities towards Africa with specific reference to the nexus between government agencies and other humanitarian NGOs (HNGOs) in constructing Turkey's "donor state" identity. The chapter compares and contrasts Turkey's development cooperation activities with those of traditional donors and rising powers in order to depict any similarities as well as differences in Turkey's humanitarianism. Oguz Gok argues that Turkey's development cooperation activities in Africa could best be described as "hybrid humanitarianism" which encompasses the aims, means and ends of both liberal humanitarianism and rising powers' emerging humanitarian efforts, yet also differs from both by its attempt to offer an alternative Turkish aid model. The chapter also elaborates the place of religion in shaping Turkey's humanitarian practices in Africa.

This religious dimension in Turkey's Africa policy is further elaborated in Chapter 11 by Elem Eyrice Tepeciklioglu. The chapter explores the evolving role of religion in formulating TFP and argues that the instrumentalization of religion as a foreign policy tool accelerated under the JDP rule. Accordingly, Turkey's use of religious practices has become an indispensable part of its African engagement. As Turkey employs religion in legitimizing its foreign policy agenda, countries with predominantly Muslim populations receive more Turkish religious initiatives. Turkey's religious outreach is implemented by public institutions including Turkey's Presidency of Religious Affairs (Diyanet), Turkiye Diyanet Vakfi (Turkish Diyanet Foundation: TDV) and the Turkish Cooperation and Coordination Agency (TIKA) as well as Turkish NGOs. Most of those NGOs operating in Africa have religious motivations and increase their aid activities in religious months. They often act in harmony with public institutions in a way to complement Turkey's Africa policy and help to spread Turkey's religious presence in the continent. The chapter concludes that this religious dimension distinguishes Turkey's engagement in Africa from many of the rising players.

In addition to Turkey's humanitarian engagement, public diplomacy initiatives and religious activities, state-controlled Turkish Airlines also contributes to Turkey's soft power capacity in Africa, increases its regional reputation and complements its rising power status. On several occasions, senior officials emphasized that Africa remains the priority for the airline company. Chapter 12 by Orcun Selcuk begins with an overview of the relationship between national airlines and foreign policy and notes that political factors have a major influence on the operations of airline companies. This includes Turkish Airlines which has traditionally been a part of the Turkish foreign policy toolkit. As the chapter examines in more detail, Turkish Airlines' use as a foreign policy tool has been more overt under the JDP government. It argues that the outline of Turkish Airlines' growth strategy is in parallel with the JDP governments' foreign policy objectives, which is visible in the increasing number of aviation routes to Africa. These new routes boost cultural connections with African people and facilitate commercial relations as well.

In expanding its presence across the continent, Turkey seeks to present itself as a country that follows a different approach than Africa's traditional partners, a discourse that frames Turkey as an ally and friend to Africa. The crucial question here is how such political discourses find resonance in African countries and how African countries respond to Turkey's engagement in Africa. The last chapter by Alexis Habiyaremye therefore examines African perceptions towards Turkey's growing influence in the continent. While the existing literature studies different dimensions of Turkey's Africa links, African views of Turkey's role and profile in the region have not been surveyed before. Arguing the long-term success of Turkey's involvement in Africa depends on its ability to shape positive perceptions among Africans, this chapter explores African attitudes by focusing on five pillars of Turkey's African engagement: diplomatic intensification, involvement in Africa's peace and security matters, development cooperation and humanitarian assistance, Turkey–Africa trade and investment bridges, and education and cultural exchanges. Despite the various challenges posed by the current global pandemic, COVID-19 (i.e. the slow data collection process, travel restrictions and the low response rate), Habiyaremye was able to collect data through key informant interviews with government officials, academics, civil society members and sector actors and through a survey that was administered to respondents based in four out of the five regional subdivisions of the continent. The research confirms that evaluations of Turkey's Africa policy by Africans tend to be mostly positive despite mutual knowledge gaps.

Taken together, the chapters in this volume cover various dimensions of Turkey–Africa relations and identify areas where further participation with African countries is possible. The book goes into some detail for areas in which Turkey is more active and questions the impact of Turkey's presence in the continent. As the contributors in this book make evident, there are some contradictions in Turkey's Africa policy, despite its rapidly expanding role in the continent. The publication of the book comes in the wake of a serious economic crisis, growing concerns over authoritarianism and democratic backsliding at home coupled with overlapping foreign policy issues. Turkey faced new and multifaceted foreign policy challenges emanating mostly from its immediate neighborhood including its involvement in the Syrian and Libyan crisis and the recent Eastern Mediterranean tension with Greece. Multiple rifts with its European partners especially over the long-lasting EU accession process and its strained relations with its long-time ally, the USA, remain as chronic problems in foreign policy. Turkey's reduced diplomatic relations with many of its neighbors also hampers its capability and lowers its credibility in the region. While Turkey was once defined as a rising soft power, its reputation and attractiveness gradually wanes in the near abroad.

Turkey's proactive and multidimensional foreign policy approach failed in many areas. The country is at loggerheads with most of its neighbors and once (strategic) partners. Nevertheless, it has managed to avoid a similar foreign policy failure in Africa. Africa continues to provide a space where Turkey can satisfy its struggle for status and test its foreign policy ambitions. However, a failing economy coupled with more immediate foreign policy concerns may well limit Turkey's soft power in the region. As the conclusion will better indicate, the recent split between the government and the Gulen movement, which has an extensive network in Africa, has also emerged as an important foreign policy challenge.

The conclusion lays out a more critical analysis of Turkey's Africa approach and discusses the domestic, regional and international impediments that may complicate its relationship with Africa. The book, however, does not aim at providing policy recommendations to respond to these various challenges but it invites readers to question if the very foundations of Turkey's Africa policy will be able to forestall the challenges to Turkey's African engagement.

The book is the product of increasing political and scholarly attention towards the continent in recent years. While there is an established literature on Turkish foreign policy towards different regions, no study has so far covered different areas concerning Turkey's African engagement in a detailed, comprehensive and theoretically grounded way. It aims to build on those earlier studies, extend its analysis into Turkey's Africa policy and contribute to the vivid discussion on Turkey's Africa partnership by providing a rich, wide-ranging and up-to-date overview of the most prominent aspects of this relationship. The fact that no other study has so far provided such a holistic account of Turkey's intensified relations with Africa makes its publication even more urgent. The book, therefore, highlights a field that shows increased intellectual attention among students, scholars and practitioners.

Notes

1 See, for example, President Recep Tayyip Erdogan's recent speech at the Third African Muslim Religious Leaders Summit held in October 19–22, 2019, in Istanbul (in Turkish; Presidency of Religious Affairs [Diyanet] 2019); Erdogan's opening speech at the Second Turkey–Africa Partnership Summit (Ministry of Foreign Affairs [MFA] n.d.); Erdogan's speech at the joint press conference with Ugandan President Yoweri Museveni (Presidency of the Republic of Turkey 2016); Erdogan's speech at the Turkish–Chad Business Forum (Presidency of the Republic of Turkey 2017); former President Abdullah Gul's speech delivered on the occasion of Africa Day in 2011 (in Turkish; Abdullah Gul Official Website 2011a); Gul's speech at the Parliament of the Republic of Ghana in the same year (Abdullah Gul Official Website 2011b). See also the article penned by the Minister of Foreign Affairs, Mevlut Cavusoglu published on the occasion of Africa Day (MFA 2018) and the seminal book of Ahmet Davutoglu, Turkey's former Prime Minister, *Strategic Depth: Turkey's International Position*, first published in Turkish in 2001. Defining the Ottoman Empire as an African state, Davutoğlu further notes that Ottoman's historical, cultural and economic ties with the region provided the basis for solidarity among Africa's anti-colonial movements (2014, 207).
2 See the synopsis of Turkey–Africa relations at the official webpage of the MFA (n.d.) "Turkey-Africa Relations." http://www.mfa.gov.tr/turkey-africa-relations.en.mfa.

References

Abdullah Gul Official Website. 2011a. "Afrika Gunu Toplantisinda Yaptiklari Konusma." http://www.abdullahgul.gen.tr/konusmalar/371/79946/afrika-gunu-toplantisinda-yaptiklari-konusma.html.
Abdullah Gul Official Website. 2011b. "Cumhurbaskani Gul Gana Parlamentosu'na Hitap Etti." http://www.abdullahgul.gen.tr/haberler/170/79276/cumhurbaskani-gul-gana-parlamentosuna-hitap-etti.html.
Atli, Altay. 2011. "Businessmen as Diplomats: The Role of Business Associations in Turkey's Foreign Economic Policy." *Insight Turkey* 13, no. 1: 109–128.
Davutoglu, Ahmet. 2014. *Strategic Depth: Turkey's International Position*. Istanbul: Kure Yayınlari.
Gumuscu, Sebnem and Deniz Sert. 2009. "The Power of the Devout Bourgeoisie: The Case of the Justice and Development Party in Turkey." *Middle Eastern Studies* 45, no. 6: 953–968. https://doi.org/10.1080/00263200903268710.
Hazar, Numan. 2011. *Küreselleşme Sürecinde Afrika ve Türkiye-Afrika İlişkileri*. Ankara: USAK Yayınları.
Hazar, Numan. 2012. "Turkiye Afrika'da: Eylem Planinin Uygulanmasi ve Degerlendirme: On Bes Yil Sonra." *Ortadogu Analiz* 4, no. 46: 29–38.
Karaca, Salih Zeki. 2000. "Turkish Foreign Policy in the Year 2000 and Beyond: Her Opening up Policy to Africa." *Foreign Policy* 25, no. 3–4: 115–119.
Karagul, Soner and Ibrahim Arslan. 2013. "Türkiye'nin Afrika Açılım Politikası: Tarihsel Arka Plan, Stratejik Ortaklık ve Geleceği." *Uluslararası Hukuk ve Politika* 9, no. 35: 21–55.
Kavas, Ahmet. 2005. *Geçmişten Günümüze Afrika*. Istanbul: Kitabevi.
Kavas, Ahmet. 2006. *Osmanlı-Afrika İlişkileri*. Istanbul: Tasam Yayinlari.
Kirisci, Kemal. 2009. "The Transformation of Turkish Foreign Policy: The Rise of the Trading State." *New Perspectives on Turkey* 40: 29–57.

Ministry of Foregin Affairs (MFA). 2018. "Article by H.E. Mr. Mevlüt Çavuşoğlu Entitled 'Turkey and Africa are Building a Solid Partnership'." http://test.mfa.gov.tr/disisleri-bakani-sayin-mevlut-cavusoglu_nun-25-mayis-afrika-g%C3%BCn%C3%BC-munasebetiyle-yayinlanan-makalesi.en.mfa.

MFA. n.d. "Turkey-Africa Relations." Accessed August 13, 2020. http://www.mfa.gov.tr/turkey-africa-relations.en.mfa.

MFA. n.d. "21 November 2014, Speech by H.E. Recep Tayyip Erdogan, the President of the Republic of Turkey." Accessed August 13, 2020. http://afrika.mfa.gov.tr/21-november-2014-speech-by-HE-recep-tayyip-erdogan-the-president-of-the-republic-of-turkey.en.mfa.

Presidency of Religious Affairs (Diyanet). 2019. "The President of the Republic of Turkey Erdogan Makes a Speech in 3rd African Summit of Muslim Religious Leaders." https://diyanet.gov.tr/en-US/Content/PrintDetail/26043.

Presidency of the Republic of Turkey. 2016. "Turkey has no History of Colonialism in Africa." https://www.tccb.gov.tr/en/news/542/44216/turkiyenin-afrikada-somurgeci-gecmisi-olmamistir.

Presidency of the Republic of Turkey. 2017. "President Erdogan in Chad." https://www.tccb.gov.tr/en/news/542/87873/president-erdogan-in-chad.

Tandogan, Muhammed. 2013. *Afrika'da Sömürgecilik ve Osmanlı Siyaseti (1800–1922)*. Turk Tarih Kurumu.

Turkish Statistical Institute. 2020. "Dis Ticaret Istatistikleri." https://biruni.tuik.gov.tr/disticaretapp/menu.zul.

Ucar, Ahmet. 2000. *140 yıllık Miras: Güney Afrika'da Osmanlılar*. Istanbul: Tez Yayinlari.

Uslu, Emrullah. 2009. "Gul's African Visit Could Indicate How Turkey Will Act in the UN Security Council." The Jamestown Foundation. https://jamestown.org/program/guls-african-visit-could-indicate-how-turkey-will-act-in-the-un-security-council/.

Part 1
Historical, theoretical and political foundations of Turkey–Africa relations

1 Theorizing Turkey's Africa policy
Turkey as a rising power

Ali Onur Tepeciklioğlu

Introduction

Turkish foreign policy (TFP) has gained momentum in the last two decades. Traditionally it was known for its status quo seeking and Western-oriented nature. Historically, apart from the Cyprus issue, Turkish governments usually sought to be on the safe side of events for the sake of preserving the status quo, even though this preference sometimes did harm their national interest. The country's almost blindfolded Westernism during the Cold War years provided it protection from Soviet threat but enabled too few foreign policy options and paths to the incumbent Turkish governments. From an IR theory perspective, this security-focused Cold War period of TFP is relatively less puzzling to conceptualize. As the country was a lesser power in terms of a neo-realist power rankings hierarchy, it did not have multiple options other than following hegemonic powers' policy preferences. Additionally, a neoliberal perspective can explain why Turkey was on the side of the Western powers but not the Soviet Union in the Cold War strife. As the country's ruling bureaucratic–military elite were historically possessed with the Western modernization model, when they captured the state apparatus after the demise of the Ottoman Empire, they were at full throttle in adapting the new Turkish state to Western world order.

Compared to Cold War TFP, theorizing post-Cold War TFP is more challenging as well as puzzling. Two interconnected reasons can explain the complexity of conceptualizing TFP. First, the change in the international climate and power distribution with the end of the Cold War resulted in an overpopulated "middle power" group of countries. In many cases, some of these countries are regarded as candidates for challenging United States' hegemony in the 2000s (Huntington 1999; Patrick 2010; Hurrell 2006). Less commonly, Turkey is also included in that group. The problem with that was there were too many countries falling into the emerging power/middle power/ USA hegemony challenger category and sometimes those countries had more differences than similarities with each other. In the end, this kind of categorization possesses a challenge in terms of the abstraction-based nature of theorizing. Moreover, it adds too little analytical value to explaining Turkey's foreign policy activism in the previous two decades.

The second reason that makes conceptualizing Turkey's untraditional foreign policy challenging is its two-way nature. The "new" TFP is not a one-way process with its fundamentals blueprinted at home and policies designed based on those fundamentals applied to the international scene. Rather, it is a bidirectional process whereby the policymaking elite reshape the basic principles of the "new" foreign policy vis-à-vis developments in the regions as well as sectors where those principles are applied. In other words, Turkey simultaneously develops its new foreign policy toolkit and implements it. So, conceptualizing TFP by focusing on particular foreign policy behavior would be a better way to understand the country's activism in international politics.

Within that framework, this chapter aims to conceptualize Turkey's foreign policy towards Africa. But it does not intend to do so just by concentrating on Turkey–Africa relations. It mainly argues that Turkey's Africa policy cannot be understood separately from its wider foreign policy agenda. Thus, any attempt to conceptualize and theorize Turkey's Africa policy would also serve the wider aim of conceptualizing Turkish foreign policy in the Justice and Development Party (JDP) era. In the last two decades, Turkey focused on refurbishing its foreign policy in a way to be more active, independent and responsive for the sake of playing a greater role in world politics. It is primarily for this reason that the country's Africa policy is not independent from the main ambitions of its wider foreign policy. Indeed, Turkey's engagement in Africa is highly integrated with its claim for a larger say in the international system. This is because the continent stands as a fruitful platform for using new foreign policy tools of the country such as humanitarian aid, direct investment, capacity building and religious diplomacy.

Adapting non-traditional instruments of foreign policy, establishing new forms of engagement with other countries and focusing on issue-specific areas in international politics are generally associated with "rising powers." Rising powers are not in the league of great powers in terms of economic and military strength. But they devote many resources to areas in which they have comparative advantage. So, rising powers have particular strengths and advantages in issue-specific areas which can be translated into the capacity of influencing outcome of some specific events in the international environment (Hart and Jones 2010, 71). China, Russia, Brazil, India, South Africa and South Korea are often described as rising powers. Less often Indonesia, Turkey and Mexico are also included in that list. This chapter, among other things, claims that Turkey's foreign policy towards Africa can be better understood and explained from a rising powers perspective. Such a conceptualization can also help us to place Turkey's African policy in its wider foreign policy ambitions.

In order to assess Turkey's rising power status, this chapter will first concentrate on the particular characteristics that are associated with rising powers. It will elaborate the various ways rising powers deal with Africa in order to provide a clearer picture of the rising power concept. Then, the chapter will turn its focus on Turkey's changing foreign policy strategies and discuss the ways TFP have been conceptualized in the extant literature. Following, the chapter will explore to what extent Turkey's involvement in the region fits the rising power conceptualization.

Conceptualizing rising powers

As noted at the outset of this chapter, international relations scholars offered various concepts to define the role played by significant powers in the newly emerging world order. Following the end of the Cold War, concepts such as middle powers (Jordaan 2003), regional powers (Godehardt and Nabers 2011), pivotal states (Chase, Hill and Kennedy 1996) as well as rising powers were coined to grasp the behavior of states that have the potential to influence the world order to a degree but not as much as great powers are able to do. Despite the similarities among these conceptualizations, the term "rising power" differs from others for defining the non-Western countries which are uncomfortable with the current Western world order. Rising power conceptualization is increasingly employed to define a group of countries that aspire to have greater status in international politics (Alden and Vieira 2005), however, the concept is mildly elusive when it comes to defining particular characteristics of the countries that fall into that category. Asking for reform in global governance mechanisms and being critical of USA hegemony and neoliberal norms that underpin that predominance can be regarded as denominators of rising powers in general. But, in particular, rising powers are typically defined by their similar foreign policy behavior (Kenkel and Cunliffe 2016, 3). Foreign aids without political conditionality, development aids to enhance peacebuilding in conflict zones, trade and investments to improve bilateral relations as well as new forms of security engagement are trademarks of rising power foreign policy behavior. All these new forms of engagement are also reflected in rising powers' involvement in Africa.

Having high ambitions to play a greater role in world politics, rising powers aim to change or reform the existing order. Most of those powers are not passionate about Western values such as democracy and human rights and normally put their national interest and sovereignty in front of international norms. These countries usually do not share neoliberal political and economic grounds of the current world order and ask for reform in international governance mechanisms such as United Nations Security Council (UNSC), the International Monetary Fund (IMF) or World Bank (Patrick 2010, 44). For Hurrell, rising powers possess significant economic and military capabilities to contribute to international order and based on that, they ask for more influential roles in world politics (Hurrell 2006, 1–2). Cornelissen (2009, 12–14) defines rising powers' demographic and economic size, their capacity to influence international economy based on that size, Southern multilateralism embodied in international organizations such as BRICS, MIKTA and IBSA, and their aspiration for more power as common characteristics. Stephen (2012, 292–293) additionally underlines these powers' desire to have a different kind of world order and defines rising powers by their qualification of being "at the center of non-Western multilateralism." Similarly, Kahler (2013, 711) stresses the rising powers' ambitions to play greater roles in a changing world order. Following the liberal interdependence theory path, some scholars argue that rising powers have leverage in some issue-specific areas thanks to the effects of globalization and interdependence (Hart and Jones 2010, 71; Larson 2018, 2). Others extend this argument and define rising powers by their characteristic of having established political ties with potential threats for Western neoliberal world order such as North Korea and Iran. For them, these ties give them an upper hand in producing regional order and acting as intermediaries between the West and those countries (Larson and Shevchenko 2010, 61).

Among other characteristics, rising powers are often described vis-à-vis their potential to play significant roles in the emergence of the new world order after the envisaged USA decline. Usually, the fundamental question about rising powers is the USA's possible ways of dealing with those powers. Although it is not the primary focus of this work, explaining rising powers' perspectives on the USA-dominated world order can shed light on their ambitions and prospective roles in a new world order. For rising powers, Western world order is exclusivist and hegemonic, and these are two interconnected unsettling characteristics.

Rising powers criticize the existing setting of the world order for being highly exclusivist because international governance mechanisms are generally restricted to countries other than the established powers. It is a club with exclusive membership and that membership largely depends on how much a country embraces democratic institutions as well as a neoliberal ideological standpoint. That is why at the center of rising powers' criticisms lies a civilizational basis. Western values that underpin current international governance mechanisms are regularly in question for rising powers (Vezirgiannidou 2013, 638; Alexandroff and Cooper 2010; Patrick 2010). Rising powers' leaders often characterize the tension between their countries and traditional powers within the framework of a "civilizational strife" (Acharya 2020, 139–140, 153). Even some featured democracies among rising powers such as Brazil and India are described as half-hearted in their approach to one of the core tenets of current order such as democracy promotion (Stuenkel 2013). Russia and China are exceptions for being UNSC members even though they are not committed to Western values. However, they are also mostly excluded from global economic governance mechanisms such as the IMF, World Bank and WTO. Rising powers other than China and Russia are also not equally represented in global governance mechanisms compared to the established powers. Voting procedures and acting bureaucrats of these organizations clearly reflect the bias. This induces strong claims from the rising powers, asking for more representation in political and economic governance mechanisms. Reform demands in international governance mechanisms are one of the most crystalized characteristics that all rising powers share. At the heart of those demand claims lie rising powers' skeptical attitude towards neoliberal values.

Alongside criticisms on exclusiveness, rising powers see the USA's hegemonic position in the current world order as being problematic. Governments of these countries argue on different platforms and occasions that the USA occupies a superfluously stronger hegemonic position than its capacity to produce order. For them, the USA's power decline is a matter of fact and it is no longer legitimate that the USA continues to have the sole say on critical issues of world politics. Indeed, the USA is waning (Layne 2009), but this is not the only ground for rising powers' multilateralism claims. The political utility of American primacy has been questioned since the early 2000s (Brooks and Wohlforth 2008, 2) because of its normative grounds and its dependency on American domestic politics (Larson 2018, 1). Together with the decline of the material power of the USA, the normative basis of the current order is also in doubt for rising powers. As explained above, rising powers seek multilateralism so that they can contribute to the international order with the help of their own strengths in issue-specific areas and comparative advantages (Kenkel and Cunliffe 2016, 2). For rising powers, being accommodated by existing global governance mechanisms is not that suitable since they are against the essence of those liberal norms regulating international politics. Thus, reform claims of rising powers are not only limited to having seats in global governance mechanisms. These powers also want change in the underpinning norms such that theirs are included (Newman and Zala 2018, 873).

The US continues to resist demands of multilateralism, despite the fact that claims are strong and the country recognizes that its hegemony is no longer absolute (Cooper and Flemes 2013, 947). Rising powers such as China and India produce large amounts of wealth and hold significant productive and military power in their hands. Russia is gradually increasing its military capacity in addition to its control over fossil energy resources and pipelines in the Euro-Asia region, India and South Korea are continuously advancing their technological capacity, and South Africa and Brazil are dynamically improving their regional leadership status. In such a setting where the USA is in material and normative power decline, rising powers hold similar views and foreign policy positions that question as well as challenge the legitimacy of US hegemony.

Rising powers in Africa

The increasing role of rising powers in different sectors irrevocably transforms Africa's international relations. There are variations in terms of rising powers' approach to Africa's development, security and economic growth. Neither do they share common interests in Africa (Shaw, Cooper and Chin 2009, 31). Nevertheless, rising powers have similar motivations in their engagement with African countries and they adopt homogenous foreign policy strategies. There are plenty of works on the different roles emerging powers play in Africa, which mostly argue that those countries establish new forms of engagement with the region, principally different than that of traditional powers. Those studies also offer new theoretical insights to explore the key drivers behind this growth and the broader implications of this relationship (Cornelissen 2009; Shaw, Cooper and Chin 2009; Vickers 2013). These new forms of engagement can be grouped by rising powers' novel approaches to development aid, peacebuilding and security, and by their parallel discourses and motivations about their engagement with the continent.

Most of the scholars converge on the view that rising powers adopt a particular development aid approach. Their development aid is different especially than that of the traditional powers for being politically unconditional and for bearing the stamp of South–South cooperation (Cornelissen 2009, 19; Cirera 2013, 3; Alden 2019, 9; Alden 2013, 7).[1] Rising powers opt for operating as equals with their African counterparts in development issues (Rowlands 2008).[2] They largely focus on infrastructure development, usually tied to interests of their national enterprises in the form of government contracts and export deals. Rising powers provide development finance to African countries with long-term, low-interest rate loans as well as development aid (Tjønneland 2015, 3–4). Their development finance differs fundamentally from that of established powers by concentrating on mutual benefits instead of simply poverty reduction (Mwase and Yang 2012). The roles played by multinational non-governmental agencies and international development institutions are minimal in comparison with the governmental institutions in rising powers' provision of development assistance. So, bilateralism is another aspect of their development aid strategy. Rather than acting through available development aid institutions and channels, rising powers often prefer to deliver development assistance through their own mechanisms/ national NGOs. Besides, in most cases, rising powers do not cooperate among themselves in delivering development assistance to Africa (Tjønneland 2015, 7).

Expanding trade relations, finding new markets for their products, supporting domestic production with African raw materials and energy resources are primary motivations of rising states in their economic engagement with Africa (Alden 2019, 5). As Cirera (2013, 3) observes, it is commonly argued that rising powers establish new forms of economic engagement with Africa that represent new economic opportunities for African countries. However, especially in international trade, rising powers are not fundamentally different than OECD countries. They import natural resources and raw materials and export value-added products to African countries (Cirera 2013, 10–12). Additionally, there is no sectoral convergence in terms of economic engagement with Africa for rising powers. Rather, domestic sectoral strengths and national economic interests are prioritized for each country.

Nevertheless, van der Merwe (2016, 31–35) points out that rising powers' economic engagement with Africa is not a singlehanded government initiative. Several established networks between business and governments in these newly emerging powers can explain why these countries focus on financial and physical African resources. As a direct result of these networks, states use various instruments to "maximize accumulation over space" and "create pro-business environments." In that sense, in several cases, rising powers' initiatives to develop economic relations with Africa clearly reflects their internal dynamics. On top of that, governments see trade and economic relations as a resource of soft power, a stepping stone to expanding their influence and attraction in the eyes of African people.[3]

For rising powers, increased economic engagement with African countries inevitably results in more involvement in Africa's peace and security agenda, as sustainable economic relations require peace and stability (Tjønneland 2014). Given that rising powers are candidates for being order-producing states in the international system in general and in Africa in particular, their genuine approaches to peacebuilding in Africa are of particular importance. The existing Western approach to peacebuilding raises rising powers' concerns since it relies heavily on contested liberal principles. For rising states, "peacebuilding has been abused by the West in order to promote and impose neoliberal principles on weak states" (de Carvalho and de Coning 2013, 4). Rising powers occasionally complied with liberal principles of peacebuilding, when there was a chance that that particular operation served their soft power capacity building (Richmond and Tellidis 2013, 2). Other than that, in terms of peacebuilding, rising powers prefer to act within the framework of SSC in which impartiality, non-resort to force and consent of the host state are guiding principles (Tardy 2012).[4] Especially "non-interference" has been a prominent principle of most, if not all rising powers. This is surely linked to rising powers' rigid position on state sovereignty. Rising powers also encourage localizing peacekeeping and peacebuilding activities in order to avert applying the same model in different parts of the world (de Coning 2013). Having a holistic peacebuilding approach, they combine their peacebuilding activities with peacekeeping, humanitarian aid, development assistance, political non-conditionality and trade with a special focus on development (de Coning and Call 2017, 3; Mawdsley 2012).

In addition to the abovementioned commonalities, rising powers draw on parallel discourses in explaining their interest in Africa. Their discourses go hand in hand with their criticism of Western order. Rising powers explicitly blame Western colonialism for Africa's problems and for them, the context in which established powers base their relations with Africa in modern times is no different than the colonial period. That is why rising powers highlight SSC and equality in their relations with Africa. In sum, rising powers aim to present themselves to African governments and people as a benevolent alternative to the West. In doing so, they largely refer to their "non-colonial" and "guilt-free" history. As Alden (2013, 9) accurately indicates, the Chinese underline their early fifteenth-century voyage to the East coast of the continent without any colonial intention, Brazilians stress their common suffering with the African people because of the slave trade and Russians promote the USSR's support for liberation movements in the twentieth century.

Conceptualizing Turkish Foreign policy

Much has been written on the recent shifts in Turkish foreign policy. One of the most prominent debates on TFP is about its orientation. Known as the "shift of axis" debate, the existing literature discusses whether Turkey's increasing expansion in different geographies and its reactive foreign policy mean a temporary or permanent diversion in its foreign policy practices or not. Especially during the JDP government's first term, the country drew near the EU, with a series of reforms aiming to strengthen democracy, human and minority rights. The decreasing influence of the military in Turkish political life, thickening of civil society, de-securitization of particular foreign policy issues, decent economic growth, remaking of political narratives, the evolution of political Islam as well as the relationship between Islam and democracy, and Turkey's active involvement in international organizations are noted as important developments that potentially bolster up its relationship with the West (Oguzlu and Dal 2013). Another parallel argument is that Turkey's rising power status should be interpreted within its Western identity and in this sense, Turkey departs from other rising powers such as BRICS countries (Cagaptay 2013). Oguzlu (2013) supports this view by underscoring that Turkey's security interests are embedded in its institutionalized relationships with the Western world and that its rise highly complies with the Western type of international order.

Some authors indicate certain diversification in Turkey's foreign policy alternatives; they explain this diversification as a natural process but not necessarily as an "axis shift." For example, the uncertainties associated with the EU membership process (Adam 2012, 148), the growing global economic trend towards the East (Babacan 2011), a stable domestic and international economic environment (Baser 2015), a desire to play more independent and active role in international affairs where BRICS-like organizations increasingly become attractive options (Onis 2011) are listed as some of the main drivers behind Turkey's foreign policy activism. On the other end of the "shift of axis" debate, some scholars see Turkey's increasing activism in terms of a dichotomy in TFP's orientation between the West and the East (Cohen 2010; Cook 2010; Taspinar 2011). Others take a step further and argue that Turkey is moving towards a pan-Islamist, Eastern orientation, especially because of the impact of the intellectual legacy of the then Minister of Foreign Affairs and Prime Minister Ahmet Davutoglu on the principles of the new TFP agenda (Ozkan 2014).

Related, but from an expanded perspective, the changing nature of TFP continues to be discussed in terms of the country's rising/middle power status.[5] A number of studies employ middle power activism or rising power status to characterize Turkey's increasing international role and they try to explain and understand the country's foreign policy behavior in the past two decades (Cagaptay 2013; Gilley 2015; Kubicek, Parlar Dal and Oguzlu 2015; Onis and Kutlay 2013; Parlar Dal 2018). They note that Turkey's status seeking behavior explains its eagerness to play a more active involvement in regional initiatives and global governance institutions. For them, the country's increasing involvement in global development assistance, its contributions to peace operations in different regions, its humanitarian diplomacy efforts and economic engagement fit the characteristics of a rising power in various ways.

As noted in the introduction, Turkey's ambitions to have a greater say in international politics is one of the primary reasons and guidelines of its Africa policy. The abovementioned characteristics of rising powers can therefore be clearly observed both in overall TFP and in Turkey's Africa policy. Turkey simply aims to develop its capacity to have more influence in international politics and sees Africa as a land for it. Hale notes that using middle power activism "is far from the only way of conceptualizing its international role, but ... it still seems the most realistic way of explaining Turkish policies" (Hale 2013). In its pursuit of better roles in world politics, Turkey needs some space where it can contribute to the changing order, use its issue-specific advantages and become an alternative path by employing new forms of engagement. These aims are all translated into activism in TFP, and that activism is particularly evident in Turkey's Africa policy. Therefore, Turkey's Africa strategy is highly integrated into its wider aim of acquiring higher status in world politics (Shinn 2015, 5). Turkey's enthusiastic interest in gaining global power status as well as its desire to become a strong regional power is strongly correlated with its Africa policy as the continent provides a fertile ground for the country's ambitions (Aglionby, Srivastava and Fick 2016; Bacik and Afacan 2013; Ozkan 2012).

Turkey as a rising power

Almost all chapters in this volume provide elaborate explanations of Turkey's rising power-like approaches in its engagement with Africa, through a range of issues ranging from public and religious diplomacy to military presence, from trade relations to foreign policy discourses. For that reason, this section of the chapter does not aim to give a detailed analysis of how Turkey engages with Africa. Rather, it will focus on how Turkey's particular forms of foreign policy actions in the continent contribute to its rising power status.

Development aid is a major field that Turkey addresses in its Africa policy. As with the other rising powers, Turkey also applies non-traditional approaches to development aid, especially as a means to include capacity building and humanitarian assistance into its development approach (Ozkan 2017). Thanks to economic recovery and political stability, combined with the proactive turn in foreign policy in the first decade of the 2000s, Turkey transformed from a recipient state to a donor state (Yardimci 2019, 357; Lepeska 2014). This enabled Ankara to have a "rising power foreign policy tool" particularly in its relations with Africa. Education, health, job creation and infrastructure improvement are the main focuses of Turkey's development aid (Idriss 2020). Turkey adopts a no political strings attached approach to its development aid and humanitarian efforts (Eyrice Tepeciklioglu 2017). As is the case with other rising powers, Turkey also uses development aid projects to create new economic opportunities for Turkish firms, especially those having strong bonds with the government. Turkey delivers a great deal of its development assistance through the Turkish Cooperation and Coordination Agency (TIKA) and Turkiye Diyanet Vakfi (TDV) instead of international institutions, another aspect that complies with rising powers' bilateralism. More importantly, Turkey uses development aid as a political tool to extend its outreach in the African continent. Besides, development aid is highly related to the Turkish governments' glorification of its Ottoman past. With strong references to Ottoman's non-colonial past in Africa, the JDP government aims to enhance the value of its "common" Turkish–African past, generate the identity of "equal partners" and promote the Islamic worldview as an alternative to current world order.[6]

Rising powers have economic incentives such as increasing their trade volume, finding new markets and energy resources in their relations with Africa. Likewise, Turkey's interest in Africa is also motivated by economic imperatives. As a grand strategy, Turkey wants to diversify its economic partners (Ozkan 2012). This was the case when it accelerated its Africa engagement at the beginning of the 2000s and it still is, as clearly demonstrated by recent economic developments. The economic factor is so crucial that for Turkey, improving economic ties is a priority even in its development aid approach, if not a must (Ozkan 2013, 139; Mehmetcik 2018, 264). The country contracts important and high-budget infrastructure projects in African countries and aims to turn these projects into business opportunities for Turkish firms. Moreover, Turkey uses its large diplomatic presence together with Turkish Airlines to increase its economic impact in the continent.[7] Turkey's economic engagement with the African continent is a textbook example of the abovementioned van der Merwe's business–government networks (van der Merwe 2016). Businessmen, mostly known as "Anatolian tigers" (Atli 2011), who provided the JDP government's electoral support base especially in the early years of its rule, have been a driving force for the government to improve its economic relationships with once neglected regions in foreign policy such as Africa, with the aim of enabling market access, providing competitive-priced raw materials and creating feasible investment opportunities. Other than that, in terms of trade relations with Africa, Turkey is not different in its export and import behavior than rising powers. Despite Turkish officials repeatedly claiming otherwise by implying that Turkey is not in Africa for natural resources but for equal partnership,

Turkey substantially imports raw materials from African countries, and exports end products to them.[8]

Peacebuilding is another field where Turkey's approach resembles that of rising powers. Showcased particularly in Somalia, Turkey adopts a holistic approach and sees the peacemaking process as linked to state-building. For this reason, infrastructure projects, technical assistance and capacity building are treated as the complementary parts of a whole. Furthermore, Turkish officials pay particular attention to national ownership of the peace process, respect the sovereignty of host nations and try to be as inclusive as possible for all stakeholders in conflict regions (Sazak and Woods 2017, 97; Sucuoglu and Sazak 2016). Like other rising powers, Turkey includes security engagement with the African countries generally in the framework of SSC. That is why Turkey does not get deeply involved in Africa's security agenda other than in North Africa which can be regarded as its immediate neighborhood. However, this does not necessarily mean that Turkey follows a completely interest-free peacebuilding approach (Akpinar 2013). Turkey's peacebuilding efforts also have a political and social dimension, notably in Somalia (Ozkan and Orakci 2015). Highlighting "humanitarianism" rooted in its culture and religion (Ministry of Foreign Affairs n.d.), the Turkish government also uses some humanitarian non-governmental organizations in peacebuilding efforts to promote Turkey, gather public support and create attraction (Aras and Akpinar 2015).[9]

Turkey's foreign policy activism and its novel ways of engagement with Africa are good fits with those of other rising powers. In addition, Turkey is also attuned to rising powers' general characteristics such as being critical of the USA-led neoliberal order and global governance mechanisms' exclusiveness. Together with Turkey's pivotal position in many volatile and troublesome issues in the Middle East, one could argue that rising power is the right term for explaining Turkey's international political behavior. The characteristics of Turkey's foreign policy actions in the last decade are manifestations of its rising power qualities. Turkey, under JDP rule regularly expresses and practically demonstrates its unwillingness to align with the West and neoliberal order, loudly voices its claims for reform in global governance mechanisms, and holds critical positions in regional and sometimes global issues.

Especially after the first half of the 2010s, the JDP government has bitterly criticized the West and frequently holds Western countries responsible for wrongdoings in world politics. For example, Turkish President Recep Tayyip Erdogan vehemently censured the attitudes of European countries in the Syrian refugee crisis, accused them of "turning the Mediterranean to a cemetery", defined their policies as "inhumane" (Melvin 2015), argued "copying the institutions, lifestyles and systems of the modern world and imposing them on the country" is destined to be an unsuccessful model of development (Hurriyet Daily News 2012) and blamed the West for siding with terrorist groups in Northern Syria (Jones 2019). Indeed, blaming the West for supporting terrorism has become a common practice in government circles in recent years (Kaliber and Kaliber 2019, 2). Erdogan also claimed that the Christchurch attack was "part of a worldwide campaign of Islamophobia" (Wintour 2019) and explicitly called Western countries for action against rising Islamophobia in the West (Aliyev and Dogantekin 2019). In Africa too, the JDP government sees Western countries as the primary source of socio-economic problems. For Erdogan, other countries are involved for the richness of the continent, for diamonds, gold and mines, while Turkey is only in for common history, friendship and brotherhood (Anadolu Ajansı 2013; Idriss 2020). He also lays the responsibility of Somalian suffering on the West, claiming that it is again the Western countries that turned a blind eye to the issue (Presidency of the Republic of Turkey 2017). All in all, Turkish foreign policy discourse has been highly preoccupied by growing anti-Westernism in the past decade.

The JDP government suggests Islamic underpinnings of the Ottoman civilization as a solution to inequality, ethnic strife, racial violence as well as economic and social underdevelopment in world politics. For the ruling Turkish elite, Islam represents a worldview of good-willing, equality and brotherhood. According to the JDP government, these qualities of the Islamic-Ottoman civilization should be represented on the world stage and in global governance mechanisms. This is one of the primary reasons for the JDP overstating so-called "pax-Ottomana" in the Middle East and North Africa as a source of order. For Ankara, Western colonialist policies damaged order and peace in the Middle East and in Africa. Turkey is portrayed as a country that is capable of ironing out the tangled issues of international politics, for being built on that rich, multiethnic, multi-civilizational Ottoman heritage (Yanik 2011). So "the new order" should definitely include non-Western (and Islamic) norms if it is to be a just, working and decent order for the Turkish government.

The Turkish government also tries new options for creating alternative policies in a post-American/post-Western hegemony setting. There are several vexed issues both in Turkey–USA and Turkey–EU relations. Turkey tries to punch above its weight by positioning itself alongside some would-be major players of the new world order such as Russia. In doing so, it does not shy away from straining its ties with the West. As crystalized by the recent S-400 crisis, Turkey adopts 'bandwagon' policies more often than before. The Turkish government's discomfort with American leadership in world politics is summed up in the "world is bigger than five" motto of Erdogan. He uses this sentence to criticize mainly the structure of the UNSC but this statement also reflects the Turkish government's reformist claims in all global governance mechanisms (Aral 2019). In critical issues such as the S-400 crisis, cross-border military operations in Northern Syria and Eastern Mediterranean rivalry with Greece where Turkey had to face harsh Western opposition, the Turkish government has strongly emphasized its independence and state sovereignty. These moves can also be read as the

Turkish government's self-ordained actions similar to other rising powers, aiming to occupy a larger place in a newly emerging post-USA hegemonic world order.

In addition, Turkey also holds critical advantages/positions in some serious issues in the Middle East region. For example, it is highly involved in the Syrian conflict, controls some Syrian soil alongside its border and actively gives wide-ranging support to some armed opposition groups in the Northern part of the country. Moreover, it hosts the largest number of Syrian refugees who remain at the highest position on the EU's security agenda.[10] Again, for the EU, Turkey remains the biggest rival of Greece in Cyprus and in Eastern Mediterranean conflicts. The Turkish government has also strengthened its ties with the UN-recognized Libyan government and vigorously supports that side in the Libyan civil war. Turkey also maintains its position as the international community's access point to Somalia. These issue-specific strengths enhance Turkey's capacity to produce order since the pivotal position that country occupies cannot be ignored by the established powers in search of a solution to these problems. In sum, despite the fact that Turkey's military capacity and interests are limited to its immediate neighborhood,[11] its economy is in dire straits and the country faces domestic social and political struggles, it still is a good match for the term "rising power" in terms of having particular strengths and advantages in issue-specific areas.

Conclusion

This study aimed to conceptualize Turkey's foreign policy activism particularly in Africa. It argued that Turkey's Africa policy should be analyzed within its wider foreign policy ambitions. Based on that argument, this chapter holds the view that "rising power" most suitably explains Turkey's foreign policy activism in the last two decades. Rising power conceptualization also allows us to make sense of the recent shifts in TFP. Turkey aspires to more power and emulates rising powers' foreign policy behavior in achieving this aim despite its long alignment with the West. Novel approaches to development aid, peacebuilding, economic engagement, emphasis on soft power and discourses on the malicious aspects of Western order are some characteristics of rising powers, especially in their relations with Africa. Given this fact, one can draw parallels between Turkey and other rising powers. Other chapters of this volume may strengthen this argument by relying on empirical evidence.

Notes

1 Please see Chapter 4 by Federico Donelli in this volume for a detailed analysis of SSC and Turkey's development aid in that framework.
2 Terms such as "win–win approach," "South–South Cooperation," "horizontal cooperation" and "African renaissance" are used by different countries to define

their development assistance to African countries. All these terms basically reflect mutual benefit, knowledge-sharing and non-interference as the key elements of development (Gu et al. 2016, 9).
3 For a further discussion of this issue, please see Chapter 6 by Samiratou Dipama and Emel Parlar Dal in this volume.
4 For a detailed analysis of rising powers' peacekeeping behavior, including that of Turkey's, please see Chapter 8 by Birsen Erdogan in this volume.
5 It should be noted that despite middle power and rising power concepts usually referring to two different groups of states, they are used interchangeably in the extant literature on Turkey's rise, in the meaning of the latter. This is probably a deliberate decision, related to the "shift of axis" debate. As "middle powers", to a great extent, comply with the Western order's principles and norms, some scholars prefer to use "middle power" instead of "rising power" in their analysis of Turkey's foreign policy activism. See, for example, Gilley 2015, Onis and Kutlay 2016, Parlar Dal 2018.
6 For a detailed analysis of Ottoman perceptions of Africa and the non-colonial legacy of the Ottomans, please see Chapter 2 by Mustafa Serdar Palabiyik in this volume.
7 For a comprehensive overview of how Turkey derives soft power and influence from Turkish Airlines' operations in Africa, please see Chapter 12 by Orcun Selcuk in this volume.
8 For a detailed analysis of trade factors in Turkey's Africa engagement, please see Chapter 6 by Samiratou Dipama and Emel Parlar Dal in this volume.
9 For a detailed account of Turkey's humanitarianism in Africa please see Chapter 10 by Gonca Oguz Gok in this volume.
10 More than three and a half million in October 2020, according to the UNHCR website. https://data2.unhcr.org/en/situations/syria/location/113.
11 For further elaboration of this argument, please see Chapter 7 by Brendon Cannon in this book.

References

Acharya, Amitav. 2020. "The Myth of the 'Civilization State': Rising Powers and the Cultural Challenge to World Order." *Ethics & International Affairs* 34, no. 2: 139–156. https://doi.org/10.1017/S0892679420000192.

Adam, Laura Batalla. 2012. "Turkey's Foreign Policy in the AKP Era: Has There Been a Shift in the Axis?" *Turkish Policy Quarterly* 11, no. 3: 139–148.

Aglionby, John, Mehul Srivastava and Maggie Fick. 2016. "The Reasons Behind Turkey Leader Recep Erdogan's Africa Tour." *Financial Times*, June 2, 2016.

Akpinar, Pinar. 2013. "Turkey's Peacebuilding in Somalia: The Limits of Humanitarian Diplomacy." *Turkish Studies* 14, no. 4: 735–757. http://dx.doi.org/10.1080/14683849.2013.863448.

Alden, Chris. 2013. "Introduction." In "Emerging Powers in Africa," edited by Nicholas Kitchen. LSE IDEAS Special Report SR016. http://wwww.lse.ac.uk/ideas/Assets/Documents/reports/LSE-IDEAS-Emerging-Powers-in-Africa.pdf.

Alden, Chris. 2019. Emerging Powers and Africa: From Development to Geopolitics. *IAI Papers* 19. https://www.iai.it/sites/default/files/iaip1923.pdf.

Alden, Chris and Marco Antonio Vieira. 2005. "The New Diplomacy of the South: South Africa, Brazil, India and Trilateralism." *Third World Quarterly* 26, no. 7: 1077–1095. https://doi.org/10.1080/01436590500235678.

Alexandroff, Alan S. and Andrew F. Cooper. 2010. "Introduction." In *Rising States, Rising Institutions: Challenges for Global Governance*, edited by Alan S. Alexandroff and Andrew F. Cooper, 1–14. Washington D.C.: Brookings Institution Press.

Aliyev, Jeyhun and Vakkas Dogantekin. 2019. "Turkey's Erdogan Strongly Condemns New Zealand Attacks." *Anadolu Ajansı*, March 15, 2019. https://www.aa.com.tr/en/turkey/turkeys-erdogan-strongly-condemns-new-zealand-attacks/1418844.
Anadolu Ajansı. "Gabon Gateway for Africa, Turkish Premier Says." January 7, 2013. https://www.aa.com.tr/en/turkey/gabon-gateway-for-africa-turkish-premier-says/288291.
Aral, Berdal. 2019. "The World Is Bigger than Five." *Insight Turkey* 21, no. 4: 71–96.
Aras, Bulent and Pinar Akpinar. 2015. "The Role of Humanitarian NGOs in Turkey's Peacebuilding." *International Peacekeeping* 22, no. 3: 230–247. http://dx.doi.org/10.1080/13533312.2015.1033374.
Atli, Altay. 2011. "Businessmen as Diplomats: The Role of Business Associations in Turkey's Foreign Economic Policy." *Insight Turkey* 13, no. 1: 109–128.
Babacan, Mehmet. 2011. "Whither an Axis Shift: A Perspective from Turkey's Foreign Trade." *Insight Turkey* 13, no. 1: 129–157.
Bacik, Gokhan and Isa Afacan. 2013. "Turkey Discovers Sub-Saharan Africa: The Critical Role of Agents in the Construction of Turkish Foreign-Policy Discourse." *Turkish Studies* 14, no. 3: 483–502. https://doi.org/10.1080/14683849.2013.832040.
Baser, Ekrem T. 2015. "Shift-of-Axis in Turkish Foreign Policy: Turkish National Role Conceptions Before and During AKP Rule." *Turkish Studies* 16, no. 3: 291–309. https://doi.org/10.1080/14683849.2015.1050958.
Brooks, Stephen G. and William C. Wohlforth. 2008. *World out of Balance: International Relations and the Challenge of American Primacy*. Princeton: Princeton University Press.
Cagaptay, Soner. 2013. "Defining Turkish Power: Turkey as a Rising Power Embedded in the Western International System." *Turkish Studies* 14, no. 4: 797–811. https://doi.org/10.1080/14683849.2013.861110.
Chase, Robert S., Emily B. Hill and Paul Kennedy. 1996. "Pivotal States and U.S. Strategy." *Foreign Affairs*: 33–51. https://www.foreignaffairs.com/articles/algeria/1996-01-01/pivotal-states-and-us-strategy.
Cirera, Xavier. 2013. "The Economic Engagement Footprint of Rising Powers in Africa: An Analysis of Trade, Foreign Direct Investment and Aid Flows." IDS Report No: 43. https://opendocs.ids.ac.uk/opendocs/handle/20.500.12413/3207.
Cohen, Ariel. 2010. "Washington Concerned as Turkey Leaving the West." *Turkish Policy Quarterly* 9, no. 3: 25–35.
Cook, Steven A. 2010. "How Do You Say 'Frenemy' in Turkish?" *Foreign Policy*, January 25, 2010. https://foreignpolicy.com/2010/06/01/how-do-you-say-frenemy-in-turkish-2/.
Cooper, Andrew F. and Daniel Flemes. 2013. "Foreign Policy Strategies of Emerging Powers in a Multipolar World: An Introductory Review." *Third World Quarterly* 34, no. 6: 943–962. https://doi.org/10.1080/01436597.2013.802501.
Cornelissen, Scarlett. 2009. "Awkward Embraces: Emerging and Established Powers and the Shifting Fortunes of Africa's International Relations in the Twenty-First Century." *Politikon* 36, no. 1: 5–26. https://doi.org/10.1080/02589340903155377.
de Carvalho, Benjamin and Cedric de Coning. 2013. "Rising Powers and the Future of Peacekeeping and Peacebuilding." Report, November, 1–8. Oslo: Norwegian Peacebuilding Resource Centre. https://www.files.ethz.ch/isn/175234/f194e6326ee12f80c3705117b151ef78.pdf.
de Coning, Cedric. 2013. "Understanding Peacebuilding as Essentially Local." *Stability* 2, no. 1: 1–6. http://doi.org/10.5334/sta.as.

de Coning, Cedric and Charles T. Call. 2017. "Introduction: Why Examine Rising Powers' Role in Peacebuilding?" In *Rising Powers & Peacebuilding*, edited by Cedric de Coning and Charles T. Call, 1–12. London: Palgrave Macmillan.

Eyrice Tepeciklioglu, Elem. 2017. "Economic Relations between Turkey and Africa: Challenges and Prospects." *Journal of Sustainable Development, Law and Policy* 8, no. 1: 1–33.

Gilley, Bruce. 2015. "Turkey, Middle Powers, and the New Humanitarianism." *Perceptions* 20, no. 1: 37–58.

Godehardt, Nadine and Dirk Nabers (eds.) 2011. *Regional Orders and Regional Powers*. London: Routledge.

Gu, J., R. Carey, A. Shankland and A. Chenoy. 2016. "Introduction: International Development, South-South Cooperation and the Rising Powers." In *The BRICS in International Development*, edited by J. Gu, A. Shankland and A. Chenoy, 1–24. London: Palgrave Macmillan.

Hale, William. 2013. *Turkish Foreign Policy Since 1774*. London and New York: Routledge.

Hart, Andrew F. and Bruce D. Jones. 2010. "How Do Rising Powers Rise?" *Survival* 52, no. 6: 63–88.

Huntington, Samuel. 1999. "The Lonely Superpower." *Foreign Affairs* 78, no. 2: 35–49.

Hurrell, Andrew. 2006. "Hegemony, Liberalism and Global Order: What Space for Would-Be Great Powers?" *International Affairs* 82, no. 1: 1–19. https://doi.org/10.1111/j.1468-2346.2006.00512.x.

Hurriyet Daily News. 2012. "Turkish PM Erdogan Slams Greediness and Wild Capitalism." March 16, 2012. https://www.hurriyetdailynews.com/turkish-pm-erdogan-slams-greediness-and-wild-capitalism-16150.

Idriss, Moustapha Abdelkerim. 2020. "Turkey-Africa Partnership: A Development-Oriented Approach." Anadolu Ajansı, January 8, 2020. https://www.aa.com.tr/en/africa/analysis-turkey-africa-partnership-a-development-oriented-approach/1696640.

Jones, Dorian. 2019. "Erdogan Criticizes Western Allies Over Syrian Operation Ahead of Putin Meeting." VOA, October 21, 2019. https://www.voanews.com/middle-east/erdogan-criticizes-western-allies-over-syrian-operation-ahead-putin-meeting.

Jordaan, Eduard. 2003. "The Concept of a Middle Power in International Relations: Distinguishing Between Emerging and Traditional Middle Powers." *Politikon* 30, no. 1: 165–181. https://doi.org/10.1080/0258934032000147282.

Kahler, Miles. 2013. "Rising Powers and Global Governance: Negotiating Change in a Resilient Status Quo." *International Affairs* 89, no. 3: 711–729. https://doi.org/10.1111/1468-2346.12041.

Kaliber, Alper and Esra Kaliber. 2019. "From De-Europeanisation to Anti-Western Populism: Turkish Foreign Policy in Flux." *The International Spectator* 54, no. 4: 1–16. https://doi.org/10.1080/03932729.2019.1668640.

Kenkel, Kai Michael and Philip Cunliffe. 2016. "Rebels or Aspirants: Rising Powers, Normative Contestation, and Intervention." In *Brazil as a Rising Power: Intervention Norms and the Contestation of Global Order*, edited by Kai Michael Kenkel and Philip Cunliffe, 1–20. New York: Routledge.

Kubicek, Paul, Emel Parlar Dal and Tarık Oguzlu (eds.) 2015. *Turkey's Rise as an Emerging Power*. London: Routledge.

Larson, Deborah Welch. 2018. "New Perspectives on Rising Powers and Global Governance: Status and Clubs." *International Studies Review* 20, no. 2: 247–254. https://doi.org/10.1093/isr/viy039.

Larson, Deborah Welch and Alexei Shevchenko. 2010. "Status Seekers: Chinese and Russian Responses to US Primacy." *International Security* 34, no. 4: 63–95. https://doi.org/10.1162/isec.2010.34.4.63.

Layne, Christopher. 2009. "The Waning of US Hegemony—Myth or Reality? A Review essay." *International Security* 34, no. 1: 147–172. https://doi.org/10.1162/isec.2009.34.1.147.

Lepeska, David. 2014. Turkey's Rise from Aid Recipient to Mega-Donor. April 25, 2014. Al Jazeera. http://america.aljazeera.com/opinions/2014/4/turkey-internationalaidafricasomaliamiddleeasterdorgan.html.

Mawdsley, Emma. 2012. *From Recipients to Donors: Emerging Powers and the Changing Development Landscape*. London: Zed Books Ltd.

Mehmetcik, Hakan. 2018. "Turkey and India in the Context of Foreign Aid to Africa." In *Middle Powers in Global Governance*, edited by Emel Parlar Dal, 255–275. Cham: Palgrave Macmillan.

Melvin, Don. 2015. "Turkish President: Europe to Blame for Drowning of 2-Year-Old Migrant." CNN, March 10, 2015. https://edition.cnn.com/2015/09/03/middleeast/turkey-president-interview/index.html.

Ministry of Foreign Affairs. n.d. "Turkey's Enterprising and Humanitarian Foreign Policy" http://www.mfa.gov.tr/synopsis-of-the-turkish-foreign-policy.en.mfa (accessed October 10, 2020).

Mwase, N. and Y. Yang. 2012. "BRICs' Philosophies for Development Financing and Their Implications for LICs." IMF Discussion Paper W12/14. Washington DC: International Monetary Fund.

Newman, Edward and Benjamin Zala. 2018. "Rising Powers and Order Contestation: Disaggregating the Normative from the Representational." *Third World Quarterly* 39, no. 5: 871–888. https://doi.org/10.1080/01436597.2017.1392085.

Oguzlu, Tarik. 2013. "Making Sense of Turkey's Rising Power Status: What Does Turkey's Approach Within NATO Tell Us?" *Turkish Studies* 14, no. 4: 774–796. https://doi.org/10.1080/14683849.2013.863420.

Oguzlu, Tarik and Emel Parlar Dal. 2013. "Decoding Turkey's Rise: An Introduction." *Turkish Studies* 14, no. 4: 617–636. https://doi.org/10.1080/14683849.2013.861112.

Onis, Ziya. 2011. "Multiple Faces of the 'New' Turkish Foreign Policy: Underlying Dynamics and a Critique." *Insight Turkey* 13, no. 1: 47–65.

Onis, Ziya and Mustafa Kutlay. 2013. "Rising Powers in a Changing Global Order: The Political Economy of Turkey in the Age of Brics." *Third World Quarterly* 34, no. 8: 1409–1426. https://doi.org/10.1080/01436597.2013.831541.

Onis, Ziya and Mustafa Kutlay. 2016. "The Dynamics of Emerging Middle-Power Influence in Regional and Global Governance: The Paradoxical Case of Turkey." *Australian Journal of International Affairs* 71, no. 2: 164–183. https://doi.org/10.1080/10357718.2016.1183586.

Ozkan, Behlul. 2014. "Turkey, Davutoglu and the Idea of Pan-Islamism." *Survival*. 56, no. 4: 119–140. https://doi.org/10.1080/00396338.2014.941570.

Ozkan, Mehmet. 2012. "A New Actor or Passer-By? The Political Economy of Turkey's Engagement with Africa." *Journal of Balkan and Near Eastern Studies* 14, no. 1: 113–133. https://doi.org/10.1080/19448953.2012.656968.

Ozkan, Mehmet. 2013. "Does 'Rising Power' mean 'Rising Donor'? Turkey's Development Aid in Africa." *Africa Review* 5, no. 2: 139–147. https://doi.org/10.1080/09744053.2013.855358.

Ozkan, Mehmet. 2017. "The Turkish Way of Doing Development Aid?: An Analysis from the Somali Laboratory." In *South-South Cooperation Beyond the Myths*, edited by Isaline Bergamaschi, Phoebe Moore and Arlene B. Tickner, 59–78. London: Palgrave Macmillan.

Ozkan, Mehmet and Serhat Orakci. 2015. "Viewpoint: Turkey as a 'Political' Actor in Africa – An Assessment of Turkish Involvement in Somalia." *Journal of Eastern African Studies* 9, no. 2: 343–352. https://doi.org/10.1080/17531055.2015.1042629.

Parlar Dal, Emel (ed.) 2018. *Middle Powers in Global Governance: The Rise of Turkey*. London: Palgrave Macmillan.

Patrick, Stewart. 2010. "Irresponsible Stakeholders? The Difficulty of Integrating Rising Powers." *Foreign Affairs* 89, no. 6: 44–53.

Presidency of the Republic of Turkey. 2017. "Peace Cannot Be Achieved in a World Where Children Are Starving to Death". April 26, 2017. https://www.tccb.gov.tr/en/news/542/74978/cocuklarin-acliktan-oldugu-bir-dunyada-huzur-ve-baris-olmaz.

Richmond, Oliver P. and Ioannis Tellidis. 2013. The BRICS and International Peacebuilding and Statebuilding. *Norwegian Peacebuilding Resource Centre Report*, 1–9. https://www.files.ethz.ch/isn/160996/5f8c6a3d43ec8fff5692d7b596af2491.pdf.

Rowlands, Dane. 2008. "Emerging Donors in International Development Assistance: A Synthesis Report." IDRC Partnership & Business Development Division. https://www.idrc.ca/sites/default/files/sp/Documents%20EN/donors-international-development-synthesis-report.pdf.

Sazak, Onur and Auveen Elizabeth Woods. 2017. "Breaking with Convention: Turkey's New Approach to Peacebuilding." In *Rising Powers & Peacebuilding. Breaking the Mold?* edited by Charles T. Call and Cedric De Coning, 93–106. Basingstoke: Palgrave Macmillan.

Shaw, Timothy M., Andrew F. Cooper and Gregory T. Chin. 2009. "Emerging Powers and Africa: Implications for/from Global Governance?" *Politikon* 36, no. 1: 27–44. https://doi.org/10.1080/02589340903155385.

Shinn, David Hamilton. 2015. "Turkey's Engagement in Sub-Saharan Africa: Shifting Alliances and Strategic Diversification." *Chatham House*, 1–20. https://www.chathamhouse.org/sites/default/files/field/field_document/20150909TurkeySubSaharanAfricaShinn.pdf.

Stephen, Matthew D. 2012. "Rising Regional Powers and International Institutions: The Foreign Policy Orientations of India, Brazil and South Africa." *Global Society* 26, no. 3: 289–309. https://doi.org/10.1080/13600826.2012.682277.

Stuenkel, Oliver. 2013. "Rising Powers and the Future of Democracy Promotion: The Case of Brazil and India." *Third World Quarterly* 34, no. 2: 339–355. https://doi.org/10.1080/01436597.2013.775789.

Sucuoglu, Gizem and Onur Sazak. 2016. "The New Kid on the Block: Turkey's Shifting Approaches to Peacebuilding." *Rising Powers Quarterly* 1, no. 2: 69–91.

Tardy, Thierry. 2012. "Emerging Powers and Peacekeeping: An Unlikely Normative Clash." *Geneva Centre for Security Policy*, 1–4. https://www.files.ethz.ch/isn/141118/Emerging%20Powers%20and%20Peacekeeping.pdf.

Taspinar, Omer. 2011. "The Three Strategic Visions of Turkey". Brookings US-Europe Analysis Series, *Brookings Institute*, 1–5. https://www.brookings.edu/research/the-three-strategic-visions-of-turkey/.

Tjønneland, Elling N. 2014. "Rising Powers in Africa: What does this Mean for the African Peace and Security Agenda?" *Norwegian Peacebuilding Resource Center Report*, 1–8. https://www.cmi.no/publications/5088-rising-powers-in-africa.

Tjønneland, Elling N. 2015. "African Development: What Role do the Rising Powers Play?" Norwegian Peacebuilding Research Centre Report. https://www.cmi.no/publications/5349-african-development.
van der Merwe, Justin. 2016. "Theorising Emerging Powers in Africa within the Western-Led System of Accumulation." In *Emerging powers in Africa*, edited by Justin van der Merwe, Alexandra Arkhangelskaya and Ian Taylor, 17–38. Cham: Palgrave Macmillan.
Vezirgiannidou, Sevasti-Eleni. 2013. "The United States and Rising Powers in a Post-Hegemonic Global Order." *International Affairs* 89, no. 3: 635–651. https://doi.org/10.1111/1468-2346.12037.
Vickers, Brendan. 2013. "Africa and the Rising Powers: Bargaining for the 'Marginalized Many'". *International Affairs* 89, no. 3: 673–693. https://doi.org/10.1111/1468-2346.12039.
Wintour, Patrick. 2019. "Erdogan shows Christchurch Attack Footage at Rallies." *The Guardian*, March 18. https://www.theguardian.com/world/2019/mar/18/erdogan-shows-christchurch-attack-footage-at-rallies.
Yanik, Lerna K. 2011. "Constructing Turkish 'exceptionalism': Discourses of Liminality and Hybridity in Post-Cold War Turkish Foreign Policy." *Political Geography* 30, no. 2: 80–89. https://doi.org/10.1016/j.polgeo.2011.01.003.
Yardimci, Aylin. 2019. "An Emerging Donor in Retrospect: Understanding Turkey's Development Assistance Activism." In *Innovating South-South Cooperation: Policies, Challenges and Prospects*, edited by Vazquez Karin Costa, et al., 349–372. Ottawa, Ontario: University of Ottawa Press.

2 Ottoman Empire and Africa in the age of colonial expansion
Appreciating the loyalty of African Muslims, debating colonial rupture

Mustafa Serdar Palabıyık

Introduction[1]

The African continent attracted the attention of the Ottoman Empire from the late fifteenth century onwards. Levant and Egypt, the two significant hubs of East–West trade routes had been controlled by the Mamluk dynasty since the mid-thirteenth century and the Ottomans began to be interested in controlling these wealthy regions. The removal of the buffer states between the Ottoman and Mamluk Empires in the late fifteenth century resulted in a fierce inter-imperial rivalry for control of the Eastern Mediterranean. The end of this rivalry with the ultimate destruction of the Mamluk Empire resulted in Ottoman control first in Egypt and then in the littoral parts of North Africa. From then on, until the early nineteenth century, most of the Mediterranean littoral of the continent was under Ottoman rule.

In addition to Ottoman direct rule over the North African provinces, particularly as a result of the will to demonstrate caliphal authority over the African Muslim community and, in some cases, upon the demand of local central and southern African Muslim states, the Ottomans diplomatically contacted these Muslim political entities from time to time. In other words, the virtual Ottoman authority in the northern parts of the continent was accompanied by a nominal caliphal authority over African Muslims.

The Ottoman Empire first encountered European colonial penetration as it became a threat to its African territories. The short-lived French attempt to control Egypt at the turn of the nineteenth century was followed by the French occupation of Ottoman Algeria in 1830. Later, French colonization of Tunisia and British occupation of Egypt in 1881–1882, and finally the loss of Tripolitania to Italy in 1912, practically ended Ottoman rule in the region.

Within this framework, this chapter has two aims. First, it intends to analyze Ottoman direct/indirect rule over North Africa as well as Ottoman diplomatic and caliphal encounters with the local Muslim political units outside the Ottoman sovereignty. Second, and more significantly, the chapter aims to present the Ottoman perception of Africa at the time of colonial penetration. In doing so, the travelogues written by the Ottoman travelers are examined; these travelers were mostly governmental agents, serving as diplomats/bureaucrats in the region, and in some cases, self-financed passengers or mere adventurers. Instead of focusing on the Ottoman intellectuals' perception of Africa, which was more or less a Eurocentric account of the continent learned from Western accounts, this chapter deliberately focuses on the Ottoman travelers, who had actually seen the continent. Because the perception of Africa by those who had actually seen it was more or less different from the perception of those who had learned about the continent through Western literature. The chapter particularly focuses on (1) the description of local Muslims' allegiance to the caliphal authority of the Ottoman Empire as well as their loyalty to the Ottoman fatherland and (2) the impact of colonial penetration in the African continent as reflected in travelers' depiction of urban duality in Northern Africa.

The chapter first argues that the Ottoman responses to European colonial penetration were twofold: On the one hand, loose administrative links with Ottoman provinces in the Maghreb were strengthened through centralization in order to prevent the loss of Ottoman territories to European colonial powers. On the other hand, African Muslims in Saharan and sub-Saharan regions were contacted through various agents sent by the Ottoman Sultans in order to demonstrate caliphal authority over local Muslim communities and to encourage them to resist against colonial penetration. Second, the chapter attempts to link the Ottoman perception of Africa with the contemporary Turkish foreign policy (TFP) perception on the continent. Particularly, in the concluding section of the chapter, it is argued that current TFP discourse approaches – particularly Northern – Africa as a part of Ottoman imperial heritage as well as an essential part of Turkish geopolitical considerations. Indeed, understanding the Ottoman travelers' perception of Africa is important for establishing leverage to assess the validity of the discursive bonds established by current Turkish decision makers with reference to the Ottoman legacy in this continent. However, it is also underlined that there are significant differences between Ottoman travelers' perception of Africa and the current TFP discourse. Particularly, nuanced Ottoman perceptions on the impact of colonial penetration in Africa and Ottoman neglect of the region gave way to a more monolithic perception of the continent in current TFP discourse as a zone of influence for Turkey as an emerging regional power. Moreover, current TFP discourse on Africa is also selective. First, it exaggerates the Ottoman heritage in the continent, since, except for Egypt, Ottoman presence in Africa had not been as strong as presented nowadays. Second, it overstates the bonds between the Ottoman Empire and Africa based on caliphal authority. Third, it overlooks some negative aspects of the Ottoman administration in Africa including negligence of infrastructure or practices such as the slave trade.

Ottoman rule in North Africa and confrontation with colonial penetration

Between the Ottoman Empire's southward expansion and the conquest of Egypt in 1517 and its occupation of Tunisia from the local al-Hafsid dynasty in 1574, North Africa was transformed into an imperial domain. While the need to control the Eastern Mediterranean for containing the two significant Mediterranean rivals of the Empire, namely the Habsburg Empire and Venice, forced the Ottomans to occupy some strategic coastal regions in Northern Africa, in the second half of the sixteenth century, the Ottomans were concerned not only about controlling the Eastern Mediterranean, but also about increasing Portuguese presence in the Indian Ocean. Portuguese penetration in the Red Sea alarmed the Ottomans who undertook to control the strategic ports of Northeastern Africa, namely Massawa and Suakin, which were captured between 1555 and 1564. These North African territories were reorganized under five provinces, being Egypt, Tripolitania, Tunisia, Algeria and Abyssinia (Kavas 2006, 46).

Considering the geographic, economic and social differences of these vast territories, the Ottomans established different modes of governance. First, these provinces were administered through a land/tax system called *saliyane*. Unlike most of the provinces in Anatolia and Rumelia, the territories of the North African provinces were not divided into smaller territorial units (*dirlik*) allocated to soldiers for cultivation to produce wealth in order to raise military troops. Rather, a predetermined amount of annual tax was imposed on these provinces. Initially, the governors appointed by the center and then the local governors had the responsibility to collect and send this tax to the central treasury (Pakalin 1993, 111–112).

Despite this common system of taxation, there were significant differences in terms of governance and center–periphery relations. The ties of Egypt with the center were the strongest, because it was the richest administrative unit of the Empire in the sixteenth century, contributing to central treasury more than any other province (Hathaway 1997, 6). These strong ties continued until the beginning of the eighteenth century. From then onwards, the rivalry between the Ottoman administration, the former Mamluk nobility, who had remained in Egypt after the conquest, and the local Arab elite loosened the Ottoman presence. This rivalry ended in 1786, when Cezayirli Gazi Hasan Pasha was sent to Egypt as governor to end the Mamluk interference with provincial administration and restore the strength of centrally-appointed governors (Holt 1968, 82–90). Unlike Egypt, Abyssinia was the least centralized administrative unit of the Empire because of its geographical distance and lack of institutional continuity. Rapid changes of governors and the absence of control over the local nomadic tribes resulted in looser ties with the center (Imber 2019, 191).

Between these two extremes, there were three Ottoman provinces named as *Garb Ocaklari* (the Western Hearths) composed of Tripolitania, Algeria and Tunisia. The administration in these provinces was based on a system called *ocak* (hearth), established by the janissary corps and the military troops brought from Western Anatolia for the maintenance of security and order in the region. This military establishment turned out to be the provincial ruling elites after a while. Since the centrally-appointed governor's short tenure (generally three years) went along with the difficult duty of collecting taxes, the internal affairs of these provinces were handled by councils that included representatives of the military establishment and local elites. Therefore, political power lay in the hands of this council (Shuval 2000, 323–344). This political balance between the centrally-appointed governor and the local council also tilted towards the latter with the gradual military decline of the Ottoman Empire in the late seventeenth and early eighteenth century. Such an authority transfer would eventually lead to almost independent provinces in the region—they even had the competence to declare war and peace towards the neighboring states, or to conclude political or economic agreements with the European states (Abun-Nasr 1993, 159–164).

The local economy in North African provinces of the Empire rested upon trade in Egypt, piracy in Algeria, Tunisia and Tripolitania and slave trade from Sudan and sub-Saharan Africa via the Red Sea and Mediterranean ports of the continent. The Ottoman slave trade in Africa was a relatively later phenomenon, since until the late seventeenth century, Ottomans either enslaved war captives or engaged in slave trade from the North via Crimean slave traders. When the Ottomans began to lose the wars with the European powers, forced enslavement began to diminish and the slave trade, this time from the African provinces of the Empire, increased. The Ottomans generally used slave labor as house servants; unlike the European experience, particularly African slave labor was not much employed in agricultural or industrial sectors (generally Circassian slaves were employed in the agricultural sector; Toledano 1998, 81). In the mid-nineteenth century, just before the abolition of the slave trade in the Ottoman Empire, the annual number of slaves transported to the Ottoman Empire was approximately 17,000. According to estimates, the total number of African slaves transported to the Empire, on the other hand, might have reached 1.3 million (Ferguson 2019, 213), a relatively small number compared to the more than 10 million slaves transported during the transatlantic slave trade (Rawley and Behrendt 2005, 16).

Ottoman rule in North Africa remained mostly uncontested until 1798. That year, the Ottoman Empire directly encountered European colonialism for the first time with the French invasion of Egypt. Although this invasion did not last long, its effects were profound. First, it resulted in the Ottoman perception that even the Ottoman territories other than borderlands were no longer secure from European penetration (Turan 2014, 309). Second, it transformed the socio-political structure of Egypt. From the post-invasion turmoil, a mighty governor, Kavalali Mehmed Ali Pasha, emerged, who would later challenge Ottoman sovereignty in Egypt and would be able to establish his dynastic rule over this province (Turan 2014, 338).

Before the Ottoman Empire's recovery from this initial shock, the province of Algeria was invaded by the French in 1830. Several lessons were drawn from this first successful colonial penetration. First, the Ottomans perceived that centralizing the remaining North African provinces was a must, because it was evident that the French invasion of Algeria was only the first step of

French colonial expansion in the region. Therefore, in 1835, Ottoman troops were sent to Tripolitania to end the *Karamanli* dynasty and to re-establish Ottoman central authority, which was consolidated particularly with the enactment of the Provincial Code in 1864. These measures proved to be effective; despite French and later English colonial ventures in North Africa, Tripolitania remained in the hands of the Ottomans until 1912. However, a similar initiative for Tunisia failed. Accordingly, in order to prevent the fall of Tunisia to French colonial rule, the Tunisians demanded that the Ottomans establish a more central administration as in the case of Tripolitania. The Ottomans responded to these demands positively and officially declared Tunisia a part of the Ottoman Empire in 1871; however, this did not prevent the province from falling under French rule a decade later (Abun-Nasr 1993, 187).

The intensification of the "scramble for Africa" after the Treaty of Berlin in 1884–1885, the French invasion of Tunisia in 1881 and the British invasion of Egypt a year later, forced the Ottoman Empire to take more serious measures. One policy was to delineate the Ottoman territories in North Africa clearly. In order to prevent further French advance in the Sahara Desert, some smaller administrative units were established in the south-western borders of the province of Tripolitania upon the request of the local people. District administrators were sent by the Porte and three districts (*kaza*) were established: Resade and Tibesti (in contemporary Chad) in 1880 and 1884, and the district of Kawar (in contemporary Nigeria) in 1911 (Hazar 1999, 124). The archives related to the establishment of Ottoman local governance in Tibesti reveal instructions of the Minister of Interior to appoint a district governor accompanied by a sufficient number of gendarmerie, and the establishment of a district government office and a police station to claim Ottoman sovereignty over the region.[2]

A second set of policy initiatives involved the use of diplomacy in order to prevent further colonial expansion. Ottoman diplomats tried to voice their protests on international platforms to protect the sovereign rights of the Empire. For instance, according to Ottoman archival correspondence dated 1901–1902, it was rumored at the time that the French were preparing an attack against the Kanem region, which was also under Ottoman sovereignty.[3] The Ottoman governor of Benghazi informed the Porte that the French had begun to collect taxes from the inhabitants of the Kanem which meant a clear violation of Ottoman sovereignty.[4] Upon these intelligence reports, the Ottoman government attempted to prepare a solid case against the French government so as to prove that Kanem was within Ottoman territory.[5]

Finally, Pan-Islamism was promoted to enhance the allegiance and loyalty of local tribes to the Ottoman sultan/caliph. Abdulhamid II contacted several religious orders, the most significant of which was the Sanusiyya order based at al-Jaghbub in the province of Tripolitania, to ensure Ottoman control over the local tribes. Especially, some former local officers, who had once served in Tripolitania, informed Abdulhamid II about the rising influence of the Sanussiya order in Northern and Central Africa.[6]

Besides Western colonial penetration, the other significant aspect of the nineteenth century was the modernization of the region either under colonial rule, or under the rule of the Ottoman or Egyptian governors. For example, Kavalali and his successors urbanized and modernized Egypt to a significant degree (Baer 1968, 135–161). In Algeria and Tunisia, the French colonial administration attempted to eliminate traditional economic and political structures to ensure the absolute and complete subjugation of the population (Stora 2001, 5–6). Finally, in the province of Tripolitania, Ottoman centralization was consolidated with modernization. Sanitary conditions improved and education developed. Particularly during the Hamidian era, tens of primary schools and a few secondary schools were opened in the province (Yazici 1995, 121–132).

All in all, in the late nineteenth and early twentieth centuries, the Ottoman presence in North Africa was very much shattered by British and French colonial penetration, as well as by the quasi-independent administration of Egypt. The limited attempts at centralization could only serve for the maintenance of Ottoman control in Tripolitania, while other Ottoman territories were gradually lost. This age of turmoil was very much reflected in the Ottoman travelogues on the region, which are examined thoroughly in the following section of this chapter.

Ottoman travelers' perception of Africa in the late nineteenth century

Although Africa was quite remote to the Ottoman center, the Ottoman travelers paid numerous visits to this continent especially during the second half of the nineteenth century. More specifically, the pan-Islamist and anti-imperialist policies of Abdulhamid II had a significant impact on this part of the world, as the rivalry of imperialist powers intensified after the 1880s. Therefore, during the late Ottoman Empire, the Ottoman travelers made their way to Africa as agents for developing good relations with the local Muslim elites to check the imperialist expansion, as soldier/bureaucrats to curb European, especially French, imperialist desires in the Sahara, or as diplomats in order to maintain friendly relations with neighboring African states. Whatever the reason for their presence in Africa, these travelers wrote and published their travel accounts and these publications help us to understand Ottoman perceptions of the continent in this volatile period.

Patriotic allegiance to the Ottoman fatherland and religious allegiance to the caliph/sultan

The Ottomans visiting Africa perceived the North African territories of the Empire as part of their fatherland instead of a colony or a dependent territory. This is interesting considering the cultural differences between the

Ottoman imperial core and its North African periphery. For example, with regard to the Sahara Desert, the Ottoman envoy to the Sanusi lodge at al-Jaghbub, Sadik el-Mueyyed wrote that the awareness that he was traveling in the Ottoman realm made him forget all the difficulties of traveling by giving "an extraordinary strength" to his body and "an unidentifiable sense of comfort and security" to his heart (El-Mueyyed 1896–1897, 45). Similarly, a journalist of a popular Ottoman newspaper, *Tanin*, Ahmed Sharif declared his feeling of peace and comfort when he entered Tripolitania, which he defined as the "holy soil of the fatherland"; he wrote that he felt as if he were at home (Sharif 1999, 242).

The perception of the remaining territories of North Africa as part of the fatherland was strengthened by the sense of pride felt for African Muslims' ultimate allegiance to the caliph. The travelers' narration of this allegiance is not peculiar to the Hamidian era, when the discourse of Pan-Islamism reached its zenith. The travelogues written before and after this period also include similar narratives. For example, as early as the 1860s, Omer Lutfi, an Ottoman scholar of Islamic jurisprudence sent to South Africa to provide local Muslims with a proper religious education, wrote that when the Muslim community of Cape Town heard of the arrival of the Ottoman mission, they gathered to express their gratitude to the caliph for answering their call by sending these scholars. This welcoming demonstration satisfied Omer Lutfi and his tutor, Ebubekir Efendi, and made them feel that they were in a friendly and familiar environment (Omer Lutfi 1868, 55–57). What is more, during their stay, an Ottoman vessel visited Cape Town and the local Muslim community declared their "joy and cheerfulness" to Omer Lutfi for hosting an Ottoman vessel in their city (Omer Lutfi 1868, 87).

The Ottoman travelers' experience of the Muslim allegiance to the caliph took its most visible form during the Friday prayers, as the *imam*s prayed for the continuation of the caliph/sultan's reign in their sermons. During these prayers, the travelers observed an intense sense of belonging to the same community. For example, Muhendis Faik, a military engineer in the Ottoman navy witnessed at Port Louis, Mauritius, a Friday prayer during which the *imam* prayed for Sultan Abdulaziz as the caliph of the entire Muslim community. After hearing this, Muhendis Faik wrote that

> we voiced our allegiance [to the Sultan] and adorned our tongues with the devotions "long live the Sultan" in order to thank for hearing the name of our eminent benefactor even in such places as a result of his imperial grace.
>
> (Faik 1868, 47)

This was also the case when Sadik el-Mueyyed, sent as an envoy to the Emperor of Abyssinia, attended a mass prayer in Harar. Almost two thousand Muslim people prayed for the caliph. Sadik el-Mueyyed (1906, 159) underlined the deep significance of caliphate in these distant lands:

Almost in all Muslim realms such a natural situation [praying for the caliph] exists. But after passing all these seas and deserts, it is impossible for a loyal subject not to be happy after seeing that the highness of that holy name [of the caliph] has always been chanted with respect and glorification.

This pattern of allegiance and loyalty of the local people was re-emphasized in the post-Hamidian era; however, this time, it was not presented as loyalty to a religious figure, namely the caliph, but to the Ottoman fatherland itself. Particularly, in Ahmed Sharif's travelogue, the allegiance to the Ottoman fatherland was expressed within the context of the Ottoman anti-imperialist quest against Italian aggression during the Tripolitanian War. Regarding the Arabs of Sfax (in contemporary Tunisia), Ahmed Sharif wrote that they expressed an extraordinary excitement against the Italian attack on the province of Tripolitania and shared his sorrow with regard to the occupation of the Ottoman fatherland by an alien outsider (Sharif 1999, 241). Similarly, he mentioned that the real wealth of the province was not its fertile soil or subsoil mineral resources, but its people who had been as loyal as the Anatolians, the inhabitants of the imperial core (Sharif 1999, 259). This comparison with the Anatolian people demonstrated how Ahmed Sharif appreciated the efforts of the local communities in defending the fatherland against colonial expansion.

In sum, narrating the allegiance of the local Muslims first to the caliph and then to the Ottoman fatherland served to create a sense of common identity, meaning that the Ottomans (including the North African people) had similar concerns and feelings with regard to the contemporary problems they had encountered. This common identity was perceived as a means to prevent the ultimate disintegration of the Empire.

"Urban duality" in North African cities: A discussion of modernity, colonialism and civilization

Another significant characteristic of the travelogues on the non-European world in general and North Africa in particular, is urban duality, in other words, the coexistence of modern European-style quarters with the old Arab/Islamic quarters in the urban space. Indeed, the concept of urban duality is a recent coinage and is used to denote the social and economic, class-based differences in the urban space. In other words, it means the division of the city along quarters or regions resided in by different groups having different socio-economic backgrounds (Hamnett 2001, 162–176). In this chapter, however, urban duality is used as a concept to denote the establishment of quarters in the urban space based on ethnic or religious divisions as well as the divisions created by colonial relationships between the colonizer and the colonized. This division of the urban space underlined the civilized/non-civilized, modern/non-modern, new/old dichotomies. For example, for the city of

Tripoli, Abdulkadir Cami underlines the contrast between the modern buildings along the coastal areas of the city and the old buildings in the old city center. While he employs positive adjectives to describe the former, he writes pejoratively about the old city (Abdulkadir Cami 1909, 12):

> The streets of the new city outside the walls are quite wide and the buildings are in good order. However, the tumult and lack of homogeneity peculiar to the East demonstrates itself here as well. One can encounter *zerbe* established by the branches of date trees peculiar to the black people within a vacant plot next to an adorned building.

Similarly, Cenap Sehabettin (1922, 74) considers that the coexistence of traditional and modern buildings challenges the very identity of Alexandria:

> Examined in whatever perspective, there is no particular characteristic of this city: One can encounter a mosque, a church, a synagogue, a Coptic monastery, or the temples of four or five communities. A large building on a new avenue is followed by an old house with bowed windows in a wide street. One street is narrow, dirty and dark; the street next to it is wide, clean, and adorned with gas lamps. There, an Egyptian sells vegetables, next to him a European deals with tailing; beyond, an Indian sells rarely-found relics, an Englishman has opened a pub, next to him there is the cabin of an Arab scribe.

In sum, the presentation of European-style and Arab/Islamic quarters by means of adjectives such as new/old, brilliant/dull, wide/narrow, enlightened/dark, ordered/tumultuous or clean/dirty serves for a more general dichotomy between civilized and uncivilized. In other words, the European quarters are presented as the embodiment of civilization while non-European quarters lack such a quality.

Their endorsement of such an account of Africa led Ottoman travelers to analyze the reasons for this division and the so-called underdevelopment of the Muslim space *vis-à-vis* the European colonial one. From the travelogues, three reasons could be discerned, related to (1) the characteristics of local people, (2) Ottoman neglect of the region, and (3) the negative implications of colonial administration.

To start with, Ottoman travelers argued that one of the reasons for this perceived backwardness was some peculiar characteristics of the local people. This argument paved the way for the reproduction of Orientalist accounts of North African people. According to Cenap Sehabettin, for instance, Egyptians did not demand much from life as they were content with their simple existence. Therefore, they did not work hard enough to benefit from the advantages of civilization (Sehabettin 1922, 116–117). To put it differently, unlike Europeans, who were continuously striving for living under better conditions, Egyptians preferred to obey the call of their desire instead of working hard for their future. Besides lack of diligence, the travelers viewed local people as being ignorant about how to benefit from the soil as well. According to Sadik el-Mueyyed (1897, 29–30) the soil of Benghazi (in contemporary Libya) was extremely fertile, but the laziness of the local people and their lack of agricultural knowledge failed to take advantage of the full potential of their lands.

The Ottoman travelers' writings on urban duality contributed to an Ottoman discourse that sounded similar to the Orientalist discourse. This resemblance was even stronger when Ottoman travelers attempted to build a racial taxonomy of local African people. Some of the Ottoman travelers, criticized European stereotyping and monolithic perception of the African people, but were nonetheless affected by the European literature on African races and influenced by the popular social Darwinist discourses as they established racial hierarchies or other categorizations based on ethnicity, religion or physiognomy (Palabiyik 2012, 207–210).

Indifference to life, laziness and ignorance were the intrinsic reasons attributed to the backwardness of local communities. However, according to the Ottoman travelers, the real reasons for underdevelopment were to be sought elsewhere. One of their explanations was the long Ottoman neglect of the region. Ottoman travelers, either indirectly or directly, stigmatized the Ottoman central administration for not dealing with these regions properly. As early as during the 1860s, Ebubekir Efendi criticized the Ottoman government for not being interested in the remote regions of Africa, although transportation had substantially improved in recent times. He also emphasized that the desire of the African Muslims to establish contact with the Ottomans and their allegiance to the caliph were very strong. Therefore, he argued, the establishment of friendly contact would be beneficial for both sides (Omer Lutfi 2006, 90–91).[7] The travelogues of the post-Hamidian era also condemned the Ottoman neglect of their own territories in North Africa. For example, Halil Halid (1906, 71) argued that instead of wasting human and financial resources for military conquests in Europe, the Ottomans should have allocated them for North Africa, which was populated by Muslims.

Ahmed Sharif (1999, 257) tried to help his readers visualize the Ottoman neglect of Africa by comparing the two sides of the Ottoman–Tunisian border. On the Tunisian side, one was to find paved roads, telegraph and telephone lines, and other traces of civilized life. The fields were properly cultivated and the soil was more fertile. On the other hand, the Ottoman side of the border could not display any such indications of civilization. The reason for this destitution was the successive Ottoman governments' disinterest in these parts of the Empire.

The Ottoman Empire was not the only actor blamed for the backwardness of the North African territories. Ottoman travelogues considered that the role of imperialist great powers, particularly France, was far more significant. Early Ottoman travelogues on Africa, particularly those concerning South

Africa did not strongly criticize colonialism, particularly the British version. Travelers found British colonial administration useful for bringing civilization to this region. For example, in one of his letters, Ebubekir Efendi wrote that the Muslims living in Cape Town were loyal to the British and hated the Dutch because of their religious intolerance during their colonial rule before the British. What's more, the Muslims felt themselves favored by the British compared to the other nomadic or settled local communities of the region. This was another factor that resulted in Muslim loyalty to the British. Ebubekir Efendi also defended British colonial administration in Mauritius as a source of civilization and appreciated it for establishing many towns and cities and for teaching the local people to raise cotton, sugar cane and other products; he perceived that the British tried to guide the local inhabitants of the region towards civilization. However, despite these efforts, the local people were so ignorant that they were not eager to learn civilization (Omer Lutfi 2006, 85). Similarly, Muhendis Faik perceived British investments in Cape Town as a contribution to the civilization of this region. He wrote that after the establishment of British control, the British spent a lot of money to develop the region with the result that Cape Town "is as improved and developed as the European countries" (Faik 1868, 96).

The travelers especially underlined the very existence of the duality between the colonizer and the colonized. For instance, Suleyman Shukri focused on the visual representations of the colonial administration through statues. In describing a French statue in Tunisia, he compared the representation of a French boy dressed in European style with a Tunisian boy dressed in traditional costume. He argued that the Tunisian boy was in an "insulting condition" both in terms of his appearance and because the French boy was depicted as teaching the French language to him. In other words, the French *mission civilisatrice* was clearly carved in stone in order to demonstrate to the Muslims that the French were in Tunisia for no other reason than to "civilize" them (Shukri 1907, 206–207).

Halil Halid and Suleyman Shukri bitterly criticized French colonial policies, particularly the religious intolerance of the French towards the Muslims despite the formers' self-proclaimed secularism. Both travelers disapproved the French prohibition of reciting the caliph/sultan's name at the Friday sermons and the implementation of this prohibition by employing French soldiers in the mosques during the prayers (Halid 1906, 48; Shukri 1907, 279). What is more, for Halil Halid, the imposition of French lifestyle in Algeria resulted in the moral decadence of the Islamic community - he concluded that the "freedom brought by French civilization undermined Islamic morality" (Halid 1906, 24).

In addition to religious intolerance and imposition of a "morally decadent" lifestyle, the segregation between the French settlers and the local Muslim community was strongly criticized. Suleyman Shukri (1907, 262) witnessed that the French were not treating the local inhabitants as equals; they did not even perceive them as human beings:

The nations that have fallen under their rule are [perceived as] nothing, regardless of the ethnic group or religious sect they belong [...] They do not perceive the ones other than their own race as human beings and they do not respect them at all.

Ottoman travelers also criticized the French policy of appointing Frenchmen only to critical governmental posts. Both Suleyman Shukri and Halil Halid criticized this policy of segregation by arguing that the Muslim community was not inferior to Frenchmen. According to Halil Halid (1906, 49–50), some Muslims were even considered superior to the officials of French origin. Likewise, according to Suleyman Shukri (1907, 279), Frenchmen occupied all the critical governmental posts, all the companies, all the fertile lands of Algeria and deprived the local people of any kind of opportunity. Although some local inhabitants of Algeria could speak French better than Frenchmen they were only employed as poorly paid translators or Arabic language clerks.

All in all, the critique of colonial administration, in general, and of the unequal treatment of the colonized people by the colonizers, in particular, features as a recurrent theme in the Ottoman travelogues written on North Africa. The backwardness of the North African communities was not solely considered as an outcome of their internal problems, but also of the colonial administration. Ottoman travelers showed some appreciation for the material development of the region as a result of colonial rule, but they generally criticized the *mission civilizatrice* for being extremely destructive for the local people.

In lieu of conclusion: The ramifications of Ottoman perception of Africa on current Turkish foreign policy discourse

The examination of Ottoman travelers' perception of Africa and African people is important because this analysis reveals the Ottoman understanding of the concepts of civilization, colonialism and race and this understanding might be utilized as leverage to comment on current TFP discourse on Africa based on the Ottoman heritage. As most of the African territories of the Empire were being lost as a result of European colonial expansion, while the remaining territories were under similar threat, Islam and Ottoman-ness were the two pillars that the Ottoman travelers extensively emphasized in their travelogues. The travelers' efforts in underlining the allegiance of local Muslims to the caliph/sultan or to the fatherland highlight how they included parts of Africa within the political/religious realm to which they also belonged. Therefore, and unlike Europeans, they did not consider African lands as territories for colonization or exploitation. Instead, they viewed the remaining African territories of the Empire as integral components of the Ottoman fatherland. They also considered that other regions of the African continent where Muslims resided were under the religious authority of the caliph. Such an understanding underlines a narrative that offers an alternative to the "Ottoman colonialism/Orientalism" literature (Makdisi 2002; Deringil 2003) and its argument that the Ottomans can also be considered as colonial masters in North Africa. Far from perceiving the region as a colony, at least at discursive level, the Ottoman travelers considered the region as an integral part of the Empire. Most of the literature on Ottoman administration in the Middle East and North Africa confuses Ottoman centralization with Ottoman colonialism. Indeed, instead of colonizing North Africa, the Ottoman administration attempted to strengthen the links between the center and North African provinces so they would not succumb to colonial powers.

The ambivalent perception of colonialism runs through the Ottoman travelogues on Africa. On the one hand, the Ottoman travelers appreciated the colonial administrations' investment in infrastructure, the establishment of modern urban centers or amelioration of sanitation and education facilities. On the other hand, they bitterly criticized the colonial mentality based on the superiority of Western/Christian/white colonizers over the colonized. The Ottoman travelers were aware of the colonial discourse aiming to rationalize and justify European colonial penetration by focusing on the lack of civilization in Africa. For this reason, they attempted to develop an alternative discourse by emphasizing the essentiality of modernization and adoption of material elements of European civilization as being strong enough to contain the threat of European colonialism. Current Turkish foreign policy discourse on Africa appreciates the latter (i.e. the Ottoman travelers' critique of colonial mentality), while totally neglecting the former (i.e. Ottoman travelers' appreciation of colonial powers for "civilizing" North Africa). In other words, the paradoxical Ottoman travelers' approach to Western colonialism no longer features in contemporary Turkish discourse. Moreover, this current discourse also overlooks, if not denies, any reference to Ottoman practices of the slave trade, Ottoman exploitation of her African territories via improper taxation practices, such as tax-farming (*iltizam*), which sometimes put excessive economic pressures on local people, or the racial taxonomy attempts by some Ottoman travelers which paradoxically made their discourse quite similar to the European/Orientalist discourse. Such practices are either found to be non-existent by most practitioners of Turkish foreign policy, or, at best, are labelled as mere exaggerations made by Western historians to denigrate Turkish presence in Africa.

The findings of Ottoman travelers still inform current Turkish foreign policy towards Africa at a discursive level. More specifically, the reference to neo-Ottomanism, associated first and foremost with former Foreign and Prime Minister Ahmet Davutoglu, carry an African dimension as well. Neo-Ottomanism found its roots in former president Turgut Ozal's discourses at the end of the Cold War. This appreciation of the imperial heritage of Turkey, which is claimed to be previously neglected, has two dimensions, one temporal and the other spatial. Temporally, neo-Ottomanism was designed as a conciliation between imperial and republican frameworks, so as to overcome the past underestimation, if not denial, of the former by the latter (Yavuz 2020: 165). Spatially, neo-Ottomanism has attracted attention to former imperial territories, over which, the heir of the Ottoman Empire, namely the Turkish Republic exerted influence based on soft power instruments (Furlanetto 2015, 176; Kalın 2012, 17–19). Neither Davutoglu, nor other prominent foreign policy advisors of Erdogan have clearly voiced that their foreign policy perception was neo-Ottomanist. Yet, the attempts of the Justice and Development Party (JDP) governments to assert Turkey's regional leadership over former imperial territories, particularly in the Balkans and the Middle East, have led researchers to label this particular foreign policy behavior as neo-Ottomanism.

Africa has not been the focus of neo-Ottomanist foreign policy, because the continent, except for North Africa, was never part of the imperial domain and, with the exception of Egypt, was connected to the imperial core through extremely loose bonds. The foreign policy discourse of JDP governments towards Africa nonetheless frequently referred to the imperial legacy.

Three major discursive debates can be identified on contemporary Turkish–African relations with regard to Ottoman heritage. First, Ottoman ties with Northern Africa have always been emphasized in a way that heralds the Ottoman-ness of the African territories as well as the African-ness of Turkey. For instance, upon his return from an official visit to Algeria in 2012, the then Foreign Minister Davutoglu mentioned that Abdulaziz Bouteflika, the President of Algeria, had told him that the Algerians were Ottomans and offered to establish an Ottoman Commonwealth (Haberturk 2012). While, according to Davutoglu, the Algerians claimed themselves to be Ottomans, Turkish identity has an African dimension as well. In one of his speeches in 2013, Davutoglu claimed that Turkey is an Afro-Eurasian country, meaning that Turkish identity has European, Asian and even African elements. Moreover, he defined Turkey as part of African history, geography, politics and economy except for a brief interlude during the twentieth century, implying the negligence of Africa in Turkish foreign policy before the JDP governments (MFA 2013). Similarly, as he visited Djibouti in 2015, President Recep Tayyip Erdogan stated that he perceived Djibouti as "a symbol land of our common civilization" referring to Islam as a common reference point for Turkey and Djibouti. He also underlined Ottoman heritage in Djibouti by saying that "our ancestors had lived together in peace and comfort on the territories of Djibouti for centuries" (TRT Haber 2015). While current Turkish foreign policy discourse emphasizes Ottoman heritage in Africa, this is somewhat ironic if one considers how some Ottoman travelers criticized Ottoman governments for neglecting their North African provinces. As mentioned above, the Ottoman governments were accused of not establishing enough physical (roads, urban facilities, etc.) and mental (education, conscience, etc.) infrastructure in the region—this would ultimately lead to the colonization of the region by the European powers. In other words, ironically, the current Turkish perception of Ottoman presence in Africa is sometimes more positive than the past Ottoman discourse on the region.

Africa has also been used as a discursive tool in recent Turkish foreign policy to criticize Western political/military interventions in the non-Western world. Emphasis has been laid on the destructive colonial presence of European powers in the continent. Accordingly, President Erdogan underlined European colonial penetration in Africa during the nineteenth and twentieth centuries in one of his recent speeches. He criticized European promotion of slavery as well as the occupation of various African territories and claimed that the Europeans attempted to convert local Muslims to Christianity by forbidding Islamic education and the Arabic language (TCCB 2019). Through this criticism of (neo)colonialism, the JDP administrations also underlined what current Turkish interest in Africa should not be. The Spokesman of the President, Ibrahim Kalin has clearly emphasized that the policy of opening towards Africa was never for colonial purposes or for the interest of Turkey solely; rather, Turkey intended to develop policies, relations and agreements for Africa to make the continent stand strong (NTV 2017).

Finally, Africa has become a significant geopolitical region for the security of Turkey. In consonance with the extension of the Ottoman Empire over three continents, the JDP political elites have argued that, even though Turkey comprises a small part of former Ottoman territories, on the basis of its imperial heritage, the defense of Turkey extends far beyond its current borders. This was the case when the 2019 Turkish–Libyan agreement was concluded on the delimitation of sea borders or when Turkey subsequently decided to send military troops to support the UN-recognized el-Sarraj government against Russian-backed Hafter forces. Ibrahim Kalin replied to the criticisms from the opposition parties by claiming that the defense of Turkey started beyond its borders. Similarly, Turkish military presence in Libya should be considered as a policy move designed to bolster the security of Turkey in the Eastern Mediterranean (Hurriyet 2019). In other words, imperial heritage is used as a discursive tool for Turkey as an emerging regional power. This is meant to enlarge the Turkish sphere of influence by linking the geopolitical security of Turkey with Africa on the one hand, and by presenting Africa as an essential component of regional leadership.

All in all, Ottoman rule in Africa and the Ottomans' encounters with colonial penetration in this continent carried significant implications for the Ottoman Empire but also for its successor, the Republic of Turkey, at least at a discursive level. Although Africa was never a central region for the Empire, cognitive representations of Ottoman rule in Africa remain relevant to African people as much as to current Turkish foreign policy makers. Caliphal authority over African Muslims can no longer be called upon, but Islam remains a common denominator between the Muslim parts of the Empire and Turkey. Ottoman resistance against colonial penetration in Africa is reproduced today as a discursive reaction against Western engagement with African conflicts, particularly in the aftermath of the Arab spring.

Although after the disintegration of the Ottoman Empire, the Balkans, Caucasus and North Africa emerged as hubs beyond the borders of Turkey, they are perceived today as significant for the security of the formal imperial core. The current Turkish drive towards Africa is conspicuous for reviving Ottoman heritage and the former grandeur of an empire that had the ability to reach and even control parts of this remote and vast continent. Yet, one should also be aware that the current TFP discourse on Africa depicts an Ottoman legacy rather stronger than the actual Ottoman presence in the region. It also overlooks the negative aspects of this presence. The frequently referred "Islamic brotherhood" discourse may conceal that the relationship between the imperial core and the African periphery was akin to a master–subject relationship, as observed elsewhere in the empire. In addition to this, current TFP discourse does not consider the Ottoman slave trade a component of the Ottoman legacy in the continent. Finally, current TFP discourse blurs the critical stance of several Ottoman travelers who complained of administrative negligence towards the empire's African provinces in terms of infrastructure building. In short, current TFP discourse on the Ottoman legacy in Africa seeks to emphasize constructive aspects of Turkey's relations with Africa. As a result, it sometimes turns a blind eye to negative Ottoman discursive and practical constructs so as to create a monolithic and positive perception of past and present relations.

Notes

1 Some parts of this chapter draw from the PhD dissertation of the author entitled "Travel, Civilization and the East: Ottoman Travellers' Perception of 'the East' in the Late Ottoman Empire," Middle East Technical University, Department of International Relations, April 2010, Ankara.
2 Presidency of the Turkish Republic Directorate of State Archives, Ottoman Archives BEO 3731/279780 (29 Rebiulevvel 1328 [10 April 1910]).
3 Presidency of the Turkish Republic Directorate of State Archives, Ottoman Archives, DH. ŞFR 317/49 (29 Saban 1319 [11 December 1901]).
4 Presidency of the Turkish Republic Directorate of State Archives, Ottoman Archives, BEO 1751/131324 (17 Saban 1319 [29 November 1901]).
5 Presidency of the Turkish Republic Directorate of State Archives, Ottoman Archives, İ. HUS. 92/80 (26 Ramazan 1319 [6 January 1902]).
6 See, for instance, Presidency of the Turkish Republic Directorate of State Archives, Ottoman Archives, Y. PRK. AZJ (22 Receb 1317 [26 November 1899]).
7 The letters sent by Ebubekir Efendi were not included in the original version of Omer Lutfi's travelogue. They were put in its transliteration by Huseyin Yorulmaz. Omer Lutfi, *Umitburnu Seyahatnamesi* (Istanbul: Kitabevi Yayinlari, 2006).

References

Abdulkadir Cami. 1326 [1909]. *Trablusgarp'tan Sahra-yi Kebir'e Dogru*. Dersaadet [Istanbul]: Unknown Publisher.
Abun-Nasr, Jamil M. 1993. *A History of the Maghrib in the Islamic Period*. Cambridge: Cambridge University Press.
Ahmed Sharif. 1999. *Arnavudluk'da, Suriye'de, Trablusgarb'de Tanin*. Transliterated and edited by Mehmet Cetin Borekci. Ankara: Turk Tarih Kurumu Yayinlari.

Baer, Gabriel. 1968. "Social Change in Egypt: 1800–1914." In *Political and Social Change in Modern Egypt*, edited by P.M. Holt, 135–161. London: Oxford University Press.

Cenap Sehabettin. 1341 [1922]. *Hac Yolunda*. Istanbul: Matbaa-i Kanaat.

Deringil, Selim. 2003. "'They Live in a State of Nomadism and Savagery': The Late Ottoman Empire and the Post-Colonial Debate." *Comparative Studies in Society and History*, 45, no. 2: 311–342. DOI: https://doi.org/10.1017/S001041750300015X.

Ferguson, Michael. 2019. "Abolitionism and the African Slave Trade in the Ottoman Empire (1857–1922)." In *The Palgrave Handbook of Bondage and Human Rights in Africa and Asia*, edited by Gwyn Campbell and Alessandro Stanziani, 209–226. New York: Palgrave Macmillan.

Furlanetto, Elena. 2015. "'Imagine a Country Where We Are All Equal': Imperial Nostalgia in Turkey and Elif Shafak's Ottoman Utopia." In *Post-Empire Imaginaries: Anglophone Literature, History and Demise of Empires*, edited by Barbara Buchenau and Virginia Richter, with Marijke Denger, 159–180. Leiden: Brill.

Haberturk. 2012. "'Osmanli Milletler Toplulugu kuralim' teklifi!" November 29, 2012. https://www.haberturk.com/gundem/haber/798565-osmanli-milletler-toplulugu-kura lim-teklifi.

Halil Halid. 1906. *Cezayir Hatiratindan*. Mısır: Matbaa-i Ictihad.

Hamnett, Chris. 2001. "Social Segregation and Social Polarization." In *Handbook of Urban Studies*, edited by Ronan Paddiso, 162–176. London: Sage Publications.

Hathaway, Jane. 1997. *The Politics of Households in Ottoman Egypt: The Rise of Qazdaglis*, Cambridge: Cambridge University Press.

Hazar, Numan. 1999. "Turklerin Afrika ile Iliskilerinin Kisa Tarihcesi." In *Turkler*, Vol. 13, edited by Hasan Celal Guzel et al., 118–131. Ankara: Yeni Turkiye Yayinlari.

Holt, P.M. 1968. "Pattern of Egyptian Political History from 1517 to 1798." In *Political and Social Change in Modern Egypt*, edited by P.M. Holt, 79–90. Oxford: Oxford University Press.

Hurriyet. 2019. "Kalin: Misak-i Milli sinirlarinin guvenligi sinirlarin otesinde baslar." December 29, 2019. http://www.hurriyet.com.tr/gundem/kalin-misak-i-milli-sinirla rinin-guvenligi-sinirlarin-otesinde-baslar-41408298.

Imber, Colin. 2019. *The Ottoman Empire, 1300–1650: The Structure of Power*, 3rd ed. London: Red Globe Press.

Kalın, İbrahim. 2012. "Turkish Foreign Policy: Framework, Values and Mechanisms." *International Journal*, 67 no. 2: 7–21. DOI: https://doi.org/10.1177/ 002070201206700102.

Karcinzade Suleyman Shukri. 1907. *Seyahat-i Kubra*. Petersburg: The Printing House of Abdurreshid Ibrahim.

Kavas, Ahmet. 2006. *Osmanli-Afrika Iliskileri*. İstanbul: TASAM Yayinlari.

Makdisi, Ussama. 2002. "Ottoman Orientalism." *The American Historical Review* 107, no. 3: 768–796. DOI: https://doi.org/10.1086/ahr/107.3.768.

MFA. 2013. "Foreign Minister Davutoglu's Inaugural Speech at the Sectoral Evaluation Meeting of African Strategies."September 3, 2013. http://www.mfa.gov.tr/disisleri-ba kani-sayin-ahmet-davutoglu_nun-afrika-stratejileri-sektorel-degerlendirme-toplanti sinin-acilisinda-yaptiklari-konusm.tr.mfa.

Muhendis Faik. 1285 [1868]. *Seyahatname-i Bahr-i Muhit*. İstanbul: Mekteb-i Bahriye-i Sahane Matbaasi.

NTV. 2017. "*Cumhurbaskanligi Sozcusu Kalin'dan Sevakin Adasi aciklamasi*." December 29, 2017. https://www.ntv.com.tr/turkiye/cumhurbaskanligi-sozcusu-ka lindan-sevakin-adasi-aciklamasi,ucpMrGmnlkSivD3Mt9iTUQ.

Omer Lutfi. 1292 [1868]. *Umitburnu Seyahatnamesi*. Istanbul: Basiret Matbaasi.
Omer Lutfi. 2006. *Umitburnu Seyahatnamesi*. Transliterated and edited by Huseyin Yorulmaz. Istanbul: Kitabevi Yayinlari.
Pakalin, Mehmet. 1993. *Osmanli Tarih Deyimleri ve Terimler Sozlugu*, Vol. 3. Ankara: Milli Egitim Basimevi.
Palabiyik, Mustafa Serdar. 2012. "Ottoman Travellers' Perception of Africa in the Late Ottoman Empire (1860–1922): A Discussion of Civilization, Colonialism and Race." *New Perspectives on Turkey*, no. 46: 187–212. https://doi.org/10.1017/S0896634600001552.
Presidency of the Turkish Republic Directorate of State Archives, Ottoman Archives, BEO 1751/131324 (17 Saban 1319 [29 November 1901]).
Presidency of the Turkish Republic Directorate of State Archives, Ottoman Archives, BEO 3731/279780 (29 Rebiulevvel 1328 [10 April 1910]).
Presidency of the Turkish Republic Directorate of State Archives, Ottoman Archives, DH. ŞFR 317/49 (29 Saban 1319 [11 December 1901]).
Presidency of the Turkish Republic Directorate of State Archives, Ottoman Archives, İ. HUS. 92/80 (26 Ramazan 1319 [6 January 1902]).
Presidency of the Turkish Republic Directorate of State Archives, Ottoman Archives, Y. PRK. AZJ (22 Receb 1317 [26 November 1899]).
Rawley, James A. and Stephen D. Behrendt. 2005. *The Transatlantic Slave Trade: A History*. Lincoln: University of Nebraska Press.
Sadik el-Mueyyed. 1314 [1896–1897]. *Afrika Sahra-yi Kebir'inde Seyahat*. Istanbul: Alem Matbaasi.
Sadik el-Mueyyed. 1322 [1906]. *Habes Seyahatnamesi*. Istanbul: Ikdam Matbaasi.
Shuval, Tal. 2000. "The Ottoman Algerian Elite and Its Ideology." *International Journal of Middle East Studies* 32, no. 3: 323–344. DOI: https://doi.org/10.1017/S0020743800021127.
Stora, Benjamin. 2001. *Algeria, 1830–2000: A Short History*. Ithaca, NY: Cornell University Press.
TCCB (Turkish Presidency). 2019. "3. Afrika Ülkeleri Dini Liderler Zirvesi'nde Yaptıkları Konuşma Yaptıkları Konuşma." October 19, 2019. https://www.tccb.gov.tr/konusmalar/353/112208/3-afrika-ulkeleri-dini-liderler-zirvesi-nde-yaptiklari-konusma-yaptiklari-konusma.
Toledano, Ehud. 1998. *Slavery and Abolition in the Ottoman Middle East*. Seattle: University of Washington Press.
TRT Haber. 2015. "Erdogan Cibuti Meclisi'ni Ziyaret Etti." January 24, 2015. https://www.trthaber.com/haber/gundem/erdogan-cibuti-meclisini-ziyaret-etti-164066.html.
Turan, Namik Sinan. 2014. *Imparatorluk ve Diplomasi: Osmanli Diplomasisinin Izinde*. İstanbul: Bilgi Universitesi Yayinlari.
Yavuz, M. Hakan. 2020. *Nostalgia for the Empire: The Politics of Neo-Ottomanism*. Oxford: Oxford University Press.
Yazici, Nesimi. 1975. "Osmanli Haberlesme Kurumu." In *150. Yilinda Tanzimat*, edited by Hakki Dursun Yildiz, 139–209. Ankara: Turk Tarikh Kurumu Yayinlari.

3 Turkey–Africa relations
A retrospective analysis

Numan Hazar and Elem Eyrice Tepeciklioğlu

Introduction

In the last few years, rising powers and their growing engagement in Africa has attracted much scholarly interest. Although Africa's traditional Western partners have strong positions in their relations with African countries, the monopoly of the West was challenged with the emergence of new actors involved in Africa, most notably, China and India. Turkey also showed recent interest in enhancing its African involvement while its growing relations with the continent gained increasing attention. Especially in the last decade, Turkey has emerged as an important provider of humanitarian aid to Africa, expanded its diplomatic presence in the continent and effectively used trade relations along with other soft power tools in order to further its relationship with Africa. As Chapter 2 exploring the Ottoman presence in Africa has revealed, Turkey's historical ties with the continent date back centuries—especially with those African countries that were once subject to Ottoman rule. Turkey appears to have significant advantages emanating mostly from its Ottoman legacy and its cultural, religious and historical affinity with some of those African countries. Presenting itself as a country having no imperial agenda in its relations with African countries, it has also long avoided becoming entangled in African conflicts—except in its recent involvement in Libya. The message reflects Turkey as a state with no colonial ambition that follows policies entirely different especially from that of its Western counterparts.

Yet, Turkey's Africa policy is also prompted by pragmatic considerations. What arouses Turkey's recent interest towards Africa is mostly economic imperatives, that is, the latter's consumer market potential for Turkish goods and services and the desire to diversify trade partnerships combined with the economic performance of a variety of African economies. Turkey's growing African engagement is also shaped by its increasing ambition in world affairs and its quest to cultivate diplomatic alliances to support its foreign policy actions. An enhanced presence in Africa can also help to transform Turkey's image at national, regional and global levels. However, interest towards the continent was minimal until the adoption of the Action Plan for Opening up to Africa in 1998.

This chapter will first discuss the determining factors that limited Turkey's engagement in Africa in the late 1990s and the formation of a robust African agenda. In doing so, it will explore how Turkey's attitude on particular incidents regarding Africa offended African nations and aroused the mistrust of those countries. The chapter will then elucidate the basic motivators that underlined the adoption of the action plan and changing patterns of relations with African countries. The final part will evaluate the major steps taken for the implementation of the plan with an additional focus on the recent developments in Turkey–Africa relations.

Why did Africa remain at the periphery of Turkish foreign policy?

Official statements place a heavy emphasis on the Ottoman presence in the continent, however, the successor of the Ottoman Empire, the Turkish Republic, placed lesser importance on relations with former Ottoman territories including those located in Africa. This is largely because the policymakers of the newly established republic were heavily preoccupied with internal issues including the implementation of domestic reforms that required urgent attention. On the other hand, foreign policy priorities were chiefly shaped by westernization efforts that long remained a constant element underpinning foreign policy. Priorities of the republican Turkey's foreign policy were also aimed at maintaining a friendship and alliance relationship with the Soviet Union, which financially and materially supported the Turkish War of Independence. As noted by Haugom (2019, 209):

> National threat perceptions in Turkey have therefore often centered on the country's unique geostrategic position and its vulnerability to great-power interests. By extension, national security has for long periods dominated matters of state and has remained a primary concern in Turkish foreign policy.

Another priority was the solution of some residual problems as well as the creation of peaceful relations with Greece. Meanwhile, the majority of African countries were still under colonial rule with few exceptions. European colonies in Africa therefore remained at the periphery of Turkish foreign policy. The establishment of an embassy in Ethiopia's capital, Addis Ababa, in 1926 was an exception during this period while the Turkish embassy in Cairo already existed.

Dealing with more imminent foreign policy issues, the Turkish leadership followed a "balanced" and "rational" foreign policy when the country was weak both in military and economic terms (MFA 2011). Combined with the vulnerability of the country in the international system, Ankara's low material capabilities restricted its ability to make "adventurous" foreign policy moves. Looking for foreign aid for national security and economic growth, Ankara received military and financial assistance from the USA (United

States of America). Meanwhile, the first wave of decolonization in Africa came in the 1950s with the independence of Northern African countries except in the case of Algeria. Having little interest in African affairs, Turkey nonetheless recognized the independence of African countries and established embassies in some of those countries including Sudan (1957), Senegal (1960), Nigeria (1962) and Ghana (1964) (Hazar 2016).

During this period, the bipolarity of the Cold War, the strategic interests of Turkey's NATO (North Atlantic Treaty Organization) allies and the need to counterbalance the perceived threats from the Soviet Union limited Turkey's African involvement and determined its behavior in particular incidents regarding Africa.[1] This includes Turkey's participation at the Bandung Conference assembled between 18–24 April 1955 and its attitude towards the non-aligned movement (NAM). Speaking at the conference as the head of the Turkish delegation, the Turkish Minister of Foreign Affairs, Fatin Rustu Zorlu advised those Asian–African countries that sought to refrain from any Cold War groupings, to align with the Western bloc: "The illusion is disastrous that by passive inactivity a country can escape from external dangers to its security ... The conference must realize the grave danger involved in a 'middle of the road' policy" (CVCE 2017).

The prevalent belief among Turkish politicians that the country could not afford to be part of the NAM due to its geographic and strategic imperatives also affected its stance towards the movement. Moreover, as a member of NATO, Turkey's security was already guaranteed as part of its alliance relationship, so Turkish officials were not interested in developing ties with NAM members (Aral 2004, 138; Baba and Ertan 2016). Seeking to increase the amount of American aid, Turkey attended the conference via American encouragement (Baba and Ertan 2016) and was later defined as a proxy of the US (Dikerdem 1977, 117–18). While Turkey's independence war could have provided it a privileged position among the other participants of the Bandung Conference,[2] the Conference increased its marginalization and distance from the non-aligned countries (Baba and Ertan 2016).

Earlier the same year, Turkey played a pioneering role in the establishment of the Baghdad Pact along with the United Kingdom, Iran, Iraq and Pakistan. The pact was a defense organization aimed at countering Soviet expansionism in the region and other regional states were expected to join. The US was not a member of the pact but it had an observer status (Cetiner 1995, iv; Yildirim 2018, 125). Although Turkey tried to enlist the number of member states as a founding member of the pact, the regional powers, most notably Egypt, had different perceptions on its formation. For example, Egyptian leader, Gamal Abd-el Nasser, explicitly opposed it from the very outset and criticized the member states for their involvement in a British initiative. Turkey's leading role in the formation of a Western-proposed regional arrangement was also perceived by most of the Arab and Northern African states as a tool to sustain Western influence in the Middle East and to prolong external involvement in regional politics (Benli Altunisik 2009,

174; Cetiner 1995). Nasser's leadership ambitions in the region also explains Egypt's position towards the pact. Nasser saw the pact as a threat to its regional hegemony and a means to dismantle Arab unity. Yet, for Turkey, the pact could guarantee its security by containing Soviet penetration in the region. As seen, diverging threat perceptions and security needs of Turkey and Arab countries help explain their drift on regional affairs (Uzer and Uzer 2005, 101).

Turkey's attitude towards the pact antagonized Egypt and its regional allies (Benli Altunisik 2009, 174) but conflicting interests between Turkey and other Arab and North African countries became more visible during the Suez Crisis. Turkey–Egypt relations deteriorated following Egypt's nationalization of the Suez Canal and Turkey's support for the British presence in the Canal. On 8 January 1954, a daily Turkish newspaper, *Vatan*, wrote: "Even today, if there were not a strong Turkey in front of Suez, a Soviet puppet would have been sitting in General Nagib's place. Egypt's independence is preserved through Turkish honor and self-respect" (Sehsuvaroglu quoted in Sanjian 1997, 262). It was also before the outbreak of the crisis when the Menderes government stated that Turkey did not take the Canal dispute as a bilateral issue between the UK (United Kingdom) and Egypt. Instead, Turkish statesmen saw it as a problem concerning NATO's overall strategy. Being convinced that the UK was acting "as guardian of an outpost of one of the key positions of the free world," Turkey feared that Egypt could not maintain the operation of the Canal (Sever 2008, 125–127).

Turkish officials were also concerned that the withdrawal of the British from the Canal would lead to regional instability and a power vacuum that could be replaced by the Soviet Union. This explains why Turkey attended the first Suez Conference held in London between 15–24 August 1956 and signed the US proposal to establish an international board for the operation of the Canal (Aldrich 1967, 542). After the failure of this conference, a second conference convened in London on 19 September 1956. Once again, Turkey supported the US-proposed Suez Canal Users Association with the majority of the conference participants. It was only after the US demanded British and French withdrawal from the Canal that Turkey reluctantly sided with the US. Not surprisingly, Turkey's alignment with the Western powers was condemned by most of the regional powers (Aldrich 1967, 543–44; Sever 2008, 127).

Another incident where the pursuit of a pro-Western foreign policy course influenced the formulation and conduct of Turkey's relations with the newly emerging nations in Africa was its attitude on the issue of Algeria. The Turkish War of Independence against the colonial powers of the time was an inspiration for Algerian leaders. The FLN (Front de Libération Nationale), even asked if Turkey could use its influence on France as a member of the Baghdad Pact (Ersoy 2012, 684–688). Yet, Turkey abstained or voted in favor of official French positions against Afro-Asian proposals calling for negotiations between the GPRA (Gouvernement Provisoire de la République

Algérienne) and France at the United Nations (UN) General Assembly (GA).[3] Turkey also voted at the UN against resolutions for the independence of Tunisia and Morocco, former French protectorates. Regarding Algerian independence as France's internal affairs, Turkey did not depict it as being within UN competence (Aral 2004, 138; Hazar 2018, 244). Turkey's Western-oriented foreign policy behavior generated resentment among the Third World countries while its diplomatic support was appreciated by the French. It was again Turkey's NATO commitments that determined its voting behavior against the Algerian independence movement. For example, Article 6 of the North Atlantic Treaty defined Algeria as part of French territory (NATO Public Diplomacy Division 2006, 372) although the North Atlantic Council modified this Treaty following the independence of Algeria. As seen, Turkey's initial attempts to enter NATO and its later membership of the organization played a decisive role in its attitude against Algerian independence given that France was an influential NATO member.

The years between 1960 and 1980 witnessed the shift towards a more multidimensional foreign policy course as the détente eased the bipolar tensions between western and eastern blocs (Oguzlu 2020). Meanwhile, domestic developments started to radically shift the political landscape. In 1960, Turkey's pro-American civilian government was overthrown by a coup d'état. As foreign policy was inextricably connected with domestic politics, the resulting regime change had important implications for Turkish foreign policy. The same year, Turkey became a co-sponsor of UNGA resolution no. 1514, "Declaration on the Granting of Independence to Colonial Countries and Peoples and voted in favor of resolution 1573(XV) which called on France to ensure the effective implementation of the principle of self-determination in Algeria. Having realized that the pro-Western stance in foreign policy led to Turkey's isolation in world politics, the military rulers sought to improve relations with the Third World countries (Aral 2004, 139; Ersoy 2012, 189) that now formed the largest voting bloc in the UN. Turkey's arduous efforts to approach those countries was mostly driven by political considerations including the need to get their diplomatic support for specific policy lines such as its Cyprus cause and to allay the impacts of its international isolation. As noted by Ulman and Dekmejian:

> it had seemed impossible to elicit such support through the perpetuation of her exclusive alliance ties with the West of the 1950s—already tangibly damaged, anyway, by the reluctance of the United States to support Turkey on her Cyprus cause in 1964.
>
> (Quoted in Aykan 1993, 102)

To this end, Turkey sent goodwill delegations to various African countries in order to explain the Turkish view on the Cyprus conflict. Among the seven delegations that were planned to visit Middle Eastern, Asian, Latin American and African countries, three of them were assigned to Africa (Bulletin of the Ministry of Foreign Affairs, Issue 3 1964, 5).[4] The underlying belief was that the development of relations with African countries could offer Turkey a new support base in international fora.

Turkey's rapprochement efforts with Africa failed to produce the desired outcomes. Turkey could not obtain the diplomatic support of those countries when the Cyprus issue was brought to the UN agenda. African countries voted against the Turkish argument while the UN General Assembly resolution of 32 Asian–African countries calling on all countries to "respect the sovereignty, unity, independence and territorial integrity of Cyprus" was accepted by 47 votes in favor on December 18 1965.[5] Those sporadic and exceptional initiatives to develop ties with African countries were not backed by a specific Africa policy. For example, in the Bulletin of the Ministry of Foreign Affairs (March 1965, 23–24), it was noted that Turkey's Asia–Africa policy should focus on establishing "friendly" relations with those newly-independent countries that are in the process of developing their foreign polices. Turkey, a member of the Western community, committed to its NATO alliance, should gain the "sympathy" of those countries without being part of the different political groupings in the non-aligned movement. However, this policy was mostly confined to the cultural sphere and aimed at promoting Turkish interests while it was firmly noted that economic or technical assistance towards those new countries was not on the agenda.

It was not until the late 1970s that the Turkish government under the leadership of Prime Minister, Bulent Ecevit, adopted a policy to outreach Africa.[6] The government has been seeking to diversify Turkey's foreign policy agenda as relations with the US deteriorated especially due to Turkish intervention in Cyprus and the following US arms embargo (Ipek and Biltekin 2013, 126). An important part of this policy was to reorganize the Ministry of Foreign Affairs by creating a desk system. The first desk created in the new administrative system within the ministry was assigned to Africa (Karaca 2000, 117). During this period, the policymakers also believed that economic relations would facilitate the development of bilateral ties with African countries, so, priority was given to commercial links. The establishment of a new department within the ministry was then followed by an economic committee formed from ministerial officials and representatives of the public and private enterprises. In early 1979, the committee visited economically powerful African countries including Nigeria, Kenya, Sudan, Uganda and Ethiopia in order to explore market opportunities. The political pillar of the opening included the increase in Turkey's diplomatic representation across the continent and the exchange of high-level visits.[7] Subsequently, two new resident embassies were opened in 1979 in Somalia's capital, Mogadishu and Tanzania's capital, Darussalam while various Turkish delegations visited the following African countries, Kenya, Nigeria, Uganda, Sudan, Tanzania, Zambia, Ethiopia and Zimbabwe in order to amplify economic and commercial relations. During this brief period, Turkey offered technical assistance to a number of African countries including the medical assistance package sent to Zimbabwe in 1978 and signed economic and technical cooperation agreements (TETs) with Egypt in 1978 and Sierra Leone in 1979 (Ipek and Biltekin 2013, 126–127).

This policy of outreach to Africa, however, was a short-lived attempt. The incumbent coalition government was dissolved following the resignation of Ecevit in late 1979. The political instability was coupled by the accelerating decline in the economy and the African opening was abandoned following the 1980 military coup. The African Desk at the Ministry of Foreign Affairs was already suffering from the lack of personnel to fulfill the duties assigned to it. After the coup, Turkey's diplomatic missions in Ghana (Accra), Somalia (Mogadishu) and Tanzania (Darussalam) were closed mainly for financial reasons (Incesu 2020; Karaca 2000, 118). The closure of embassies is a clear indicator of the waning political interest towards Africa; however, this would soon be replaced by a new attentiveness to Africa's economic potential.

It was in the early 1980s that Turkey introduced an economic liberalization program in order to integrate the Turkish economy with world markets. A critical figure behind this policy was Turgut Ozal who served respectively as the deputy prime minister responsible for economic affairs (1980–1982), the prime minister (1983–1989) and the president of Turkey (1989–1993). The political stability of the 1980s was instrumental in the recovery from the economic crisis (Onis 2004, 113). In addition to the neoliberal structuring of the Turkish economy, economic growth enabled the following of a more multidimensional and balanced foreign policy in the mid-1980s when Turkey approached different regions including the Middle East, and the Eastern Bloc countries in an effort to cultivate relations with them. The new bourgeoisie that emerged during this liberalization period also supported the opening to new geographies. This increased the attractiveness of African markets to Turkish businesses, seeking new investment opportunities and alternative destinations. The Ozal government enjoyed the support of this newly-emerging business community—the business–state partnership continued under the JDP government. So, this period has not only seen the diversification of Turkey's foreign relations but it has also witnessed the increasing role of Turkey's private sector in formulating the foreign (economic) policies of the country.

Ozal's foreign policy vision had repercussions on Turkey's Africa policy as well. This is evidenced in the delivery of Turkey's first comprehensive aid package to Africa. It was part of the Sahel Project developed by the State Planning Organization in 1987. Targeting the following African countries, namely, Somalia, Sudan, Chad, Niger, Mali, Mauritania, Burkina Faso, Senegal, the Gambia, Guinea, Guinea Bissau and Cape Verde, Turkish aid amounted to US$10 million (Birtek 1996, 37). In March 1988, Turkey hosted the UN Seminar on the International Responsibility for the Independence of Namibia that aimed at mobilizing concerted action for Namibian independence. In his Opening Statement, Professor Ali Bozer, the Minister of State and the Acting Foreign Minister, said that the seminar reflected "a renewed expression" of Turkey's support for the Namibian cause (Ataov 1988, 13).

It is important not to underestimate economic considerations when exploring the Ozal-era initiatives towards Africa. Because the same year, Ozal sent delegations to several African countries including Senegal, Gambia, Gabon, Nigeria and Cameroon in order to explore the possibilities to facilitate trade relations with African countries (Bleda 2000, 184–190). Between 1987 and 1989, Turkey also signed cooperation and TET agreements with seven African countries, namely, Uganda, Nigeria, Botswana, Chad, Djibouti, the Gambia and Zambia (Ipek and Biltekin 2013, 127). Through such agreements, Turkey sought to explore the opportunities African markets could provide for Turkish companies and business associations that had been lobbying the government to expand commercial ties with the continent and supporting the country's integration with world markets (Kirisci and Kaptanoglu 2011, 713). Having their roots in small-scale businesses in Anatolia, these Anatolian businessmen later, in 1990, formed MUSIAD (Independent Industrialists' and Businessmen's Association) which played an active role in the JDP (AKP: Justice and Development Party) from its establishment (Tur 2011).

The end of the Cold War improved Turkey's maneuvering capability in foreign policy (Oguzlu 2020). It not only allowed Turkey to follow a more autonomous foreign policy in different regions but it also eroded its strategic value for its Western allies. Oguzlu (2020) notes that:

> the 1990s could be seen as a period in which Turkey tried to strike a balance between pursuing a more independent/multidirectional foreign policy stance on the one hand and increasing its efforts to solidify its presence in the western international community on the other.

As Turkey sought to diversify its external relations, priority was given to former Soviet territories in the Balkans and Central Asia along with Turkey's relationship with its Middle Eastern neighbors. In order to coordinate aid projects in the newly emerged Central Asian states with which Turkey has strong historical and cultural ties, the Turkish Cooperation and Coordination Agency (TIKA) was established in 1992 during Turgut Ozal's presidency.

However, Turkey's regional aspirations to form a Turkic community under its own leadership were not received with the same enthusiasm by those newly established countries. Combined with the rejection of its EU candidacy at the 1997 Luxembourg Summit, this has led to Turkey's outreach policies towards remote regions through the "Action Plan for Latin America and the Caribbean" and the "Action Plan for Opening up to Africa" adopted in 1998. The latter started a new chapter in Turkey–Africa relations in a period when relations between those two parties was at its nadir. It was initiated by the then Minister of Foreign Affairs, Ismail Cem, who was keen to enhance Turkey's international profile by pursuing an active and independent foreign policy. Cem, however, faced resistance even from his own ministry (Kirisci and Kaptanoglu 2011, 713). The action plan was not fully implemented due to this lack of political support, coupled with the subsequent economic crisis, unstable political environment and the absence of sufficient financial resources until the JDP assumed power with the 2002 elections. Having strong political and economic incentives to expand Turkey's engagement in Africa, the JDP built on the previous Africa policy and gave a new orientation to Turkey's relations with Africa.

The implementation of the action plan and recent developments

Contemporary Turkey–Africa relations can be characterized by a long period of reciprocal ignorance. This was followed by sporadic interests guided by the primary concerns of foreign policy. Thus, until 1998, there was a lull as far as Turkey–Africa relations were concerned. The comprehensive plan of action adopted under the leadership of Ismail Cem aimed at upgrading Turkey's relationship with Africa at all levels. Upon the invitation of Cem, Ambassador Numan Hazar, the general director for Africa and the Middle East, was personally involved in preparing the plan.[8]

The plan, which suggested several measures to improve the Turkey–Africa relationship, was prepared at the end of a series of meetings in consultation with multiple actors including senior government officials, Turkish ambassadors in Africa, honorary consuls of African countries as well as representatives from the private sector and civil society. Prior to those meetings, the Undersecretary of the Ministry of Foreign Affairs, Korkmaz Haktanir invited Hazar and asked him to form a delegation that would visit African countries in order to explain Turkish views on the Cyprus question. Haktanir believed that Hazar's diplomatic experience in both Cyprus and Africa could serve as an advantage in getting African support for Turkey's Cyprus cause in international fora.[9] Referring to previous goodwill delegations Turkey sent to African countries in the 1960s, Hazar said that the real problem was the lack of a coherent Africa policy despite the existing potentialities. Noting that African nations may find it hard to understand the Turkish position on Cyprus due to historical reasons as well as the ethnic, tribal or religious diversity prevalent in many African countries, Hazar suggested that the development of bilateral relations would eventually lead Africans to have a better understanding of Turkish foreign policy concerns. The action plan therefore included a separate section on the Turkish Republic of Northern Cyprus (Section IX), which stipulated that: "Any opening policy to Africa should include the Cyprus issue and contribute to Turkey's Cyprus cause" (MFA 1999, 14).

Overall, the plan aimed at increasing Turkey's diplomatic representation in Africa, promoting high-level visits, establishing political consultation mechanisms and providing humanitarian assistance especially through UN technical assistance programs (political measures); concluding agreements of trade, technical, economic and scientific cooperation, prevention of double taxation, mutual promotion and protection of investments, implementing business visits, establishing joint business councils or chambers of commerce and realizing Turkey's membership of the African Development Bank (AfDB) as a non-regional donor country (economic measures); the signing of cultural cooperation agreements, promoting cooperation and interaction between Turkish and African universities and increasing the number of grants and scholarships provided to African students (educational and cultural measures); cooperation in the field of the defense industry, contribution to the UN peacekeeping missions in Africa, promotion of air links and maritime transportation and implementing visits by high-ranking military officials (military measures). Some of those measures also aimed at introducing Africa to Turkish people—and vice versa—and increasing public and scholarly awareness of African issues (MFA 1999).

Despite all the attempts at implementation of the plan, the document remained "a wish list" (Wheeler 2011, 46). As discussed before, various domestic challenges including the devastating 1999 Marmara earthquake, a serious financial crisis and political instability led by weak coalition governments relegated Africa's status in foreign policy (Wheeler 2011, 46) and prevented the effective implementation of the action plan. Following the JDP's coming to power with the 2002 parliamentary elections, Turkish foreign policy underwent a major transformation. Relations with Western countries was still a primary concern but Turkey also sought to reach out to distant geographies.

Shortly after it assumed power, the JDP took firms steps in order to expand its engagement with Africa. For example, in 2003, the Undersecreteriat of the Prime Ministry for Foreign Trade prepared the document, the "Strategy for Development of Economic Relations with Africa," in order to complement the economic component of the action plan. The year 2005, which was proclaimed by the Turkish Government as "the Year of Africa," was a turning point in Turkey's relations with the continent. While the first presidential visit to sub-Saharan Africa had taken place when Cevdet Sunay visited Ethiopia in 1969, no Turkish prime minister had visited SSA until 2005 when Recep Tayyip Erdogan paid official visits to South Africa and Ethiopia. Erdogan's trip raised a number of questions by some commentators—namely, if this would distract Turkey's attention from its European path. This period has seen Turkey's European orientation continued despite also looking for alternative connections. It is also true that Erdogan's visit, accompanied by a group of business people, provided a new impetus for enhanced engagement with Africa. Observers argued that the visit to SSA was to ensure African support for Turkey's bid for a non-permanent seat in the UNSC but another motive was to further economic ties with African countries (Uslu 2009). Not long after that visit, Turkey was accorded observer status in the African Union (AU).

The second half of the 2000s brought a significant turn in Turkey's relationship with Africa. During this period, Turkey started an ambitious diplomatic campaign for its candidacy for the UNSC membership and lobbied extensively. In 2008 voting, it was elected to the Security Council as a temporary member with the support of all but two African countries. The same year, Turkey was confirmed as strategic partner of the AU at its 10th Summit, became a non-regional member of the AfDB and organized the first Turkey–Africa Summit in Istanbul, Turkey. The summit was attended by 49 African countries and produced a declaration and a cooperation framework. Turkish embassies across the SSA have significantly increased following the summit that laid down the institutional framework for Turkey's relations with the continent. Turkey had resident embassies in Northern African countries before the action plan.[10] Turkish embassies in Abidjan (Ivory Coast) and Dar es Salaam (Tanzania) were opened in 2009 but among the 42 Turkish embassies in Africa, 23 of them were opened between 2010 and 2014. Efforts are underway to open a resident embassy in other African capitals including Monrovia (Liberia), Ligongve (Malawi), Lome (Togo) and Bangui (Central African Republic). Table 3.1 provides a detailed account of Turkey's diplomatic representation across the continent.

The second Turkey–Africa summit took place in Malabo, Equatorial Guinea in 2014 under the theme of "A New Model of Partnership for the Strengthening of Sustainable Development and Integration." In his keynote speech delivered at the summit, Erdogan declared that Turkey has completed the opening-up process to Africa with the summit hailing a new stage based on partnership (MFA 2014a). The final declaration adopted at the summit by the Turkish and African leadership confirmed the starting of a new stage while the implementation plan projected a comprehensive cooperation for the benefit of both parties (MFA 2014b).

Along with those summit-level meetings, relations were also reinforced with intensifying high-level visits to the continent, as appeared in the opening

Table 3.1 The list of Turkey's diplomatic missions in sub-Saharan Africa

Year	Country
Before 2010	Ethiopia (1926), Sudan (1957), Senegal (1960), Nigeria (1962–1984, 2000), Ghana (1964–1981), Kenya (1968), Democratic Republic of the Congo (1974), Somalia (1979–1991), South Africa (1994), Tanzania (1979–1994, 2009), Ivory Coast (2009)
2010	Angola, Cameroon, Ghana (reopened), Madagascar, Mali, Uganda
2011	Gambia, Mauritania, Mozambique, Somalia (reopened) South Sudan, Zambia, Zimbabwe
2012	Burkina Faso, Gabon, Namibia, Niger
2013	Chad, Djibouti, Eritrea, Guinea
2014	Benin, Botswana, Republic of the Congo, Ruanda
2018	Burundi, Equatorial Guinea, Sierra Leone

Source: Data abstracted by the authors from the Turkish Ministry of Foreign Affairs, www.mfa.gov.tr.

Table 3.2 Presidential and prime ministerial visits to Africa between 2002 and 2020

Year	Country	
	Prime ministerial visits	*Presidential visits*
2002	–	South Africa (A.N. Sezer)
2003	–	Tunisia (A.N. Sezer)
2004	Egypt (R.T. Erdogan)	-
2005	Tunisia, Morocco, Ethiopia, South Africa (R.T. Erdogan)	Egypt (A.N. Sezer)
2006	Sudan, Egypt, Algeria (R.T. Erdogan)	–
2007	Ethiopia (R.T. Erdogan)	–
2008	–	Tanzania, Republic of Congo, Democratic Republic of the Congo (A. Gul)
2009	Egypt (R.T. Erdogan)	Tanzania, Kenya (A. Gul)
2010	Libya (R.T. Erdogan)	Cameroon, Democratic Republic of the Congo, Nigeria (A. Gul)
2011	Egypt, Libya, Somalia, Tunisia, South Africa (R.T. Erdogan)	Gabon, Ghana (A. Gul)
2012	Egypt (R.T. Erdogan)	Tunisia (A. Gul)
2013	Gabon, Niger, Senegal, Morocco, Algeria, Tunisia (R.T. Erdogan)	Egypt (A. Gul)
2014	–	Equatorial Guinea, Algeria (R.T. Erdogan)
2015	–	Somalia, Djibouti, Ethiopia (R.T. Erdogan)
2016	–	Senegal, Ivory Coast, Somalia, Kenya, Uganda, Guinea, Nigeria, Ghana (R.T. Erdogan)
2017	–	Tanzania, Mozambique, Madagascar, Sudan, Chad, Tunisia (R.T. Erdogan)
2018	–	Mali, Senegal, Mauritania, Algeria, Zambia, South Africa (R.T. Erdogan)
2019	–	Tunisia (R.T. Erdogan)
2020	–	Senegal, Gambia, Algeria, (R.T. Erdogan)

Source: Data abstracted by the authors from the Turkish Ministry of Foreign Affairs, www.mfa.gov.tr and Presidency of the Republic of Turkey, https://www.tccb.gov.tr/.

policy. Table 3.2 reveals that Erdogan has made 52 visits to 28 African countries under his tenure as prime minister and president in the last 15 years. Erdogan paid five visits to Tunisia, Egypt and Algeria, four visits to Senegal, three visits to Ethiopia, Somalia and South Africa and two visits to Sudan, Libya and Morocco. Former President Abdullah Gul also visited ten African countries during his service as president. Several high-profile African leaders have also been welcomed in Ankara. Since Erdogan succeeded Gul as president in 2014, no prime ministerial visits have been paid to the continent.

The economic measures included in the action plan were to a large extent implemented. The strengthening economic relationship is evidenced by the increase in the trade volume with African countries. Turkey–Africa trade increased almost sevenfold between 1997 and 2019 and stood at US$21.5 billion. However, this is far below the target of US$50 billion that does not seem achievable at least in the near future. The "Strategy for Development of Economic Relations with Africa" adopted in 2003 was also updated during the Turkey–Africa Partnership Summit in 2014. A major outcome of the Strategy was the increase in the number of trade and cooperation agreements with African countries. While the number was 23 in 2003, it increased to 46 in 2018 (Durul 2018). Having commercial counselors in 26 African countries, Turkey also enjoys double taxation agreements with eight countries (Tunisia, Algeria, Egypt, Sudan, Morocco, South Africa, Ethiopia and Gambia) and free trade agreements (FTAs) with four countries (Morocco, Egypt, Tunisia and Mauritius) while FTAs signed with Sudan and Ghana are under ratification process (Ergocun 2019; Ministry of Trade 2019; Turkish Revenue Administration 2016). Turkey's Foreign Economic Relations Board of Turkey (DEIK) also has business councils in 45 African countries (DEIK n.d.). The majority were established after 2014 following DEIK's restructuring of Law No. 6552 of 11 September 2014 which put DEIK under the control of the Ministry of Economy.

As envisaged in the action plan, Turkey also enhanced its military cooperation with African countries, expanded its participation in UN peacekeeping operations (UNPKO) and special political missions deployed in the continent, Turkish police and military experts provided military training to their counterparts both in Turkish institutions and on African soil while the Turkish government also donated military equipment in order to support their armed forces (i.e. Libyan, Gambian and Somalian armed forces benefited from these training programs). As of August 2020, Turkey contributes to UNAMID (United Nations–African Union Hybrid Operation in Darfur) and UNMISS (United Nations Mission in South Sudan) with 42 police personnel (United Nations 2020a). Other UN peacekeeping missions Turkey has contributed after the action plan include MONUC (Democratic Republic of Congo), UNAMSIL (Sierra Leone), UNMIL (Liberia), UNOCI (Ivory Coast), UNMIS (Sudan), UNIOSIL (Sierra Leone), MINURCAT (Central African Republic and Chad), MONUSCO (Democratic Republic of Congo), MINUSMA (Mali) and MINUSCA (Central African Republic) (Eyrice

Tepeciklioglu 2019, 34–35). Most of the rising powers including India, China and Indonesia have become key contributors to UNPKO in recent years but Turkey's contribution to those missions is meager when compared to those powers.[11]

The Turkish Armed Forces also has military attachés in 17 African countries (Turkish Armed Forces 2019) with military cooperation agreements signed with ten African countries after the 1998 action plan. Turkey's growing military presence in the continent is most visible in the opening of its largest overseas military (training) base in Somalia's capital, Mogadishu, in 2017 and its active role in the country's post-conflict reconstruction process. Turkey's recent intervention in the Libyan conflict is also seen as another sign of its increasing military footprint in the region. Turkey overtly supports the Tripoli-based Government of National Accord (GNA) against the Khalifa Haftar's Libyan National Army (LNA) while Turkish intervention in Libya's conflict has been instrumental in the withdrawal of Haftar's forces from Tripoli. The security and military cooperation agreement signed with the GNA in 2019 allows Turkey to sell arms and military equipment to the UN-backed Libyan government.

Despite being less discussed, the opening plan also urged the expansion of cultural relations and educational interaction with African countries. Accordingly, Turkey increased the number of scholarships provided to African students. Various institutions, most notably the Presidency for Turks Abroad and Related Communities provide scholarships to African students at high school, graduate and undergraduate levels. When Turkey adopted the action plan in the late 1990s, the number of scholarships provided to African students was only 204 (MFA 1999, 8). According to recent data released by the Higher Education Council, 21,556 African students received undergraduate and graduate education at Turkish universities during the 2018–2019 period (Council of Higher Education 2020). The interaction between Turkish and African universities and the number of visiting academics from African countries also increased in the last few years (MFA, n.d.).

The cultural measures also included the establishment of a research center devoted to Africa attached to a university in order to shape Turkey's policymaking. It was not until 2008 that an African Studies Center was founded at a public university in Turkey's capital, Ankara. The center was unveiled with the participation of the then president, Abdullah Gul and Prof. Dr. Melek Firat, the first director of the center, accompanied Gul during his official visits to Kenya and Tanzania in 2009. There are now ten other African studies centers affiliated with both state and private foundation universities. Located in eight different cities, they all aim to gather information about Africa in order to guide foreign policymaking towards the continent.

As part of Turkey's cultural diplomacy efforts, the Yunus Emre Institute, established in 2007 with the aim to promote Turkish culture around the world, opened cultural centers in eight African countries (Yunus Emre Institute, n.d.).[12] Other state agencies that further Turkey's African engagement include the Directorate of Religious Affairs (Diyanet), the Turkish Maarif Foundation (TMV), TIKA and Turkish Airlines. Diyanet enhances Turkey's religious influence in the continent through increasing ties with Africa's Muslim societies (see Chapter 11 in this book). TMV, established in 2016 in order to take over the schools affiliated with the Gulen network, opened schools, educational centers and dormitories in African countries (Chapter 9). As Turkey intensified its aid efforts in Africa, Turkey's international aid agency, TIKA, increased the number of its humanitarian projects in the continent, implemented through its program coordination offices in 22 African countries. TIKA cooperates with a range of government institutions and civil society organizations including relevant ministries, the Turkish Red Crescent and Disaster and Emergency Management Presidency (AFAD; Chapter 10). Turkey's national airline company, Turkish Airlines expanded its destinations to Africa (Chapter 12) and contributed to Turkey's soft power in the continent. Flying to 55 destinations and more than 35 countries in Africa, it became the major international airline connecting the continent to the world. On the other hand, Turkey's Africa policy involves different players other than the state and public institutions. The activities of those non-state actors including business groups and NGOs generally play a complementary role in advancing Turkey's African policy.

Conclusion

This chapter sought to provide an overview for the trajectory of Turkey's relations with Africa and argued that Ankara has several motives to engage with Africa more intensely. While its aspiration for a greater role in regional and global politics steer the contemporary interest towards Africa, this is combined with the search for new partners to advance its political causes and enhance its economic benefits. Turkey's engagement with the continent has gained tremendous momentum especially following the first Turkey–Africa Summit and significant achievements have been recorded in the implementation of the measures projected in the action plan. Despite all these achievements, there are many areas that need to be developed.

For example, as proposed in the action plan, Turkey's diplomatic presence in the continent has significantly increased. Yet, some of those embassies face a shortage of human resources and budgetary problems. The relevance of opening resident embassies in each African country in order to maintain bilateral diplomatic relations is also questionable. Economic exchanges with African countries are also on the rise while Turkish contractors concluded major infrastructure contracts especially in the Horn of Africa. When compared with other emerging powers, mostly visibly, China and India, Turkey's economic presence in the continent is less impressive. On the other hand, it appears that the lack of interest and knowledge towards African issues still prevails among the Turkish media and even in government circles. The break-up of the government's alliance with the Gulen movement also has the potential to tarnish Turkey's image as the latter largely maintains its well-established network in the continent. Despite its historical inheritance in some parts of the continent, Turkey's capabilities to realize the full potential of the action plan are limited in the presence of other regional and international actors. Therefore, it would be over-simplistic to frame Turkey's African engagement as a success story as widely claimed by many senior officials. Yet, Turkey has steadily increased its investment in the continent to an unprecedented level with firm determination to further this engagement especially in cases where its national interests are at stake, including Libya.

Notes

1 On the one hand, Turkey sought Western support against the Soviet demands for military bases on the Straits and territorial demands in eastern Anatolia. The quest for Western help against the Soviet threat explains Turkey's bid for NATO membership. On the other hand, it was not able to overtly support the decolonization process, as the colonial powers were its NATO allies.
2 Here, it should be noted that the Turkish War of Independence was noted by African intellectuals with keen interest. For an overview, see Doster 2008.
3 Turkish help came clandestinely when Turkey provided weapons and military equipment to Algerian freedom fighters, first through Libya in 1957, then through Tunisia in 1959 (Ataov 1977, 133–134).
4 In late 1964, the first delegation started their visit to the former French colonies of Guinea, Ivory Coast, Niger, Dahomey (today's Benin), Togo, Cameroon, Gabon, Republic of the Congo, Central African Republic and Chad. In early 1965, the East Africa delegation visited Ethiopia, Kenya, Somalia, Burundi, Ruanda, Tanzania, Malawi and Madagascar in addition to Sudan, Libya and Tunisia. The third delegation also initiated their visits in early 1965 to the following African countries of Algeria, Morocco, Mauritania, Liberia, Ghana, Nigeria, Sierra Leone and Senegal (Bulletin of the Ministry of Foreign Affairs, Issue 5 1965, 38–47). The delegations were formed from ministers, ambassadors, academics and journalists.
5 For details, see Bulletin of the Ministry of Foreign Affairs, Issue 5 (1965) and Issue 15 (1965).
6 The extant literature mostly refers to the 1998 document of the Africa Action Plan as the first attempt to design a coherent Africa policy while there is almost no reference to the 1978 action plan. Although it is true that the 1998 document was more ambitious to enhance Turkey's presence in Africa, its predecessor should be given enough credit for laying down its groundwork.
7 The details of the 1978 opening were mostly abstracted from Selcuk Incesu's newspaper article published in a popular Turkish newspaper, *Cumhuriyet* (2020). Here, it should be noted that Incesu was appointed as the Head of the Africa Department at the Ministry of Foreign Affairs established in 1978.
8 During his service as the Turkish Ambassador in Lagos, Nigeria from 1995 to 1998, Hazar was also accredited to eight other West African countries, since there were no resident embassies in those countries. In his various reports to the Foreign Ministry, Hazar underlined the potential of developing relations with African countries. After the completion of his term of office in Nigeria, he was given responsibility for relations with Africa in the Ministry of Foreign Affairs together with the Islamic Cooperation Organization.
9 Here, it should be noted that the negotiations between South Cyprus and EU officials on the EU membership of the former started in March 1998 (Sertoglu

and Ozturk 2003, 64) following the Luxembourg Summit in December 1997 that announced the countries eligible for membership. As noted, Turkey was excluded as a candidate in the same summit.
10 Since 2013, diplomatic relations with Egypt are maintained at the level of chargés d'affaires.
11 For example, India's contribution to those missions with police and staff officers, military experts and contingent troops makes it the fifth largest contributor to UNPKO in 2020 while Indonesia ranked eighth and China ninth out of 119 countries in terms of peacekeeping contributions (United Nations 2020b).
12 These are: Algeria, Morocco, Egypt, Sudan, Somalia, South Africa, Senegal and Tunisia.

References

Aldrich, Winthrop W. 1967. "The Suez Crisis – A Footnote to History." *Foreign Affairs* 45, no. 3: 541–552. https://doi.org/10.2307/20039255.
Aral, Berdal. 2004. "Fifty Years On: Turkey's Voting Orientation at the UN General Assembly, 1948–97." *Middle Eastern Studies* 40, no. 2: 137–160. https://doi.org/10.1080/00263200412331302017.
Ataov, Turkkaya. 1977. *Afrika Ulusal Kurtulus Mucadeleleri* [National Liberation Struggles in Africa]. Ankara: Ankara Universitesi Siyasal Bilgiler Fakultesi Yayinlari.
Ataov, Turkkaya. 1988. "The United Nations Istanbul Seminar on The International Responsibility for The Independence Of Namibia." *Ankara universitesi SBF Dergisi* 43, no. 1: 13–27.
Aykan, Mahmut Bali. 1993. "Turkey and the OIC: 1984–1992." *The Turkish Yearbook of International Relations* 23: 101–131.
Baba, Gurol and Senem Ertan. 2016. "Turkey at the Bandung Conference: A Fully-Aligned among the Non-Aligned." Paper presented at ISA Asia-Pacific Conference, Hong Kong, June 2016. http://web.isanet.org/Web/Conferences/AP%20Hong%20Kong%202016/Archive/64185d87-7a01-44f1-acbc-1566b192398f.pdf.
Benli Altunisik, Meliha. 2009. "Worldviews and Turkish Foreign Policy in the Middle East." *New Perspectives on Turkey* 40 (Spring): 171–194. https://doi.org/10.1017/S0896634600005264.
Birtek, Nuri. 1996. "Turkiye'nin Dis Yardimlari ve Yonetimi." MSc Thesis, Bilkent University.
Bleda, Tansug. 2000. *Maskeli Balo*. Istanbul: Dogan Kitap.
Bulletin of the Ministry of Foreign Affairs, Issue 3. 1964. (October–December).
Bulletin of the Ministry of Foreign Affairs, Issue 5. 1965. (February).
Bulletin of the Ministry of Foreign Affairs, Issue 6. 1965. (March).
Bulletin of the Ministry of Foreign Affairs, Issue 15. 1965. (December).
Cetiner, Yusuf Turan. 1995. "*The Baghdad Pact: An Anglo-American Quest for Policy in the Middle East*." MSc Thesis, Bilkent University.
Council of Higher Education. 2020. "Higher Education Information Management System." https://istatistik.yok.gov.tr/.
CVCE (Centre Virtuel de la Connaissance sur l'Europe). 2017. "Summary of the Introductory Speeches at the Bandung Conference (18–19 April 1955)." https://www.cvce.eu/content/publication/2015/10/20/831656d3-62e4-4978-a44f-c043c8fb9011/publishable_en.pdf.

DEIK. n.d. "Business Councils." Accessed October 1, 2020. https://www.deik.org.tr/business-councils.
Dikerdem, Mahmut. 1977. *Ortadogu'da Devrim Yillari*. Istanbul: Istanbul Matbaasi.
Doster, Baris. 2008. "*Atatürk ve Türk Devrimi'nin Asya ve Afrika'daki Etkileri.*" (The Influence of Atatürk and Turkish Revolution on Asian and African Nations.) Paper presented at the 38th ICANAS International Congress of Asian and North African Studies, Ankara, September 2007. https://www.ayk.gov.tr/wp-content/uploads/2015/01/DOSTER-Bar%c4%b1%c5%9f-ATAT%c3%9cRK-VE-T%c3%9cRK-DEVR%c4%b0M%c4%b0%e2%80%99N%c4%b0N-ASYA-VE-AFR%c4%b0KA%e2%80%99DAK%c4%b0-ETK%c4%b0LER%c4%b0.pdf.
Durul, Tevfik. 2018. "Türkiye-Afrika ilişkileri 2018'de hız kazandi." Anadolu Ajansi. December 23, 2018. https://www.aa.com.tr/tr/turkiye/turkiye-afrika-iliskileri-2018de-hiz-kazandi/1346417.
Ergocun, Gokhan. 2019. "2020 to be Africa Year for Turkey, Says Trade Minister." Anadolu Agency. December 12, 2019. https://www.aa.com.tr/en/economy/2020-to-be-africa-year-for-turkey-says-trade-minister/1668261.
Ersoy, Eyup. 2012. "Turkish Foreign Policy toward the Algerian War of Independence (1954–62)." *Turkish Studies* 13, no. 4: 683–695. https://doi.org/10.1080/00263200412331302017.
Eyrice Tepeciklioğlu, Elem. 2019. *Türk Dış Politikasında Afrika: Temel Dinamikler, Fırsatlar ve Engeller*. Ankara: Nobel Yayincilik.
Haugom, Lars. 2019. "Turkish Foreign Policy under Erdogan: A Change in International Orientation?" *Comparative Strategy* 38, no. 3: 206–223. https://doi.org/10.1080/01495933.2019.1606662.
Hazar, Numan. 2016. *Turkiye-Afrika İliskileri: Türkiye'nin Dost Kitaya Acilim Stratejisi*. Ankara: Akcag Yayinlari.
Hazar, Numan. 2018. *Sovyet Tehdidinin Golgesinde Turk Dis Politikası: Kuzey Afrika Ornegi*. Ankara: Dis Politika Enstitusu.
Incesu, Selcuk. 2020. "Afrika Acilim Politikasi." *Cumhuriyet*. January 30, 2020. https://www.cumhuriyet.com.tr/yazarlar/olaylar-ve-gorusler/afrika-acilim-politikasi-1717211.
Ipek, Volkan and Gonca Biltekin. 2013. "Turkey's Foreign Policy Implementation in Sub-Saharan Africa: A Post-International Approach." *New Perspectives on Turkey* 49: 121–156. https://doi.org/10.1017/S0896634600002065.
Karaca, Salih Zeki. 2000. "Turkish Foreign Policy in the Year 2000 and Beyond: Her Opening Up Policy to Africa." *Dis Politika* 25, no. 3–4: 115–119.
Kirisci, Kemal and Neslihan Kaptanoglu. 2011. "The Politics of Trade and Turkish Foreign Policy." *Middle Eastern Studies* 47, no. 5: 705–774. https://doi.org/10.1080/00263206.2011.613226.
MFA. 1999. "*Afrika'ya Acilim Eylem Plani.*" Revised 2nd Edition.
MFA. 2011. "Turkish Foreign Policy during Ataturk's Era." http://www.mfa.gov.tr/turkish-foreign-policy-during-ataturks-era.en.mfa.
MFA. 2014a. "21 November 2014, Speech by H.E. Recep Tayyip Erdogan, the President of the Republic of Turkey." http://afrika.mfa.gov.tr/21-november-2014-speech-by-HE-recep-tayyip-erdogan-the-president-of-the-republic-of-turkey.en.mfa.
MFA. 2014b. "The Summit." http://afrika.mfa.gov.tr/summit.en.mfa.
MFA. (Turkish Ministry of Foreign Affairs). n.d. "Turkey-Africa Relations." Accessed July 3, 2020. http://www.mfa.gov.tr/turkey-africa-relations.en.mfa.
Ministry of Trade. 2019. "Yururlukte bulunan STA'lar." https://ticaret.gov.tr/data/5b872ada13b8761450e18f4b/STA%20tablosu.pdf.

NATO Public Diplomacy Division. 2006. "*NATO Handbook.*" Brussels.

Oguzlu, Tarik. 2020. "International System and Turkish Foreign Policy." Foreign Policy Institute. http://foreignpolicy.org.tr/international-system-and-turkish-foreign-policy/.

Onis, Ziya. 2004. "Turgut Özal and His Economic Legacy: Turkish Neo-Liberalism in Critical Perspective." *Middle Eastern Studies* 40, no. 4: 113–134. https://doi.org/10.1080/00263200410001700338.

Sanjian, Ara. 1997. "The Formulation of the Baghdad Pact." *Middle Eastern Studies* 33, no. 2: 226–266.

Sertoglu, Kamil and Ozturk, Ilhan. 2003. "Application of Cyprus to the European Union and the Cyprus Problem." *Emerging Markets Finance and Trade* 39, no. 6: 54–70.

Sever, Aysegul. 2008. "A Reluctant Partner of the US over the Suez? Turkey and the Suez Crisis." In *Reassessing Suez 1956: New Perspectives and Its Aftermath*, edited by Simon C. Smith, 123–132. London and New York: Routledge.

Tur, Ozlem. 2011. "Economic Relations with the Middle East Under the AKP—Trade, Business Community and Reintegration with Neighboring Zones." *Turkish Studies* 12, no. 4: 589–602. https://doi.org/10.1080/14683849.2011.622515.

Turkish Armed Forces. 2019. "The Offices of the Military Attachés of the TAF in Foreign Countries." https://www.tsk.tr/Sayfalar?viewName=MilitaryAtachesOfTaf.

Turkish Revenue Administration. 2016. "Yururlukte Bulunan Cifte Vergilendirmeyi Onleme Anlasmalari." http://www.gib.gov.tr/sites/default/files/uluslararasi_mevzuat/VERGIANLASMALIST.htm.

United Nations. 2020a. "Summary of Contribution to UN Peacekeeping by Country, Mission and Post: Police, UN Military Experts on Mission, Staff Officers and Troops, 31/08/2020." https://peacekeeping.un.org/sites/default/files/03_country_and_mission_28.pdf.

United Nations. 2020b. "Summary of Troops Contributing Countries by Ranking: Police, UN Military Experts on Mission, Staff Officers and Troops." https://peacekeeping.un.org/sites/default/files/02_country_ranking_28.pdf.

Uslu, Emrullah. 2009. "Gul's African Visit Could Indicate How Turkey Will Act in the UN Security Council." The Jamestown Foundation. https://jamestown.org/program/guls-african-visit-could-indicate-how-turkey-will-act-in-the-un-security-council/.

Uzer, Umut and Ayse Uzer. 2005. "Diverging Perceptions of the Cold War: Baghdad Pact as a Source of Conflict Between Turkey and the Nationalist Arab Countries." *Turkish Yearbook of International Relations* 36: 73–100.

Wheeler, Tom. 2011. "Ankara to Africa: Turkey's Outreach since 2005." *South African Journal of International Affairs* 18, no. 1: 43–62. https://doi.org/10.1080/10220461.2011.564426.

Yildirim, Ozgur. 2018. "The Attitude of Egypt towards Baghdad Pact." *Journal of Atatürk and the History of Turkish Republic* 1, no. 3: 125–146.

Yunus Emre Institute. n.d. "*Our Cultural Centers.*" Accessed October 10, 2020. https://www.yee.org.tr/en/corporate/yunus-emre-institute.

4 Being "Southern" without being of the Global South

The strange case of Turkey's South–South cooperation in Africa

Federico Donelli

Introduction

The world is gradually changing from a Western-dominated system to one in which power is more diffuse, and the rules of the game are beginning to shift. Changes in the post-Cold War global order have also shaped trends in the field of development cooperation. The end of the bipolar balance has paved the way for new emerging players who have rapidly gained both economic and political power. These trends seem to have led African countries to realize that development can take place relatively quickly following different paths of growth. Indeed, the rapid economic growth, proactive diplomatic approach and enlargement of the areas of interest of these emerging–or (re)merging–players have transformed the landscape of international development cooperation by making it even more fluid (Mawdsley 2012). As underlined by de Renzio and Seifert (2014, 1860) "[these players] have significantly increased their engagement in development assistance and technical cooperation, and questioned the predominance and legitimacy of more traditional forms of development cooperation." Both the scientific literature and the media tend to group these players into a variety of categories, including "new development partners" (Park 2011), "non-traditional donors" (Kragelund 2012), "emerging donors" (Mawdsley, Savage and Sung-Mi 2014) and "Southern providers" (Bracho 2015). In some cases, countries labelled as emerging donors have a very long history of development assistance. For example, China had already started development programs in Africa in the mid-1950s. For this reason, according to some scholars, what is considered emergent is their impact on global politics (Sato et al. 2010, 2).

Regardless of the label, these countries share the rejection of all, or only part, of the Development Assistance Committee (DAC) countries' principles and practices. Throughout the years, DAC members have institutionalized value commitments such as (1) a definition of "official development assistance" (ODA) that excludes military and commercially driven aid; (2) the common belief that ODA requires coordinated effort in which individual donors restrain their activities to contribute to the whole; (3) the emphasis on the importance of transparency of aid activities and the idea that the critique and monitoring of mutual activities can further improve development performance. Besides, the DAC countries have also developed common criteria for the evaluation of development assistance that comprises: purpose of evaluation, impartiality and independence, credibility, usefulness, participation of donors and recipients, donor cooperation, design and implementation of evaluations, reporting, dissemination and feedback.[1]

The emerging players adopt and apply only partially these principles and integrate them with alternative approaches. These countries support their actions through rhetoric that promotes a different kind of relationship with the countries to which they assist. Among these emerging actors there are many who have adopted the South–South cooperation (SSC) approach. The SSC is essentially based on solidarity, horizontality, non-interference in domestic affairs and mutual prosperity. This approach allows developing countries to pursue their individual or shared objectives of national capacity building through the exchange of knowledge, skills, resources and technical expertise.

In the emerging multi-order system, also Turkey has increased its commitment to development cooperation. The motivations that led Turkey to increase efforts in the field of development cooperation match those of other emerging powers: market access, natural resource demands and diplomatic and political support on global issues are all significant to the emerging economies. Besides the regional and global factors, ideological preferences of the ruling party—grounded on conservative principles with pragmatic implementation—have defined this different route for Turkish foreign policy towards the so-called Global South. This southern route posits a normative and responsible stance as a middle emerging power by taking a more global and accountable approach to world politics emphasizing the ways to overcome global inequality. The southern dimension of Turkish foreign policy has placed Turkey in an intermediate—bridge—position, no longer as in the past between the West and the East, but between high-income and low-income economies. A position that has found its expression in Turkey's development cooperation policy through the promotion of an alternative paradigm: the Ankara consensus. Although Turkey does not consider itself a member of the South of the world, its development paradigm recalls elements that can be traced back to the principle of horizontality typical of SSC. This chapter analyzes the main features of the Turkish application of SSC, highlighting its place in the promotion of the development cooperation policy towards African countries. It aims to understand whether it is possible to define the Turkish approach as a South–South one.

South–South cooperation: A solidarity paradigm or a realist strategy?

The SSC gained political relevance in the developing world during the Cold War, when the concept of solidarity between developing countries became increasingly popular. However, it is only with the end of the Cold War and the progressive reshaping of the global economic system that the SSC has acquired greater theoretical and practical relevance. The process of maturation of the SSC has been far from straightforward, alternating phases of slowdown with sudden speed-ups. The first milestone in this long-term process was the Bandung Conference held in Indonesia in April 1955. Turkey was one of the countries that joined the conference. However, Ankara's presence was not the result of ideological conviction but a political strategy coordinated with its American ally. The Turkish delegation, indeed, went to Bandung following an American demand to support the Western bloc's cause. A decision that did not achieve the desired outcomes and, rather, aroused suspicion and mistrust by developing countries.[2] Since Bandung, the process of institutionalization of the SSC has progressed through further steps including the Belgrade Conference (1961), with the establishment of the Non-Aligned Movement (NAM); the United Nations Conference on Trade and Development (UNCTAD) in 1964, at whose end 77 developing countries established the Group of 77 (G77); the program of a New International Economic Order (NIEO) was launched in 1974. The latter was a highly ambitious plan aimed to create and institutionalize a global redistributive order founded on a new binding rule. However, although some of the NIEO's principles were adopted by the UN General Assembly, its reformation momentum faded in the mid-1980s. The second milestone was the adoption of the Buenos Aires Plan of Action for Promoting and Implementing Technical Cooperation among Developing Countries (BAPA) by 138 UN Member States in 1978. The plan established a scheme of collaboration among least developed countries, mostly located in the south of the planet (South–South), and triangular cooperation—between Northern and Southern partners—globally and within the UN. It recognized in a multilateral context the importance of technical cooperation and development assistance ties among Southern countries.[3] The BAPA formalized, for the first time, a framework for this type of cooperation and incorporated in its practice the founding principles of the SSC: respect for sovereignty, non-interference in internal affairs and equality of rights, among others (Modi 2011; Gray and Gills 2017). The following two decades ('80s and '90s) were shaped by the affirmation of neoliberalism and the resetting of international post-Cold War balances. With the new millennium, the rise of the small groups of large developing countries such as BRICS gave new impetus to the SSC.[4] This group of non-traditional or emerging donors have shared some similarities, such as being emerging powers with a recent history of economic growth and successful development, combined with an interest in expanding their international footprint and influence. Another common feature of the majority of emerging donors was that in some cases they were still relying on external aid to address poverty problems in their own country. For this reason, the emerging powers usually reject the notion of "donor" and "recipient" countries and are not members of the DAC.

Although the scope of the development programs promoted within the SSC framework has grown dramatically over the last two decades, opening up stage 3.0 of the SSC according to Mawdsley (2019), there is still a lack of a common and shared definition. The term "South–South" is not understood as a geographical category, because several key SSC actors (e.g. China) are located in the northern hemisphere. Rather, as expressed in the outcomes statement that emerged at the end of the Fourth High-level Forum on Aid Effectiveness held in Busan (2011), the term South–South refers to technical cooperation, knowledge exchange and financial assistance between couples in developing countries. The cornerstone of this approach is the concept of mutual benefit. It is a tool used by states, international organizations, academics, civil society and the private sector to collaborate and share knowledge, skills and successful initiatives in specific areas such as agricultural development, human rights, urbanization, health, and climate change. The promotion of SSC has been conceptualized as a way of pursuing common economic interests and trade as part of efforts to advance economic independence from former colonial powers, thereby overcoming the exploitative nature of North–South relations.[5]

The aid of emerging donors is frequently not labelled "aid" but, rather, as a form of SSC, which differs from Western aid because of its lack of conditionality and its "untied" nature (Woods 2008). Moreover, in many cases, including the one discussed in this study, the SSC's "brand" serves to mark the difference between North–South cooperation and the principles and practices promoted by DAC countries.

Despite the hugely successful expansion of the SSC, many critical issues and doubts have also emerged among practitioners and scholars. In the current global system, the motivations behind the South–South relationship established by the emerging powers are attributable to pragmatic and interest-oriented evaluations rather than solidarity. The development aid programs promoted by emerging economies—from China to India—are driven by vital national interests, for example energy security, and by commercial concerns, such as the search for new markets (Bergamaschi, Moore and Tickner 2017). They provide aid in the form of "packages," including grants, preferential loans, credit lines, debt relief and preferential trade and investment programs (Rampa, Bilal and Sidiropoulos 2012). A different approach in form to the one adopted by traditional donors but not so different in essence. Furthermore, further clarification is necessary. While the literature and media oversimplify the SSC approach by treating it as a single strategy, in practice, the emerging donors adopt different strategies for development assistance. Each country, indeed, declines its policy, tailoring it to its national interests and specificities. In the case of Turkey, if the material gains have been one of the drivers of African policy, the selection of countries and areas to invest in has also considered cultural proximity. This choice to give relevance to religious affinities reflects both the opportunity to develop B2B relations with African counterparts more easily, and the need to substantiate the investment in the eyes of the Turkish public. Especially for the conservative segments of Turkish society, development assistance, and humanitarian intervention for African Muslim communities is often considered as a duty, an expression of Islamic charity.

Turkey's shifted paradigm: From the DAC model to the Southern donors' model

While it is possible to trace a general framework of the SSC, it should be stressed that there is no single way of implementing this cooperation. Indeed, each emerging country engaged in development cooperation has applied these principles according to its interests and peculiarities. For this reason, the literature usually divides non-traditional or emerging donors into several subcategories (Zimmermann and Smith 2011). Among these categorizations, the most commonly used is the Center for Global Development (CGD), which distinguishes among: (a) new donor countries that broadly follow the DAC model; (b) Arab countries and funds; and (c) other Southern donors including the BRICS, except for Russia.[6] In the African context more than elsewhere, some emerging donors exploit a common discourse of contrast—at least partially—to the DAC model, and present themselves as representatives of the Global South and claim to pursue the interests of developing countries on the international scene. These countries present themselves as providers of an alternative model of development assistance, a model based on fairer partnerships that include not only technical and financial assistance, but also a strengthening of trade and investment, and the sharing of knowledge and experience closer and more relevant to the low-income countries to which they assist (de Renzio and Seifert 2014; Gray and Gills 2016). For the beneficiary African countries, a distinction must be made between the perception of civil society and that of the governments, the former being concerned about respect for human rights and the latter being reassured by the lack of political conditionality (Gray and Gills 2017). In general terms, however, the SSC is popular in Africa because it is considered a "softer" way in which emerging powers do business, showing respect in their dialogue with local populations, the acceptance of the principle of representation at the same administrative, political or diplomatic level for both sides in political discussions (unlike European powers) and their sharing of backgrounds and experiences both as donors and aid recipients (Rampa, Bilal and Sidiropoulos 2012, 156). The ever increasing involvement of the emerging powers in Africa has inevitably led to a reassessment and reconfiguration of the continent's relationship with the traditional powers. Many Africans believe that among the positive effects of development support by emerging powers, there is also the different attitude adopted towards them by the traditional donors (Tjønneland 2015). In particular, African countries have expectations that the growing centrality given to Africa by emerging players will lead traditional powers to acknowledge the global role of the continent and to recognize the aspirations of the people who live on it.

In the picture so far, Turkey holds a very unusual role. Based on the CGD's classification, Turkey is considered within the sub-group of the new donor countries (a). Within this cluster, Turkey is often associated with Russia and Israel, which are countries that have longstanding aid programs, and are pursuing a closer relationship with the DAC. Turkey, indeed, has some unique characteristics: it is a member of the OECD but not of the DAC, in which it has the status of observer. Moreover, Turkey does not intend to become a full member of OECD/DAC although it meets all necessary criteria and was offered membership in 2012 (UNDP 2013). Several considerations determined Ankara's choice to refuse DAC membership: the willingness to maintain the status of a beneficiary country and the access to concessional loans at lower costs; to be able to operate more autonomously, both in terms of budget and political preferences; and, for the existence of a linguistic gap because many of the Turkish actors do not speak English, which is the language of most international coordination meetings (Binder 2014). One of these motivations, namely the search for greater autonomy, is among the factors that have led Turkey to move progressively away from the new donors' group (a) and closer to that of the Southern donors (c). A shift that was conditioned by the decision to reorientate the country's foreign policy after the outbreak of the 2011 uprisings, by increasing the relevance of the southern routes (Donelli and González Levaggi 2018). Despite its proximity to the DAC, Turkey uses the SSC label for its development assistance activities. Turkey voluntarily signed the DAC's aid effectiveness declarations and participated in the Busan Forum and the founding of the Global Partnership for Effective Development Cooperation (GPEDC). These choices have led Turkey to become an uncommon player in the field of development cooperation. Indeed, beyond the labels, it is in practice that Turkey has reconfigured its development cooperation taking inspiration from the providers of SSC. More specifically, Turkey has implemented pragmatically its model of development cooperation in which aspects of the SSC are combined with traditional DAC procedures. This phenomenon has increased the interest of scholars who have begun to relate the concept of SSC to the development policies promoted by Turkey (Stearns and Sucuoglu 2017; Ozkan 2018). A deeper analysis suggests that Turkey has maintained different characteristics of the typical new donors by cloaking them in a SSC operational framework and narrative. Therefore, as underlined by de Renzio and Seifert (2014, 1868) "Turkish development cooperation, seems to be aimed at fulfilling the function of a mediator between Northern and Southern positions and players by placing itself in neither camp." An approach that mirrors the changing foreign policy of recent years, increasingly oriented to assume a non-aligned position in the global context (Aydıntasbas 2020). This very unusual pathway has shaped the outlines of the Ankara consensus, the paradigm of Turkish development cooperation.

A mixed paradigm: The Ankara consensus

Even though it is not a well-defined concept, the Ankara consensus can be conceived of as a model for economic, political and social development of the African countries, alternative to both the so-called Washington consensus[7]—US- and European-dominated neoliberal economic and developmental discourse—and the most recent Beijing consensus as state-led economic growth and prioritization of stability over democracy.[8] Despite the neoliberal model remaining the most appreciated and followed by African leaders, a broader crisis of confidence in it, particularly after the 2008 financial crisis, has paved the way for the rise of the Chinese model (Lekorwe et al. 2016). The fact that many African leaders consider alternative development models less risky for their power than the neoliberal model has contributed to their appeal. Turkey has attempted to promote a middle way, or a third way, through the implementation of a win-win policy in Africa which includes peacebuilding efforts and a policy of mutual empowerment. At the same time, Ankara's idea neither refuses nor denies benefits and opportunities of global capitalism. Therefore, Turkey seeks to share with African countries its own development paradigm or formula that has proved successful in its rapid economic growth. Rather than creating new relations of dependence—as traditional donors tend to do but also some emerging ones like China—Turkey's approach, particularly in states that are trying to get out of crises such as Somalia, tends to focus on political equality, mutual economic development and a long-term social partnership. As pointed out by Cannon (2017, 99):

> Turkey has shown less interest in an attempt to craft expensive, long-term solutions that are short on detail and involve the usual suspects of foreign-funded civil society organizations, NGOs and consultancies. These result in conferences and policy papers but rarely offer anything concrete such as medical facilities or roads.

Even though until the three-year period 2008–11 the SSC remained a marginal component in Turkish discourse and practice, the analysis of the net disbursement shows that between 2002 and 2008 the budget allocated by Turkey to countries of the so-called "Global South" grew exponentially (Ozkan 2018, 569). The purpose of this increment was, however, precise and limited in time. In those years, indeed, the Turkish government aimed to be elected as a non-permanent member of the United Nations Security Council. This target was achieved by Turkey in 2009–2010, thanks also to the votes of many of the African recipient countries of Turkish aid.[9] This stage was a testing period for Turkey which gradually integrated elements of the SSC into its development aid program. Turkey subsequently modified its approach to development programs by extending and institutionalizing aspects of the SSC. In 2011, the Turkish state's decision to intervene in the humanitarian crisis in Somalia gave further impetus to this trend. Since then, Somalia, which at the time was completely isolated (and ignored) by the international community, has become a laboratory for Turkey, a clean slate on which it can test its capacity not only in humanitarian emergencies (Baird 2016; Donelli 2015) but also in conflict mediation (Akpinar 2015; Kadayifci-Orellana 2016), the state-building process (Ozkan 2014; Cannon 2016) and development programs (Donelli 2017b). Nowadays, Turkey's approach has several components ascribable to the SSC. Indeed, the philosophy behind the SSC emerges from the notion of mutual growth, and the underlying principle is to support each other for a win–win partnership on all sides (Quadir 2013). The main tenets of Turkish assistance efforts reportedly have much in common with the principles of SSC: respect for national ownership, mutual benefit, solidarity, context-specific, and demand-driven assistance.

The similarities of the Turkish approach to the principles of the SSC can be assessed more precisely thanks to a framework for assessing the quality of SSC that has been recently developed by the Network of Southern Think Tanks (NeST).[10] The NeST framework defines the quality of the SSC based on a qualitative analysis of the performance of the actors on several issues: a) inclusive national ownership; b) horizontality; c) self-sufficiency and sustainability; d) accountability and transparency; e) development efficiency. By applying this tool to the Turkish case, it is possible to highlight certain traits of the Turkish approach that makes Turkey a kind of hybrid because it mixes SSC tools with traditional donor practices. With regards to inclusive national ownership (a), the Turkish approach indicates respect for non-conditionality, non-interference and respect for sovereignty, as well as demand-led assistance. The horizontality of the aid (b), is expressed in terms of mutually beneficial cooperation for both parties, as evident in the Turkish approach both in practice and in the narrative, where concepts such as solidarity, mutual trust and partnership are often stressed. Regarding self-sufficiency and sustainability (c), it has been explicitly indicated several times as one of the main targets of Turkish aid initiatives in a crisis. Specifically, fostering self-reliance and sustainability has been declared as one of the most important objectives of Turkish aid to sub-Saharan Africa. Emblematic of this approach has been the activism in Somalia where both state institutions—Ministry of Foreign Affairs, the Turkish Cooperation and Coordination Agency (TIKA), the Ministry of Education—and non-governmental actors—NGOs, charity foundations, business associations—have stressed the focus on capacity building, the concentration on education through scholarships and building leadership skills, the manifestation of long-term interest through building embassies and consulates, support to institutions and training of state officials, such as diplomats, investing in Mogadishu city through roads, infrastructure and employing local Somalis in several projects including private sector efforts. As pointed out by Sucuoglu and Sazak (2016, 82) "Turkey's efforts have really been remarkable in these areas, and in alignment with SSC principles of solidarity, capacity building and technology/knowledge transfer, and use of local systems and resources."

On accountability and transparency (d), Turkey is one of the few emerging powers that shares its development assistance data with OECD-DAC, including those related to non-governmental organizations and more sporadically reports to OCHA's financial monitoring services.[11] However, there are many doubts about effective transparency. Reports do not always present a geographical and sectoral breakdown and, as specified in the following paragraph, there is no standardized model for monitoring and evaluating projects in the field. Turkey has not developed quantifiable indicators and targets to measure the real impact and progress of its projects and initiatives. Finally, as far as development efficiency (e) is concerned, the presence in the field of Turkish practitioners—belonging to state and non-state agencies—alongside local communities and indigenous civil society has allowed Turkish actors to be more adaptable to local conditions, needs and desires (Donelli 2018). In other words, the Turkish approach has proven to hold a higher degree of resilience on the ground.

Compared to other emerging players that are active in Africa following the SSC approach, Turkey includes a religious meaning to its assistance. Turkey, in its development model, also takes some elements from the Arab model, including the religious significance attributed to aid and the close link between aid and foreign policy strategy. As briefly mentioned, most of the works carried out by Turkish NGOs are promoted as Islamic duties (Ozkan 2013, 48). Turkey gives a religious dimension to its assistance and, following the Arab model of development aid, concentrates on Muslim African communities.[12] This is the case in Somalia, which is a member of the Arab League and, as well as Turkey, is also a member of the OIC. Arab aid is distinct from the DAC model, as it remains primarily concentrated regionally and is more openly influenced by social solidarity and religious ties. Further, the Arab aid has traditionally been very generous, yet also very volatile, both because of the uncertainty of Arab countries' oil and gas export earnings and because of the strategic use of aid in support of their foreign policies. Initially, in the early years of foreign assistance the Arab solidarity was the decisive factor and the primary objective in directing aid. Subsequently, however, aid has become an important foreign policy tool, and the Arab donors have expanded to sub-Saharan Africa.[13]

The Ankara consensus takes these two aspects from the Arab model—religious meaning and aid as a foreign policy tool—and puts them together with other elements including an important feature of the Beijing consensus: the non-conditionality principle. Conditionality refers to the conditions attached to the provision of loans, debt relief or foreign aid by the provider to the recipient, which is usually a sovereign government. In other words, recipient nations must meet prerequisites to receive aid. The application of clear political and economic conditionalities in aid and assistance to push for normative principles and values, especially in human rights, is one area of divergence between more traditional donors and non-traditional aid providers. Aiming to attract developing nations, China adopted a policy of no political preconditions for receiving aid.[14] Turkey's agenda adheres to the principle of non-conditionality in its support for African countries. By refraining from imposing political conditions, Turkey demonstrates that it can engage with recipient governments in a spirit of solidarity while not sacrificing effectiveness and efficiency (Sucuoglu and Sazak 2016). The lack of political conditionality, moreover, allows Turkey to keep channels open with all kinds of African regimes. This approach has enabled the development of pragmatic relations, focusing on mutual gains and, in some cases, underpinned by the existence of ideological and religious affinities.

Turkish storytelling

Turkey's African policy pays lip service to a normative element, on behalf of a more egalitarian world politics, fostered by the narrative of Turkish officials during their visits. By criticizing the development policies of traditional donors, Turkey distances itself from them, emphasizing the novelty of its approach based on a mutually beneficial and sustainable partnership between donors and recipients (Murphy and Woods 2014, 10). During the 2015 Sustainable Development Summit, the then Prime Minister Ahmet Davutoglu brought forward Turkey's SSA policy as an example of the driving force for the positive outputs resulting from combining humanitarian and development assistance programs within a collective strategy. The Ankara consensus is emphasized by the narrative that backs up Turkish activism, strengthening the perception of Turkey as a unique actor in the sub-Saharan context. The Turkish South–South narrative is blended with faith-based elements, humanitarianism, some references to a particular kind of Third-Worldism, and Neo-Ottomanism.

South–South

Even though traditionally its sights have been focused on the West—and thus, considered to be close to the Global North—Turkey is aware of its position between the North and the South due also to the strong identity/security nexus that has characterized its developmental path. Therefore, like other emerging powers, Turkey refuses to use the dominant language of official development, which tends to rationalize the hierarchical relationship between North and South (Dreher, Nunnenkamp, and Thiele 2011). Furthermore, Turkey displays such rhetoric in every bilateral and multilateral meeting in which it emphasizes that the Turkish goal is to help the African nations in their policy of "African solutions to African problems." As President Erdogan underlined during the Second Economic and Business Forum, "We [Turks] want to improve our relations, built on mutual respect, in all areas on the basis of win–win and equal partnership."[15] Despite this strong SSC rhetoric, Turkey's South–South credentials have not proven to be fully reliable.

Humanitarianism

In a global context, Turkey's humanitarian-oriented approach is used as a way to live up to the expectations of international solidarity and problem-solving initiatives that come with the status of being a rising power. Since 2008, Turkey's humanitarian diplomacy has grown and its reputation as a humanitarian state rings louder over all sub-Saharan Africa (Hasimi 2014; Donelli 2017a). For the Turkish government, humanitarian aid was and still is a means to strengthen bilateral relations with governments. The religious element is especially evident in the humanitarian dimension of Turkish efforts. Indeed, during the last decade, Turkey's humanitarianism aimed to restore the bond between Turkey and Muslim countries, and it was articulated with a perceived Turkish responsibility towards Muslim communities outside of its borders (the *ummah*). In recent years, however, this *ummah* focus has been replaced by an Islamic internationalism that suggests having cross-border humanitarian engagement as a vessel of Islamic religious identity (Cevik 2014). Theoretically, it means that even though Turkish NGOs do not discriminate based on religion and ethnic origin in their aid activities, a strong Islamic identity shapes their approach to their actions (Celik and İseri 2016). The main limit of this discourse is that this image of a moral state, which Turkey has fed into the international arena, is a mismatch with the decreasing level of democratic standards within the country following the coup attempt of mid-2016.

Third-Worldism

Finally, a sort of Turkish Third-Worldism is traceable to the revision project of global—political and economic—governance institutions and structures, and in particular to the United Nations Security Council (UNSC), International Monetary Fund (IMF) and the World Bank.

In some circumstances, Turkey's government rhetoric seems very harsh against globalization, considering it as a new form of Western colonialism and modern slavery.[16] However, statements with a significant media impact are more related to the current anti-Western domestic political discourse rather than true belief. Such discourse does not go against the globalization process and its economic and financial effects, as in the position of the traditional post-Marxist wave, but it implies a broader and deep criticism of international governance. Yet, this rhetoric does not reflect the nature of traditional "Third World" political movements such as the NAM or the G-77.[17] Despite the last six years, where Turkey has been trying to become elected to a non-permanent seat on the UN Security Council—after its successful bid of 2008—it has been increasingly critical of the UN, labelling the intergovernmental organization body as "unfair." President Erdogan and other Turkish senior diplomats use the ethical discourse based on the motto "the world is greater than five" that finds strong resonance in Africa. This narrative represents a radical critique of the existing status quo in the international system that is inspired by the notions of global good and responsibility. The call to reform the architecture and representation mechanism of the UN carries a strong message to African leaders and people. At the same time, this anti-systemic discourse is connected to the increasing isolation the Ankara government has faced in the post-Arab upheavals era (Bilgin 2015).

Neo-Ottomanism

From the beginning of its involvement in Africa, Turkey has understood that an opening-up policy to the continent would not be complete or sustained without religious connections which are also directly linked with the Ottoman past in Africa. Consequently, the two elements—Islam and Ottoman past—reinforce the idea of "clean slate." Whereas the historical past is an obstacle for Western powers, Turkey can emphasize its imperial past and use it to retrieve old historical and identity links. Significantly, and moreover in terms of Turkish relations with the Global South, Turkish foreign policy-makers have stressed that the Ottoman Empire never engaged in the full-fledged colonialism of European powers. The anti-colonial discourse has emerged several times in the tones used by the Turkish elite, assuming in some cases an anti-European connotation. As stressed by Langan (2017, 1403), "the Neo-Ottoman identity is presented as a benevolent force in contrast to Western hegemony, within an 'anti-colonial' narrative."

Conclusion

Throughout the study of the development policies promoted and implemented by Turkey in Africa, the chapter wanted to explore the similarities in both practice and narrative between the Turkish approach and South–South cooperation. Even though Turkey's development agenda is increasingly associated with many Southern donors, mainly due to several common traits—mutual benefit, no conditionalities and anti-imperialist rhetoric—the study highlighted how Turkey has shaped its development model adopting the peculiarities of both traditional donors (DAC) and the SSC. The uniqueness of the Turkish development model, referred to as the Ankara consensus, places Turkey in a middle position, namely a gateway between the North and the Global South. A role that Turkey has shown to want to explore in particular in the African context. For this reason, while it is not correct to speak of Turkish adoption of the SSC tout court, it is also appropriate to consider the leverage that the SSC has on the Turkish development cooperation agenda and policies. The effective impact of Turkish policies on the development pathways of African countries shall be evaluated over a mid-term time horizon. Meanwhile, it should be noted that Turkey's Southern strategic projection has shown the first evidence of structural failure after the initial momentum. The domestic democratic backsliding, the economic slowdown and the involvement in regional crises—Syria, Libya—have constrained Turkey to re-orientate resources towards other priorities. All these developments jeopardize the Turkish attempt to be a Southern player without being from the Global South.

Notes

1. OECD. 1991. "DAC Principles for Evaluation of Development Assistance." Paris. http://www.oecd.org/development/evaluation/2755284.pdf.
2. For an in-depth analysis of this issue see Baba and Ertan 2017.
3. The full text of the BAPA is available for consultation, URL: https://www.unsouthsouth.org/bapa40/documents/buenos-aires-plan-of-action/.
4. Although in previous decades SSC volumes had been marginal, they have since grown in importance and influence; they were estimated to be about 10% of global development assistance flows in 2010 and are expected to reach up to 15–20% in the coming years (de Renzio and Seifert 2014, 1862).
5. Naohiko Omata. 2019. "South–South Cooperation in International Organizations: Its Conceptualization and Implementation within UNDP and UNHCR." Southern Responses to Displacement, June 19. https://southernresponses.org/2019/06/17/south-south-cooperation-in-international-organizations-its-conceptualization-and-implementation-within-undp-and-unhcr/.
6. Russia is aggregated to group (a). For more detail about this categorization see, https://www.cgdev.org.
7. The Washington consensus is a set of economic policy recommendations for developing countries that became popular during the 1980s. Essentially, the Washington consensus advocates, free trade, floating exchange rates, free markets and macroeconomic stability. For more details, see Babb 2013.
8. The term is used to identify a series of economic and social doctrines, born in China after 1978, opposed to the neoliberal policies of development and the influence that these are finding in developing countries. For more details, see Cooper Ramo 2004; Hsu, Wu and Zhao 2011.
9. A few years later, in 2014, the Turkish candidacy was not so successful. Among the main motives was European lobbying in favor of the Spanish candidacy, which won at the third round.
10. NeST is a forum of think tanks and academics from the Global South committed to generating, systematizing and sharing knowledge on South–South approaches to international development cooperation. See http://southernthinktanks.org/index.html.
11. https://fts.unocha.org.
12. For an in-depth analysis of the issue, see Chapters 10 and 11.
13. For further details about the Arab model see Villanger 2007.
14. The only political condition required by China to receive its aid is that the recipient state has no official links with Taiwan (Huang and Peiqiang 2012).
15. Erdogan's speech at the Turkey Africa Second Economic and Business Forum, hosted by the Ministry of Trade and organized by Foreign Economic Relations Board of Turkey (DEIK) in collaboration with the African Union (AU), began in Istanbul on October 10, 2018.
16. Editorial. 2016. "Globalization New Form of Colonialism, President Erdogan Says." *Daily Sabah* (online), November 2. https://www.dailysabah.com/economy/2016/11/02/globalization-new-form-of-colonialism-president-Erdoğan-says.
17. By "Third World" the present study means states in Asia, Africa, Latin America and the Caribbean, and other regions that were either full colonies or semi-colonies of Western powers (Kessler and Weiss 1991).

References

Akpinar, Pınar. 2015. "Turkey Peacebuilding in Somalia: The Limits of Humanitarian Diplomacy." In *Turkey's Rise as an Emerging Power*, edited by Paul Kubicek, Emel Parlar Dal and Tarik Oguzlu. Abingdon: Taylor & Francis.

Aydıntasbas, Asli. 2020. *The Turkish Sonderweg: Erdogan's New Turkey and its Role in the Global Order*. Istanbul: Istanbul Policy Center Sabancı.

Baba, Gurol and Senem Ertan. 2017. "*Turkey at the Bandung Conference: A Fully-Aligned among the Non-Aligned.*" Paper presented at ISA International Conference 2017, Hong Kong. http://web.isanet.org/Web/Conferences/AP%20Hong%20Kong%202016/Archive/64185d87-7a01-44f1-acbc-1566b192398f.pdf.

Babb, Sarah. 2013. "The Washington Consensus as Transnational Policy Paradigm: Its Origins, Trajectory and Likely Successor." *Review of International Political Economy* 30, no. 2: 268–297.

Baird, Theodore. 2016. "The Geopolitics of Turkey's 'Humanitarian Diplomacy' in Somalia: A Critique." *Review of African Political Economy* 43, no. 149: 470–477.

Bergamaschi, Isaline, Phoebe Moore and Arlene B. Tickner, eds. 2017. *South–South Cooperation Beyond the Myths. Rising Donors, New Aid Practices*. London: Palgrave Macmillan.

Bilgin, Ayata. 2015. "Turkish Foreign Policy in a Changing Arab World: Rise and Fall of a Regional Actor?" *Journal of European Integration* 37, no. 1: 95–112.

Binder, Andrea. 2014. "The Shape and Sustainability of Turkey's Booming Humanitarian Assistance." *Revue Internationale de Politique de Développement* 5, no. 2. https://doi.org/10.4000/poldev.1741.

Bracho, Gerardo. 2015. In Search of a Narrative for Southern Providers. In *Discussion Paper*. Bonn: German Development Institute.

Cannon, Brendon J. 2016. "Deconstructing Turkey's Efforts in Somalia." *Bildhaan: An International Journal of Somali Studies* 16, no. 14: 98–123.

Cannon, Brendon J. 2017. "Turkey in Africa: Lessons in Political Economy." *Florya Chronicles of Political Economy* 3, no. 1: 93–110.

Celik, Nihat and Emre İseri. 2016. "Islamically Oriented Humanitarian NGOs in Turkey: AKP Foreign Policy Parallelism." *Turkish Studies* 17, no. 3: 429–448.

Cevik, Senem. 2014. "The Rise of NGOs: Islamic Faith Diplomacy." CPD Blog, USC Center on Public Diplomacy. May 27, 2014. https://uscpublicdiplomacy.org/blog/rise-ngos-islamic-faith-diplomacy.

Cooper Ramo, Joshua. 2004. *The Beijing Consensus: Notes on the New Physics of Chinese Power*. London: Foreign Policy Centre.

de Renzio, Paolo and Jurek Seifert. 2014. "South–South Cooperation and the Future of Development Assistance: Mapping Actors and Options." *Third World Quarterly* 35, no. 10: 1860–1875. doi:10.1080/01436597.2014.971603.

Donelli, Federico. 2015. "Turkey's Presence in Somalia a Humanitarian Approach." In *The Depth of Turkish Geopolitics in the AKP's Foreign Policy: From Europe to an Extended Neighbourhood*, edited by Alessia Chiriatti, Emidio Diodato, Salih Dogan, Federico Donelli and Bahri Yilmaz, 35–51. Perugia: Università per Stranieri Perugia.

Donelli, Federico. 2017a. "Features, Aims and Limits of Turkey's Humanitarian Diplomacy." *Central European Journal of International and Security Studies* 11, no. 3: 59–83.

Donelli, Federico. 2017b. "A Hybrid Actor in the Horn of Africa. An Analysis of Turkey's Involvement in Somalia." In *The Horn of Africa since the 1960s. Local*

and *International Politics Intertwined*, edited by Aleksi Ylönen and Jan Záhořík, 158–170. London: Routledge.
Donelli, Federico. 2018. "The Ankara Consensus: The Significance of Turkey's Engagement in Sub-Saharan Africa." *Global Change, Peace & Security* 31, no. 2: 57–76. doi:10.1080/14781158.2018.1438384.
Donelli, Federico and Ariel S. González Levaggi. 2018. "From Mogadishu to Buenos Aires: The Global South in the Turkish Foreign Policy in the Late JDP Period (2011–2017). In *Middle Powers in Global Governance: The Rise of Turkey*, edited by Emel Parlar Dal, 53–73. London: Palgrave Macmillan.
Dreher, Axel, Peter Nunnenkamp and Rainer Thiele. 2011. "Are 'New' Donors Different? Comparing the Allocation of Bilateral Aid Between non DAC and DAC Donor Countries." *World Development* 39, no. 11: 1950–1968.
Gray, Kevin and Barry K. Gills. 2016. "South–South Cooperation and the Rise of the Global South." *Third World Quarterly* 37, no. 4: 557–574. https://doi.org/10.1080/01436597.2015.1128817.
Gray, Kevin and Barry K. Gills, eds. 2017. *Rising Powers and South–South Cooperation*. London: Routledge.
Hasimi, Cemalettin. 2014. "Turkey's Humanitarian Diplomacy and Development Cooperation." *Insight Turkey* 16, no. 1: 127–145.
Hsu, S. Philip, Yu-Shan Wu and Suisheng Zhao, eds. 2011. *In Search of China's Developmental Model: Beyond the Beijing Consensus*. Milton Park: Routledge.
Huang, Meibo and Ren Peiqiang. 2012. "China's Foreign Aid and Its Role in the International Architecture." *International Development Policy* 3, no. 3. doi:10.4000/poldev.1004.
Kadayifci-Orellana, Ayse S. 2016. "Turkish Mediation in Somalia for Peace and Stability." In *Turkey as a Mediator: Stories of Success and Failure*, edited by Doga Ulas Eralp, 99–124. Lanham, MD: Lexington Books.
Kessler, Meryl A. and Thomas G. Weiss, eds. 1991. *Third World Security in the Post-Cold War Era*. Boulder: Lynne Rienner.
Kragelund, Peter. 2012. "The Revival of Non-Traditional State Actors' Interests in Africa: Does it Matter for Policy Autonomy?" *Development Policy Review* 30, no. 6: 703–718. https://doi.org/10.1111/j.1467-7679.2012.00595.x.
Langan, Mark. 2017. "Virtuous Power Turkey in Sub-Saharan Africa: The 'Neo-Ottoman' Challenge to the European Union." *Third World Quarterly* 38, no. 6. https://doi.org/10.1080/01436597.2016.1229569.
Lekorwe, Mogopodi, Anyway Chingwete, Mina Okuru and Romaric Samson. 2016. China's Growing Presence in Africa Wins Largely Positive Popular Reviews. In Afrobarometer Dispatch: Afrobarometer. https://www.afrobarometer.org/publications/ad122-chinas-growing-presence-africa-wins-largely-positive-popular-reviews.
Mawdsley, Emma. 2012. *From Recipients to Donors: Emerging Powers and the Changing Development Landscape*. New York: Zed Books.
Mawdsley, Emma. 2019. "South–South Cooperation 3.0? Managing the Consequences of Success in the Decade Ahead." *Oxford Development Studies* 47, no. 3: 259–274. doi:10.1080/13600818.2019.1585792.
Mawdsley, Emma, Laura Savage and Kim Sung-Mi. 2014. "A 'Post-Aid World'? Paradigm Shift in Foreign Aid and Development Cooperation at the 2011 Busan High Level Forum." *Geographical Journal* 180, no. 1: 27–38. https://doi.org/10.1111/j.1475-4959.2012.00490.x.
Modi, Renu, ed. 2011. *South–South Cooperation. Africa on the Centre Stage*. London: Palgrave Macmillan.

Murphy, Teri and Auveen Elizabeth Woods. 2014. *Turkey's International Development Framework Case Study: Somalia*. Istanbul: Sabanci University Istanbul Policy Center.

Ozkan, Mehmet. 2013. "Turkey's Religious and Socio-Political Depth in Africa" In "*Emerging Powers in Africa.*" LSE IDEAS Special Report 16: 45–50.

Ozkan, Mehmet. 2014. *Turkey's Involvement in Somalia: Assessments of a State-Building in Progress*. Ankara: SETA Publications.

Ozkan, Mehmet. 2018. "Turkey in South–South Cooperation: New Foreign Policy Approach in Africa." *Vestnik Rudn International Relations* 18, no. 3: 565–578. doi: http://dx.doi.org/10.22363/2313-0660-2018-18-3-565-578.

Park, Kang-Ho. 2011. "New Development Partners and a Global Development Partnership." In *Catalyzing Development: A New Vision for Aid*, edited by Homi Kharas, Koji Makino and Woojin Jung, 38–60. Washington: Brookings Institution Press.

Quadir, Fahimul. 2013. "Rising Donors and the New Narrative of 'South–South' Cooperation: What Prospects for Changing the Landscape of Development Assistance Programmes?" *Third World Quarterly* 34, no. 2: 321–338. ttps://doi.org/10.1080/01436597.2013.775788.

Rampa, Francesco, Sanoussi Bilal and Elizabeth Sidiropoulos. 2012. "Leveraging South–South Cooperation for Africa's Development." *South African Journal of International Affairs* 19, no. 2: 247–269. doi:10.1080/10220461.2012.709400.

Sato, Jin, Hiroaki Shiga, Takaaki Kobayashi and Hisahiro Kondoh. 2010. "How do "Emerging" Donors Differ from "Traditional" Donors? An Institutional Analysis of Foreign Aid in Cambodia." JICA-RI Working Paper. Tokyo: JICA Research Institute. https://www.jica.go.jp/jica-ri/publication/workingpaper/jrft3q00000022dd-att/JICA-RI_WP_No.2_2010.pdf.

Stearns, Jason and Gizem Sucuoglu. 2017. South–South Cooperation and Peacebuilding: Turkey's Involvement in Somalia. Policy Insights 43. South African Institute of International Affairs. https://www.jstor.org/stable/resrep25981.

Sucuoglu, Gizem and Onur Sazak. 2016. "The New Kid on the Block: Turkey's Shifting Approaches to Peacebuilding." *Rising Powers Quarterly* 1, no. 2: 69–91.

Tjønneland, Elling N. 2015. "African Development: What Role do the Rising Powers Play?" Norwegian Peacebuilding Research Centre Report. https://www.cmi.no/publications/5349-african-development.

UNDP. 2013. "Turkey is on the Way of OECD DAC Membership." www.tr.undp.org/content/turkey/en/home/presscenter/news-from-new-horizons/2012/05/turkey-is-on-the-way-of-OECD-DAC-membership.

Villanger, Espen. 2007. *Arab Foreign Aid: Disbursement Patterns, Aid Policies and Motives*. Bergen: Chr. Michelsen Institute.

Woods, NGaire. 2008. "Whose aid? Whose influence? China, Emerging Donors and the Silent Revolution in Development Assistance." *International Affairs* 84, no. 6: 1205–1221.

Zimmermann, Felix and Kimberly Smith. 2011. "More Actors, More Money, More Ideas for International Development Co-Operation." *Journal of International Development* 23, no. 5: 722–738. https://doi.org/10.1002/jid.1796.

Part 2
Economic relations and military strategies

5 The political economy of Turkey–Africa relations

Hüseyin Emrah Karaoğuz and Selman Emre Gürbüz

Introduction

Turkey closed its embassies in sub-Saharan Africa (SSA) because of economic concerns in the 1980s[1] and the country was represented by only 12 embassies in Africa in 2005. Yet, Turkey established 30 new embassies in the region in the following 15 years. The country's economic relations with Africa were also institutionalized to a certain degree and intensified. The Foreign Economic Relations Board of Turkey (DEIK) established 34 new business councils with sub-Saharan African countries between 2008 and 2018 (there was only one with South Africa in 1997). While the total volume of trade with Africa was only 4.3 billion USD in 2002, it increased to 23.5 billion USD in 2019.[2] Likewise, the volume of Turkish foreign direct investment (FDI) in Africa (stock) spectacularly rose to 55 billion USD in 2019 from a mere 100 million USD in 2003 (Parlar Dal and Dipama 2020, 256). In short, Turkish governments and civil society organizations have shown an unprecedented interest in developing political and economic ties with many African countries, especially since 2005.

Turkey's new activism in Africa has attracted scholarly attention, albeit more effort is needed to better understand the country's novel "opening" to the region. In this chapter, we elaborate Turkey–Africa relations from a political economy perspective. We emphasize two points by also engaging with the literature on the political economy of Turkish foreign policy. First, many studies note that Turkey's neoliberal transformation in the 1980s and the new elite's willingness to find new markets for its allies in the economy in the 2000s have been crucial in shaping Turkey's growing interest in Africa. We briefly provide a political economy background to these explanations. Turkey's neoliberal restructuring set the scene for its Africa initiative two decades later; and small and medium sized enterprises' (SME) historical exclusion from resource allocation mechanisms (secular vs. conservative cleavage) incentivized Turkey's new ruling elite to find new investment sites for its allies in the new millennium. Then, we put Turkey's engagement with Africa into a context by examining domestic and external developments that first enabled, and then undermined, Turkey's economy-driven foreign policy in the 2000s. We highlight that many global, regional and domestic developments have conditioned the realization of Turkey's rising power ambitions in Africa and beyond.

Turkey's neoliberal restructuring in the 1980s

Turkey faced a severe economic crisis in the late 1970s, ending the country's roughly 40-years-long experimentation with import-substitution-industrialization (ISI) strategy. The economy grew by 6.8 percent on average between 1967 and 1977 (Barlow and Senses 1995, 111), and ISI seemed to deliver what was expected of it during the post-war's "golden age of capitalism." However, because of apparent inefficiencies in the ISI model, policy failures and adverse external shocks such as the oil crisis, Turkey's main macroeconomic indicators deteriorated after 1976 (Aricanli and Rodrik 1990). The growth rate of gross national product (GNP), for instance, decreased to -1.1 percent in 1980 from 2.9 percent in 1978; the inflation rate rose to 50 percent (1977) from 18 percent (1970–1975); and Turkey's external indebtedness increased from 3 billion USD in 1973 to 15 billion USD in the following six years (Barlow and Senses 1995, 111). Having also faced a devastating social unrest and political instability, Turkey switched to export-oriented-industrialization (EOI) strategy with the 24 January decisions announced in 1980.[3] Then, the country pursued a stabilization and structural adjustment program under the supervision of the International Monetary Fund (IMF) and the World Bank.

The main objective of Turkey's ruling elite was to solve the country's pressing macroeconomic problems and restore its creditworthiness by liberalizing the economy—and most importantly—by structurally limiting the state's excessive role in the economy to be able to create a well-functioning free-market economy. On that note, one key goal was to boost Turkish exports to rationalize economic behavior, and to reap the benefits of "comparative advantage" as advocated by the mainstream economic theory. Accordingly, policies were executed to encourage exports by creating and institutionalizing a liberal economy, that is, real exchange rate depreciation, export subsidies and import liberalization. For instance, the exchange rate was instantly devalued by 48.6 percent with the 24 January decisions, adjusted daily after May 1981 and the rate of the Turkish lira's annual depreciation was recorded as 4.2 percent on average between May 1981 and May 1987 (Baysan and Blitzer 1990, 11). Tax rebates, credit subsidies and foreign exchange allocations (enabling intermediate goods' and raw materials' duty-free import) were among the instruments of export promotion. The average tax rebate, for instance, increased to 23 percent in 1983 from 9 percent in 1980, and the rebate system's total coverage (share of manufactured exports qualified for rebates) increased to 87 percent from 61 percent in the same period (Baysan and Blitzer 1990, 13–15). Import liberalization was also essential: reductions in stamp duty (reduced to 1 percent from 25 percent in

1980), relaxations in import restrictions, simplifications in import procedures and abolishment of the import quota list were among the policies implemented at the initial stage of import liberalization (Baysan and Blitzer 1990, 15–23). These policies were followed by major revisions in the tariff structure. At the end of the day, there was a

> spectacular increase in [Turkish] exports unparalleled by any other country in the protectionist and largely stagnant international environment of the 1980s [...] [and Turkish] exports registered nearly a five-fold increase in only eight years rising from $2.3 billion in 1979 to $10.2 billion in 1987, accounting in 1985 for 14.9 percent of GNP.[4]
> (Senses 1990, 60)

Finally, it is with this neoliberal restructuring that business began to play more active roles in policymaking processes in Turkey, conservative economic elites also known as "Anatolian Tigers" emerged as an influential actor in the political economy, and influential associations began to be established to represent the interests of Turkey's business at home and abroad. For instance, DEIK was founded in 1985 with the goal of "compiling information on opportunities of commercial cooperation and presenting it to entrepreneurs; providing coordination at international level for various forms of commercial and economic cooperation; ensuring the appropriate political environment for the realization of the existing potential" (Atli 2011b, 113). We briefly elaborate the long-term consequences of these developments from a political economy perspective in the following sections.

From neoliberalism to Turkey's "Africa opening"

Turkey's neoliberal transformation in line with the propositions of what was later referred to as the "Washington consensus" led to sea changes in the Turkish political economy (Onis 2004). One of the most important consequences was that Turkey's typical inward-looking economy was integrated into the global markets. Along with the global triumph of neoliberalism, it gave rise to an entirely new socio-economic environment. In fact, many authors elaborated the causes and consequences of the global shift to neoliberalism in depth. One influential examination that is particularly important in our context is Rosecrance's "trading state" conceptualization (Rosecrance 1986). In short, Rosecrance noted that states can either act like a "territorial state" or a "trading state" depending on incentive structures—the equilibria shaped by domestic and external conditions.[5] On the one hand, a "territorial state" seeks control over new territories through the exercise of military power because it lacks the motivation to generate wealth through economic engagement. On the other hand, a "trading state" prioritizes international trade and transactions, since its ability to accumulate wealth is highly dependent on the creation and consolidation of economic ties with other economies. Rosecrance argued that the new liberal order incentivizes states to act more like a "trading state" than a "territorial state," since the opportunity cost of military engagement and conflict is unacceptably high under neoliberalism. That is to say, states functioning in a globalized political economy irrationally endure significant welfare losses if they act like a "territorial state." It would also be difficult to legitimize military aggression to domestic audiences because the alternative seems more appealing in democratic settings.

Rosecrance's approach is drawn on to offer a complementary political economy reading of Turkey's "new foreign policy" in the 2000s (Kirisci 2009; Kirisci and Kaptanoglu 2011). It is also used to evaluate Turkey's new interest in SSA (Parlar Dal and Dipama 2020). In brief, there was a U-turn in Turkish foreign policy behavior in the 2000s with the Justice and Development Party's (JDP) coming to power in 2002. In contrast with the previous decade, when Turkey's foreign policy outlook was highly securitized, the ruling elite promoted an economy-driven foreign policy in the 2000s. Turkey's chief objective was to reduce conflict in its neighborhood by boosting interstate economic activities, which was frequently called "zero-problems with neighbors" policy (Aras 2009; 2014). The rapprochement with Armenia and Greece, and Turkey's willingness to mediate between countries such as Afghanistan and Pakistan, and Israel and Syria, were the manifestations of the country's new foreign policy stance (Kirisci 2009). This change in Turkey's foreign policy approach was the puzzle that was to be explained. For Kirisci (2009) and many others, the shift in orientation was mainly a political economy consequence of Turkey's neoliberal turn in the 1980s.[6] Under neoliberalism, both in Turkey and in the world, economic welfare became more and more dependent on the private sector's degree of innovativeness and international competitiveness, finding new markets for domestic firms emerged as an important determinant of economic, and therefore political success, capital notably increased its power vis-à-vis the state under new international political economy conditions—especially with financial liberalization and the overwhelming power of finance capital, new actors willing to further the liberalization process emerged, and finally economic concerns began to occupy a more central role in the formulation of countries' foreign policies. It is this structural change that is said to have established the pillars of Turkey's trade-induced foreign policy between 2002 and 2011. Turkey's good record on democratization, promising developments regarding EU membership process, and successful macroeconomic performance also contributed to Turkey's prioritization of soft power in its international affairs. For instance, on business' influence on policy-making processes in Turkey under new international political economy conditions, Kirisci (2009, 46–47) noted:

> These interest groups [including main business associations] not only interact with various government agencies, but also have direct access to

the government itself and are capable of shaping public opinion. They are also able to form alliances with government agencies as well as their counterparts in other countries, for the purposes of lobbying in support of policies typically associated with a trading state.

It is in this political economy context that Turkey–Africa relations gained momentum in the 2000s. As Parlar Dal and Dipama (2020, 251) aptly noted, for instance, "Turkey's opening to the SSA region in the early years of the 2000s should be considered as part and parcel of its evolving 'trading state' status." To illustrate, there was a sharp increase in the volume of Turkey's overall trade with Africa in the 2000s: It increased from 5.4 million USD in 2003 to 21.5 million USD in 2018—North Africa being Turkey's main trading partner.[7] In SSA, Turkey's two out of top ten trading partners were in South Africa (South Africa and Angola), three in East Africa (Sudan, Ethiopia and Tanzania), four in West Africa (Nigeria, Senegal, Cote d'Ivoire and Ghana) and one in Central Africa (Cameroon; Parlar Dal and Dipama 2020, 256). There was also a visible increase in the volume of Turkish FDI stock in Africa as indicated. In fact, many Turkish firms invested in Africa, contributing to the creation of economic interdependencies between Turkey and the region. Summa Holding's construction facilities in Senegal, MNG Holding's gold mining activities and Origin Group's seed horticulture sector in Burkina Faso, Limak Holding and Sanko Holding's joint facilities in the cement factory sector and Yildirim Holding's naval transportation sector in Ivory Coast, Kazancı and Karadeniz Holdings' energy plant construction sector in Ghana, Yıldız Holding and Elvan Holdings' biscuit factory construction facilities in Nigeria, and finally Ayka Textile Incorporations' textile factory in Ethiopia are some examples in this regard (Ipek 2017, 226).

As noted at the outset, Turkey's economic relations with Africa were also institutionalized to a certain degree. When the JDP came to power in 2002, Turkey had no free trade agreements (FTAs) with African countries. The country signed four FTAs in the following decade with Tunisia (2004), Morocco (2004), Egypt (2005) and Mauritius (2011).[8] Turkey acquired observer status in the African Union in 2005, was declared a strategic partner in the African Union Summit in 2008 and became a non-regional member of the Africa Development Bank (Ozkan 2010, 534). Influential business organizations played a crucial role in deepening and institutionalizing Turkey–Africa affairs. To exemplify, while DEIK had five business councils with African countries in the 1990s (Algeria, Egypt, Morocco, South Africa and Tunisia), the organization founded 40 new councils in the following two decades.[9] DEIK established 34 new councils with sub-Saharan African countries between 2008 and 2018. The Turkish Confederation of Businessmen and Industrialists (TUSKON), JDP's trusted ally until the rift between the party and the Gulenist movement, was also an important player in initiating Turkey's "Africa opening" (Ozkan 2012, 124; Bacik and Afacan 2013, 496–497; Eyrice Tepeciklioglu 2017, 11; Alkan and Mercan 2013).

Indeed, TUSKON was praised by Turkey's high-state officials because of its contributions to the country's economic growth and visibility in the world.[10] Besides organizing high-level summits between Turkey and African countries to improve economic relations, TUSKON operated business matchmaking programs to introduce Turkey's SMEs to the African market—that is, it "took more than five thousand small- and medium-sized Turkish entrepreneurs to various African countries as part of its business matchmaking programs" (Bacik and Afacan 2013, 496). Likewise, MUSIAD, established in 1990 to represent Anatolia's conservative capitalists, and which later developed organic ties with JDP, also played important roles in facilitating relations with Africa. The organization declared 2018 the "Year of Africa," aimed to maintain bilateral relations to expand business networks, hosted foreign trade delegations in coordination with the Ministry of Foreign Affairs, and organized business forums, seminars, fairs and conferences to set the standards for imports and exports (Ngwa 2019, 28). In short, Turkey–Africa relations gained momentum after 2005 in a political economy context that was favorable for the rise of the so-called Turkish trading state.

Political economy constraints and limitations of Turkey's "Africa opening"

Many external and internal developments undermined Turkey's economy-driven foreign policy approach post-2011, while the country's foreign policy stance had been securitized with each passing day. In fact, for many observers, the intriguing question was: "How Turkey went from 'zero problems' to zero friends" foreign policy outlook post-2011?[11] To start with, the Syrian civil war, Arab spring and havoc in the MENA region tested the durability of Turkey's economy-led integration attempts. Turkey relied on its hard power amid growing security threats, that is, conducting military operations on foreign soil to fight against terrorist groups. Uprisings and political turmoil also resulted in "state capacity" problems in the region, in the sense that Turkey's trading partners could no longer provide security to their citizens by exercising state authority—the first and foremost prerequisite of economic activity (Kutlay 2016). At home, backsliding of democracy (Esen and Gumuscu 2016), a failed coup attempt in July 2016 and its political economy consequences (Parlar Dal and Dipama 2020, 247), and the Turkish economy's enduring structural weaknesses (Orhangazi 2019; Subasat 2014; Onis and Kutlay 2013) contributed to the weakening of Turkey's trading state vision. The rate of growth slowed down, the inflation rate rose to two-digit numbers as in the 1990s and high unemployment began to pose major problems. Turkey could not achieve industrial upgrading despite political will and effort (Kutlay and Karaoguz 2018) and thus failed to overcome the middle-income trap by solving its chronic current account deficit problem. Politically motivated interventions to the bureaucracy and independent regulatory agencies also hindered the formulation and implementation of effective policies (Karaoguz 2018; Ozel 2012). In fact, the institutional foundations of Turkey's so-called trading state were weak even in the 2002–2011 period: Failure to implement technological upgrading stemmed from weak developmental governance, the fragmented nature of state–business relations, and weak financial statecraft in supporting domestic business in their economic activities abroad (Kutlay and Karaoguz 2020b). Thus, it is in this broad political economy context that Turkey's "Africa opening" lost momentum, in the sense that economic interdependencies between Turkey and Africa were not intensified and institutionalized as expected of them in the heyday of Turkey's economy-led integration attempts. As such, for instance, Turkey's volume of trade with Africa remained dwarfed in cross-country comparisons (Parlar Dal and Dipama 2020, 265); Turkey's trade shares in Africa did not exceed 8 percent of its overall trade (Eyrice Tepeciklioglu 2017, 26). As aptly emphasized, "although the low level of attention paid to African issues has changed, the pace of the development of relations with Africa is still slow and more steps have to be taken to further improve relations with African countries" (Eyrice Tepeciklioglu 2017, 1).

Nature of state–business relations in Turkey and implications for Turkey–Africa affairs

It is often noted by experts that Turkey's growing interest in Africa was primarily because of the new ruling elite's willingness to find new markets and investment sites for its allies in the economy in the 2000s. The new elites supported Anatolia's conservative capitalists and business associations to be able to increase their power vis-à-vis the secular elite in politics and in the economy. These conservative firms were largely SMEs, and one of their main objectives was to access new markets in the Middle East and in Africa—regions that were not traditionally targeted by the secular economic elite in Turkey, that is, the Turkish Industry and Business Association (TUSIAD). In this section, we first provide a political economy background to this issue by also elaborating on the persistence of clientelist relations in Turkish politics. Then, we briefly examine the nature of state–business relations in Turkey with its implications for the political economy of Turkey–Africa affairs.

Historical roots of clientelism in Turkey and SMEs' exclusion from distribution mechanisms

Clientelism has been a central attribute of Turkish politics and society since the 1920s (Sayari 2014).[12] Locally influential notables, who molded clientelist relations with the peasants by safeguarding them against the unforeseen behavior of state officials in the Ottoman period, reinforced their socio-economic status in the early years of the Republic. They played important roles in the newly formed Republican People's Party and sustained their alliance with local officials (Gunes Ayata 1994). The regime, in return, controlled the periphery through these notables (Sayari 2011). This traditional patron–client form of clientelism mostly faded away with the transition to multiparty politics in the late 1940s. With millions of people participating directly in politics for the first time under free elections and universal suffrage in Turkey, a new form of clientelism emerged based on the delivery of goods and services in exchange for votes (Sayari 2014, 658–660). The allocation of state resources in return for political support became an indispensable mechanism of nurturing popular support (Sayari 1977; Ozbudun 1981). For instance, after its electoral victory in the 1950 general elections, the conservative Democratic Party (DP) forged clientelist relations to broaden its popular support among its constituencies. While the DP awarded its electoral base with infrastructural investments (road, water, electricity, etc.), it punished those who voted for the opposing party by excluding them from allocation processes. The DP also relied on the then dominant state economic enterprises to keep its electoral base intact (Bayar 1996). Since then, "the distribution of goods and services in exchange for votes through political clientelism and patronage" has been an important determinant of voter preference in Turkey (Sayari 2014, 665).

Clientelism also refers to particularistic distribution of public resources to favored groups in the economy in exchange for their political support. This type of clientelism has also been a traditional aspect of the Turkish political economy. For instance, large and diversified business groups emerged as the key player of economic development in the ISI period, both in the world and in Turkey, because the ISI strategy was based on the productive potential of concentrated capital in the hands of the few. Although this was not in itself the main problem, the ruling elite's selective allocation of rents to their friends in the economy (in an inefficient manner) was the problem in Turkey in the 1960s and the 1970s. As Krueger (1974, 294) estimated, for instance, rents from import licenses alone were approximately 15 percent of GNP in Turkey in 1968. Furthermore, governments' control over state economic enterprises was one of the main mechanisms of coalition building via clientelism. As noted, the governments' command over prices in the ISI period "was seen as a way of directing assistance to [...] sectors of the economy in return for political support" (Onis and Riedel 1993, 102). In short, SMEs were largely excluded from the "winning coalition" in Turkey in the post-war period under the conditions of ISI.

The exclusion of SMEs from allocation processes squarely overlapped with a crucial cleavage in the Turkish context: marginalization of Anatolia's conservative businesspeople, who were mainly small business owners. It is also because of this exclusion that the Islamic-leaning political parties tried to raise the voices of SMEs in Turkey. For instance, one of the reasons for the first religious party's establishment in Turkey in 1970, the National Order Party, was to represent the interests of Anatolian SMEs. The party aimed to challenge the then Justice Party government, which had close ties with large business groups. The National Salvation Party, replacing the National Order Party in 1972, likewise represented the conservative economic elites and

SMEs. That is to say, the constituent SMEs of Islamic-leaning parties were "discontented with the allocation of state resources to large businesses in the major cities and demanded state protection and support for themselves in order to receive 'their due share of the expanding economic pie'" (Baskan 2010, 401).

An institutional constraint: Fragmented nature of state–business relations

Many studies suggest that the JDP also forged clientelist relations with the electorate and interest groups in the 2000s (Yildirim 2020; Bugra and Savaskan 2014). The party's effective use of formal and informal distributive mechanisms in exchange for political support is noted as a crucial factor in its unprecedented electoral success in Turkey (Sayari 2011; Onis 2012; Komsuoglu 2009; Ark Yildirim 2017). More importantly, the JDP is said to nurture its own allies in the economy to be able to counter the secular elite's influence in the political economy (Bugra and Savaskan 2014; Esen and Gumuscu 2018). On that note, some authors claimed that the party successfully energized the unutilized entrepreneurial potential of Asia Minor by integrating previously discouraged devout businesspeople to the system. This upward social mobility, provided to those Islamic-leaning businesspeople who were previously excluded from resource allocation processes by the secular elite, is said to contribute to Turkey's successful macroeconomic performance. Accordingly, the JDP supported conservative business groups like MUSIAD and TUSKON, who played leading roles in shaping the country's foreign economic policy in the heyday of Turkey's economy-led integration strategy (Atli 2011b; Tur 2011). They also assumed significant roles in fostering economic relations with Africa (Ozkan 2012, 124; Eyrice Tepeciklioglu 2017, 11). It is known that MUSIAD and JDP had organic and close ties, and the organization played a role in JDP's foundation process (Baskan 2010, 408).

In this political economy context, two issues held back the consolidation of Turkey's "new foreign policy" in the 2000s (Kutlay and Karaoguz 2020b), and its attempts to create economic interdependencies with Africa and the Middle East. First, the new ruling elite could not succeed in getting everyone on board regarding its economy-driven integration strategy. As aptly noted, for instance:

> there are certain limits and constraints of employing political economy factors as a driving force in the Turkish foreign policy activism [...] [which are related to] industrial capacity in terms of competitiveness, the state-business and business–business synergy, and the societal coherence in terms of domestic and foreign policy priorities.
>
> (Kutlay 2011, 67, 82)

Perhaps most importantly, TUSIAD, the biggest umbrella business organization in Turkey representing Istanbul-based capitalists, did not wholeheartedly support Turkey's multidimensional foreign policy (Unay 2010, 34). Also, high-state officials' sharp criticisms levelled against TUSIAD post-2011 revealed the nature of the growing conflict between the JDP and TUSIAD.[13] Furthermore, there were politically motivated attempts by the ruling elite to punish those non-compliers in the economy who raised their voices against the ruling party. For instance, shortly after the Gezi Park Protests, tax agencies audited companies affiliated with Koc Holding, a leading TUSIAD member, which was claimed to host protestors in one of its hotels during the protests (Esen and Gumuscu 2018, 359). Examples of politically motivated initiatives as such can be proliferated. In short, these political economy dynamics, which were also related to Turkey's volatile relations with the EU,[14] is aptly summarized by Arda (2015, 216) such as in the following:

> The shift in the interest of the government away from the EU [...] went in parallel with the government's distancing itself from [...] TUSIAD [...] which [...] is linked mostly to Western oriented big business, is strongly and actively supporting the EU accession process and is avidly secular. The relations further soured with TUSIAD's pronouncements criticizing the government on its handling of human rights and some legal processes in Turkey. This led to the rise of TUSKON and MUSIAD, two business associations with bases fundamentally in Anatolia and espousing traditional values, including religious ones.

Second, even though business gained strength and assumed more significant roles in the formulation and implementation of foreign (economic) policy in Turkey post-1980, its agency has always been questionable in the sense that it has never been strong and autonomous enough to exert its influence on the country's foreign (economic) policy to push it in a direction that is not first embraced by the ruling political elite. In other words, neither the neoliberal transformation nor the increasing trade volumes paved the way for the business world to appear as an autonomous actor and to direct the country's foreign (economic) policy in a direction not previously approved by the politicians. As Atli (2011b, 125, emphasis added) noted, for instance, "business associations such as DEIK and TUSKON are important actors in Turkey's foreign economic policy, and they are likely to maintain this position *as long as they remain loyal partners to state actors.*" Indeed, while DEIK effectively became a governmental organization with a last-minute change in an omnibus bill in September 2014, TUSKON was shut down after the failed coup attempt in July 2016 since it was declared a terrorist organization (Kutlay and Karaoguz 2020b). Or, Tur (2011, 600, emphasis added) noted,

> the first potential roadblock [for more economic activity with the Middle East] may be the primacy of political issues in driving economic ones; there is a need for the business relations to take root and develop their own dynamism such that they may become more institutionalized.

Likewise, in the case of TUSIAD, the organization's inclusion in economic policymaking processes were "contingent upon its relationship with the government, where, in fact, the presence of a tension mostly result[ed] in exclusion due to the absence of institutionalized incorporation of business into policy-making" (Ozel 2013, 1097). This trait of Turkish political economy is crucial for the following reason: For Turkey to successfully pursue its rising power ambitions (in Africa) in a shifting international order via creating durable economic interdependencies, the business should have the required autonomy and strength to participate in foreign (economic) policymaking processes. Otherwise, any external shock will be more likely to drive Turkish foreign (economic) policy towards a security-oriented axis.[15]

Conclusion

This chapter examined Turkey–Africa relations from a political economy perspective. First, it contextualized and provided a political economy background to Turkey's growing interest in Africa in the 2000s by revisiting the country's neoliberal transformation in the 1980s and SMEs' historical exclusion from resource allocation mechanisms. While political economy factors that were set into motion by Turkey's neoliberal restructuring conditioned the country's Africa opening, SMEs' exclusion from resource allocation mechanisms (secular vs. conservative cleavage) was one of the reasons why Turkey's new ruling elite aimed to find new markets and investment sites for its allies in the economy in the 2000s. From a broader perspective, it was also the case that new markets in the Middle East and Africa, rather than Europe, were where Turkey's new economic elite and SMEs had a chance to be competitive. This also conditioned and drove Turkey's new ruling elite's growing interest in finding new markets in the Middle East and in Africa. Then, the chapter contextualized Turkey's engagement with Africa by elaborating on external and domestic developments that first enabled, and then undermined, Turkey's economy-driven foreign policy in the new millennium. In the 2002–2011 period, Turkey adopted a foreign policy stance that prioritized the creation of economic interdependencies with its neighbors and beyond, which is frequently called "zero-problems with neighbors" policy. Favorable global (economic) conditions, promising relations with the EU, encouraging macroeconomic performance and a good record on democratization contributed to the emergence of Turkey's trade-induced foreign policy. It is in this political economy context that Turkey–Africa relations gained momentum, especially after 2005. However, adverse external shocks, such as the Syrian civil war, the Arab spring, and the 2008 global economic crisis; worsening relations with the EU, backsliding of democracy, poor macroeconomic performance stemming from the economy's structural weaknesses, and weaknesses in the institutional pillars of economy-led integration attempts led to the securitization of Turkey's foreign policy. Despite positive steps and progress, Turkey's "Africa opening" lost momentum under this new political economy climate. In other words, Turkey–Africa relations were not intensified and institutionalized as anticipated in the heyday of Turkey's Africa opening. In consequence, many external and domestic political economy factors conditioned the realization of Turkey's rising power ambitions, both in general and in the context of Africa.

Finally, it should be emphasized that the examination of external and domestic conditions that African countries faced in the new millennium is a must for a better account of the political economy of Turkey–Africa relations. As noted almost a decade ago,

> the response from the African side, by and large, has been a mixture of confusion and hope. Whether such an African interest and Turkish eagerness may converge in future is an important issue that will define the future of Turkey's opening to Africa.
>
> (Ozkan 2012, 121)

This is still an important point. Furthermore, what Turkey should do to improve relations with Africa is yet another question. As noted, for instance:

> [Turkey's] action plan applied for the whole African continent should be customized to each country, and the national or regional differences should be taken into consideration. Otherwise, the foreign policy instruments, which work seamlessly for South Africa, might not work for Algeria, Cote d'Ivoire or Uganda.
>
> (Afacan 2013, 54)

This is also a crucial point, requiring further elaboration.

Notes

1 Republic of Turkey Ministry of Foreign Affairs. n.d. "Turkiye-Tanzanya Siyasi İliskileri." Accessed June 14, 2020. http://www.mfa.gov.tr/turkiye-tanzanya-siyasi-iliskileri.tr.mfa and Republic of Turkey Akra Büyükelçiliği. n.d. "Buyukelcilik." Accessed June 14, 2020. http://akra.be.mfa.gov.tr/Mission/About.
2 Republic of Turkey Ministry of Foreign Affairs. n.d. "Turkiye-Afrika İliskileri." Accessed June 14, 2020. https://www.mfa.gov.tr/turkiye-afrika-iliskileri.tr.mfa.
3 The 24 January decisions, with which Turkey liberalized its economy through structural reforms and neoliberal policies, are considered to be a milestone in the Turkish economy. It is still celebrated by proponents of liberal economy. See, for instance, Anadolu Agency. 2020. "40th year of Turkey's transition to liberal economy." Accessed October 26, 2020. https://www.aa.com.tr/en/economy/40th-year-of-turkeys-transition-to-liberal-economy/1711449.
4 For more on Turkey's neoliberal restructuring, see Onis and Senses (2009).
5 For a review of the trading state, see Parlar Dal and Dipama (2020, 240–243) and Kutlay and Karaoguz (2020a, 571–572).
6 For more on business associations and Turkey's foreign economic policy in the 1980s, also with an emphasis on Turgut Ozal's role in the process, see Atli (2011a). Ozal was one of the most influential figures of Turkey's neoliberal restructuring.

Ozal's "unique background involving exposure to public, private and transnational organizations, at successive phases of his career, clearly proved to be a major asset for Ozal during his subsequent rise to political power" (Onis 2004: 115). Ozal acted as the Prime Minister between 1983 and 1989, and the President between 1989 and 1993.
7 See Chapter 6 by Samiratou Dipama and Emel Parlar Dal in this volume for a thorough analysis of Turkey–Africa trade relations.
8 Republic of Turkey Ministry of Trade. 2019. "Free Trade Agreements." Accessed September 8, 2020. https://www.trade.gov.tr/free-trade-agreements.
9 DEIK, 2020. "African Business Councils." Accessed September 4, 2020. https://www.deik.org.tr/african-business-councils?pm=28.
10 Sabah. 2012. "Basbakan TUSKON'da konustu." Accessed September 8, 2020. https://www.sabah.com.tr/ekonomi/2012/03/31/basbakan-erdogan-konusuyor.
11 Davutoglu, Ahmet. 2010. "Turkey's Zero-Problems Foreign Policy." *Foreign Policy*, May 20 2010.
12 Also see Karaoguz (2016, 140–145) for a brief review of clientelism in Turkey.
13 *Hurriyet Daily News*. 2014. "Turkish PM Erdogan slams top business group head for probe warnings." Accessed September 8, 2020. https://www.hurriyetdailynews.com/turkish-pm-erdogan-slams-top-business-group-head-for-probe-warnings-61543.
14 For more on Turkey–EU relations, see Aydın and Acıkmese (2007), Onis (2008) and Saatcioglu (2020).
15 Kutlay and Karaoguz (2020b) claim that the fragmented nature of state–business relations in Turkey is one of the political economy factors that undermined the longevity of Turkey's trading state.

References

Afacan, Isa. 2013. "The African Opening in Turkish Foreign Policy." *Ortadoğu Analiz* 5, no. 52: 46–54.
Alkan, Haluk and Muhammet Huseyin Mercan. 2013. "Yeni Burjuvazi, Ekonomik Kalkınma ve Afrika: TUSKON Afrika Ticaret Kopruleri." *Marmara Universitesi Siyasal Bilimler Dergisi* 1, no. 1: 25–41.
Aras, Bulent. 2009. "The Davutoglu Era in Turkish Foreign Policy." *Insight Turkey* 11, no. 3: 127–142.
Aras, Bulent. 2014. "Davutoglu Era in Turkish Foreign Policy Revisited." *Journal of Balkan and Near Eastern Studies* 16, no. 4: 404–418. https://doi.org/10.1080/19448953.2014.938451.
Arda, Mehmet. 2015. "Turkey – The Evolving Interface of International Relations and Domestic Politics." *South African Journal of International Affairs* 22, no. 2: 203–226. https://doi.org/10.1080/10220461.2015.1050448.
Aricanli, Tosun and Dani Rodrik, eds. 1990. *The Political Economy of Turkey: Debt, Adjustment and Sustainability*. New York: Palgrave Macmillan.
Ark Yildirim, Ceren. 2017. "Political Parties and Grassroots Clientelist Strategies in Urban Turkey: One Neighbourhood at a Time." *South European Society and Politics* 22, no. 4: 473–490. https://doi.org/10.1080/13608746.2017.1406431.
Atli, Altay. 2011a. "Business Associations and Turkey's Foreign Economic Policy: From the 'Ozal Model' to the AKP Period." *Bogazici Journal* 25, no. 2: 171–188.
Atli, Altay. 2011b. "Businessmen as Diplomats: The Role of Business Associations in Turkey's Foreign Economic Policy." *Insight Turkey* 13, no. 1: 109–128.
Aydın, Mustafa and Sinem A. Acıkmese. 2007. "Europeanization through EU Conditionality: Understanding the New Era in Turkish Foreign Policy." *Journal of*

Southern Europe and the Balkans 9, no. 3: 263–274. https://doi.org/10.1080/14613190701689944.

Bacik, Gokhan and Isa Afacan. 2013. "Turkey Discovers Sub-Saharan Africa: The Critical Role of Agents in the Construction of Turkish Foreign-Policy Discourse." *Turkish Studies* 14, no. 3: 483–502. https://doi.org/10.1080/14683849.2013.832040.

Barlow, Robin and Fikret Senses. 1995. "The Turkish Export Boom: Just Reward or Just Lucky?" *Journal of Development Economics* 48, no. 1: 111–133. https://doi.org/10.1016/0304-3878(95)00031-00033.

Baskan, Filiz. 2010. "The Rising Islamic Business Elite and Democratization in Turkey." *Journal of Balkan and Near Eastern Studies* 12, no. 4: 399–416. https://doi.org/10.1080/19448953.2010.531207.

Bayar, Ali H. 1996. "The Developmental State and Economic Policy in Turkey." *Third World Quarterly* 17, no. 4: 773–786.

Baysan, Tercan and Charles Blitzer. 1990. "Turkey's Trade Liberalization in the 1980s and Prospects for Its Sustainability." In *The Political Economy of Turkey: Debt, Adjustment and Sustainability*, edited by Tosun Aricanli and Dani Rodrik, 9–36. New York: Palgrave Macmillan.

Bugra, Ayse and Osman Savaskan. 2014. *New Capitalism in Turkey: The Relationship Between Politics, Religion and Business*. Cheltenham: Edward Elgar.

Esen, Berk and Sebnem Gumuscu. 2016. "Rising Competitive Authoritarianism in Turkey." *Third World Quarterly* 37, no. 9: 1581–1606. https://doi.org/10.1080/01436597.2015.1135732.

Esen, Berk and Sebnem Gumuscu. 2018. "Building a Competitive Authoritarian Regime: State–Business Relations in the AKP's Turkey." *Journal of Balkan and Near Eastern Studies* 20, no. 4: 349–372. https://doi.org/10.1080/19448953.2018.1385924.

Eyrice Tepeciklioglu, Elem. 2017. "Economic Relations between Turkey and Africa: Challenges and Prospects." *Journal of Sustainable Development Law and Policy (The)* 8, no. 1: 1–33. https://doi.org/10.4314/jsdlp.v8i1.2.

Gunes Ayata, Ayse. 1994. *CHP: Orgut ve İdeoloji*. Ankara: Gundogan Yayınları.

Ipek, Volkan. 2017. "Turkey's Foreign Policy Towards Sub Saharan Africa." In *Turkish Foreign Policy: International Relations, Legality and Global Reach*, edited by Pınar Gozen Ercan, 217–235. Cham: Palgrave Macmillan.

Karaoguz, Huseyin Emrah. 2016. *"The Political Economy of Innovation: Technological Nationalism, Executive Interference, and Neo-Populism in the R&D Sector in Turkey."* PhD Dissertation, Central European University.

Karaoguz, Huseyin Emrah. 2018. "The Political Dynamics of R&D Policy in Turkey: Party Differences and Executive Interference during the AKP Period." *Journal of Balkan and Near Eastern Studies* 20, no. 4: 388–404. https://doi.org/10.1080/19448953.2018.1385928.

Kirisci, Kemal. 2009. "The Transformation of Turkish Foreign Policy: The Rise of the Trading State." *New Perspectives on Turkey* 40: 29–56. https://doi.org/10.1017/S0896634600005203.

Kirisci, Kemal and Neslihan Kaptanoglu. 2011. "The Politics of Trade and Turkish Foreign Policy." *Middle Eastern Studies* 47, no. 5: 705–724. https://doi.org/10.1080/00263206.2011.613226.

Komsuoglu, Aysegul. 2009. "Birimiz Hepimiz, Hepimiz Birimiz Icin Mi - Daginik Bir Siyasetin Topluma Sundugu Elde Kalan Tutkal: Klientalist Aglar." *Toplum ve Bilim*, no. 116: 21–54.

Krueger, Anne. 1974. "The Political Economy of the Rent-Seeking Society." *American Economic Review*, 291–303.
Kutlay, Mustafa. 2011. "Economy as the 'Practical Hand' of 'New Turkish Foreign Policy': A Political Economy Explanation." *Insight Turkey* 13, no. 1: 67–88.
Kutlay, Mustafa. 2016. "Whither the Turkish Trading State? A Question of State Capacity." The GMFUS on Turkey Series. https://books.apple.com/us/book/whither-turkish-trading-state-question-state-capacity/id1082369116.
Kutlay, Mustafa and Huseyin Emrah Karaoguz. 2018. "Neo-Developmentalist Turn in the Global Political Economy? The Turkish Case." *Turkish Studies* 19, no. 2: 289–316. https://doi.org/10.1080/14683849.2017.1405727.
Kutlay, Mustafa and Huseyin Emrah Karaoguz. 2020a. "Regionalism in the Middle East: Turkish Case in Perspective." In *The Routledge Handbook to Global Political Economy*, edited by Ernesto Vivares, 569–580. New York: Routledge.
Kutlay, Mustafa and Huseyin Emrah Karaoguz. 2020b. *"The Ties That Don't Bind: Interdependence, Trading States, and State Capacity."* (unpublished manuscript.)
Ngwa, Neba Ridley. 2019. "Turkish-African Relations: An Institutionalist Approach of Turkish Foreign Policy Towards Africa." *Uluslararası İliskiler ve Diplomasi Dergisi/Journal of International Relations and Diplomacy* 2, no. 2: 23–43.
Onis, Ziya. 2004. "Turgut Ozal and His Economic Legacy: Turkish Neo-Liberalism in Critical Perspective." *Middle Eastern Studies* 40, no. 4: 113–134. https://doi.org/10.1080/0026320041001700338.
Onis, Ziya. 2008. "Turkey-EU Relations: Beyond the Current Stalemate." *Insight Turkey* 10, no. 4: 35–50.
Onis, Ziya. 2012. "The Triumph of Conservative Globalism: The Political Economy of the AKP Era." *Turkish Studies* 13, no. 2: 135–152. https://doi.org/10.1080/14683849.2012.685252.
Onis, Ziya and Mustafa Kutlay. 2013. "Rising Powers in a Changing Global Order: The Political Economy of Turkey in the Age of Brics." *Third World Quarterly* 34, no. 8: 1409–1426. https://doi.org/10.1080/01436597.2013.831541.
Onis, Ziya and James Riedel. 1993. *Economic Crises and Long-Term Growth in Turkey*. Washington, DC: World Bank.
Onis, Ziya and Fikret Senses, eds. 2009. *Turkey and the Global Economy: Neo-Liberal Restructuring and Integration in the Post-Crisis Era*. London and New York: Routledge.
Orhangazi, Ozgur. 2019. "Structural Problems of the Turkish Economy, Financial Fragilities, and Crisis Dynamics." *Mulkiye Dergisi* 43, no. 1: 111–137.
Ozbudun, Ergun. 1981. "Turkey: The Politics of Political Clientelism." In *Political Clientelism, Patronage, and Development*, edited by S. Shmuel Noah Eisenstadt and Rene Lemarchand, 249–268. Beverly Hills: Sage.
Ozel, Isik. 2012. "The Politics of De-Delegation: Regulatory (in)Dependence in Turkey." *Regulation & Governance* 6, no. 1: 119–129. https://doi.org/10.1111/j.1748-5991.2012.01129.x.
Ozel, Isik. 2013. "Is It None of Their Business? Business and Democratization, the Case of Turkey." *Democratization* 20, no. 6: 1081–1116. https://doi.org/10.1080/13510347.2012.674369.
Ozkan, Mehmet. 2010. "What Drives Turkey's Involvement in Africa?" *Review of African Political Economy* 37, no. 126: 533–540.
Ozkan, Mehmet. 2012. "A New Actor or Passer-By? The Political Economy of Turkey's Engagement with Africa." *Journal of Balkan and Near Eastern Studies* 14, no. 1: 113–133. https://doi.org/10.1080/19448953.2012.656968.

Parlar Dal, Emel and Samiratou Dipama. 2020. "Assessing the Turkish 'Trading State' in Sub-Saharan Africa." In *Turkey's Political Economy in the 21st Century*, edited by Emel Parlar Dal, 239–270. Cham: Palgrave Macmillan.
Republic of Turkey Akra Büyükelçiliği. n.d. "Buyukelcilik." Accessed June 14, 2020. http://akra.be.mfa.gov.tr/Mission/About.
Republic of Turkey Ministry of Foreign Affairs. n.d. "Turkiye-Afrika İliskileri." Accessed June 14, 2020. https://www.mfa.gov.tr/turkiye-afrika-iliskileri.tr.mfa
Republic of Turkey Ministry of Foreign Affairs. n.d. "Turkiye-Tanzanya Siyasi İliskileri." Accessed June 14, 2020. http://www.mfa.gov.tr/turkiye-tanzanya-siyasi-iliskileri.tr.mfa.
Rosecrance, Richard. 1986. *The Rise of the Trading State: Commerce and Conquest in the Modern World*. New York: Basic Books.
Saatcioglu, Beken. 2020. "The European Union's Refugee Crisis and Rising Functionalism in EU-Turkey Relations." *Turkish Studies* 21, no. 2: 169–187. https://doi.org/10.1080/14683849.2019.1586542.
Sayari, Sabri. 1977. "Political Patronage in Turkey." In *Patrons and Clients in Mediterranean Societies*, edited by Ernest Geller and John Waterbury, 103–113. London: Duckworth.
Sayari, Sabri. 2011. "Clientelism and Patronage in Turkish Politics and Society." In *The Post-Modern Abyss and the New Politics of Islam: Assabiyah Revisited—Essays in Honor of Serif Mardin*, edited by Faruk Birtek and Toprak Binnaz, 81–94. Istanbul: Bilgi University Press.
Sayari, Sabri. 2014. "Interdisciplinary Approaches to Political Clientelism and Patronage in Turkey." *Turkish Studies* 15, no. 4: 655–670. https://doi.org/10.1080/14683849.2014.985809.
Senses, Fikret. 1990. "An Assessment of the Pattern of Turkish Manufactured Export Growth in the 1980s and Its Prospects." In *The Political Economy of Turkey: Debt, Adjustment and Sustainability*, edited by Tosun Aricanli and Dani Rodrik, 60–77. New York: Palgrave Macmillan.
Subasat, Turan. 2014. "The Political Economy of Turkey's Economic Miracle." *Journal of Balkan and Near Eastern Studies* 16, no. 2: 137–160. https://doi.org/10.1080/19448953.2014.910396.
Tur, Ozlem. 2011. "Economic Relations with the Middle East Under the AKP—Trade, Business Community and Reintegration with Neighboring Zones." *Turkish Studies* 12, no. 4: 589–602.
Unay, Sadik. 2010. "Economic Diplomacy for Competitiveness: Globalization and Turkey's New Foreign Policy." *Perceptions* XV, no. 3–4: 21–47.
Yildirim, Kerem. 2020. "Clientelism and Dominant Incumbent Parties: Party Competition in an Urban Turkish Neighbourhood." *Democratization* 27, no. 1: 81–99. https://doi.org/10.1080/13510347.2019.1658744.

6 Interplay between identity and trade in Turkey–Africa relations

Samiratou Dipama and Emel Parlar Dal

Introduction

The globalization phenomenon which experienced its peak stage in the 1980s has increased the interdependency among states in the international system. This growing interdependency has led to states' increasing awareness about the necessity to increase interstate cooperation on economic, political and societal issues. Economic globalization is by far one of the most important facets of the globalization phenomenon and as such particular importance has been attached to trade and economic-related issues in interstate interactions. States' efforts to enlarge and deepen the scope of their external trade relations is not only based on the obvious economic interests associated with trade exchanges but also on the idea that trade is one of the instruments of soft power. This argument is particularly valid for rising powers which are persistently in search of wider recognition and acceptance of their rising powers status at the regional and international levels.

In this context, Turkey is generally cited as one of the examples of rising powers, which, has used trade as an instrument of foreign policy and status enhancing, especially since the late 1990s and early 2000s. Turkey has used trade as a means to normalize relations with its immediate neighboring countries, to build relations with faraway countries in Africa, Latin America and Asia and boost its international status. This article delves into the assessment of the nexus between trade and identity in Turkey's relations with Africa. It investigates whether there exists a parallelism between Turkey's new identity building process and its trade relations with African countries and tries to assess if trade plays a subordinate role or not in its African policy as a whole. The relevance and timeliness of this question are grounded in the recent developments of Turkey's political economy and the increasing threats to the economic globalization dynamics brought about by the growing trade restriction policies used by some Western powers. Although many studies in the literature have attempted to examine the trade factor in Turkey's foreign policy, most restrained their scope of examination to Turkey's neighboring countries in the Middle East and Central Asia and few investigated the interlinkage between trade and identity. Filling this gap in academia through extending the scope and framework of analysis to the African continent is the main aim of this chapter.

In doing so, it first analyzes Turkey's trade objectives in Africa by using a social constructivist approach in order to locate Turkey as a newly constructed trading partner of Africa among other developing/emerging countries having already engaged in Africa in terms of both diplomacy and trade. Second, it aims to understand the main patterns and features of the trade–identity nexus in Turkey–Africa relations through the use of statistical data. In the final analysis, it aims to grasp the risks and opportunities associated with the interplay between identity and trade in Turkey's engagement with the African continent. Throughout the analysis, this paper will also try to show how Turkey's foreign policy towards sub-Saharan Africa is similar and/ or different from its trade engagement with North Africa. This paper contends that despite existing challenges in the trade–identity nexus factor in Turkey's trade relations with Africa, Turkey remains an ambitious actor which is likely to increase its assertiveness and to consolidate its identity as an emerging trading partner in Africa.

Turkey as a newly constructed trade actor in Africa: A social constructivist perspective

Social constructivism assumes that a country's foreign policy agenda is primarily shaped by immaterial factors such as ideas, role identities, norms and values. This theory considers international relations as norm-governed and state interests as constructed through a "fluid and interactive process of identity formation" which leads to "particular norms coming to be seen as appropriate, that is genuinely embedded in belief systems rather than adhered to for merely instrumental reasons" (Youngs 2001, 6). In this sense, states' identities are not fixed and unchangeable but are rather constructed and subject to possible changes over time. Alexander Wendt rightly put the connection between identity and interests in the following: "interests presuppose identities because an actor cannot know what it wants until it knows who it is" (Wendt 1999, 231), which in turn depends on their social relationships (Jeferson, Wendt and Katzenstein 1996, 59). Wendt pursues that "actors do not have a 'portfolio' of interests that they carry around independent of social context; instead, they define their interests in the process of defining situations" (Wendt 1992, 398).

Regarding the nexus between trade and identity, social constructivists would argue that a given country's decision to start trade relations with another country is not primarily based on obvious material interests but rather on ideational interests. Put differently, a state's decision to engage in trade with other countries goes hand in hand with its own identity. Thus, states aiming at getting an international recognition of their status are likely to expand their trade relations with the outside world as prosperous economic relations are likely to spill over into political relations. States in quest of the recognition of their rising powers status are likely to have recourse to trade instruments as one of the main means through which they can increase acceptance of the legitimacy of their political actions and serve their own economic interests. Therefore, the pursuit of economic interests through trade engagements with the outside world is shaped by the state's identity to an extent that a change in the identity of the state results in a change in the state's trade policies.

The trade dimension in Turkey's foreign policy towards Africa could be analyzed from a social constructivist perspective. Turkey's opening to Africa is part and parcel of the country's changing identity in the last two decades. In fact, until the end of the Cold War, Turkey observed a monolithic Western orientation and security-oriented perspective, which means that Turkey concentrated most of its foreign policy efforts on strengthening its ties with the West with timid openness to the non-Western world and prioritized security issues over economic ones. Yet, this trend changed drastically in the post-Cold War era, especially under the current Justice and Development Party (JDP). Turkish foreign policymakers have redefined Turkish identity and foreign policy orientation. The newly constructed Turkish identity is active, autonomous and multidimensional with a strong soft power blueprint. As a consequence of this new identity, Turkey's perceptions of world politics changed significantly. Turkey partly based this new identity on the idea that due to its geostrategic location, the country cannot and should not be centered on the Western world or the Eastern world but should behave as a bridge and middle country lying in between the East and the West. In this context, Turkey made efforts to normalize relations with its Middle Eastern and Asian neighboring countries through its zero-problem policy. Turkey also assigned itself the role of regional security provider and stabilizer in the Middle East through the conduct of various mediation activities between political actors. In parallel, Turkish political elites were quite decisive in diversifying their external partners, especially in the sphere of economics in order to decrease their traditional dependency vis-à-vis the West.

The launch of Turkey's policy of "opening to Africa" dates back to the year 1998 under the auspices of Ismail Cem, but its effective implementation came later on at the beginning of 2000 (Parlar Dal and Dipama 2020), where "initial assessments of Africa's potential were made and lower-level meetings were held between Turkish officials and their African counterparts" (Ozkan 2016, 1–14). Since then, the world has witnessed an increasingly active involvement of Turkey in Africa in multidimensional spheres including diplomacy, economics, and humanitarian and development assistance (Parlar Dal and Dipama 2020). The revival of Turkey's relations with Africa should be considered as one of the end results of the ongoing multidimensional feature of Turkey's foreign policy and the manifestation of the "new strategic identity" of Turkey prioritizing the diversification of trade partners. At the same time, Turkish foreign policy activism in Africa played a significant role in shaping and nourishing this ongoing process of new Turkish identity building.

Although the trade dimension occupies a key place in Turkey's opening to Africa, it is worth mentioning that Turkey has initially used non-economic instruments, namely diplomacy and development assistance to serve its economic objectives of deepening trade ties with Africa (Parlar Dal and Dipama 2020). This argument is corroborated by the increasing evidence provided by statistics that the volume of Turkey's bilateral trade with Africa has kept increasing since the implementation of the opening to Africa policy with total trade volume jumping from 810 million USD in 2002 to 19.5 billion USD in 2015 (Turkish Ministry of Foreign Affairs n.d.). The opening of diplomatic representations and the provision of humanitarian and development assistance are also manifestations of Turkey's newly (re)established identity built upon historical, cultural (Ottoman-Islamic identity essentially based on brotherhood and generosity) and humanitarian factors which prompts Turkey to provide help to countries in crisis and suffering people without any discrimination.

Turkish political elites do not miss any opportunity to stress that their approach to Africa is totally different from the neocolonial powers because their relations with Africa would be based on equality, mutual respect, and win–win partnership and not on exploitation and assimilation. This means a Turkish "self" in opposition to the "others" (mostly Western powers) has been constructed in connection with trade relations with Africa. The Turkish "self" is one that is not exploitative, mutually respects its African peers as equal partners and has a win–win orientated, honest and brotherhood spirit towards development issues in Africa. The "others" are imperialistic, asymmetric, exploitative, egoistic and care minimally about the development of sub-Saharan Africa (SSA). Turkey argues that it cannot exploit the African continent as Westerners are doing because this is not consistent with its historical and cultural legacy. To illustrate this point, the former Turkish President, Abdullah Gul, stressed during an address to Ghanaian officials that Turkey is different from Africa's European partners because she does not look after raw materials but rather focuses on sharing its experiences, knowledge and technologies with African countries and investing in capacity building in Africa (Abdirahman 2011, 66). Likewise, the current Turkish President, Recep Tayyip Erdogan underlined that Turkey does not have a colonial past in Africa and that its approach towards Africa is based on equal partnership rather than on the exploitation of the continent's natural resources (*Al Jazeera* 2016). Through such groundbreaking role conception, African leaders expect Turkey to act and behave in a way consistent with its constructed identity and Turkey's actions on the continent will be evaluated according to its self-role conception.

In sum, this paper argues that the increase in trade relations with Africa since the opening policy is an indication of Turkey's changing identity and role in international politics. The newly acquired Turkish identity combined both norms and interests in the sense that extensive humanitarian aid provided to African countries contributed to the achievement of Turkey's foreign economic agenda of diversifying its external economic partners and

Interplay between identity and trade 113

entering the dynamic African market (Parlar Dal and Dipama 2020). One scholar underlines Turkey's use of humanitarian aid as a legitimizing instrument in its economic ambitions in Africa in the following: "Turkey wants to legitimize its role on the world stage and make out that it is not interested in just trade and economics, but humanitarian issues too" (Bacik cited in Christie-Miller 2012).

Features of Turkey–Africa trade relations: A statistical overview

This part mainly uses statistical data to highlight the main features and patterns of Turkey's trade relations with Africa taking into consideration the trade–identity nexus factor. The volume of overall trade exchange, geographical and sectoral distribution are considered in the analysis.

Turkey's trade in volume with Africa

It follows from Table 6.1 that despite a slight decrease in Turkey's total trade volume with Africa from 2013 to 2015, Turkey's total trade with Africa has overall increased from 5.4 million USD in 2003 to 21.5 million USD in 2018. This sharp increase clearly illustrates that trade plays an important role in strengthening Turkey's newly constructed foreign policy with a multi-dimensional stance. While in 2003 and 2006, the total volume of Turkey's imports from Africa exceeded its total volume of exports to Africa, the years 2009, 2013, 2015 and 2018 show that Turkey exports more to Africa than it imports from Africa. Thus, whereas Africa experienced a slightly positive trade balance with Turkey at the very beginning of the launch of the opening to Africa policy, the trend is increasingly reversing towards a negative trade balance at the expense of Africa. The observed asymmetry in Table 6.1 challenges the arguments upon which the newly (re)constructed Turkish identity is built with respect to economic relations with Africa, which were meant to be more balanced compared to economic relations Africa has experienced with other actors.

Yet, despite an increase in the volume of Turkey's total trade with Africa, Africa is still not among Turkey's top trading partners in the world. It is

Table 6.1 Turkey–Africa import, export and total trade volume in million USD

	2003	2006	2009	2013	2015	2018
Export	2.1	4.5	10.179	14.146	12.449	14.452
Import	3.3	7.3	5.700	6.031	5.099	7.048
Total trade	5.4	11.8	15.879	20.177	17.500	21.500

Sources: Data extracted from: Turkish Ministry of Trade. "Turkey-Africa Trade and Economic Relations," https://www.trade.gov.tr/multinational-relations/turkey-africa-economic-and-business-forum/turkey-africa-relations and Turkish Ministry of Trade. "Foreign Trade Statistics," available at https://ticaret.gov.tr/istatistikler/dis-ticaret-istatistikleri/ulkelere-gore-dunya-ticareti-2005-2019.

clear from Table 6.2 that the bulk of Turkey's export and import exchanges are made with European countries. In 2018 for instance, EU countries shared about half of Turkey's total exports to the world. Given the long historical economic ties existing between the EU and Turkey (notably the customs union), it is not surprising that the EU remains the first top trading regional partner of Turkey in the world. The ongoing first place occupied by the EU amongst Turkey's world trade partners further indicates that there might be some disconnection between Turkish political discourses to diversity its economic partners as one manifestation of its changing identity and the implementation of these discourses in practice. Historical and cultural ties (the Ottoman Empire) and geographical proximity could also justify the fact that the Middle East and Asian region rank interchangeably as the second and third top trading partner region of Turkey in the world in 2014, 2016 and 2018. Table 6.2 shows that Africa's share of Turkey's total trade from 2014 to

Table 6.2 Share of Turkey's imports, exports and total trade: Breakdown by region (%)

	2014			2016			2018		
	Exp.	Imp.	Total	Exp.	Imp.	Total	Exp.	Imp.	Total
EU countries (28)	43.5	36.7	80.2	48.0	39.0	87.0	50.0	36.2	86.2
Other EU countries	9.6	15.0	24.6	6.8	11.0	17.8	7.0	13.2	20.2
African countries	8.7	2.5	11.2	8.0	2.7	10.7	8.6	3.2	11.8
North America	4.6	5.7	10.3	5.2	6.0	11.2	5.7	6.4	12.1
Central America and Caribbean	0.6	0.5	1.1	0.6	0.5	1.1	0.9	0.4	1.3
South America	1.2	1.6	2.8	0.8	2.1	2.9	1.1	3.5	4.6
Near and Middle Eastern countries	22.5	8.5	31	22.0	6.9	28.9	17.4	8.0	25.4
Other Asian countries	7.4	23.3	30.7	6.8	27.3	34.1	7.5	23.1	30.6
Australia and New Zealand	0.4	0.3	0.7	0.5	0.3	0.8	0.5	0.5	1
Other countries and regions	0.1	5.6	5.7	0.1	3.4	3.5	0.1	5.0	5.1
Total world	100	100	100	100	100	100	100	100	100

Source: Turkish Ministry of Trade. "Foreign Trade Statistics," available at https://ticaret.gov.tr/istatistikler/dis-ticaret-istatistikleri/ulkelere-gore-dunya-ticareti-2005-2019.

2018 has not significantly increased (11.2 to 11.8%) and this share has even decreased in 2016 from 11.2 to 10.7%. Another significant difference in the trade patterns between Turkey and Africa on the one hand and Turkey and the other regions on the other hand is that the asymmetry in Turkey's trade exchange with Africa is much more pronounced compared to the other regions because Africa's share of Turkey's total exports to the world is threefold more than its share of Turkey's total imports from the world. These data show some limits in Turkey's ambition to use trade as an instrument of its newly adopted foreign policy stances and identity.

Geographical and sectoral distribution of Turkey's trade with Africa

With respect to the geographical distribution of Turkey's trade exchanges with the African region, Table 6.3 indicates that out of Africa's share of Turkey's total imports and exports between 2013 and 2018, North Africa holds the largest share both for imports and exports. For instance, in terms of exports, in 2013 out of Africa's 9.3% share of Turkey's total exports, North Africa holds 6.6% while sub-Saharan Africa only holds 2.7%. In the same manner, in 2018, North Africa holds 5.6% of Africa's 8.6% share of Turkey's total exports to the world (see Table 6.3). The same holds for imports. Table 6.3 shows that in 2013 out of Africa's 2.4% share of Turkey's total imports, North Africa holds 1.4% while sub-Saharan Africa only holds 1%. In the same manner, in 2018, North Africa holds 2.1% of Africa's 3.2% share of Turkey's total exports to the world (see Table 6.3). Considering the longer historical ties and deeper cultural proximity existing between Turkey and North Africa, this paper argues that the first ranking of North Africa follows constructivist logic according to which states' interests are primarily shaped by their identity.

Nonetheless, when looking at the trend over the years, it becomes evident that while the share of North Africa in Africa's total share of Turkey's total exports to the world decreased from 6.6% in 2013 to 5.6% in 2018, the opposite trend is observed in the case of sub-Saharan Africa with the share increasing from 2.7% in 2013 to 3.0% in 2018 (see Table 6.3).

The same gap is not observed in the case of imports. While the share of North Africa in Africa's total share of Turkey's total imports from the world increased considerably from 1.4% in 2013 to 2.1% in 2018, SSA's share has timidly increased from 1% in 2013 to 1.1 % in 2018 (see Table 6.3).

Regarding the top trading partners of Turkey in Africa, Table 6.4 indicates that out of the top six trading partners of Turkey in Africa, five are all from North Africa and the only one from SSA is South Africa. In terms of share of total trade, in 2018 Egypt ranks first as the top trading partner of Turkey in Africa (24.39%) followed respectively by Algeria (14.74%), Morocco (12.58%), South Africa (8.91%), Libya (8.67%) and Tunisia (5.05%). The five North African countries made up about 65% of Turkey's total trade volume in Africa. This first-ranking of North African countries could be easily explained by the fact that compared to SSA countries, North African countries enjoy stronger

Table 6.3 Share of North and sub-Saharan African countries in Turkey's total exports and imports (%)

	2013		2014		2015		2016		2017		2018		2013–2018 change	
	Exp.	Imp.	Exp.	Imp.	Exp.	Imp.	Exp.	Imp.	Exp.	Imp.	Exp.	Imp.	Exp.	Imp.
Africa's share of Turkey's total exports	9.3	2.4	8.7	2.5	8.7	2.5	8.0	2.7	7.4	3.1	8.6	3.2	23.8	-1.8
North Africa	6.6	1.4	6.2	1.4	5.9	1.5	5.4	1.6	4.8	1.8	5.6	2.1	26.0	+10.9
Sub-Saharan Africa	2.7	1.0	2.5	1.0	2.7	1.0	2.6	1.1	2.6	1.3	3.0	1.1	19.8	-19.1

Source: Turkish Ministry of Trade. "Foreign Trade Statistics," available at https://ticaret.gov.tr/istatistikler/dis-ticaret-istatistikleri/ulkelere-gore-dunya-ticareti-2005-2019.

Table 6.4 Turkey's top six trading partners in Africa, in 2018, in million USD

	Export	Import	Total	Share (%) Turkey's total trade with Africa
Africa	14.452	7.048	21.500	
Egypt	3.054	2.191	5.245	24.39
Algeria	2.032	1.138	3.170	14.74
Morocco	1.990	716	2.706	12.58
South Africa	534	1.382	1.916	8.91
Libya	1.498	367	1.865	8.67
Tunisia	904	182	1086	5.05

Source: Turkish Ministry of Trade. "Foreign Trade Statistics," available at https://ticaret.gov.tr/istatistikler/dis-ticaret-istatistikleri/ulkelere-gore-dunya-ticareti-2005-2019.

Table 6.5 Sub-Saharan Africa product exports and imports from Turkey in 2018

	Import products from Turkey Share (%)	Export products to Turkey Share (%)
All products	100	100
Capital goods	23.58	3.81
Consumer goods	35.04	38.86
Intermediate goods	37.89	14.09
Raw materials	2.58	43.16
Animal	0.76	0.18
Chemicals	6.26	1.55
Food products	8.85	18.75
Footwear	0.21	0.00
Fuels	6.89	47.51
Hides and skins	0.08	0.68
Metals	15.50	7.25
Minerals	7.69	7.11
Miscellaneous	4.19	0.23
Plastic and rubber	5.85	1.03
Stone and glass	1.58	0.98
Transportation	6.15	0.85
Vegetables	8.36	7.46
Wood	2.44	0.98

Source: The World Bank. "World Integrated Trade Solution, Sub-Saharan Africa Product exports and imports from Turkey 2018," https://wits.worldbank.org/CountryProfile/en/Country/SSF/Year/2018/TradeFlow/EXPIMP/Partner/TUR/Product/all-groups.

and deeper historical and cultural ties with Turkey as constructivists predict. Nonetheless, material aspects such as geographical proximity and industrialization level are also important factors that could explain this trend.

One other evident point in Table 6.4 is that South Africa presents a very particular case among Turkey's largest trading partners in Africa because data in 2018 shows that South Africa is the only country among the six where Turkey imported more than it exported. This trend breaks the overall existing imbalance in Turkey's trade exchange with African countries and at the same time reduces the explanatory power of identity in Turkey's trade engagement with Africa because although South Africa does not enjoy deeper historical ties with Turkey in comparison to North African countries, it nevertheless benefits from more balanced trade relations with Turkey.

Table 6.5 on sectoral distribution indicates that in 2018 intermediate goods constitute the bulk of Turkey's export items to SSA since they represent 37.89% of Turkey's total export products to SSA. Consumer goods and capital goods represent respectively 35.04 and 23.58% of Turkey's export items to SSA and occupy the second and third place after intermediate goods. In terms of import items, the table showcases also that in 2018 nearly half of Turkey's import products from SSA are made up of fuels (47.51%). Fuel products are followed by raw materials which represent 43.16% of Turkey's import items from SSA.

Table 6.6 Main export and import items in Turkey's trade with North Africa

	Main export products	*Main import products*
Egypt	Crude petroleum-derived products, textile fiber and textile products, iron and steel, metal products and road transport vehicles.	Plastics and plastic products, fertilizers, textile fiber and textile products, crude petroleum-derived products and organic chemicals
Morocco	Iron and steel, textile products, vehicles	Vehicles, gold, gold plating, silver and base metal, inorganic chemicals, rare elements composites
Tunisia	Textile products, confectionary, vehicles	Fertilizers, inorganic chemicals, confectionary
Algeria	Road transport vehicles, iron and steel, machineries, textiles and confectionery	Mineral fuels, sugar and products, inorganic chemicals
Libya	Textile, furniture, carpets, jewelry, cement and medicine	Petroleum products, gold, scrap metals, aluminum

Source: Turkish Ministry of Foreign Affairs Website, www.mfa.gov.tr.

Interplay between identity and trade 119

Contrary to the case of SSA where the majority of Turkish import items is made up of raw materials, Table 6.6 shows that the import items of Turkey from North African countries are not exclusively composed of raw materials and fuels but also include non-negligible finished products such as vehicles, sugars, plastics, etc. Thus, this paper deducts that in comparison to North Africa, identity seems to play a more minimal role in shaping Turkey's trade relations with SSA because an extensive focus on raw materials and fuel imports is likely to deepen the already existing asymmetric trade relationship and to undermine Turkey's ongoing new identity building process based on brotherhood and solidarity and is portrayed to be different from the exploitative status-quo powers' foreign policy towards SSA.

Assessing the risks and opportunities of the identity–trade dimension in Turkey–SSA relations

The growing inclusion of the trade–identity dimension in Turkey–Africa relations presents both some risks and opportunities which will be elaborated in this section.

Strengths and opportunities

Since the launch of its opening to Africa policy in the late 1990s, Turkey has tirelessly worked to impose itself as a key player in Africa and in multiple areas, including trade. This assertiveness of Turkey has relatively produced impressive results in the field of trade especially as demonstrated by the sharp increase in the volume of Turkey's trade exchanges with the African continent in a relatively short period of time, although compared with other rising powers like China, the volume of Turkey's trade exchanges with the continent is still minimal.

One of the main factors behind such non-negligible success is that Turkey has well prepared the ground in Africa for the flow of trade relations through the use of non-economic means, namely diplomacy and humanitarian aid instruments. Indeed, as mentioned in the sections above, Turkey's trade engagement with the African continent should be analyzed in the context of its newly (re)constructed identity with historical, cultural, humanitarian and multidimensional features. Therefore, the prevalence of this newly constructed identity in Turkey's trade engagement with Africa explains why Turkey did not directly start with trade in its opening policy but rather primarily focused on diplomatic and humanitarian policies as the means through which its identity could be strengthened and trade relations could flourish easily. Consequently, the revival (for those African countries which were part of the Ottoman empire) or starting (for those African countries which did not have previous relations with the Ottoman empire) of Turkey's relations with the African continent has been achieved through progressive steps starting with the provision of humanitarian aid to countries and people in need and the opening of Turkish embassies and diplomatic relations in

African countries. These first steps have contributed significantly to build and maintain a positive and singular image of Turkey in the eyes of the African people and elites and to reinforce its global humanitarian actorness.

Through putting diplomatic and humanitarian actions at the very first stage, Turkey has shown its intentions to establish long-term relations with the African continent based on the sense of brotherhood and solidarity. These have contributed to increasingly shape Africans' positive perceptions of the intentions behind Turkey's sudden opening to Africa policy. In turn, positive perceptions by African people and elites have ensured the warmhearted entrance of the "Anatolian tigers" and other business groups onto the African continent to conduct their business activities. In this vein, development and humanitarian aid represents "the main tool for Turkey to gain a foothold in African countries" (Kucuk 2015, 24) and to prepare a fertile ground for the "Anatolian tigers" to conduct prosperous economic activities in Africa (Parlar Dal and Dipama 2020). Turkish business groups have not missed the opportunity offered to them to exploit the new African markets which possess huge potentials and opportunities for the flourishing of business.

Unlike the case of Turkey, most of the remaining emerging powers have tried to simultaneously develop political, humanitarian and economic relations with the African continent and this has significantly damaged their image in the eyes of African people and elites over time who are increasingly developing suspicions about their good intentions towards the continent. The simultaneous development of relations with the African continent in all spheres seems to be less effective because it does not give time to the African partners and people to learn their peers' identity, culture and history, which is nonetheless a necessary stage to establish the basis for the acceptance of the legitimacy of rising powers' (economic) actions in the continent. The case of China is especially remarkable because of its aid for economic development policy which led to increasing conviction among Africans that Chinese aid is being poisoned. China has been accused of demanding significant economic benefits in return for providing development and humanitarian assistance to African countries.

Second, Turkey's trade engagement with the African continent is based on the principle of exploiting the economic potentials of each side. Turkish political elites and business groups have somehow contributed to the increasing awareness of Africans about the huge economic potentials they have and the urgency to exploit these potentials in a win–win partnership with external partners. Turkey is making efforts to help the continent value its economic potentials through technical capacity and the share of knowhow. Turkey is aware of the fact that helping Africa develop its potentials will also benefit Turkey as it will increase the scope and volume of trade exchanges between and to the benefit of both parts. The fruits of Turkey's approach are already visible in the exponential increase in its trade volume with the African continent in the last 15 years (see Table 6.1).

Third, the creation of various economic exchange networks by Turkish business groups contributes to increase trade relations between Turkey and

Africa. Hence, Turkish business associations such as the Foreign Economic Relations Board (DEIK), the Independent Industrialists' and Businessmen's Association (MUSIAD) and the Turkish Industry and Business Association (TUSIAD) regularly organize business meetings, trips and trade fairs to encourage commercial exchanges between Turkey and Africa and to help both parts exploit and value their economic potentials (Parlar Dal and Dipama 2020). Institutionally speaking, further steps have been taken by DEIK with the establishment of business councils in many African countries whose purpose is "to help increase and diversify Turkey's exports to African countries, and to encourage host countries to engage in joint investments" through the organization of joint meetings and trade fairs. The business councils organize joint meetings in their respective countries and support Turkish export fairs to promote products made in Turkey (DEIK n.d.). Thus, business groups contribute to strengthen the legitimacy of Turkey's new identity in the eyes of its African peers through exporting to Africa trade revisionist discourses based on solidarity, brotherhood and equality. The argument that Turkey uses diplomatic channels to advance Turkey's economic interests in Africa is further substantiated by the fact that commercial counsellors are regularly assigned to Turkish embassies opened in Africa by Turkish authorities with the main duty of promoting, guiding, facilitating and increasing the scope and volume of trade exchanges with African business partners (Parlar Dal and Dipama 2020).

Fourth, the signing of free trade agreements (FTAs) and other trade facilitation instruments with African countries constitutes another opportunity for Turkey to strengthen trade relations with Africa and to nurture its newly constructed identity. Since Turkey's new identity is also about diversifying trade partners, the signing of trade agreements contributes to consolidate this identity because trade agreements are meant to decrease trade barriers between both parties and to increase trade exchanges. Accordingly, FTAs have been concluded with Morocco (2004), Tunisia (2004), Egypt (2005) and Mauritius (2011; Bacchi 2016, 16), the FTA ratification process is ongoing with Sudan and Ghana, four FTA negotiation processes are ongoing with the Democratic Republic of Congo, Cameroon, Seychelles, Chad, Djibouti and Libya and there are ongoing talks for the opening of new FTA negotiations with Algeria and South Africa (Turkish Ministry of Trade n.d.). Turkey has also increased the number of African countries with which she has signed a Trade and Economic Cooperation Agreement from 23 in 2003 to 45 in 2017 (Parlar Dal and Dipama 2020). The number of African countries with which Turkey has signed Prevention of Double Taxation Agreements, jumped also from 4 in 2003 to 13 today (Parlar Dal and Dipama 2020).

Risks and challenges

Despite the above-mentioned opportunities, Turkey's trade engagement with Africa presents some risks and challenges for its newly constructed identity.

First, although the volume of Turkey's trade exchange with Africa has increased tremendously since the early 2000s, it is clear that Turkey is far from occupying a primordial place in the African trade sphere. Africa's share of Turkey's total trade volume is very modest and has timidly increased over the years. Contrary to the intention of diversifying trade partners expressed in various Turkish political elites' discourses as part of its new identity building, the evidence based on statistics is that up to today Turkey's trade exchanges mostly concentrate on its traditional European partners which share about 80% of Turkey's total trade with the world. Thus, there is a gap in discourse between the intention to open up to the African continent to reinforce its new identity and the practice of actually increasing trade ties with the African continent on the ground. Turkey needs to encourage more Turkish business groups and African partners in increasing their trade exchanges through increasing the scope of free trade agreement with African countries. During her address at the consultation meeting of African Business Councils organized by DEIK, Turkish Ministry of Trade, Ruhsar Pekcan, acknowledged that although some important increases in Turkey's bilateral trade with Africa have been observed in the last decade, current export figures between Turkey and Africa still remain below Turkey's trade ambitions with Africa and that Turkey should increase its proactive role in the African market (Anadolu Agency 2019).

In the same manner, Africa's trade exchanges with the world mostly concentrate on its traditional Western partners and the "old" emerging powers in the continent. Turkey as a "new" emerging power is still lagging behind in terms of Africa's key trading partners in the world. Table 6.7 shows that China is the first largest import and export partner of African countries and India ranks as the second largest import partner and third largest export partner of Africa. Traditional trade partners, namely the Netherlands and USA occupy respectively the third and fourth rank in terms of Africa's top import partners, behind India and China. Regarding Africa's top export partners, the USA and Germany rank respectively as the fourth and fifth largest partners behind Southern partners, namely India, South Africa and China. This shows that Southern partners are increasingly playing a key role in Africa's trade sphere (see Table 6.7). Although Turkey's trade exchange with Africa has increased significantly since the opening to Africa policy, it is

Table 6.7 Africa's top five import and export partners in 2018 (%)

Top import partners	Top export partners
China (13.33%)	China (16.47%)
India (9.34%)	South Africa (6.93%)
Netherlands (5.25%)	India (5.73%)
USA (5.19%)	USA (4.84%)
South Africa (4.53%)	Germany (4.74%)

Source: IMF Trade Statistics, available at https://data.imf.org/regular.aspx?key=61013712.

still far from being a key trade partner of Africa with the likes of China and India because its share of Africa's total imports and exports is still very low comparative to the performance of China and India. According to IMF Statistics, in 2018, Turkey's share of Africa exports was 0.98% and its share of Africa's imports was 1.66%. Thus, should Turkey aim to use trade as an instrument of its newly adopted foreign policy objectives, more effort should be made to push up trade exchanges with the African continent.

Second, Turkey's trade exchanges with the African continent show an imbalance at the expense of the African continent. Since 2006, statistics have demonstrated that Turkey exports threefold more to Africa than it imports from Africa. This has led to a trade deficit for the African continent with evident negative impacts on its development. Yet, that Turkey exports more to Africa than it imports is understandable to a certain extent because the lack of technological developments limits the capacity of the continent to transform its raw materials into finished products and sell them to the global markets. Africa then also has to purchase significant finished products for its own consumption from Turkey and other emerging markets. Since Turkey–Africa relations have been based on African people's and elites' perception about the positive distinctiveness of Turkey as an emerging actor in Africa, persisting asymmetry in trade relations could jeopardize the value of Turkey's constructed positive identity in the continent.

Third, the statistics above have also indicated that Turkey's trade exchanges with the African continent mostly concentrate on North African countries. Although this prevalence of North African countries could be justified by longer historical ties, geographical proximity and relatively higher level of industrialization of these countries, a continuation of this trend is likely to damage Turkey's credibility and legitimacy in the eyes of its sub-Saharan African partners and to challenge the legitimacy of its newly constructed identity in the SSA region. The fact that free trade agreements have been concluded with three (out of five) North African countries whereas very few are signed with SSA countries (one concluded so far) is one of the main factors behind the gap in the volume of trade exchanges between North Africa and SSA. Concentrating trade exchanges mostly on North Africa challenges the performance of Turkey with respect to the trade–identity nexus in Turkey–Africa relations as this prevents Turkey from rising to the top of the African trade sphere and to fully use the trade instrument to raise its status and identity in Africa. To be counted among Africa's top trading partners in the upcoming years with the likes of China and India, Turkey needs to increase trade ties with SSA. Turkey could, for instance, increase the number of FTA signings with SSA countries and perhaps establish a customs union with African regional economic organizations.

Last, the sustainability of Turkey's engagement with SSA constitutes another factor that could challenge the sustainability of the trade factors in Turkey–Africa relations. Turkey's opening policy to the African continent has been activated under the current JDP government. It is part of the current government's political agenda and newly-defined Turkey's identity. A change of government is likely to lead to a redefinition of Turkey's identity which in turn would impact the place of Africa in Turkey's foreign policy priorities. If the incoming power does not share the same foreign policy perceptions and interests as the outgoing power and prioritizes a return to the old Western-centric Turkish identity, Turkey–Africa relations in all spheres, especially in the trade sector, might be set back.

Conclusion

This chapter has analyzed the trade–identity nexus dimension in Turkey–Africa relations using a three-layered framework of analysis. In the first layer, it theorized Turkey's trade objectives in Africa from a social constructivist perspective and argued that the engagement of Turkey in Africa in the trade sector has been one aspect of its constructed multidimensional, humanitarian and autonomous foreign policy since the early 2000s. Turkey's new strategic identity with its independence, activeness and multidimensional features has pushed it to reach geographically distant parts of the world, including Africa. Turkey's new identity combines both normative and realist characteristics, especially in the case of Africa where trade relations have been preceded by the conduct of strong diplomatic and humanitarian actions.

In the second layer of analysis, this paper illustrated Turkey–Africa trade relations in numbers. The statistics have shown that despite a sharp increase in Turkey's trade with Africa in the past decade, it remains nonetheless low compared to other emerging powers intervening in Africa, and Turkey's top trading partners are still concentrated in Europe. The geographical distribution data showcases also that the North African region holds more than half of the share of Turkey's total trade with the African continent and that trade volume with SSA is still comparatively low despite some increases over the years. In terms of sectoral distribution, whereas the bulk of Turkey's trade with SSA relies on raw materials, its trade with North Africa includes some finished products in terms of import items from Africa.

Regarding the third layer on risks and opportunities of the trade–identity dimension in Turkey–Africa relations, this paper mainly argues that Turkey's engagement in the sphere of trade in Africa is still weak compared to other external actors intervening in Africa, and presents some challenges related to persisting trade barriers, the North–SSA gap in trade volume and doubt about the sustainability of Turkey's trade engagement in SSA, all factors which limit its ability to use trade as an instrument to strengthen its newly established identity and foreign policy orientations. Nonetheless, there are some strengths and opportunities linked with Turkey's trade engagement in Africa, which contribute to reinforce the identity building process in its trade relations with SSA. These opportunities pertain to the use of non-economic means to prepare a fertile ground for the activation and strengthening of trade relations with Africa, the increasing number of signed FTAs and other trade facilities, and the increasing establishment of various exchange and cooperation frameworks by business groups to facilitate and encourage the development of business activities between Turkish businessmen and their African peers.

Overall, this paper contends that despite existing challenges, Turkey remains nevertheless an ambitious actor which is likely to increase its assertiveness as a rising trading partner in Africa and both Turkey and Africa are fertile soils with huge trade opportunities that need to be exploited at most for the benefit of both sides.

References

Abdirahman, Ali. 2011. "Turkey's Foray into Africa: A New Humanitarian Power?" *Insight Turkey* 13, no. 4 (fall): 65–73.

Al Jazeera. 2016. "Erdoğan: Türkiye'nin Afrika'da Sömürgeci Geçmişi olmadı." June 1, 2016 http://www.aljazeera.com.tr/haber/erdogan-turkiyenin-afrikada-somurgeci-gecmisi-olmadi.

Anadolu Agency. 2019. "2020 to be Africa Year for Turkey, Says Trade Minister." December 9, 2019. https://www.aa.com.tr/en/economy/2020-to-be-africa-year-for-turkey-says-trade-minister/1668261.

Bacchi, Eleonora. 2016. *"The Strategic Guidelines of Turkey's Foreign Policy according to Ahmet Davutoglu- Turkey's Opening to Africa Policy: The Case of Ethiopia"*. PhD Dissertation, Università degli Studi di Perugia.

Christie-Miller, Alexander. 2012. "Turkey Takes Lead in Rebuilding Somalia". *The Christian Science Monitor*, June 5, 2012. Accessed October 20, 2019. http://www.Csmonitor.Com/World/Middle-East/2012/0605/Turkey-Takes-Lead-In-Rebuilding-Somalia.

DEIK. n.d. "Business Diplomacy-Business Councils." Accessed January 5, 2020. https://www.deik.org.tr/business-councils.

International Monetary Fund. n.d. "IMF Trade Statistics." Accessed April 10, 2020, https://data.imf.org/regular.aspx?key=61013712.

Jeferson, L. Ronald, Alexander Wendt and Peter J. Katzenstein. 1996. "Norms, Identity, and Culture in National Security." In *The Culture of National Security: Norms and Identity in World Politics*, edited by Peter J. Katzenstein, 33–75. New York: Colombia University Press.

Kucuk, Y. Kenan. 2015. *"Ten Years of Turkish Engagement with Africa: Discourse, Implementation and Perception in Somalia."* MSc Thesis, University of Oxford.

Ozkan, Mehmet. 2016. "Turkey's African Experience: From Venture to Normalization." *Istituto Affari Internazionali (IAI)* working paper 16, no. 20: 1–14.

Parlar Dal, Emel and Samiratou Dipama. 2020. "Assessing the Turkish 'Trading State' in Sub-Saharan Africa." In *Turkey's Political Economy in the 21st Century*, edited by Emel Parlar Dal, 239–270. Cham: Palgrave Macmillan.

The World Bank. n.d. "World Integrated Trade Solution, Sub-Saharan Africa Product Exports and Imports from Turkey 2018." Accessed March 10, 2020. https://wits.worldbank.org/CountryProfile/en/Country/SSF/Year/2018/TradeFlow/EXPIMP/Partner/TUR/Product/all-groups.

Turkish Ministry of Foreign Affairs. n.d. "Turkey-Africa Relations." Accessed January 5, 2020. http://www.mfa.gov.tr/turkey-africa-relations.en.mfa.

Turkish Ministry of Trade. n.d. "Free Trade Agreements." Accessed January 5, 2020. https://www.trade.gov.tr/free-trade-agreements.

Turkish Ministry of Trade. n.d. "Serbest Ticaret Anlaşmaları." https://ticaret.gov.tr/dis-iliskiler/serbest-ticaret-anlasmalari.

Wendt, Alexander. 1992. "Anarchy is what States Make of it: The Social Construction of Power Politics". *International Organization* 46, no. 2: 391–425.

Wendt, Alexander. 1999. *Social Theory of International Politics*. Cambridge: Cambridge University Press.

Youngs, Richard. 2001. "Democracy Promotion: The Case of European Union Strategy." CEPS Working Paper, No.167. https://www.ceps.eu/ceps-publications/democracy-promotion-case-european-union-strategy/.

7 Turkey's military strategy in Africa

Brendon J. Cannon

Introduction

This chapter defines the parameters of Turkey's military and security interactions with the continent of Africa—both North and sub-Saharan Africa—and analyzes their impetuses, effects and aims. It places Turkey's military interactions with African states firmly in the literature of rising powers. The chapter's findings demonstrate no clear military strategy for Turkey across the length and breadth of the African continent. Instead, a combination of Turkey's national security and business interests inform its relations with and actions in North Africa. In contrast, Turkey's security interactions in sub-Saharan Africa have generally been ad hoc and opportunistic, exhibiting four basic features: military facilities or bases, peacekeeping, security assistance and training and, last, arms sales.

Turkey is a middle power experiencing—albeit in fits and starts—significant economic, political and military growth. As a G20 member, Turkey now clubs with other rising powers and great powers. Yet, Turkey's political and economic successes on the global stage are relatively recent and date to the waning days of the Cold War when Turkey began to economically liberalize in the early 1980s, and then politically during the 1990s. Because of Turkey's Cold War alliance against the Soviet Union, it was an early member of NATO and its military was professionally trained to NATO standards. It also had access to and used largely American-made weaponry from the 1950s onward. Turkey's military was—and remains—primarily a land army, focused on the defense of its borders and maintaining Turkey's sovereignty at all costs (Yavuz 2003, 45; Cannon 2016b, 211–214).

For much of its history, the Turkish Armed Forces (TAF) were not necessarily known for their innovation or weapons development and manufacture. Beyond deployments during the Korean War (1950–1953) and Ankara's military intervention in Cyprus (1974), Turkey's military largely stayed at home and focused on internal threats, mainly from the political Left or the conservative religious Right (resulting in three coups d'état) as well as Kurdish separatists, and keeping Soviet Russia out. As the Cold War ended, Turkey's political relationship with the West began to change because of systemic shifts to global distributions of power as well as Turkey's own domestic and political economic liberalization. Circa 2000, these changes rapidly accelerated as the military's political sway was curtailed by the democratically elected Justice and Development Party (JDP) governments led by then-Prime Minister (now President) Recep Tayyip Erdogan.

In a similar fashion, Turkish businesses and manufacturers were freed from state-run and regulated practices and began to manufacture all sorts of items—such as white goods—that had been previously imported. In the process, some Turkish businesses and manufacturers saw efficacy in arms production, particularly as the state increasingly championed such efforts. Ankara did so by funding research, placing orders and buying the resulting products—all at great cost and, Janus-faced, in a way that mixed a free-market economics with an increased emphasis by Turkey's JDP government on autarky in arms (Bagci and Kurc 2017, 40–41).

These major changes—economic, social and political—dovetailed with, indeed they engendered, a resurrection of Turkish power and, thereby, an entrance onto the world stage in a way Turkey had not done since Ottoman times. This, in turn, was driven by two contingencies. First, as Turkey's relationship with first Europe and then the US changed and increasingly became strained, Ankara found its options for sophisticated and fast-developing weaponry increasingly out of reach or with cumbersome strings attached.[1] Second, one of the hallmarks of great powers historically has been the production of their own weaponry (Kinsella 1998). In the case of Turkey, historically traumatic memories of military equipment being requisitioned still rankle.[2] Thus, achieving autarky in the design, manufacture and, therefore, the sales of weaponry would not only bolster the country's self-reliance but also its pride and rising power status (Bagci and Kurc 2017, 58). Autarky in armaments production theoretically frees states from potential coercion by supplier states and ensures they are not excluded from fast-evolving military technologies.[3] Yet, this is considered by many to no longer be possible (Devore 2013, 532; Bitzinger 2011). "Go-it-alone [arms] production is no longer an option for most [states]. The processes associated with defense-industrial globalization combined with the ever-rising costs of producing leading-edge weapons systems present huge disincentives for autarky in armaments" (Rossiter and Cannon 2019a, 353). Despite these obstacles, however, Turkey not only launched its own effort to achieve greater self-reliance in armaments production but also has accelerated it over the past decade.

During the 1980s, the foundations were laid for an indigenous defense industry through major investments in the major Turkish arms manufacturers operating today: Turkish Aerospace Industries (TAI) as part of the F-16 Falcon venture in 1984, Nurol Makina as part of the Advanced Infantry Fighting Vehicle project in 1988, Havelsan in military software, Aselsan in military electronics and Roketsan in missiles. Yet success was by no means quick in coming and importing military equipment remained dominant throughout the 1980s and 1990s (Bagci and Kurc 2017, 43).

Patterns in business practices, research and development and funding were also laid in the 1980s as Turkish manufacturers such as TAI focused on supplying weapons to their primary customer: the Turkish military. In this, Turkish defense manufacturers are no different than most other defense manufacturing states: defense is a monopsony in which the single buyer, the government, is also the regulator that lays down procurement procedures (Kovacic and Smallwood 1994, 101).

As Turkish manufacturers and entrepreneurs began to move from co-development in the 1990s to local production in the 2000s, with significant bumps in government funding, the push to develop small arms, drones, rockets and land systems for the Turkish military corresponded with a move to sell them externally to absorb steep costs. At the same time, arms imports from external defense manufacturing states, primarily the US, slowly dropped or, in the case of armed drone technologies, were prohibited. By 2011, 52 percent of the Turkish military's defense equipment was being assembled in-country. Three years later, it was 60 percent (Bagci and Kurc 2017, 44). For some, the changing political landscape in Turkey coupled with these developments provided empirical evidence that the country was rapidly becoming a great power again (Cagaptay 2013; Celik 2016). Indeed, the desire for influence and prestige—whether that comes about via economic, political or military means—provides great explanatory power for Turkey's seemingly sudden interest beyond its near abroad, to include Africa. In addition, Turkey, by the mid-2000s, had the tools (goods, money and political will) to demonstrate its interest. It is because of these multiple variables and opportunities that Turkey "found" Africa (Ozkan 2010; Cannon 2016a; Donelli 2018; Parlar Dal and Dipama 2020).

Turkey's involvement in Africa, historically, has been mixed and it remains so today. Militarily speaking, Turkey never had nor does it currently have an "Africa strategy" simply because of its primary national security interests and limited hard power capabilities. Instead, Ankara wishes to influence outcomes informed by its interests. The closer those interests are to home, such as disputed gas reserves in the eastern Mediterranean, the more Turkey will expend its resources to influence outcomes. As such, Ankara continues to revise its eastern Mediterranean strategies that necessarily touch on the North Africa littoral, particularly Tunisia, Libya and Egypt. Beyond these traditional spheres of interest and influence (the Ottomans ruled much of North Africa, de facto or de jure, for centuries), Turkey has demonstrated little interest until recently.

What separates Turkey's current from its previous interests are its relative economic, political and military capabilities in its Mediterranean neighborhood, in part because of Turkey's burgeoning defense manufacturing sector and available defense products. This chapter's exploration of Turkish hard power capabilities and policies necessarily separates North Africa from points further south. Turkey's relationship, for example, with sub-Saharan African states should be understood as largely opportunistic and ad hoc. In contrast, business and national security interests in a common Mediterranean space inform its relations with North African states. The tyranny of both physical and strategic geography simply means that Turkey must take its more proximate North African neighbors into its calculations more than sub-Saharan Africa.

Turkey's military interactions in North Africa

Turkey has robust interests in North Africa for historical, economic and security reasons. Turkey is a Mediterranean state and therefore views the security of its maritime near abroad as integral to its own power, prosperity and, thus, sovereignty. Considered an Ottoman lake for hundreds of years, the Mediterranean necessarily figured less in Republican Turkey's foreign policies because of its loss of power and territories in the region and its refocus on terrestrial threats from Soviet Russia. Despite this, economic actors, particularly Turkish construction firms, remained active in places like Egypt, Libya and Algeria, especially after the Turkish economy began to liberalize in the 1980s (Giritli, et al. 1990). Arms sales were never on offer, however, because Turkey's defense sector is relatively new and Turkey only sold arms to Libya, for example, in the final days of Muammar Gaddafi's rule (Feinstein 2011). Indeed, it was Gaddafi who courted Turkey and reportedly sold it spare parts for US-made aircraft after Turkey was embargoed in 1974 (US Department of State 2001, 711).

As the Turkish economy, industrial capacity and output grew in the new millennium, Erdogan's nationalist policies aimed at reducing Turkey's dependency on imported weapons became not only a priority, but a possibility. In turn, Turkey's souring relations with the West continued, assisted by misunderstandings about Iraq in 2003, Israel in 2010 and the July 2016 attempted coup aimed at removing Erdogan. After the coup attempt, Erdogan placed the Turkish arms industry directly under his control as president and showered it with more funding. The Turkish Armed Forces Foundation (TSKGV), which owns majority shares in Turkey's top defense companies, now reports to the president and not to the defense minister. This is also the case for Turkey's largest defense company TAI, military electronics specialist Aselsan, missile-maker Roketsan and military software specialist Havelsan (Bekdil 2017).

With the president firmly backing, funding and controlling defense autarky efforts, Turkey's lofty goal is to domestically produce 75 percent of its military needs by 2023, the centenary of the founding of the Turkish Republic, for both domestic prestige and political gains (Kurc 2017, 261; Aboulafia 2019). The perception among Turkey's JDP elite and much of the electorate supporting it is that Turkey is again becoming a regional economic and political power to be reckoned with.

> Turkey has been striving to become a regional power ... and a military force that enables power projection without inference from [its Western]

Allies ... In sum, the local production and indigenization of weapon systems have become the core principles in Turkish defense procurement as defense industrialization was justified in terms of pursuit of power, wealth and prestige.

(Bagci and Kurc 2017, 39)

Turkey began to test its new power and capabilities as the Arab Spring uprisings began in 2011. Turkey now had armed drones and armored vehicles, both areas where Turkish-made defense products rival the best competitors but at a cheaper price. These were now for sale to state and non-state actors whose interests dovetailed with that of Ankara's. In turn, an era of intensely personal and confrontational relations with neighbors such as Egypt, Israel and Syria occurred just as technological advances made the extraction of contested gas reserves in the eastern Mediterranean affordable.

Erdogan visited Tunisia, Egypt and Libya in 2011 as their populations attempted to overthrow decades-old leaders. In Egypt, Erdogan fostered a close relationship with its Muslim Brotherhood-supported leader, Mohamed Morsi. Erdogan offered arms, aid and diplomatic support but Morsi was overthrown in 2013 and Turkey's relationship with Egypt soured quickly as Cairo's new military government won the support of the anti-Muslim Brotherhood Arab Gulf States. Egypt also provoked Turkey by starting talks with Greece to exploit natural gas reserves and undercut Turkish maritime influence in the eastern Mediterranean.

Next door, Gaddafi was overthrown, and Libya devolved into civil war. Turkey largely remained on the sidelines until Cairo, Athens and others began prospecting for gas in earnest. At this point, Turkey began providing a variety of Turkish-made arms to Tripoli's Government of National Accord (GNA). Drones,[4] military personnel and armored vehicles were emoluments to the GNA encouraging it to sign on the dotted line in late 2019 in a deal between Tripoli and Ankara that attempted to establish a joint maritime border in order to disrupt Egypt's, Greece's and Israel's extraction of gas resources under agreements that firmly exclude Turkey.

What of other North African states and Turkey's military influence and power? Tunisia's mildly Islamist governments, in power since 2011, have remained relatively warm to Turkey and Turkish arms sales have increased. Tunisia awarded TAI a US$240 million contract for six Anka-S drones, three ground control stations and an unspecified level of technology transfer (Bekdil 2020). TAI's competitor, drone manufacturer Baykar, may establish a drone maintenance center in Tunisia with the reported aim of breaking into the increasingly lucrative sub-Saharan African drone market (Africa Intelligence 2020a). Turkish drones, whether made by TAI or Baykar, are generally much cheaper than those of their Western counterparts, but also technologically advanced and, crucially, battle-tested.[5] In addition, American and European drone manufacturers may, at times, be chary to sell armed drones to certain states. In this regard, Turkey can fill the gap, albeit in the face of a host of competing defense manufacturing states such as China and Israel.

Beyond drones, Tunisia, along with next-door Algeria, has reportedly purchased Cobras, an infantry mobility vehicle developed by Turkish firm Otokar, a subsidiary of the powerful and decades-old Turkish family conglomerate Koç Holding (Sanchez and Morgan 2019). In addition, Tunisia purchased 100 BMC-made[6] Mine-Resistant Ambush Protected (MRAP) Kirpi vehicles in 2014, 70 Nurol Makina-made Ejder Yalcin armored vehicles in 2017, and ordered nine BMC-made Vuran 4x4 Medium Class Multi-Purpose Armored Vehicles (MPAVs), with reports of a production facility in Tunisia for Nurol Makina-made armored vehicles and vests in the works in order to supply the Tunisian security services, and for export to West African markets (Africa Intelligence 2020b).

Turkey's military and other security interactions with North Africa, which mainly involve arms sales, are products of savvy business persuasion, cheaper cost and the willingness of the Turkish state to offer loans (such as those to Tunisia) that encourage the arms transfers. In the case of Libya, the Turkish drones and other materiel are directly supporting Turkish interests in the eastern Mediterranean and thus an extension of Turkish foreign policy in its near abroad. Ankara has gambled that the GNA will retain control of Tripoli and possibly reclaim some of Libya's oil-producing regions and facilities. If so, Turkey may have a much-needed ally with which to prosecute its claims in the eastern Mediterranean as well as regaining what was an important market, prior to 2011, for Turkish construction work and products.

Military interactions in sub-Saharan Africa

Turkey's entry into sub-Saharan Africa has focused on certain regions and states. Turkey's relationship with Somalia, for example, has received a great deal of attention from the rest of the world. Somalia, however, pales in comparison to next door Ethiopia or, a continent away, Nigeria in terms of Turkish investment. In both these states, and a multiplicity of others such as South Africa and Kenya, Turkey's relationship has been largely fostered through the language of business, encouraged and assisted in their endeavors by the JDP and government institutions such as the Turkish Cooperation and Coordination Agency (TIKA) (Ozkan and Orakci 2015; Cannon 2016a, 115; Langan 2017; Parlar Dal and Dipama 2020). It is noteworthy, for example, that many of the Turkish businesspeople involved in Senegal, Niger and Guinea such as Summa's Selim Bora are close friends and supporters of President Erdogan and the JDP (Dombey 2013). They also have developed close personal ties with powerful African leaders such as Ghanaian ex-president John Kufuor and Niger's Mahamadou Issoufou (Africa Intelligence 2019).

Turkey certainly has developed multiple Africa policies over the past 20 years, and Turkish efforts—from air connectivity with Turkish Airlines to business partnerships to the opening of embassies in 42 countries—have had a marked impact. Turkey is generally liked and unthreatening to African leaders because it is geographically distant and a medium power. Turkey's JDP leadership values Africa because they have created myths of deep historical relations with the continent coupled with a dynamic geographical depth (Davutoglu 2008, 78–79).

Particularly since the attempted coup and the arms embargo imposed by some EU states on account of Turkey's military intervention in Syria, "reducing dependency on the West and working with different strategic actors independently" has become the lodestar guiding Turkey's growing relations with sub-Saharan Africa (Siradag 2018, 318). However, implying causality between the actions of Turkish businesses and diplomats on the continent on the one hand, and some sort of structured, straightforward Turkish security interests and related policies, on the other, may be folly. Rather, much like Turkey's actions in Somalia since 2011, which evolved from a humanitarian venture to an economic one and then to the political, the focus of Turkey's security interests in sub-Saharan Africa have dovetailed with those of some African states' political elites and the security of their regimes. African leaders often engage Turkey's leaders and businesses first, rather than the contact coming from Istanbul or Ankara.[7] Because this is the case, it explains a great deal about the way Turkish military and security interactions have developed south of the Sahara and why they markedly differ to its north. In other words, Turkish security interactions have little to do with Turkey's national security interests in its near abroad and therefore have generally been ad hoc and opportunistic, exhibiting four basic features: military facilities or bases, peacekeeping, security assistance and training and, last, arms sales.

Military facilities or bases

Some have argued that Turkey, after a decade of intense soft power peddling on the continent, is intent on applying hard power to protect its economic investments, expand its military presence—particularly in the Horn of Africa—and open new markets for Turkish military equipment (Shabana 2017). To this end, Turkey has built or will build military bases in Somalia and Sudan. Turkey's actions have accordingly "facilitated geopolitical tensions and regional rivalries that risk militarizing the region and impacting human security" (Kabandula and Shaw 2018, 2328), in part, because:

> The Iranians can now use the new Turkish base [at Suakin] in Sudan to send more arms and equipment to [the] Houthis [in Yemen], while Turkey can use its newfound military presence to send more troops to Qatar, or meddle further in the affairs of Egypt.
>
> (Moubayed 2017)

Turkey's base in Mogadishu, because it has already been built and has been operational since 2017, is of the greatest import. The word "base" calls to mind heavily fortified, Cold War facilities that constitute a part of a state's infrastructure for war-making; that is, a critical means through which states project military power abroad. A traditional base is a site where forces are permanently deployed to deter foes, provide the initial reaction to military threats and to reassure allies (Lostumbo et al. 2013). In Somalia, however, the TAF have deployed its military personnel for a training mission rather than to project hard power. A cadre of over 100 Turkish military instructors have been stationed there to provide a standardized military curriculum to Somali soldiers, non-commissioned officers and officers. The remaining Turkish troops—another 200 or so—protect the site from attack. In functional terms, the Turkish military presence is not an overseas base, even though it is referred to as such in both the Turkish and international media (Rossiter and Cannon 2019b, 170).

This "base" is popularly viewed as part of Turkey's relatively new forward-basing posture, a string of strategic ports and bases aimed at reconfiguring the security architecture of the Mediterranean–Red Sea corridor (Tanchum 2019). That is, some see connections between Turkey's deployed military personnel in Northern Cyprus, northern Iraq, Syria, Qatar and Somalia as evidence of Turkey's "backdoor strategy to reclaim former Ottoman territories" (Lin 2019). The problem with comparing the training facility in Mogadishu with bases in Cyprus or Iraq is that their purposes are different. The TAF is in Mogadishu to train the Somalia National Army (SNA), not project power. Its resources, scope, declared mission and activities over the past three years do not indicate otherwise. However, it is certainly worth highlighting that even if Ankara had the intention to reclaim Ottoman territories (in which Somalia and the majority of the Horn of Africa never figured) and project hard power to the Horn of Africa as part of some effort to "protect its investments," its base in Mogadishu would not necessarily provide the requisite facilities to do so. In addition, Turkey's own military capabilities, while significant for a medium power, are insufficient as well as ill-prepared for expeditionary activities and, in any event, will remain deployed closer to home to protect against critical national security threats in its near abroad (Cannon and Donelli 2020).

North of Mogadishu, on Sudan's Red Sea coast, Erdogan signed a 2017 deal with Sudan's then-President Omar al-Bashir to restore Suakin, a ruined Ottoman port town on Sudan's Red Sea coast. The agreement also reportedly gave Turkey the right to build a naval dock to maintain civilian and military vessels. Three years later, there are doubts as to how much work Turkey will do beyond restoring the Ottoman town.[8] However, certain regional states are uncomfortable with what they see as the apparent consolidation of a permanent Turkish presence in the region, thereby feeding a process of perceived securitization in and around the Red Sea (Cannon and Donelli 2019).

Away from the Horn of Africa, Turkey has enlarged its security footprint through peacekeeping actions, security sector assistance and training as well as arms sales.

Peacekeeping

Turkey's economic and political landscapes changed significantly, as noted, from the end of the Cold War. Accordingly, its rather limited conceptualization of security, as defined by its Western partners against the USSR, progressively expanded and was designed according to new economic and political developments in Turkey. This meant, by 2000, the inclusion of "new threats, challenges and opportunities, such as international terrorism, climate change, migration ... [and] peacekeeping" (Siradag 2013, 26). While admittedly unfocused, Turkey did send staff in support of UN, EU, NATO and other peacekeeping operations around the word, to include Africa.[9] Turkish staff have been deployed to Cote d'Ivoire, South Sudan, Liberia, Darfur in Sudan and Congo (DRC) as well as to Central Africa Republic (CAR) and Mali.[10] In addition to Ankara's support of terrestrial peacekeeping missions, Turkey has been an active participant in EU and UN anti-piracy operations in the Gulf of Yemen and western Indian Ocean, deploying four frigates, as of 2018, consecutively to the region (Ozkan 2018, 574). While limited in number, Turkish support for peacekeeping operations pays dividends for Ankara in terms of prestige and international visibility, thereby becoming "a pragmatic political tool for the Turkish political elite to further Turkey's interests, especially in the Middle East and Africa" (World Politics Review 2015). Despite the JDP's efforts to portray Turkey as a newly responsible actor internationally, analysis demonstrates that while Turkey's foreign policy priorities may have shifted post-Cold War, their contributions to peacekeeping operations were only slightly more robust after the election of JDP governments from 2002 than from 1988–2001 (Yalcinkaya et al. 2018, 480).

Security assistance and training

Turkey's pragmatic peacekeeping support on the continent has been complemented by Ankara's use of its highly skilled and trained security service personnel as trainers (Sazak and Woods 2017; Bayer and Keyman 2012; Oguzlu 2007). Turkish training missions, beyond that mentioned in relation to Turkey's military training facility for soldiers of the SNA, have proliferated across the continent since the first such experiment in the Republic of Gambia (1991–2005). The results of that mission and Turkish influence in West Africa offer telling lessons because the highly personal ties built decades ago have proved remarkably resilient. For example, one of the Gambian trainees, Major General Yankuba Drammeh, is currently in command of the Gambian armed forces, in charge of the personal security of the Gambian leader, Adama Barrow, and formerly served as a military attaché in Ankara.

Gambia was the recipient of military hardware from Ankara in 2018 and, as a sign of mutual affinity, Drammeh is reportedly a major proponent of Turkish military assistance to West Africa (Darboe 2018; Africa Intelligence 2020e).

By 2018, Turkey had reportedly

> signed agreements with more than 25 African countries in the fields of defense and security, training nearly 900 foreign police officers and soldiers from more than 20 countries since 2007 under the 'International Police Training Cooperation Project.' More than 10 African countries have received security training in Turkey as part of the abovementioned security project.
>
> (Siradag 2018, 318–319)

In Somalia, since 2011, Turkey dedicated a budget of nearly US$3 million for the restructuring of the Somali army and its police forces. In addition, police teams have been brought to Turkey, resulting in more than 500 police officers being trained in the period 2014–2017 (Ozkan 2018, 574).

Turkey has also promised US$5 million to the G5 Sahel (Burkina Faso, Chad, Mali, Mauritania and Niger) to assist in the training and equipping of 5,000 troops fighting terrorist groups such as Boko Haram and al-Qaeda (Gulf News 2018). Additional support has been offered to the Sahelian states battling lawlessness. A Turkish security firm was reportedly contracted by Nigerian authorities to install all the security equipment at Niamey's international airport, recently renovated and modernized as part of a project fully financed and executed by Selim Bora's company, Summa (The Republic of Niger 2019).

Arms sales

International arms sales are a priority for Turkey's defense industry and government. This is for reasons of international and domestic prestige, as noted earlier, and to offset high costs in what, currently, remains a loss-making industry (Kurc 2017, 270–272). The strategic plan for 2019–2023 of Turkey's Presidency of Defence Industries (SSB) has the goal of increasing exports to near US$10.2 billion by 2023 (Sariibrahimoglu 2019). Sub-Saharan Africa figures in Ankara's calculus and Turkey has made limited inroads, mainly through personal ties and the savvy politicking, assisted by frequent state visits, trade shows and conferences, that have come to define Turkey's actions on the continent. What does Turkey have to show for its efforts? The figures worldwide show a major jump in Turkish arms sales. However, some nuance is necessary. Low levels of R&D spending coupled with weak innovation capabilities contribute to the fact that "Turkish [arms] exports are well below the expected levels and not even close to cover [the major expenses needed] for a significant portion of arms imports [to keep

Turkey's defense industry running]" (Bagci and Kurc 2017, 58–59). Nonetheless, in sub-Saharan Africa, Ghana purchased 36 Otokar Cobras over the course of 2018–2019. Burkina Faso's army purchased 40 Cobra IIs in 2018, Senegal purchased 25 Nurol Makina-manufactured Ejder Yalcin off-road vehicles and six Ejder Toma riot control trucks (Africa Intelligence 2020c). Mauritania reportedly also purchased six Turkish-made armored vehicles, likely Otokar Cobras, as have Rwanda and Nigeria (de Cherisey 2019; Defence Web 2019). Turkey also exported hundreds of small arms to Burkina Faso, Ghana and Cameroon (UNROCA 2018). Turkey's Katmerciler reportedly received a US$20 million export order from Uganda for the company's Hizir light armored personnel carriers (APCs; Africa Intelligence 2020d).

Turkey's powerful textile industry is spearheading another form of profitable security cooperation: uniforms. Barer Holding, for example, reportedly produces uniforms and military equipment in Kaduna, Nigeria for the Nigerian military and security services and neighboring countries (Barer Holding 2020). Barer Holding also signed a deal with the Chadian government in early 2019 to co-manage the Manufacture of Military Equipment (*Manufacture des Equipements Militaires,* MANEM) in the supply of uniforms and other military equipment to the Chadian military. In mid-2019, Turkey had reportedly begun construction of a factory to produce uniforms for the country's military in Mogadishu, Somalia (Goldberg 2019).

Erdogan's highly visible and frequent visits to sub-Saharan Africa over the past decade have likely had a positive effect and direct impact on Turkey's arms sales and related contracts. However, neither the numbers, types of weaponry or monetary amounts of Turkish arms sales to sub-Saharan Africa should be overstated. Turkey has not, for example, sold drones south of the Sahara—at least not publicly. Turkey's defense sales are also minimal to nonexistent south of the Sahel, with Rwanda's and Uganda's recent purchases of Turkish armored vehicles being the exceptions to the rule. Indeed, it is worth noting that Turkish arms sales were small in comparison to its well-established competitors such as Russia and France (Sanchez and Morgan 2019).

The reality of Turkish autarky in arms, however, is seriously in question because of a combination of inefficiency in industry and investment (Bitzinger 2011, 2013) as well as weak planning, the ongoing difficulties in Turkey's civil–military relations, the propensity of Turkish defense manufacturers to cooperate internationally as well as Turkey's desire to emulate the US, an impossibility given Turkey's size and resources (Kurc 2017, 261). However, Turkey's drones and armored vehicles do seem to have the right combination of price, capabilities and reputation and therefore will likely continue to be purchased by militaries in Africa. Those sales will not, in and of themselves, correct the structural problems with Turkey's defense industry nor will they make it profitable soon. Contextually, this is not necessarily problematic, many of the world's defense manufacturing states are loss makers, particularly when the state that orders, funds and uses most of these weapons is a medium or small state.

Conclusion

Turkey's involvement in Africa, historically, has been mixed and it remains so today. Turkey's interests, particularly in Egypt, Libya and Tunisia are centuries old and involve both military/strategic aspects as well as business interests, as demonstrated by its actions in all three states over the past decade. Ankara's relations with sub-Saharan African states, in contrast, are relatively new as well as mostly ad hoc and opportunistic. They exhibit four basic features: military facilities or bases, peacekeeping, security assistance and training and, last, arms sales. Turkey's interesting combination of business with political backing from Ankara and arms sales—ranging from Senegal to Niger to Somalia—is increasingly visible and exhibits both the strengths and weaknesses of Turkey's defense sector in its current state. In terms of niche weaponry such as armed drones or armored vehicles, African leaders both north and south of the Sahara may increasingly look to Turkey as an option, even an ally.

Notes

1 During the first period of the JDP government (2002–2007), Turkey focused mostly on Europeanization efforts with a strong commitment to Western orientation. The second term of the JDP government (2007–2011) saw the weakening commitment to Turkey's EU membership due to disappointments concerning its EU candidacy process. Post-2011, a toxic combination of mistrust between Ankara and the EU, issues of migration, market access and Kurdish separatism and an attempted coup in July 2016 harmed relations. Turkey's relations with the US similarly soured, based on almost willful misunderstandings on both sides, vis-à-vis the Syrian crisis, Kurdish separatism and power and arms sales/transfers.
2 Three days prior to the UK declaring war on Germany in 1914, two Ottoman-commissioned warships were confiscated by the UK government—even after full payment by Istanbul and as Ottoman crews arrived to pilot them to Istanbul (Rogan 2016). One hundred and five years later, in 2019, the US removed Turkey from its F-35A fighter jet program and refused to begin delivery of 100 F-35As because of Turkey's purchase of Russia's S-400 missile system. The fighter jets, however, are already formally owned by Turkey, which participated and partially funded the F35A fighter program (Mehta 2019).
3 The 1974 arms embargo imposed by its NATO allies was the earliest factor motivating Turkish arms autarky (Bagci and Kurc 2017, 43). The US decision not to export armed drone technology encouraged Turkey to develop its own drone program in 2007 (Sukhankin 2020).
4 Several medium-altitude-long-distance (MALE) Bayraktar TB-2 drones have been delivered to the GNA. They are reportedly operated by Turkish military personnel. The Bayraktar TB-2 drone can spend 24 hours over a target.
5 Several Bayraktars, for example, attacked and destroyed two Ilyushin Il-76 military transport aircraft in Libya used to ferry weapons to the GNA's opponents, the Libyan National Army (LNA) along with a hangar. Senior LNA officers were

reportedly killed in the attack (Arabian Aerospace 2020). A combination of cheap, but highly effective Turkish drones pounded the Syrian army in early March 2020, showcasing again the power and worth of Turkish-made drones (Prothero 2020). The Turkish offensive was reportedly carried out using drone-launched missiles and precision artillery strikes leveraging drone artillery spotters (Roblin 2020).
6 BMC is Turkey's largest commercial and military vehicle manufacturer. It was founded in 1964 as a partnership with British Motor Corporation. It is currently 51 percent Turkish-owned and 49 percent Qatari-owned.
7 The Gambians, for example, approached Turkey in 1991 and asked for it to provide training; first, to its gendarmerie and then, by the late 1990s, to its navy, air force and army (Varoglu, Cakar and Basim 2009). The first official contact between Turkey and Somalia occurred when then-Prime Minister Erdogan attended the African Union (AU) Summit in Addis Ababa in January 2007 and met Somalia's then-President Abdullah Yusuf Ahmed. Erdogan reportedly asked him to submit a proposal to Ankara related to Somalia's needs. Subsequently, the former Transitional Federal Government (TFG) President Sharif Sheikh Ahmed made three visits to Turkey before Erdogan paid his first official visit to Somalia in August 2011 (Siradag 2016, 92).
8 When al-Bashir was deposed during a popular uprising in 2019, his government's agreements with numerous countries, to include the Suakin deal with Turkey, were called into question.
9 Turkey did support UN peacekeeping in Africa on a limited basis prior to 2000 in places like Somalia, Sierra Leone and Congo (DRC).
10 For more detailed information on Turkish support for peacekeeping missions see (Yalcinkaya et al. 2018).

References

Aboulafia, Richard. 2019. "Turkey After the F-35: Choice for Alternative Fighter will help Shape Country's Future." *Forbes*, July 21, 2019. https://www.forbes.com/sites/richardaboulafia/2019/07/21/turkey-after-the-f-35-choice-for-alternative-fighter-will-help-shape-countrys-future/#1ea780724326.

Africa Intelligence. 2019. "Selim Bora, the Businessman with the Ear of the Presidents." *Africa Intelligence Newsletter*, Issue 795, February 27, 2019.

Africa Intelligence. 2020a. "Turkish Drone-Maker Baykar Teams Up with Avionav After Losing Out to TAI." *Africa Intelligence Newsletter*, March 6, 2020.

Africa Intelligence. 2020b. "Erdogan's Arms Merchants Increasingly Well-Ensconced." *Africa Intelligence Newsletter*, Issue 817, February 5, 2020.

Africa Intelligence. 2020c. "Koc and Nurol Target the Land Armies." *Africa Intelligence Newsletter*, Issue 815, January 8, 2020.

Africa Intelligence. 2020d. "Kampala gets Katmerciler APCs as Part of Erdogan's Military-Diplomatic Drive." *Africa Intelligence Newsletter*, March 6, 2020.

Africa Intelligence. 2020e. "Erdogan's Sahelian Manoeuvres." *Africa Intelligence Newsletter*, Issue 1375, February 5, 2020.

Arabian Aerospace. 2020. "Libya's Deadly Game of Drones." *Arabian Aerospace*, March 19, 2020. https://www.arabianaerospace.aero/libya-s-deadly-game-of-drones.html.

Bagci, Huseyin and Caglar Kurc. 2017. "Turkey's Strategic Choice: Buy or Make Weapons?" *Defence Studies* 17, no. 1: 38–62. https://doi.org/10.1080/14702436.2016.1262742.

Barer Holding. 2020. "Companies." https://www.barerholding.com/en/Companies/3.
Bayer, Resat and Emin Fuat Keyman. 2012. "Turkey: An Emerging Hub of Globalization and Internationalist Humanitarian Actor." *Globalizations* 9, no. 1: 73–90. https://doi.org/10.1080/14747731.2012.627721.
Bekdil, Burak Ege. 2017. "Turkey's Erdogan Decrees Sweeping Defense Procurement Takeover." *Defense News*, December 27, 2017. https://www.defensenews.com/industry/2017/12/27/turkeys-erdogan-decrees-sweeping-defense-procurement-takeover/.
Bekdil, Burak Ege. 2020. "Turkey's TAI Sells Six Anka-S Drones to Tunisia." *Defense News*, March 16, 2020. https://www.defensenews.com/unmanned/2020/03/16/turkeys-tai-sells-six-anka-s-drones-to-tunisia/.
Bitzinger, Richard A. 2011. "China's Defense Technology and Industrial Base in a Regional Context: Arms Manufacturing in Asia." *The Journal of Strategic Studies* 34, no. 3: 425–450. https://doi.org/10.1080/01402390.2011.574985.
Bitzinger, Richard A. 2013. "Revisiting Armaments Production in Southeast Asia: New Dreams, Same Challenges." *Contemporary Southeast Asia* 35, no. 3: 369–394.
Cagaptay, Soner. 2013. "Defining Turkish power: Turkey as a Rising Power Embedded in the Western International System." *Turkish Studies* 14, no. 4: 797–811. https://doi.org/10.1080/14683849.2013.861110.
Cannon, Brendon J. 2016a. "Deconstructing Turkey's Efforts in Somalia." *Bildhaan: An International Journal of Somali Studies*, 16, no. 1: 98–123.
Cannon, Brendon J. 2016b. *Legislating Reality and Politicizing History: Contextualizing Armenian Claims of Genocide*. Offenbach am Main: Manzara Verlag.
Cannon, Brendon J. and Federico Donelli. 2019. "Middle Eastern States in the Horn of Africa: Security Interactions and Power Projection." Istituto per gli Studi di Politica Internazionale (ISPI), April 30, 2019. https://www.ispionline.it/en/pubblicazione/middle-eastern-states-horn-africa-security-interactions-and-power-projection-22943.
Cannon, Brendon J. and Federico Donelli. 2020. "Asymmetric Alliances and High Polarity: Evaluating Regional Security Complexes in the Middle East and Horn of Africa." *Third World Quarterly* 41, no. 3: 505–524. https://doi.org/10.1080/01436597.2019.1693255.
Celik, Omer. 2016. "Turkey's Great Transformation: An Influence-Multiplier for the Future of Europe and Beyond." *Rising Powers Quarterly* 1, no. 2: 35–53.
Darboe, Mustafa. 2018. "Turkey Donates Military Hardware to Gambia." Anadolu Agency, September 24, 2018. https://www.aa.com.tr/en/africa/turkey-donates-military-hardware-to-gambia/1263577.
Davutoglu, Ahmet. 2008. "Turkey's Foreign Policy Vision: An Assessment of 2007." *Insight Turkey* 10, no. 1: 77–96.
de Cherisey, Erwan. 2019. "Ghana Army Shows New Otokar Cobra Vehicles." *Jane's Defence Weekly*, November 13, 2019. https://www.janes.com/article/92548/ghana-army-shows-new-otokar-cobra-vehicles.
Defence Web. 2019. "Otokar Targets African growth." *Defence Web*, January 23, 2019. https://www.defenceweb.co.za/land/land-land/otokar-targets-african-growth/.
Devore, Marc R. 2013. "Arms Production in the Global Village: Options for Adapting to Defense-Industrial Globalization." *Security studies* 22, no. 3: 532–572. https://doi.org/10.1080/09636412.2013.816118.
Dombey, Daniel. 2013. "Turkey Flexes its Economic Muscle in Africa." *Financial Times*, January 6, 2013. https://app.ft.com/cms/s/d9b175de-4849-11e2-8aae-00144feab49a.html.

Donelli, Federico. 2018. "The Ankara Consensus: The Significance of Turkey's Engagement in Sub-Saharan Africa." *Global Change, Peace & Security* 30, no. 1: 57–76. https://doi.org/10.1080/14781158.2018.1438384.

Feinstein, Andrew. 2011. "Where is Gaddafi's Vast Arms Stockpile?" *The Guardian*, October 26, 2011. https://www.theguardian.com/world/2011/oct/26/gadaffis-arms-stockpile.

Giritli, Heyecan, Zeynep Sozen, Roger Flanagan and Peter Lansley. 1990. "International Contracting: A Turkish Perspective." *Construction Management and Economics* 8, no. 4: 415–430.

Goldberg. 2019. "Turkey to Construct Military Uniforms Factory for Somali National Army in Mogadishu." Strategic Intelligence, June 18, 2019. https://intelligencebriefs.com/turkey-to-construct-military-uniforms-factory-for-somali-national-army-in-mogadishu/.

Gulf News. 2018. "Turkey Announces $5m for Sahel Anti-Terrorist Force." *Gulf News*, March 1, 2018. https://gulfnews.com/world/mena/turkey-announces-5m-for-sahel-anti-terrorist-force-1.2181246.

Kabandula, Abigail and Timothy M. Shaw. 2018. "Rising Powers and the Horn of Africa: Conflicting Regionalisms." *Third World Quarterly* 39, no. 12: 2315–2333.

Kinsella, David. 1998. "Arms Transfer Dependence and Foreign Policy Conflict." *Journal of Peace Research* 35, no. 1: 7–23.

Kovacic, William E. and Dennis E. Smallwood. 1994. "Competition Policy, Rivalries, and Defense Industry Consolidation." *Journal of Economic Perspectives* 8, no. 4: 91–110.

Kurc, Çaglar. 2017. "Between Defence Autarky and Dependency: The Dynamics of Turkish Defence Industrialization." *Defence Studies* 17, no. 3: 260–281.

Langan, Mark. 2017. "Virtuous Power Turkey in Sub-Saharan Africa: The 'Neo-Ottoman' Challenge to the European Union." *Third World Quarterly* 38, no. 6: 1399–1414.

Lin, Christina. 2019. "Neo-Ottoman Turkey's 'String of Pearls.'" *Asia Times*, October 14, 2019. https://asiatimes.com/2019/10/neo-ottoman-turkeys-string-of-pearls/.

Lostumbo, Michael J., Michael J. McNerney, Eric Peltz, Derek Eaton and David R. Frelinger. 2013. *Overseas Basing of US Military Forces: An Assessment of Relative Costs and Strategic Benefits*. Washington, DC: Rand Corporation.

Mehta, Aaron. 2019. "Turkey Officially Kicked Out Of F-35 Program, Costing US Half A Billion Dollars." *Defense News*, July 17, 2019. https://www.defensenews.com/air/2019/07/17/turkey-officially-kicked-out-of-f-35-program/.

Moubayed, Sami. 2017. "Turkish Base in Sudan a Problem for Arab Powers." *Gulf News*, December 28, 2017. https://gulfnews.com/world/mena/turkish-base-in-sudan-a-problem-for-arab-powers-1.2148443.

Oguzlu, Tarik. 2007. "Soft Power in Turkish Foreign Policy." *Australian Journal of International Affairs* 61, no. 1: 81–97. https://doi.org/10.1080/10357710601142518.

Ozkan, Mehmet. 2010. "What Drives Turkey's Involvement in Africa?" *Review of African Political Economy* 37, no. 126: 533–540.

Ozkan, Mehmet. 2018. "Turkey in South-South Cooperation: New Foreign Policy Approach in Africa." *Vestnik RUDN. International Relations* 18, no. 3: 565–578.

Ozkan, Mehmet and Serhat Orakci. 2015. "Turkey as a "Political" Actor in Africa–An Assessment of Turkish Involvement in Somalia." *Journal of Eastern African Studies* 9, no. 2: 343–352.

Parlar Dal, Emel and Samiratou Dipama. 2020. "Assessing the Turkish 'Trading State' in Sub-Saharan Africa." In *Turkey's Political Economy in the 21st Century*, edited by Emel Parlar Dal, 239–270. Palgrave Macmillan. doi:10.1007/978-3-030-27632-4.

Prothero, Mark. 2020. "Turkey Used a New Weapon in Syria That Was So Effective It Looks Like Russia Won't Dare Confront Turkey Directly." *Insider*, March 10, 2020. https://www.insider.com/turkey-drones-syria-russia-wont-confront-directly-2020-3.

Roblin, Sebastien. 2020. "Turkish Drones and Artillery are Devastating Assad's Forces in Idlib Province-Here's Why." *Forbes*, March 2, 2020. https://www.forbes.com/sites/sebastienroblin/2020/03/02/idlib-onslaught-turkish-drones-artillery-and-f-16s-just-destroyed-over-100-armored-vehicles-in-syria-and-downed-two-jets/#20e12bf66cd3.

Rogan, Eugene. 2016. "World War I and the Fall of the Ottomans: Consequences for South East Europe." In *Balkan Legacies of the Great War: The Past is Never Dead*, edited by Othon Anastasakis and David Madden, 59–65. London: Palgrave Macmillan.

Rossiter, Ash and Brendon J. Cannon. 2019a. "Making Arms in India? Examining New Delhi's Renewed Drive for Defence-Industrial Indigenization." *Defence Studies* 19, no. 4: 353–372. https://doi.org/10.1080/14702436.2019.1685880.

Rossiter, Ash and Brendon J. Cannon. 2019b. "Re-Examining the 'Base': The Political and Security Dimensions of Turkey's Military Presence in Somalia." *Insight Turkey* 21, no. 1: 167–188. https://doi.org/10.25253/99.2019211.09.

Sanchez, Wilder Alejandro and Scott Morgan. 2019. "Arms Sales in Africa: A Buyer's Market." *Geopolitical Monitor*, December 16, 2019. https://www.geopoliticalmonitor.com/arms-sales-in-africa-a-buyers-market/.

Sariibrahimoglu, Leyla. 2019. "Turkey to Increase Domestic Content and Exports of Defence Equipment." *Jane's Defence Weekly*, December 11, 2019. https://www.janes.com/article/93121/turkey-to-increase-domestic-content-and-exports-of-defence-equipment.

Sazak, Onur and Auveen E. Woods. 2017. "Thinking Outside the Compound: Turkey's Approach to Peacebuilding in Somalia." In *Rising Powers and Peacebuilding*, edited by Charles T. Call and Cedric de Coning, 167–189. Basingstoke: Palgrave Macmillan.

Shabana, Ayman. 2017. "Reasons Behind Turkey's Military Base in Somalia." *Future for Advanced Research and Studies*, April 11, 2017. https://futureuae.com/m/Mainpage/Item/2686/dimensions-of-the-turkish-role-reasons-behind-turkeys-military-base-in-somalia.

Siradag, Abdurrahim. 2013. "The Making of the New Turkish Foreign and Security Policy Towards Africa." *Africa Insight* 43, no. 1: 15–31.

Siradag, Abdurrahim. 2016. "Turkish-Somali Relations: Changing State Identity and Foreign Policy." *Inquiry-Sarajevo Journal of Social Science* 2, no. 2: 89–106.

Siradag, Abdurrahim. 2018. "Turkey-Africa Alliance: Evolving Patterns in Security Relations." *African Security Review* 27, no. 3–4: 308–325.

Sukhankin, Sergey. 2020. "Is Turkey Becoming a Drone Superpower?" *Gulf State Analytics*, May 5, 2020. https://gulfstateanalytics.com/is-turkey-becoming-a-drone-superpower/.

Tanchum, Michael. 2019. "Turkey's String of Pearls: Turkey's Overseas Naval Installations Reconfigure the Security Architecture of Mediterranean-Red Sea Corridor." Austria Institut für Europa-und Sicherheitspolitik (AIES), April 2019.

The Republic of Niger. 2019. "Inauguration of the Renovated and Modernized Diori Hamani International Airport." https://niger.dk/inauguration-of-renovated-and-modernized-the-diori-hamani-international-airport/.
UNROCA. 2018. Turkey 2018: UNROCA Original Report. New York: United Nations Register of Conventional Arms, 2019. https://www.unroca.org/turkey/report/2018/.
US Department of State. 2001. *Foreign Relations of the United States 1969–1976*. Vol. 10865. Washington, DC: Government Printing Office.
Varoglu, Abdulkadir, Mehmet Cakar and Nejat Basim. 2009. "An Unusual Bi-National Military Cooperation: The Case of Turkish–Gambian Relations." In *Military Cooperation in Multinational Peace Operations*, edited by Joseph Soeters and Philippe Manigart, 131–142. London and New York: Routledge.
World Politics Review. 2015. "Turkey Takes Pragmatic Approach to International Peacekeeping." *World Politics Review*, January 20, 2015. https://www.worldpoliticsreview.com/trend-lines/14895/turkey-takes-pragmatic-approach-to-international-peacekeeping.
Yalcinkaya, Haldun, Emre Hatipoglu, Dilaver Arikan Acar and Mitat Celikpala. 2018. "Turkish Efforts in Peacekeeping and the Introduction of the TUBAKOV Dataset: An Exploratory Analysis." *International Peacekeeping* 25, no. 4: 475–496. https://doi.org/10.1080/13533312.2018.1492342.
Yavuz, M. Hakan. 2003. *Islamic Political Identity in Turkey*. Oxford: Oxford University Press.

8 Turkey and UNPKO in Africa
Reluctant multilateralism

Birsen Erdoğan

Introduction

This chapter argues that Turkey's reluctant contribution to the United Nations Peacekeeping Operations (UNPKO) is a result of Turkey's identity constructions of itself and of Others. The chapter overall aims at explaining identity formations by analyzing the discourses and debates especially in the Turkish parliament regarding UNPKO in Africa. Discourse analysis here is inspired by the Essex School and Laclau and Mouffe (Erdogan 2017).

According to Laclau, agents identify with something because there is something lacking in their identity in the first place (Laclau 1996, 92). Using a Lacanian logic, Laclau asserts that search for identity is a search to fill this lack. Inspired by Laclau and Mouffe, proponents of this approach study an unfinished, incomplete and unstable character of the identity (Torfing 2005, 8). Perception of a unified self is an imaginary construct (Epstein 2010, 334) through which the self tries to make sense of itself and its existence.

In this understanding, the world outside is meaningful only through discourses (Howarth 2000, 100–102) and so are the actions. Discourse is a performance embedded in social practices (Butler 1990). Discourses consist of articulations about objects and subjects; they tell us about the perceived identity of Self and its relationship with the Other. As Hansen noted, actors do not have pre-given fixed identities which determine their foreign policies (2006, 26). But agents might refer to their perceived self-identities to justify their actions. If, for instance, justification about peacekeeping is also in conformity with the perceived identity, then the policy will have more support and consistency.

Discourses act in a social realm with other discourses, sometimes in a competing relationship. Every agent has a particular way of interpreting itself, its other, an issue or a situation and this is not necessarily the same as the Other's articulation. Discourses might oppose or clash or they might ignore each other. Discourses rarely stay the same, and so with identities. Institutions or norms, such as "peacekeeping," "democracy" or "state" gain their meanings through discourses and practices. Discourses establishing binaries and antagonistic relationships are more susceptible to challenges and contestation. Laclau and Mouffe state that "there is not one discourse or one system of categories through which the real might speak without mediation" (Laclau and Mouffe 2001, 3). In short, as Torfing stated, there is never closure for discourses, and they are subject to change because of social and political struggles (1999, 89).

Hegemonic discourses set certain expectations and norms for the actors. For instance, democratic states should act in a certain way or "peacekeeping" should be understood in a specific way. In this sense, identities are stuck between their self-preferences and dictates of their political environments. Most of the time subjects identify with their "subject positions" which are pro-status quo to avoid turmoil or tension. However, in times of political crisis, major transformations and changes, subjects might find an opportunity to become political agents (also known as "political subjectivity"; Howarth and Stavrakakis 2000, 20; Aslan 2012, 162). A structural change, an opening in the hegemonic discourse can give subjects an opportunity to reformulate their identities or create new ones. Such as the rising political agency of women in the West in the last two centuries together with changes in multiple realms. In such times, marginalized discourses/identities might claim a place in the realm of legitimate discourses and challenge the status quo. Unsurprisingly, Turkey either acted in accordance with the expectations of the Western hegemonic discourse or challenged them, acting as a political subject in times of individual, regional and global transformations (end of the Cold War, September 11, rapid economic growth, Arab Spring, Syrian war, and so on). Often, it was both at the same time. Thus, an agent takes a political discourse/action to confirm or to challenge or both. But none of these positions is permanent.

As a chosen method here, post-structuralist discourse analysis helps to detect and analyze the link between identities and justifications for actions. It also investigates how subjects try to fix a meaning, an identity, a position or a truth in a competitive and complicated discursive realm called foreign policy. For this purpose, the author analyzed the proceedings of debates on Turkey's contribution to the UNPKO in the Turkish parliament (TBMM). Not every UNPKO was brought to the parliament's attention. In this study, debates for three peacekeeping (PK) operations are analyzed: Somalia, Congo, Mali and Central African Republic (together). The parliament's role was important because the government needed the majority's vote to be able to send troops abroad. The objective is to see how the foreign policy elite and government represented itself, UNPK, Africa and others (such as the West) and how these narratives were challenged by the opposition.[1]

The next section briefly mentions some literature about the rising powers and their contributions to the UNPKO. Then, debates in the Turkish parliament about three operations mentioned above will be analyzed. The chapter will end with some observations and conclusive remarks.

Peacekeeping and rising powers

According to the literature, there may be several reasons for sending troops to the UNPKO. For instance, Bellamy and Williams (2012, 3–6) indicate political (such as concerns for prestige, increasing influence or pressure from allies), economic (such as monetary compensation), security (such as perceived security interests or geographical proximity), institutional (such as domestic factors in decision making and the role of the armed forces), normative rationales (such as self-image) and habitualization of peacekeeping (path-dependency). They also mention possible reasons why countries would not contribute to the UNPK. Those reasons are other security priorities, institutional preferences, financial costs, discomfort with the expanding UNPK agenda, exceptionalism, absence of pressure to contribute, difficult domestic context, risks for national reputation, military resistance and weakness in the UN-force generation system (Bellamy and Williams 2012, 6–8). According to them, a considerable number of states are "token contributors," with small contributions (less than 40 uniformed personnel; Bellamy and Williams 2013, 440). Turkey can be considered within this group, as will be explained later.

Ninety-two percent of the military and police contributions to the UNPKO come from countries in Asia, Africa and Latin America, especially after the 2000s. Weiss and Kuele mention three main reasons for this: Concerns for regional interests and cooperation, search for international recognition and prestige and, finally, the possibility of financial benefits (2019). Interestingly, while they were major troop contributors during the Cold War, Western countries showed a more hesitant attitude towards the UNPKO after the failures in Somalia, Rwanda and Srebrenica in the 1990s.[2] Countries from the Global South on the other hand, contributed to the UNPKO almost consistently after 2010 (IPI Peacekeeping Database n.d.), Bangladesh, Ethiopia, Rwanda, Nepal and India being the top five troop contributors in August 2020 (UNPK 2020a).

There is extensive academic research on UNPK and the contributions of developing states or rising powers.[3] Most developing countries and rising powers such as Brazil and South Africa send their troops to conflicts in their region proving the geographical proximity argument (such as Brazil in Haiti, South Africa in Congo). Some countries in the Global South take an active role in peacekeeping to increase their influence and reputation to have a greater say in regional and global security and at the United Nations Security Council (UNSC; such as India, as explained by Beri 2008 and Blah 2017; Pakistan, by Krishnasamy 2001).

According to some scholars, China's changing position towards UNPK especially after 2003 from no-involvement to active participation has several reasons. One concerns changes in China's perception of UNPK (Teitt 2011). Another is China's changing foreign policy behavior to appear as a "responsible" and normative power, while trying to expand its influence and test its power projection (Pang 2005; Hirono and Lanteigne 2011). More recently, it is suggested that China's main aim in joining UNPKO is less about status, more about rational economic calculations (Cho 2019; Best 2020). Using constructivist arguments, Huang suggests that China's greater involvement in PK and its increasing interaction with the world led to its socialization to accept certain norms such as peacekeeping (2011). Some scholars analyzed China's changing role and identity by looking at the discourses (Kuo 2020; Carrozza 2019). According to research, regional powers sometimes contested the UNPKO and voiced their frustration with the asymmetrical power relations at the UNSC (Abdenur 2019, 53–54; Blah 2017).

Looking at the conflict management behaviors of the rising powers, Parlar Dal found some common patterns: considerations of self-interests, regional priorities, normative costs calculations and their status (2018a, 2209). In this sense, rising powers usually criticize the unjust Western world order while being attached to the Westphalian state system (Parlar Dal 2018a, 2209). They challenge this order only if the perceived costs are low, otherwise they work within the existing order (Parlar Dal 2018a, 2211).

Although most academic research is still dominated by the rational actor approaches, there are more studies analyzing discourses, identities, social context and role of ideational factors. These compilations discuss how traditional Western concepts have been re-articulated, challenged and transformed by the rising powers (Call and de Coning 2017). These discourses sometimes reinforce and mimic the traditional notions of UNPK, but they also present a different perspective and introduce novel practices (de Coning and Peter 2019).

Turkey in UN peacekeeping

Academic research presents different arguments on Turkey's involvement in the UNPKO. While some studies show a widening geographical interest over the years with the missions in the African and Asian continents (Yalcinkaya et al. 2018, 490) some mention the contributions of these operations to Turkey's image abroad in bringing it closer to the Western institutions such as NATO and the EU (Oguzlu and Gungor 2006). According to Satana, Turkey's involvement is linked to factors such as regional security, normative considerations and its multidimensional and proactive foreign policy (2012). Parlar Dal (2018b) mentions that Turkey's contributions are mostly connected to its immediate security concerns in its own region or to its institutional commitments (to NATO or the EU). Consequently, she argues that it is not realistic to assume an increase in Turkey's involvement in UNPK, given the fact that Turkey's own security concerns have been prioritized in recent years.

Turkish official discourses give the perception that Turkey is one of the main supporters of the UNPKO and promote Turkey's self-image as a major contributor to peacekeeping (see, for instance, TRT Haber 2015, Anatolian Agency 2018; MFA 2019; 2020a, 122; Turkish Armed Forces 2020). However, relative to other developing states and rising powers (except Russia), Turkey's contribution to the UNPKO has been rather modest. By August 2020, Turkey was the 64th largest troop contributor to the UNPKO with 132 troops in the list of 119 countries (UNPK 2020a).[4] Turkey's contributions to the largest PKO (UNMISS in South Sudan and MONUSCO in Congo, more than 13,000 troops each) are only 21 and none respectively. The third and fourth largest missions (MINUSMA in Mali and MINUSCA in Central African Republic, more than 11,000 troops each) have no personnel from Turkey. Turkey's contribution is mainly in UNIFIL in Lebanon (88 contingent) followed by UNAMID for Darfur (21). Turkey has two personnel in Kosovo (UNMISS) and none in Somalia (UNPK 2020b, 2020c).[5]

Turkey's first military involvement in a United Nations (UN)-mandated international operation took place in 1950 in Korea. Turkey sent a significant army unit of 15,000 soldiers to Korea (Kocer 2006). The reason was mainly linked to the lack of Turkish agency and autonomy back then. Turkey simply followed the US-led coalition, which at the end made Turkey's membership to the Western defense alliance possible. After the Korean War, Turkey's participation in any international military operation came to a halt until the end of the Cold War. In the post-Cold War period, Turkey took a slightly more active role not only in United Nations operations but also in several NATO, European Union (EU) and Organization of Security and Cooperation in Europe (OSCE) operations. However, its contribution remained limited both quantitatively and qualitatively. In recent years, it is observable that Turkey's unilateral interventions abroad have increased considerably together with its political subjectivity (agency) and ambitions with the opening spaces in its region and elsewhere. One should note that Turkey's contributions did not show any stability over the years changing from two soldiers in 1990 to 1,497 in 1994, from 196 in 2001 to 962 in 2007, and from 196 in 2014 to 130 in 2019. Most of these troops were positioned in Kosovo or in Lebanon, with only a few in Africa.

What can explain Turkey's (limited) contribution to the UN peacekeeping operations (UNPKO)?

Small contributions by states are called "token" in the literature and Turkey fits this definition in a technical and quantitative sense as mentioned above. Token contributions are preferred because they are low-cost and low-risk for the troop-sending countries, however they still provide some advantages such as familiarization with the UNPK, hence acting as a stepping stone for the future, or generating prestige (Bellamy and Williams 2013, 440). The UN welcomed such contributions even though they do not add anything to the operation, to make countries familiar with the UNPK structure and operations. Indeed, using such rationalist accounts one can explain why Turkey sends more troops to areas where self-interest is involved but not to places where advantages are limited, and risks appear high. However, Turkish official discourses contradict this argument. Discourses present Turkey as an important contributor to UNPK and they confirm the importance of such missions. In the discourses, traces of self-gain, costs and self-interest can be found but not that often. Moreover, it looks like constructivist socialization, habitualization or familiarization arguments fail in the Turkish case. In addition to these, one should note that Turkey became more active in places where the UN was previously involved. As will be shown in this book, Turkey has developed intense military, diplomatic, commercial, humanitarian, political and cultural relations with a group of states in Africa (Somalia and Sudan being at the top of this list) and with intergovernmental organizations in the continent (such as the African Union). This indicates that even though on the ideational level UNPK might be praised and supported, on the behavioral level Turkey still chooses not to act with the UNPKO, if an autonomous action, an independent foreign policy, a smooth, direct relationship are possible. In other words, if self (Turkey) has an agency and if this is not challenged, it prefers acting on its own with its own terms by making its own story.

First encounters in Somalia

The headline of a daily newspaper dated 13 October 1993 reflected the shock and anger at the catastrophic events and concerns for the well-being of 300 Turkish soldiers positioned to protect the UN Headquarters in October 1993 in Somalia (Milliyet 1993a). This contradicts the news from February 1993, on the arrival of the Turkish mission in this country. Even the Vice Prime Minister, Erdal Inonu paid an official visit to the country then which was reported in a completely different tone: "Muslim" Somalians warmly welcomed the Turkish politicians and troops (Milliyet 1993b).

On 8 December 1992, the coalition government, which was composed of the Social Democratic Populist Party (SDPP) and the central right True Path Party (TPP) asked the permission of the parliament to send troops to Somalia for the purposes of assisting aid delivery to the "starving" Somalian people and contributing to the establishment of peace and security based on the UN Security Council Resolution 743. Speaking on behalf of the government, Hikmet Cetin, Minister of Foreign Affairs claimed that the Resolution was legitimate, and Turkey had a responsibility towards another Muslim country with which it had historical ties (TBMM 1992, 252). Several speakers from the opposition parties such as the center-right Homeland Party (HP), social democratic Republican People's Party (RPP) and left-wing Democratic Left Party (DLP) mentioned that they would vote in favor of the proposal, whereas religious conservative parties such as the Welfare Party (WP) and Nation Party (NP) voted against (TBMM 1992). However, almost all MPs also criticized the Security Council (TBMM 1992). Some MPs such as Kamran Inan from the center-right HP and Oguzhan Asilturk from the Welfare Party even mentioned the hegemonic and imperialist objectives for interventions (TBMM 1992, 226, 236). They called for more support for Muslims in Northern Cyprus and Bosnia by accusing the Western states of being selective and inconsistent (TBMM 1992, 227, 236). Almost all speakers, both from the government and from the opposition asserted that this was mainly an aid operation for a brotherly "Muslim" country, thus it was justified on humanitarian grounds (TBMM 1992, 223, 228, 230, 231, 236). The same day, the parliament discussed another proposal on Bosnia (TBMM 1992, 204). This proposal was about giving the necessary competence to the government to be able to contribute to any military enforcement measure taken by the Security Council for the aim of halting atrocities in Bosnia-Herzegovina. This was a topic on which all parties agreed that the international community, great powers and Turkey should act more decisively. Bosnia, located in Turkey's neighborhood and significant for cultural, historical and political reasons received much more attention than Somalia. Some parties including the left DLP even wanted the government to give conditional support—or no support—for Somalia unless Bosnia received more attention and involvement from Western states. For instance, Bulent Ecevit, the leader of the DLP issued a statement asking for the separation of the two issues. His party supported any contribution, involvement and effort for the resolution of the conflict in Bosnia, while being against or conditionally in favor of contributing to the Somalian peacekeepers (TBMM 1992, 261). Additionally, some MPs from the opposition, such as Oguzhan Asilturk from the conservative religious WP criticized the government for obeying America's orders unquestioningly and risking the lives of Turkish soldiers to protect Americans (TBMM 1992, 237–238). He mentioned that the new world order under the American leadership was an order of oppression and injustice. American interest in the region was serving the material gain of the Western powers to exploit the natural resources in Africa (uranium in the case of Somalia; TBMM 1992, 237). Kamran Inan from the center-right HP mentioned the emergence of unipolarity in the world order and rise of US power globally and also in international institutions (TBMM 1992, 224). However, almost nobody mentioned logistical, material and cost-related issues. All party and government representatives including left and social democratic parties referred to religion (Muslim Somalia). All parties voted in favor of Bosnia resolution, but religious parties (WP and NP) voted against the Somalia proposal (266 in favor, 24 against).

Between May 1993 and January 1994, a Turkish General took the command post of the UNOSOM II. This was celebrated with pride and joy in the society and media in the spring and summer months of 1993. Yet, this joyful moment was soon overshadowed by the infamous "Battle of Mogadishu" on 3 and 4 October 1993. In October 1993, the opposition parties in particular started objecting to Turkey's involvement in Somalia. In a heated debate on 26 October 1993 at the parliament, speakers from the opposition WP of

Islamic/conservative orientation put forward an inquiry against the government alleging that Turkish troops were in the middle of a dirty fight between the UN troops and Muslim Somalians—implying that they were going to choose the UN over Muslim Somalians. In their inquiry they asked for withdrawal from Somalia (TBMM 1993, 21).

This time, almost everyone in the opposition ranging from left to right was against Turkey's continuous presence in Somalia. The main arguments were the radical change in the situation on the site which was no longer a simple "aid delivery" (for instance, Sevket Kazan from the religious conservative WP; TBMM 1993, 23) and under these circumstances the UN mandate was impossible to achieve anyway. Turkey was helping the ambitions of the Western states to control Somalia and its riches. Moreover, some MPs stated that many Western states were pulling out of this "swamp," and so should Turkey (Engin Guner from the center-right HP; TBMM 1993, 30–31). Speakers from the opposition, such as Istemihan Talay of the social democratic RPP and also from the government, such as Hikmet Cetin, the Minister of Foreign Affairs mentioned that the situation in Somalia was out of control and Turkey had no direct "interest" there unlike in other places such as Bosnia, Cyprus and Azerbaijan (TBMM 1993, 36, 45).

Even though MPs from the coalition parties such as Irfan Demiralp from the TPP and the Minister of Foreign Affairs tried to convince the opposition by arguing that there were not only Americans, but also many Muslim nations contributing to the operation, many states did contribute with more troops than Turkey—even small states like Belgium—and the Turkish commander was proof of how appreciated, trusted and respected Turkey was (TBMM 1993, 34–50), they also promised that if the situation was worse (and it was worse), they would withdraw.

Following the events of October 1993, countries gradually called their soldiers back home. In 1994 and 1995, the withdrawal of all foreign troops including 300 Turkish soldiers under the mandate of UNOSOM II was completed. This was the end of UNOSOM II. The portrayal of Somalia in the press changed from "warm welcoming Muslim nation" to "hell" and then finally the decision to bring the Turkish soldiers was celebrated (Milliyet 1994).

In the case of Somalia, the Turkish government followed the Western powers and the UN agencies in a rather passive role. This is also how Turkish foreign policy looked before the 2000s. Figure 8.1 shows this in a simplified way.

The first episode of Turkey's involvement in Somalia was over but there were going to be new chapters. The image of Somalia remained in the Turkish discourse as a poor Muslim country which was exploited for centuries and torn by civil wars and famine. The next episode would start with a nationwide humanitarian campaign in Somalia in 2011. Moreover, negative memories of the events in Somalia also reinforced the Turkish idea that military interventions were not always desirable. Somalia contributed to

Figure 8.1 Turkey as a passive actor. This figure shows Turkey as a passive actor which is almost at the periphery of the Western alliance throughout a considerable part of the twentieth century. Turkey had neither an independent position, nor subjectivity. Turkish foreign policy after the 2000s started changing

Turkey's positive self-image as a reliable caregiver. But it also reinforced the negative image of the West, especially the USA and its actions in Africa. Somalia was to re-emerge as a humanitarian and peacebuilding project in 2011, as explained elsewhere in this book. Somalia is the best example of Turkish geographical imagination and its wide borders. Somalia will also be a catchphrase to prove Turkey's political subjecthood, its rising agency and its exemplary foreign policy, which is in direct contrast with Western policies.

Turkey's increased political subjecthood

Turkish foreign policy entered a new era and transformed itself dramatically after the election of the Justice and Development Party (JDP) in 2002. This transformation has manifested itself in several avenues but especially in expanding the vision and sphere of interest when it comes to Turkey's international relations and its role in the region and in the world. Turkey's foreign policy has changed rapidly, especially after the appointment of Ahmet Davutoglu to the post of Minister of Foreign Affairs in 2009 (then serving as Prime Minister between 2014 and 2016). The period following 2009 marked Turkey's active, comparatively autonomous, multidimensional, diplomatically proactive and trade-centric foreign policy. However, this did not mean a significant increase in participation in the UNPKO.

In this period, the Turkish parliament discussed only two proposals to send Turkish soldiers abroad under the UNPK mandate: Congo and Mali and Central African Republic (CAR) (discussion took place on the same day for both missions). Turkey participated with a small presence in the missions in Sudan, Darfur, South Sudan and Somalia but these missions were not discussed in parliament. A further two proposals related to international military operations taking place in Africa in the Gulf of Aden and Libya, however these were not UNPK operations. Below, the parliamentary debates on Congo, Mali and CAR missions are summarized and briefly analyzed.

Congo: A ticket to Europe?

The period from the mid-2000s to 2010 has marked itself as a period when the Turkish governments formed by the JDP gave priority to European Union membership. Accordingly, in June 2006 the government brought a bill asking permission of the parliament to contribute to the EU's election observation mission in the Democratic Republic of Congo (EU-EOM 2006). The mission was authorized by UNSC Resolution 1279 to support the UNPKO in Congo (MONUC). The EU asked for contributions from its member states and from NATO members, including Turkey.

Mehmet Vecdi Gonul, the Minister of Defense asked for the support of MPs in the Turkish parliament in a session dated 27 June 2006 (TBMM 2006, 44-46). He presented two reasons for support: first, Turkey's contribution was small (just a military transport aircraft and its personnel for four months) and did not include any combat role (TBMM 2006, 46); second, this contribution would make a positive impact on the EU thus helping Turkey's membership bid, reminding them that the contribution to the Korean War helped Turkey's membership of NATO (TBMM 2006, 46).

The opposition, consisting of the social democratic Republican People's Party (RPP) and Democratic Left Party (DLP), the far-right Nationalist Action Party (NAP), center-right True Path Party (TPP), center-right Homeland Party (HP) and religious conservative Felicity Party (FP) supported the proposal yet still made critical speeches emphasizing certain points. For instance, an MP from the center-right HP said that Turkey's case for Cyprus should be defended more compellingly before the EU and UN (TBMM 2006, 49). An MP from the opposition social democratic RPP mentioned that Western states failed badly in Srebrenica and could not solve the Cyprus issue. Moreover, they had exploited "black" Congo for decades (for instance, an MP from the social democratic RPP; TBMM 2006, 51). Yet, the proposal was still accepted by the majority vote.

It is important to note a couple of things at this point. Turkey's contribution to the EU mission in Congo has not been a subject of heated or major debate in society. The parliamentary talks centered on a couple of issues on which almost everyone agreed. Among these issues, the fact that the mission was too small and symbolic was highlighted. The contribution was perceived as just small enough to be seen but too insignificant to pose any threat to anyone or constitute any burden on the Turkish government or Armed Forces. Moreover, this mission was deployed in a country where Turkey did not have any direct interests, unlike Western states. This eliminated allegations of material interests and neocolonialism. Furthermore, the mission was legitimate and legal (TBMM 2006, 54–55).

However, almost all the opposition MPs mentioned that the Western-led international order was no longer legitimate. Turkey was presented as the victim of unfair and unjust policies of international organizations and the EU (especially for the Cyprus issue and delayed EU membership; TBMM 2006, 47, 51, 58). Other victims were the Muslim nations (such as Bosnians and Turkish Cypriots) and "black" Africa (such as Congo). Still, the general consensus was that a small contribution like a transport aircraft would increase Turkey's status and prestige in the EU and would move Turkey closer to the EU's military and political decision making.

Overall, the Congo decision was the result of a wrong calculation based on a perception that military contributions would increase Turkey's prestige and status. At least in the case of Congo, Turkey has not gained any leverage with the European Union. However, it should also be noted that Turkey's norm-following behavior, generosity and dignified attitude have been confirmed by the Turkish political elite's positive view of themselves. Moreover, Africa's black-ness, insecurities and suffering have been reinstated and reproduced in the political imagination. Africa was once more a passive actor exploited by the white West.

Mali and Central African Republic: Token contributions

In November 2014, the Turkish parliament—composed of the majority JDP and the opposition social democratic RPP, the nationalist conservative far-right Nationalist Action Party (NAP) and the Kurdish-left Peoples' Democratic Party (PDP)—discussed a proposal to contribute a handful of personnel to the European Union's missions in Mali (EUCAP Mali and EUTM Mali) and the Central African Republic (CAR) (EUFOR RCA). Both countries were neither on Turkey's radar nor in the public debate before 2014 as mentioned by Hasip Kaplan, an MP from the Kurdish-left PDP in the proceedings (TBMM 2014, 400). Although Turkish governments increased their efforts to be more present in the African continent especially after 2005 (African Opening) and 2011 (Somalia aid campaign and Arab Spring), contributions to the missions in Mali and CAR were not directly about Turkey's policies in these two states. Moreover, after 2014, Turkey's overall contribution to UNPK started declining. Thus, UNPK started losing its appeal.

In the background, 2014 was one of the most turbulent periods in Turkey's near region. In this period, the government under the leadership of Davutoglu and the foreign policy elite looked for like-minded states to receive help for Syrian refugees and to ease Turkey's security concerns if necessary with military solutions.[6] In the parliament, the Kurdish-left Peoples' Democratic Party (PDP) in particular emerged as a consistent opponent (BBC 2014). This period marked the increasing insecurities of Turkey due to the transformations in its region and increasing protests and opposition both at home and abroad. At the end, acting mostly on its own, Turkey turned to a more aggressive and less predictable foreign policy after 2016 in a pursuit for more security and recognition.[7] This pursuit showed itself clearly not only in Syria but also in Africa.

In November 2014, good relations with the EU and NATO still mattered as they were Turkey's allies. The proposal signed by Ahmet Davutoglu, the Minister of Foreign Affairs referred to the fact that relations with Western allies and contributions to the Mali and CAR missions would bring the EU and Turkey closer (TBMM 2014, 392). Sirin Unal from the majority JDP stated that Turkey's active participation in such missions—no matter how small—increased its reputation and status with European and NATO states (TBMM 2014, 405–406). Moreover, such contributions provided Turkey with important military and operational experience in the field, added to its knowledge of the region and increased its credibility in the continent. Additionally, the MP reminded parliament that especially in Mali, the majority were Muslims.

Some of the opposition parties such as the far-right Nationalist Action Party (NAP) and social democratic RPP voted in favor of the proposal. Their main justification was to help peace and stability in war-torn countries. However, they also criticized the government for following religion and kinship-oriented foreign policy (especially the social democratic RPP; TBMM 2014, 395) and for not being decisive enough in areas which are essential to Turkey (especially the nationalist NAP). The nationalists, that is the NAP, was very critical of the Western states for their exploitative and imperialist policies which are causing these conflicts. Mustafa Erdem from the NAP portrayed Africa in these words: "Africa is a drama of humanity. Africa is the shame for humanity. Africa is a space of attraction, battle, and portioning. African is poor, sufferer and victim" (TBMM 2014, 397).

In this vein, Hasip Kaplan from the Kurdish left PDP expressed the reasons for their "rejection" of the proposal. These were mainly the criticisms of the government for its unprincipled foreign policy, for not consulting the parliament or civil society sufficiently on security matters, and for following the Western states and their wishes unquestioningly (TBMM 2014, 400). The MP also mentioned the need to prioritize solving the internal problems in Turkey before taking small and irrelevant parts in Western states' strategic calculations.

All speakers from the government and opposition alike, mentioned a couple of similar points such as the responsibility of the Western states for the problems in Africa and their ambitions for the continent's natural resources. They agreed that Turkey needed to follow a proactive, autonomous and independent foreign policy. Opposition parties especially stated that Turkey's foreign policy should be humanitarian, credible, consistent, accountable and humble (TBMM 2014, 398, 402, 410). Moreover, Turkey's priority should be solving domestic problems. In foreign policy, Turkey should be active in matters concerning its direct interests (Cyprus, Syria, Palestine; TBMM 2014, 394, 398, 399, 401, 403, 408). They also agreed that any involvement abroad should be legitimate, legal, short and risk-free.

Some speakers from the nationalist NAP also referred to the Ottoman past, religion and cultural values that Turkey possessed and shared with the African states (TBMM 2014, 397, 399, 411). While Hasip Kalpan, the MP from the Kurdish left PDP criticized the government for neo-Ottoman expansionism and Ottoman discourses (TBMM 2014, 400). Vice Prime Minister Bulent Arinc responded to such allegations by stating that Turkey has been a European, Asian and African state since Ottoman times (TBMM 2014, 411). For Arinc, joining such operations was not only a strategic prerogative but also a source of pride and honor.

On 2 August 2016, the Turkish parliament discussed the extension of the mandate for limited troop numbers in Mali (MINUSMA) and CAR (MINUSCA). This time, Fikri Isik, the Minister of National Defense did not make much reference to relations with the EU indicating that the EU was falling out of favor (TBMM 2016, 271).

In the government's narrative, certain things were different than 2014. First, as a novelty Turkey was portrayed as an Afro-Eurasian nation by the Minister of Defense, which should have a say in the security and stability of this region (TBMM 2016, 275). Terrorism had a more central place in the speeches. The importance of stability in these two states to halt the spread of terrorism was mentioned more frequently (TBMM 2016, 274–275). Finally, Sirin Unal, an MP from the JDP claimed that such missions were in conformity with Turkey's proactive foreign policy and historical role (TBMM 2016, 289).

Nationalist and social democratic opposition supported the extension mainly due to the security concerns (linked to terrorism), while the Kurdish-left PDP voted against. Ayhan Bilgen, an MP from PDP mentioned inconsistencies in the foreign policy discourses of the government: On one hand, Turkey was being presented as a major supporter to UNPK (although its contribution was mostly and ridiculously with a small number of troops), while on the other hand the government was using every platform to loudly criticize the UN, its composition and its policies (TBMM 2016, 283). By emphasizing the lack of transparency and accountability, Bilgen questioned peacekeeping in general and Turkey's contributions specifically.

In the session dated 17 July 2017, the Turkish contribution to both peacekeeping operations was extended one more time. This time, an MP from the JDP explained the improvements in Turkey–Africa relations in all sort of fields extensively and in an understanding of partnership (TBMM 2017, 516–517). He also said (TBMM 2017, 518):

> We have always seen African nations as our companion and mates. Even though our languages, values, ethnic origins and external appearances are different, we felt ourselves and Africans as passengers of the same boat ... We have seen the pain of Africa not from the political, strategic, interest-centric lenses; we have approached them always with humanitarianism and conscientiousness ... It has been central to the Turkish Foreign Policy that African countries are independent, free and in peace and security and they determine their own fate.

In addition to this, all speakers mentioned the expansion of terrorism in Africa, that contributed to the securitization of Africa (TBMM 2017, 516, 518, 522). This session was also marked by debates on Turkey's increasing insecurities in recent years.[8]

Observations and conclusions

In line with the theoretical framework and data analysis, it is possible to make some observations. Before the JDP consolidated its power, Turkish discourses on the UNPK helped to represent Turkey as a compliant state, which wanted to follow Western values and institutions. Even though there were audible anti-Western discourses in the political realm, Turkey's subject position did not really challenge the Western or UN order. With the JDP's increasing sense of power, its political subjectivity has also increased, as shown in Figure 8.2.

In the discursive realm, both Europe and the USA have been represented as Turkey's antagonistic Others. Africa presented itself as an open and available terrain for the JDP's broadened foreign policy and its increased sense of agency. Power vacuums, isolation, exclusion and consequences of protracted conflicts especially in countries like Sudan and Somalia paved the way for the discourses of "Turkish protector–African protected" and added these territories to the Turkish sphere of interest—without much challenge and contestation. As such, Turkey was portrayed as generous, righteous, fair and emancipatory (positive self-image) as opposed to the

158 *Erdoğan*

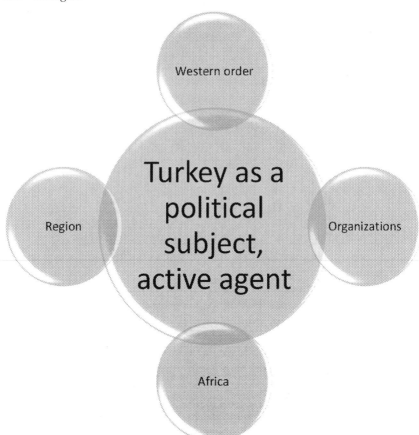

Figure 8.2 Turkey as a political subject and active agent. After the 2000s, Turkey's self-perception has gradually improved as a political subject, active agent and autonomous actor. Turkey in this new identity seemingly determines its own foreign policy. It decides itself when, where and how it will act. In this view, Turkey is in the center and options are multiple. Moreover, Africa has been added as an alternative region in recent years to the options

self-centric, greedy, exploitative and unfair West (difference) as shown in Figure 8.3.

Africa in general was articulated as a continent suffered from centuries-long exploitation, marginalization and pain and now was ready to be reconstructed and protected. Emotional discourses concerning the peoples of Africa have changed from narratives of hunger or poverty to people who were Turkey's siblings and its family (equivalence; MFA 2020b). Religious, cultural, historical and geographical bonds have been emphasized. Policies were evolved from the discourses of charity and assistance, then to economic, strategic and security cooperation.

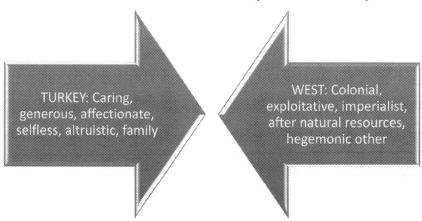

Figure 8.3 Turkey's antagonistic relationship with the West

Regarding the UNPK in the Turkish context, one can conclude that even though the idea of PK has positive associations and all norm-following states should support it, it is being abused by the great Western states for self-interest. Interestingly and against constructivist research, Turkey has not internalized or habitualized the practice of contributing to UNPK. In a declining trend, Turkey's contributions to UNPK are even less in recent years, whereas its unilateral operations multiplied. The Turkish self feels safer, especially in recent years, if it is on its own. All multilateral institutions including the UNSC are highly criticized and questioned. Thus, the problem with UNPK is derived from the perceived world order and Turkey's new political subjectivity which desires to challenge it.

As a last word, one can observe that Turkey's sense of agency has been critically damaged especially after the domestic and regional developments and upheavals These changes have led to a sense of insecurity for its identity but also to an endeavor to search for new terrains where it might feel comfortable and safe. It looks as if Europe is not that terrain. But Africa can be. It is presented as the world might have left Africa, but Turkey has found it.

As noted in the introduction, state actors try to build their foreign policies around certain seemingly stable foundations such as a unified identity. Since these foundations are usually ambiguous or too idealistic and since the state actor is constantly under criticism and social–political surveillance; the identity finds it hard to fix a meaning for itself. In times of crisis and rising opportunities, actors start renegotiating, reconfiguring and reconstructing meanings and policies. Turkey expanded its imagined geography to the African continent in recent years. These were not direct results of Turkey's contributions to the UNPKO but more Turkey's increasing sense of agency and autonomy in recent years. Turkey keeps its symbolic contributions to the UNPKO and yet remains as an invisible and insignificant actor in multilateral peacekeeping. Elsewhere, Turkey has found more visibility and significance.

As a final word, more direct confrontations between the Turkish subject and other political subjects over Africa will most probably be observed in the coming years, as Africa becomes more visible to other actors and/or African nations gain more agency. Turkey's Africa policies are right now consistent with its perceived self-identity and its perception of Africa; but none of these are permanent, secure and/or stable.

Notes

1 One should note that in almost all cases mentioned above, party members voted in line with their party's position.
2 However, during and in the aftermath of the Yugoslavian wars and after 9/11, the Western alliance was involved in military operations (under the UN or NATO mandate). Moreover, some Western states sent troops to Africa due to escalation of conflicts there. But this trend moved downward again after 2010 (see http://www.providingforpeacekeeping.org/wp-content/uploads/2017/04/Contributors.png).
3 By "rising powers," the author means countries which gained a substantial sense of confidence and political subjectivity (agency) especially after a transformation, growth or change which opened a way for new discursive reconfigurations and identity articulations. These states in their discourses show signs of empowerment, intentions of expansion of their influences, glorify themselves and follow more ambitious foreign policy than before. Even though they discursively might challenge the Western hegemonic discourses, they usually still act within the status quo.
4 After states such as Italy, Spain, Tunisia, Poland, Argentina, Brazil, Burkina Faso, Cambodia, Chad, Egypt (3,093 troops), Indonesia (2,837), South Africa (1,151), Jordan (484), Portugal and China (2,531). See troop and police contributors at https://peacekeeping.un.org/en/troop-and-police-contributors.
5 Of 132 total personnel, three are female and 129 are male; 44 are police officers, 86 are troops, one is expert and two are staff officers. See https://peacekeeping.un.org/sites/default/files/03_country_and_mission_28.pdf.
6 For more information see Al-Jazeera 2014; BBC 2014; CFR 2014; Radikal 2014; CNN 2014.)
7 For an extensive analysis of events, see Erdogan 2017.
8 One should note that this session took place right after the coup attempt against the Government on 15 July. This shocking incident can be considered as one of the biggest, most hideous and serious attacks against the Turkish state, its identity and its legitimacy. Challenging the foundations of political power and its discourses, the coup attempt deeply scared the Turkish self. After the coup attempt, the sense of insecurity understandably increased. The state and its existential identity were being contested. As a response, the state re-established its power and reaffirmed its subjectivity more fiercely. Friends and foes were rearticulated, internal and foreign policies were reconfigured. At the end, new antagonistic relationships emerged putting Turkey in a tense and unstable position in a realm of competing and opposing discourses.

References

Abdenur, E. Adriana. 2019. "UN Peacekeeping in a Multipolar World Order: Norms, Role Expectations, and Leadership." In *United Nations Peace Operations in Changing Global Order*, edited by Cedric de Coning and Mateja Peter, 45–64. Cham: Palgrave. https://doi.org/10.1007/978-3-319-99106-1.

Al-Jazeera. 2014. "Turkey can Save Kobane from ISIL." October 7, 2014. http://america.aljazeera.com/articles/2014/10/7/turkey-kobane-intervention.html.

Anatolian Agency. 2018. "Contribution of the Turkish Armed Forces to the World Peace." January 1, 2018. https://www.aa.com.tr/tr/turkiye/turk-silahli-kuvvetlerinden-dunya-barisina-katki/1019887.

Aslan, Ali. 2012. "The Foreign Policy-Hegemony Nexus: Turkey's Search for a 'New' Subjectivity in World Politics and Its Implications for US-Turkish Relations." *Perceptions*, 17, no. 4: 159–184. http://sam.gov.tr/pdf/perceptions/Volume-XVII/winter-2012/7Ali_Aslan.pdf.

BBC. 2014. "Syria-Iraq Proposal Accepted at the Parliament (in Turkish)." 2 October, 2014. http://www.bbc.com/turkce/haberler/2014/10/141002_tezkere_canli.

Bellamy, J. Alex and Paul D. Williams. 2012. "Broadening the Base of UN Troop- and Police-Contributing Countries." International Peace Institute. https://www.ipinst.org/wp-content/uploads/publications/ipi_pub_broadening_the_base.pdf.

Bellamy, J. Alex and, Paul D. Williams. 2013. "UN Force Generation: Key Lessons and Future Strategies." In *Providing Peacekeepers: Politics, Challenges and the Future of the UN Peacekeeping Contributions*, edited by Alex J. Bellamy and Paul D. Williams, 437–445. Oxford: Oxford University Press. doi:10.1093/acprof:oso/9780199672820.001.0001.

Beri, Ruchita. 2008. "India's Role in Keeping Peace in Africa." *Strategic Analysis* 32, no. 2: 197–221. https://doi.org/10.1080/09700160801994852.

Best, Lucy. 2020. "What Motivates Chinese Peacekeeping?" Council on Foreign Relations. January 7. https://www.cfr.org/blog/what-motivates-chinese-peacekeeping.

Blah, Montgomery. 2017. "India's Stance and Renewed Commitment to UN Peacekeeping." *Strategic Analysis* 41, no. 3: 257–272. https://doi.org/10.1080/09700161.2017.1295605.

Butler, Judith. 1990. *Gender Trouble: Feminism and the Subversion of Identity*. New York and London: Routledge.

Call, Charles T. and Cedric de Coning, eds. 2017. *Rising Powers and Peacebuilding: Breaking the Mold*. Cham: Palgrave. doi:10.1007/978-3-319-60621-7.

Carrozza, Ilaria. 2019, "Chinese Diplomacy in Africa: Constructing Security-Development Nexus." April 7, 2019. E-International Relations. https://www.e-ir.info/2019/04/07/chinese-diplomacy-in-africa-constructing-the-security-development-nexus/.

CFR. 2014. "Turkish President on ISIS and Regional Security." Council on Foreign Relations, 22 September, 2014. https://www.cfr.org/event/turkish-president-erdogan-isis-and-regional-security.

Cho, Sunghee. 2019. "China's Participation in UN Peacekeeping Operations since the 2000s." *Journal of Contemporary China* 28, no. 117: 482–498. https://doi.org/10.1080/10670564.2018.1542216.

CNN. 2014. "Turkey Willing to Put Troops in Syria If Others Do Their Part." October 6, 2014. http://edition.cnn.com/2014/10/06/world/meast/amanpour-davutoglu-interview/.

de Coning, Cedric and Mateja Peter, eds. 2019. *United Nations Peace Operations in A Changing Global Order*. Cham: Palgrave. https://link.springer.com/book/10.1007%2F978-3-319-99106-1.

Epstein, Charlotte. 2010. "Who speaks? Discourse, the Subject and the Study of Identity in International Politics." *European Journal of International Relations* 17, no. 2: 327–350. https://doi.org/10.1177/1354066109350055.

Erdogan, Birsen. 2017. *Humanitarian Intervention and Responsibility to Protect: Turkish Foreign Policy Discourse.* Cham: Palgrave. doi:10.1007/978-3-319-47683-4.

EU-EOM. 2006. "EU Election Observation Mission in Congo". October 30, 2006. https://eeas.europa.eu/topics/election-observation-missions-eueoms_en/26170/EU%20election%20observation%20mission%20to%20the%20Democratic%20Republic%20of%20Congo%20in%202006.

Hansen, Lene. 2006. *Security as Practice: Discourse Analysis and the Bosnian War.* Abingdon: Taylor and Francis. https://doi.org/10.4324/9780203236338.

Hirono, Miwa and Marc Lanteigne. 2011. "Introduction: China and UN Peacekeeping." *International Peacekeeping* 18, no. 3: 243–256. https://doi.org/10.1080/13533312.2011.563070.

Howarth, David. 2000. *Discourse.* Buckingham: Open University Press.

Howarth, David and Yannis Stavrakakis. 2000. "Introducing Discourse Theory and Political Analysis." In *Discourse Theory and Political Analysis: Identities, Hegemonies and Social Change,* edited by David Howarth, Aletta Norval and Yannis Stavrakakis, 1–37. Manchester: Manchester University Press.

Huang, Chin-Hao. 2011. "Principles and Praxis of China's Peacekeeping." *International Peacekeeping* 18, no. 3: 257–270. https://doi.org/10.1080/13533312.2011.563554.

IPI Peacekeeping Database. n.d. "Providing Peacekeeping." Accessed June 27, 2020. http://www.providingforpeacekeeping.org/peacekeeping-data-graphs/.

Kocer, Gokhan. 2006. "The Support of Turkey to the Peacekeeping Operations (in Turkish)." *Uluslararası İliskiler/International Relations* 3, no. 11: 47–70.

Krishnasamy, Kabilan. 2001. ""Recognition' for Third World Peacekeepers: India and Pakistan." *International Peacekeeping* 8, no. 4: 56–76. https://doi.org/10.1080/13533310108413920.

Kuo, Steven. 2020. *Chinese Peace in Africa: From Peacekeeper to Peacemaker.* Oxon: Routledge.

Laclau, Ernesto. 1996. *Emancipation(s).* London: Verso.

Laclau, Ernesto and Chantal Mouffe. 2001. *Hegemony and Socialist Strategy: Towards a Radical Democratic Politics.* 2nd Edition. London: Verso.

MFA (Ministry of Foreign Affairs). 2019. "Our Proactive and Humanitarian Foreign Policy at the Entry of 2020." http://www.mfa.gov.tr/site_media/html/2020-yilina-girerken-girisimci-ve-insani-dis-politikamiz.pdf.

MFA (Ministry of Foreign Affairs). 2020a. "Our Approach to the UNPKO and Our Contributions." http://www.mfa.gov.tr/birlesmis-milletler-baris-operasyonlarina-ya klasimimiz-ve-katkilarimiz.tr.mfa.

MFA (Ministry of Foreign Affairs). 2020b. "Turkey-Africa: Solidarity and Partnership." http://www.mfa.gov.tr/turkey_africa_-solidarity-and-partnership.en.mfa.

Milliyet. 1993a "Love for Turks" (in Turkish). February 20, 1993. http://gazetearsivi.milliyet.com.tr/Ara.aspx?araKelime=somali%20erdal%20inonu&isAdv=false.

Milliyet. 1993b. "Are We Going to Stay in This Hell (in Turkish)?" October 13, 1993. http://gazetearsivi.milliyet.com.tr/GununYayinlari/bXEMy9yFf_x2F_TFmoBr1Fp7Wg_x3D__x3D_.

Milliyet. 1994. "Turkish Soldiers are Counting Days (in Turkish)." December 12, 1994. http://gazetearsivi.milliyet.com.tr/GununYayinlari/KsDc5fT4BMlxmfZ6yfwuwg_x3D__x3D_.

Oguzlu, H. Tarik and Ugur Gungor. 2006. "Peace Operations and the Transformation of Turkey's Security Policy." *Contemporary Security Policy* 27, no. 3: 472–488. https://doi.org/10.1080/13523260601060388.

Pang, Zhongying. 2005. "China's Changing Attitude to UN Peacekeeping." *International Peacekeeping* 12, no. 1: 87–104. https://doi.org/10.1080/1353331042000286597.
Parlar Dal, Emel. 2018a. "Rising Powers in International Conflict Management: An Introduction." *Third World Quarterly* 39, no. 12: 2207–2221. https://doi.org/10.1080/01436597.2018.1503048.
Parlar Dal, Emel. 2018b. "UN's New Peacekeeping Action and Turkey's Reaction." Anadolu Ajansi, October 2, 2018. https://www.aa.com.tr/tr/analiz-haber/bm-nin-yeni-barisi-koruma-aksiyonu-ve-turkiye-nin-yaklasimi/1270583.
Radikal. 2014. "This Issue Cannot be Resolved Without a Ground Operation (in Turkish)." October 7, 2014. http://www.radikal.com.tr/politika/kara-harekti-olmadan-bu-is-cozulmez-1217413/.
Satana, Nil. 2012. "Peacekeeping Contributor Profile: Turkey." Providing for Peacekeeping. http://www.providingforpeacekeeping.org/2014/04/03/contributor-profile-turkey/.
TBMM. 1992. Tutanaklar. December 8, 1992. Session no. 36. https://www.tbmm.gov.tr/tutanaklar/TUTANAK/TBMM/d19/c022/tbmm19022036.pdf.
TBMM. 1993. Tutanaklar. October 26, 1992. Session no. 20. https://www.tbmm.gov.tr/tutanaklar/TUTANAK/TBMM/d19/c042/tbmm19042020.pdf.
TBMM. 2006. Tutanaklar. June 27, 2006. Session no. 120. https://www.tbmm.gov.tr/tutanaklar/TUTANAK/TBMM/d22/c125/tbmm22125120.pdf.
TBMM. 2014. Tutanaklar. November 20, 2014. Session no. 17. https://www.tbmm.gov.tr/tutanaklar/TUTANAK/TBMM/d24/c092/tbmm24092017.pdf.
TBMM. 2016. Tutanaklar. August 2, 2016. Session no. 121. https://www.tbmm.gov.tr/tutanaklar/TUTANAK/TBMM/d26/c022/tbmm26022121.pdf.
TBMM. 2017. Tutanaklar. July 17, 2017. Session no. 112. https://www.tbmm.gov.tr/tutanaklar/TUTANAK/TBMM/d26/c048/tbmm26048112.pdf.
Teitt, Sarah. 2011. "The Responsibility to Protect and China's Peacekeeping Policy." *International Peacekeeping* 18, no. 3: 298–312. https://doi.org/10.1080/13533312.2011.563085.
Torfing, Jacob. 1999. *New Theories of Discourse: Laclau, Mouffe, and Zizek*, Oxford: Blackwell.
Torfing, Jacob. 2005. "Discourse Theory: Achievements, Arguments and Challenges." In *Discourse Theory in European Politics: Politics, Identity, Policy and Governance*, edited by David Howarth and Jacob Torfing, 1–31. London: Palgrave. doi:10.1057/9780230523364.
TRT Haber. 2015. "Turkish Armed Forces are Always Ready for the Training of the PK Troops." 29 September, 2015. https://www.trthaber.com/haber/gundem/tsk-baris-gucu-askerlerinin-egitimi-icin-her-zaman-hazir-205884.html.
Turkish Armed Forces. 2020. "Turkey's Contributions to the PKO." https://www.tsk.tr/Sayfalar?viewName=BarisiDestekleme.
UNPK. 2020a. "Summary of Troops Contributing Countries by Ranking: Police, UN Military Experts on Mission, Staff Officers and Troops." https://peacekeeping.un.org/sites/default/files/02_country_ranking_28.pdf.
UNPK. 2020b. "Summary of Contribution to UN Peacekeeping by Country, Mission and Post: Police, UN Military Experts on Mission, Staff Officers and Troops 31/08/2020." https://peacekeeping.un.org/sites/default/files/03_country_and_mission_28.pdf.
UNPK. 2020c. "Summary of Military and Police Personnel by Mission and Posts: Police, UN Military Experts on Mission, Staff Officers and Troop 31/08/2020." https://peacekeeping.un.org/sites/default/files/06_mission_and_post_28.pdf.

Weiss, Thomas G. and Giovanna Kuele. 2019. "The Global South and UN Peace Operations." E-International Relations. https://www.e-ir.info/2019/02/03/the-global-south-and-un-peace-operations/.

Yalcinkaya, Haldun, Emre Hatipoglu, Dilaver Arıkan Acar and Mitat Celikpala. 2018. "Turkish Efforts in Peacekeeping and the Introduction of the TUBAKOV Dataset." *International Peacekeeping*, 25, no. 4: 475–496.

Part 3
Turkey's soft power

9 "The voice of the voiceless"
Turkey's public diplomacy in Africa

Senem B. Çevik

Introduction

Although Turkey and the African continent share an extensive and complex history predating the establishment of the Turkish Republic, Turkey's most notable interest in Africa began with the Africa Opening Plan in 1998. The turning point in relations between Turkey and African states was in 2005 with the announcement of The Year of Africa under the *Adalet ve Kalkinma Partisi* (Justice and Development Party, JDP/AKP; Donelli and Levaggi 2016). Elements of Turkish soft power such as image management, cultural diplomacy, educational exchanges and developmental assistance were integrated into the Africa opening to ensure successful relations (Wheeler 2011). Since the implementation of the Africa opening plan, there has been a gradual increase in relations with African states on economic, political and cultural fronts (Tepeciklioglu, Tok and Basher 2017). These various elements of Turkish soft power are part and parcel of Turkey's global aspirations and its efforts to situate itself among rising powers. Thus, it is rooted in Turkey's interest in being a more influential actor in global politics. Turkey has significantly invested in multiple avenues of outreach in the African continent. Although the country's engagement with Africa does not compare to the efforts of more prominent actors such as China, it is considered among newest actors.

As the cornerstone of Turkey's proactive foreign policy, Turkey's engagement particularly with Sub-Saharan African states received noteworthy attention within Turkey and has been covered extensively in academic literature (Ozkan 2011; Ipek 2014). However, there has been limited research on Turkey's public diplomacy in Africa. Particularly, the impact of the AKP–Gulen movement split has not received significant attention, in part due to the Gulen movement's contested nature in Turkey and academic self-censorship.[1]

This chapter aims to contribute to the existing literature on Turkey's engagement with Africa by introducing a public diplomacy layer. It aims to investigate Turkey's public diplomacy toolkit in Africa with an emphasis on cultural, educational exchanges and broadcasting. The chapter looks at whether Turkey's 1998 Africa Opening Plan, thus its aspirations to be a rising power, is actualized through its public diplomacy initiatives and in what ways the Gulen–AKP coalition as well as the split shaped its public diplomacy practice.

New regions, new horizons: Roots and motivations in Turkey's Africa outreach

Turkey is a relatively new actor in its institutionalized public diplomacy practice. Public diplomacy, the craft of engaging with foreign publics, is integral to foreign policy and has found fertile ground in the foreign policies of emerging powers. There are a number of intertwined drivers behind Turkey's growing interest in public diplomacy which have shaped Turkey's public diplomacy activities in Africa.

First, Turkey's budding economy in the second half of the 2000s, has enabled her to establish new institutions for her foreign outreach (Atli 2011; Kirisci 2011; Parlar Dal and Dipama 2020). Together with the economic prosperity, Turkey invested in establishing various state institutions undertaking educational exchanges, international broadcasting, advocacy and cultural diplomacy (Sancar 2015). For example, the Yunus Emre Institute (YEE) and Presidency for Turks Abroad and Related Communities (YTB) were established during this time to serve Turkey's public diplomacy apparatus. Furthermore, business groups dubbed as Anatolian Tigers became prominent conveyors of Turkey's newly found ambitions. Particularly, the Gulen-affiliated Turkish Confederation of Businessmen and Industrialists (TUSKON) and Independent Industrialists' and Businessmen's Association (MUSIAD) with close ties to the AKP paved the way for Turkey's relations with Africa (Cevik 2015). Consequently, Turkey's relative economic progress prompted the expansion of its diplomatic presence in Africa, while the expansion of air travel routes on Turkish Airlines (THY) have contributed to Turkey's soft power capacity (Selcuk 2013).

Second, Turkey's new foreign policy vision laid the groundwork of its public diplomacy toolkit (Arkan and Kinacioglu 2016). Ahmet Davutoglu, during his tenure as minister of foreign affairs kickstarted Turkey's public diplomacy efforts as a systematic approach to foreign policy. His strategic depth vision, a policy approach that draws from Turkey's historical, geographical and cultural ties to former Ottoman territories served as a blueprint to establish public diplomacy as a new approach for Turkey's global engagement (Davutoglu 2012, 2013; Murinson 2006; Ozkan 2014).[2] Subsequently, cultural affinity with Central Asia and the Balkans has been an important factor in reaching out to those areas (Sevin 2017). In addition to Turkey's natural geographical vicinity, Africa became a focal point in Turkey's engagement. The Ottoman heritage in Yemen, Sudan, Somalia, Eritrea and parts of North Africa has been the anchor for Turkey–Africa relations. Although diplomatic relations with these countries were well established, public diplomacy level engagement was still lacking. Therefore, the AKP government under Recep

Tayyip Erdogan and Davutoglu unofficially assigned Turkey's public diplomacy to the Gulen network, their political ally at the time. The Gulenist schools, trade unions, their cultural organizations and think tanks were major components of establishing Turkey's international communication network and creating long-lasting relationships across the globe. Africa constituted a significant part of that relationship where the Gulen network was well established. Gulen-affiliated organizations such as its trade network TUSKON, humanitarian aid organization *Kimse Yok Mu?* and numerous charter schools in the region became semi-official representatives of Turkey on the ground. The Gulen network had established an exclusive channel of communication with local authorities over years of being active in Africa, which was very convenient for the Turkish authorities. In this respect, Turkey's economic prosperity and foreign policy outlook were intertwined with the Gulen network and its organizations, which in turn facilitated state organizations to expand their presence in Africa. Turkey's foreign policy in Africa was accompanied by the expansion of new Turkish Airlines destinations through which the flagship carrier became Turkey's leading global brand (please see Chapter 12 by Selcuk in this volume). An important layer of Turkey's public diplomacy in Africa is Turkey's global and regional ambitions. Turkey's aspiration to be a rising power, to be considered amongst the league of emerging powers, was stimulated by its economic progress in the mid-2000s. This aspiration, weaved into its foreign policy doctrine, was initially facilitated by numerous foreign and humanitarian aid initiatives particularly in the former Ottoman provinces in Africa. Most notable of these, is Turkey's efforts in rebuilding Somalia with the help of state and non-state actors. By way of rebuilding Somalia, Turkey is not only establishing grassroots relations with the Somali public but also crafting its nation brand as a humanitarian actor (Cevik and Sevin 2017). Turkey's humanitarianism in the African continent pertains to both its actions and discourse. In this respect, Turkey's aspirations to become a rising power serve as a platform to galvanize its nation brand in both domestic and international dimensions.

Third, the AKP–Gulen split starting in 2013 and the coup attempt in July 2016 have proven to be critical thresholds for Turkey's public diplomacy in Africa. The African continent has been a battlefield for Turkey's public diplomacy owing to the extensive power the Gulen network has had in Africa. The fallout of former political allies unearthed the lack of state resources invested in public diplomacy. The AKP government's gradual disenchantment with the Gulen network created a vacuum in Turkey's global outreach. This alarming revelation encouraged decision makers to adopt new strategies and establish new organizations to revamp Turkey's public diplomacy apparatus. The establishment of TRT World in 2015, the Maarif Foundation in mid-2016 and TRT Swahili in 2020 characterize the post-Gulen era. The coup attempt involving a group of fringe military personnel was the last straw in the AKP–Gulen split. Although the details of the failed coup attempt are still unclear to this day, the state of Turkey considers the

Gulen network as the sole responsible party and has immediately classified its one-time ally as a terrorist organization. The coup attempt, which many critics argue was conducted by a multitude of stakeholders, was successfully thwarted by the government and people of Turkey. Nevertheless, the coup attempt catalyzed the government's approach in reactive public diplomacy. Following the coup attempt, the Turkish government engaged informing foreign publics with various activities in regard to the Gulen network and their role in the coup attempt. Since 2016, Turkey has invested more heavily in building its own public diplomacy infrastructure, strengthening those that already exist and engaging in a communication offense. The coup attempt reframed Turkey's public diplomacy efforts as a reactive stance where Turkey emphasized advocacy in order to combat negative news flow about Turkey and shape public opinion in favor of its government. In addition to numerous advocacy-based public diplomacy such as websites, print and online publications in multiple languages Turkey also utilized its international broadcasting. TRT World and Anadolu Agency are two avenues Turkey utilized more strategically after the coup attempt in aims to curb the influence of the Gulen network. Simultaneously, Turkey invested in long-term public diplomacy via expanding the network of Maarif Foundation schools. Today, Turkey employs both long-term and short-term public diplomacy strategies in its outreach to Africa.

To conclude, the objectives and strategy of Turkey's public diplomacy in Africa have changed in the last decade. Previously aimed at expanding its sphere of influence, Turkey's more recent goal has been explaining its message to shape public opinion. The cumulative economic and political drivers of Turkey's public diplomacy have prompted the establishment of institutions emphasizing cultural and educational exchanges with regions of strategic importance to Turkey. For example, YEE, Turkey's own version of cultural foundations and YTB, Turkey's diaspora agency are byproducts of this former era. Endeavors during the strategic depth/zero problems era underscored Turkey's relations with its immediate region and aimed to make Turkey more appealing as a role model in the Middle East and beyond. On the other hand, Turkey's public diplomacy in Africa following the AKP–Gulen fallout initially shifted its public diplomacy angle towards an information-based approach. Then, Turkey gradually balanced those initiatives with long-term relationship building efforts through educational and cultural exchanges.

Public diplomacy engagement in Africa

A growing number of researches examine Turkey's broader public diplomacy practice situating these initiatives within Turkey's foreign policy framework. However, only a few address public diplomacy as part of Turkey's Africa engagement (Sevin 2017; Cevik 2015). None of these compilations specifically addresses Turkey's public diplomacy in Africa. Eyrice Tepeciklioglu,

Tepeciklioglu and Unal (2018) describe Turkey's public diplomacy in sub-Saharan Africa looking at various cultural initiatives. Nonetheless, the authors omit the apparent Gulen–AKP split, which is a noteworthy factor in the way Turkey's public diplomacy has shifted. This chapter furthers existing discussions on Turkey's public diplomacy in Africa investigating Turkey's cultural, educational and international broadcasting initiatives under the consecutive AKP governments. In doing so, it will examine the dramatic shift of Turkey's public diplomacy in Africa from proactive to reactive public diplomacy.

Cultural exchanges

Public diplomacy scholar and historian Nick Cull (2019, 5) describes cultural diplomacy as "an actor's attempt to manage the international environment through facilitating the export of an element of that actor's life, belief or art." Cultural exchange, on the other hand, puts an emphasis on mutual learning, which can be facilitated through cultural capacity building, cultural information and cultural dialogue (Cull 2019). Cultural exchanges are critical in Turkey's public diplomacy in Africa whether to maintain existing relations or to establish new ones. Prior to the government restructuring, the Prime Ministry Office of Public Diplomacy served as a hub for Turkey's cultural exchanges. Facilitating journalist, youth and diplomat exchanges, the Directorate of Public Diplomacy laid the groundwork for Turkey's official public diplomacy. Despite its novel efforts, the Directorate of Public Diplomacy was a short-lived endeavor and became engulfed in Turkey's systemic changes. Currently, the Directorate of Communications under the Presidency undertakes some of the initiatives of the Directorate of Public Diplomacy such as professional exchanges.

The YEE is Turkey's leading cultural diplomacy actor established in 2007. A partner in the Global PDNet, YEE oversees cultural exchanges such as concerts, calligraphy workshops, film festivals and various art classes (Yunus Emre Institute n.d.). It operates in 47 offices around the globe and is gradually expanding in regions that are critical to Turkey's interests. These local cultural centers, akin to that of the British Council or Goethe Institute, offer language courses as well as cultural activities. Bringing students across the globe for Turkish Summer School, a month-long program in intensive Turkish classes in Turkey, YEE aims to build bridges with students from different parts of the world by providing a platform for experiential and cultural exchanges.

The YEE has eight cultural centers in Africa as of 2020, which have been expanding its presence since 2010 with the establishment of its first center in Cairo, Egypt. The inauguration of Yunus Emre Cultural Centers in Rabat, Morocco (2013) and Algiers, Algeria (2013) correspond with Turkey's growing interest in Africa. Cultural centers in Khartoum, Sudan (2016), Mogadishu, Somalia (2016), Johannesburg, South Africa, Tunis, Tunisia (2017)

Table 9.1 Yunus Emre Cultural Centers in Africa

City	Year opened
Cairo	2010
Rabat	2013
Algiers	2013
Khartoum	2016
Mogadishu	2016
Johannesburg	2017
Tunis	2017
Dakar	2020

Source: Compiled from Yunus Emre Institute website, https://www.yee.org.tr.

and Dakar, Senegal (2020) reflect Turkey's efforts in countering the Gulen network's public diplomacy. These cultural centers promote the Turkish culture by way of language courses, film festivals, movie screenings, art and craft events and sponsoring college-level Turkish programs. They are in effect Turkey's window to these countries. Given Turkey's interest in Africa and the existing conflict with the Gulen network, the YEE Cultural Centers are vital cultural avenues to influence foreign publics in favor of Turkish culture. However, YEE does not have offices in countries with relatively high trade and political engagement such as Nigeria, Ethiopia, Ghana, Kenya and Tanzania. This track record indicates that with the exception of South Africa, a country with which Turkey historically has high trade volume, YEE opened cultural centers in majority Muslim nations. The current scope of YEE cultural centers underscores Turkey's heightened engagement with the global Muslim community and its utilization of religion in its foreign policy orientation (see Chapter 11 by Eyrice Tepeciklioglu in this volume). In this respect, although Turkey's cultural exchanges in Africa accompany its public diplomacy apparatus, the narrow geographical scope of the YEE cultural centers poses a limitation to its aspiration to be a rising power in Africa (Table 9.1).

Educational exchanges

Educational exchanges are the foundation of relationship building that relies on the process of teaching the culture through lived experiences. This way, the knowledge acquired is internalized by the participant and a personal bond is created on the basis of this experience (Cull 2019). It is expected that educational exchanges render positive outcomes following a satisfactory experience. This is not always the case, especially under circumstances in which the exchange is a humiliating experience or feels like an unwelcoming one. With the hope to create favorable experiences to shape positive public opinion of Turkey, the state has created a number of programs for international students, Turkey's diaspora communities and Turks wanting to study abroad. Although Turkey has long been part of other international exchanges such as ERASMUS and Fulbright, the Turkish state discovered the merits of educational exchanges along with the establishment of Turkic states after the fall of the Soviet Union (Sancar 2015). While there have been programs to invite students from these newly independent states, Turkey did not have a holistic approach when it came to new regions such as Africa and Latin America. Although Turkey has programs for professional exchanges such as diplomat and journalist trainings as well as youth exchanges, this chapter focuses on higher education exchanges. The YTB, established in 2010, launched the *Turkiye Burslari* (Turkey Scholarships) program in 2012 to foster international student mobility to Turkey. While there were scholarships available for international students under bilateral agreements going back to the 1960s, Turkiye Scholarships is the most comprehensive scholarship program funded by the Turkish state. The undergraduate programs of Turkiye Scholarships are aimed at students in the affinity regions (The Balkans, Middle East, Caucasus, Central Asia) and Africa (Turkiye Scholarships n.d.). This program aims to build relationships and at the same time create networks of future leaders in developing nations who will gain appreciation for Turkey through their experiences as exchange students. In the pre-Gulen fallout, the Gulen network offered scholarships to African countries training them in Gulen-affiliated universities such as Fatih University, then sending the graduates back to their home countries as future leaders. In essence, the Turkish state needed to counter the Gulen influence in Africa. Turkiye Scholarships has become an important vehicle to facilitate that transition. The YTB's Turkish government scholarship program contributes to the diffusion of Turkish culture and improvement of credibility of Turkey amongst the participants of the program (Aras and Mohammed 2019).

Based on the data gathered from official statistics during the consecutive AKP governments, Turkey hosted a growing number of students from African states, significantly students from Somalia, who consist of an overwhelming majority of the students enrolled in Turkish universities. Mostly Muslim majority countries such as Egypt, Libya, Nigeria, Morocco, Cameroon and Sudan follow Somalia. These statistics indicate that there has been a significant increase, more than threefold, since 2013 and a major rise in 2018. An increase in the number of students choosing to study in Turkey is a positive factor in improving relations between the host country and guests. However, whether these exchanges can create meaningful interactions to render positive outcomes, in other words favorable public opinion about Turkey, is rather questionable. Inadequate knowledge and interaction with Africans in Turkey results in stereotypes and biases. Where universities are expected to offer cultural engagement, this reality can in fact undermine Turkey's efforts in utilizing educational exchanges to build long-term relations with African students (Figure 9.1).

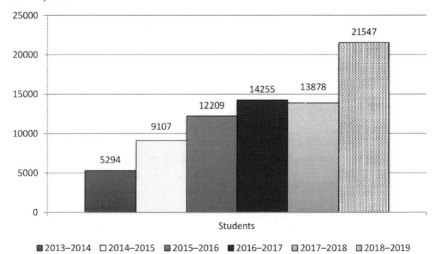

Figure 9.1 International students from Africa
Source: Compiled from Turkish Higher Educational Council Statistics, https://ista tistik.yok.gov.tr.

A fairly new development in Turkey's educational exchanges is the establishment of The Turkish Maarif Foundation (TMF) in order to curb the influence of the Gulenist network in Africa and Central Asia (Turkiye Maarif Foundation n.d.).[3] Maarif Schools are private schools run by the Turkish government. The Maarif Foundation's motto "Our aim is to raise goodwilled people around the world" conveniently overlaps with Turkey's self-acclaimed role as a value-oriented, benevolent nation (Maarif Foundation Board of Trustees).[4] Prior to the establishment of the Maarif Foundation, there were a large number of Gulen network-affiliated schools in several African countries.[5] These schools educate the elite of the countries they operate in. Immediately after the establishment of the Maarif Foundation, with the efforts of President Erdogan, Turkey convinced several of these African states to shut down or hand over Gulen-affiliated private schools (Czerep 2019). As of 2020, there are 143 Maarif Foundation Schools and 16 dormitories across Africa. Nonetheless, the efforts of the Turkish government to persuade African governments to hand over Gulenist schools have not been very successful given the political connections Gulenists established with local figures. Moreover, Turkey's vacillating approach towards the Gulenist network in Africa over the years has created a contradiction about the credibility of its argument (Table 9.2).

International broadcasting

States have traditionally sought control over information as they competed for global power and were in need of avenues to express stories from their

Table 9.2 Maarif Foundation Schools in Africa

Country	School	Dormitory
Burundi	2	N/A
Djibouti	2	N/A
Chad	6	1
Equatorial Guinea	4	N/A
Ethiopia	4	1
Ivory Coast	4	N/A
Gabon	4	N/A
Gambia	3	N/A
Ghana	1	N/A
Guinea	10	2
Cameroon	14	4
Congo	4	N/A
DRC	4	N/A
Madagascar	3	N/A
Mali	21	N/A
Mauritania	9	N/A
Niger	10	2
Senegal	13	N/A
Sierra Leone	2	N/A
Somalia	7	3
Tanzania	6	2
Tunisia	4	1
Total	137	

Source: Compiled from Turkiye Maarif Vakfi, https://turkiyemaarif.org/page/42-dunyada-tmv-16.

perspective. Control over information has historically been advantageous to nations as was the case during the height of the British Empire. Flow and spread of information became even more important in the competition to shape public opinion during the two world wars. The pivotal role of public opinion in global affairs has ushered dominant world powers to invest in communication technologies, in particular broadcasting. International broadcasting is state-sponsored media relying on journalism and information to both inform foreign audiences and promote goodwill to the sponsoring countries (Powers and Youmans 2012). Cull (2019) argues that international broadcasting has a role in advocacy, cultural diplomacy and exchanges. State-sponsored news is one avenue of international broadcasting, which has been mastered by broadcasters such as the BBC World Service, Voice of America and Deutsche Welle. These broadcasters, attached to the twentieth century's great powers are currently challenged by newcomers such as China's CCTV, Russia's Russia Today or Qatar's Al Jazeera.

Turkey is certainly not new to international broadcasting and is aiming to shape public opinion by way of its communication outlets. The Anadolu Ajansi (Anadolu Agency/AA), Turkey's national press agency, was established in 1920 to broadcast Turkey's voice in the international arena. Similar to its counterparts, Associated Press and Reuters, the Anadolu Agency was established with the intention to influence domestic and international public opinion in favor of the Turkish War of Independence. The AA helped announce the first legislation by the Turkish parliament and inform the world about Turkey's defense against occupation. Therefore, the AA has been integral to the establishment and international recognition of the Republic of Turkey (Anadolu Agency n.d.). Turkey's recent security concerns pertaining to the threat from the Gulenist network (designated as FETO by the Turkish state) and threats from PKK/YPG terror organizations paved the way for the restructuring of the AA.

Given the acute crises and the pressing need to share Turkey's position on key issues, Turkey launched an aggressive campaign to redesign its international broadcasting structure following the failed coup attempt and recurring attacks from PKK/YPG. In the past few years, AA has expanded its base in new regions and diversified the number of languages in which it covers news. Operating in 31 countries, the Anadolu Agency expanded its news services in 13 languages. This newly gained vision is integral to Turkey's public diplomacy, in particular to its relations with Turkey's regional proximity and to sharing Turkey's perspective with the rest of the world (Sancar 2015). The AA is also active in the digital sphere by posting infographics, news snippets and news photos on social media platforms. Turkey's expansion into the international broadcasting market accelerated in the aftermath of the fallout between the Gulen network and the government. The failed coup attempt and Turkey's difficulties in its foreign affairs gave an impetus for Turkey to put an emphasis on international broadcasting. Anadolu Agency's outreach in Africa has expanded to 15 local offices in the region and 13 global languages reporting from the ground. AA's network in Africa allows viewers to get a genuine perspective, presenting news directly from the ground. In addition to having local reports and offices, AA's services in English and French are two platforms for Turkey's outreach in Africa (Table 9.3).

TRT, Turkey's public broadcaster, was established in 1964 and its first international office was established in Berlin in 1998. TRT opened its offices in Cairo, Egypt in 2000. TRT's multilingual news website www.trtvotworld.com now operates in 41 languages since its establishment in 2008. TRT Hausa, Swahili, Arabic, French and Portuguese are news websites that cater to various African nations. TRT-ETTURKİYE was launched in 2010 and started to operate under TRT-El Arabiya in 2015. Turkey's most recent broadcasting avenue, TRT World was established as a result of these developments as part of Turkey's English language public broadcasting network. TRT World is an English language 24-hour news channel based in Istanbul, Turkey with the aim to provide new perspectives on world events (TRT

Table 9.3 Anadolu Agency in Africa

City/country	Broadcast studio	Representative	Offices
Addis Ababa	x	N/A	N/A
Abuja	N/A	N/A	x
Cairo	N/A	N/A	x
Rabat	N/A	N/A	x
Khartoum	N/A	N/A	x
Mogadishu	N/A	N/A	x
Johannesburg	N/A	N/A	x
Algeria	N/A	x	N/A
South Africa	N/A	x	N/A
Kenya	N/A	x	N/A
Libya	N/A	x	N/A
Nigeria	N/A	x	N/A
Somalia	N/A	x	N/A
Yemen	N/A	x	N/A
Tunis	x	N/A	N/A

Source: Compiled from AA Yurt Dışı Bürolar, https://www.aa.com.tr/tr/p/yurt-disi-burolar.

World n.d.). TRT World's angle in offering new perspectives particularly relates to the way Africa is covered in the news by mainstream news outlets. TRT World and TRT news websites try to offer an unbiased take on issues related to Africa, with efforts to remedy the mostly unfavorable representation the continent receives in Western news outlets.

Turkey's efforts in international broadcasting have expanded significantly after 2000. The current vast network in multiple languages and channels enables Turkey to connect and communicate with African communities. Although research on whether these news outlets have an actual audience in Africa does not exist, Turkey's attempts to launch programs geared towards Africa, presenting news from the ground complements Turkey's ambitions to become a rising power.

Conclusion

Despite being relatively new to the practice, Turkey has a diverse public diplomacy toolkit. Turkey places more emphasis on advocacy, cultural diplomacy, educational exchanges and international broadcasting rather than listening.[6] Within Turkey's public diplomacy apparatus geared towards Africa, listening constitutes the least weight where in fact an elaborate listening could prove beneficial in terms of Turkey's rising power ambitions. Without detailed studies of African perception of Turkey's public diplomacy efforts, these initiatives run the risk of falling on deaf ears. This is a major drawback of Turkey's public diplomacy in Africa. Other factors that hamper Turkey's engagement with Africa are the *Erdoganization* of the public diplomacy apparatus and an emphasis on Muslim religious kinship. The institutions spearheading Turkey's public diplomacy initiatives have strong political affiliations with the AKP government and President Erdogan. Therefore, oftentimes Turkey's public diplomacy is conducted on behalf of AKP and President Erdogan's office rather than the state of Turkey.

Turkey's transition into a presidential system in 2018 resulting in a mass power grab by the presidential seat further strengthened ties between institutions and their allegiance to the leadership. President Erdogan currently represents the state and the government. As a result, Turkey's public diplomacy has a dual agenda to advocate *Erdoganism* and promote Turkey in Erdogan's image. Turkey's public diplomacy structure is therefore centralized within the president's office. Political allies and associates enabling the aforementioned dual agenda occupy many seats that oversee Turkey's public diplomacy. As a result, Turkey's public diplomacy overall has an important domestic agenda to promote Turkey's initiatives domestically in efforts to rally pro-AKP supporters. Consequently, the discourse about Turkey's public diplomacy in Africa, in other words communication about public diplomacy, is integral to Turkey's engagement in Africa. President Erdogan's manifestation that Turkey is "the voice of the voiceless in Africa" derives from the idea that Turkey is a values-driven state aiming to be the custodian of moral conduct towards people.

The interweaved mechanism of party politics and public diplomacy actors introduces a strong domestic dimension to Turkey's public diplomacy. This means, Turkey's public diplomacy actors and institutions are prone to Turkey's domestic developments whether it be a clash between different political groups or ideologies. For example, Turkey's post-2013 public diplomacy has an important layer of agenda setting given the fallout with the Gulen movement.

Particularly, Davutoglu's departure from office and the permanent crisis mode in Turkey resulted in a de-emphasis on soft power and an emphasis on disseminating information. In this regard, current public diplomacy, particularly the 2016 post-coup attempt, reflects a shift to a more situational and reactive communication structure that is grounded in crisis communication. Turkey's public diplomacy in broadcasting and advocacy is a reflection of public affairs that is shaped by the domestic dimension.

Following the fallout between the AKP government and the Gulen movement, Turkey lost its access to various communities in the world, particularly in Central Asia, South Eastern Europe, Africa and the United States (Ozturk 2017). This significant loss has been shaping Turkey's public diplomacy in Africa. Since 2016, has Turkey invested heavily in three areas to curb the Gulen movement's access: educational exchanges, cultural diplomacy and international broadcasting.

Although Turkey's pre-coup and post-coup public diplomacy differ in strategy, they both address the 1998 Africa opening and are anchored in

Turkey's ambitions to become a rising power. In this respect, engagement with Africa by way of scholarships and cultural exchanges builds bridges between Turkey and Africa. Simultaneously, Turkey's efforts in international broadcasting highlight Turkey's narrative and take on global events. Nonetheless, there are uncertainties about Turkey's public diplomacy capacity in Africa given its volatile economy, lack of qualified human resources and more importantly, a lack of long-term public diplomacy strategy.

Notes

1 Fethullah Gulen is a self-exiled Turkish Islamic clergyman who has a vast support network of followers across the globe, particularly in African countries, which has helped Turkey to open up to new markets. His network in Turkey was in a de facto political alliance in the early stages of AKP rule, however their diverging political stance on several key issues caused a gradual fallout resulting in a conflict in 2013. The government of Turkey accuses Gulen followers of inciting the coup attempt and has designated it as a terrorist organization. Many of the top-level Gulen supporters have left Turkey while others remaining have been prosecuted or purged.
2 Ahmet Davutoglu is the former chief foreign policy advisor to then Prime Minister Erdogan (2002–2009), former Minister of Foreign Affairs (2009–2014) and former Prime Minister (2014–2016) serving under consecutive AKP governments. As the Minister of Foreign Affairs, he led Turkey's foreign policy by his zero-problems policy and strategic depth doctrine, two frameworks he introduced in his previous academic work. The strategic depth doctrine, situated Turkey as a regional power, a center country, and an order instituting country building on humanitarian responsibility, including that of foreign aid. Thus, Turkish policymakers, led by Davutoglu, have argued that Turkey's foreign policy was grounded in moral values and that it drew on historical responsibility. Based on this doctrine, Turkey undertakes a strategic role in the global Muslim community and acts as a protector of Muslim nations. Therefore, an underlying reason for Turkey's foreign policy activism and public diplomacy towards the Ottoman territory has certain ideological roots.
3 The Gulenist network has hundreds of affiliated K-12 and college level-institutions. Following the coup attempt in 2016, the Turkish state initiated negotiations with numerous countries in Africa, Central Asia and the Balkans to hand over the administration of Gulen-affiliated schools to the TMF. This demand by the Turkish government has caused a rift between some African states and Turkey. To this day, TMF has been able to take over only a fraction of Gulen-affiliated schools.
4 Please see the message from the Chairman of the Board of Trustees: https://turkiyemaarif.org/page/65-board-of-trustees-5, accessed on April 21, 2018.
5 Based on his field research, David Shinn argues the number of Gulen-affiliated schools in 2015 was approximately 96 (Shinn 2015). Due to the Gulen movement's shadowy and inexplicit organization structure, it is not possible to know the exact number of schools.
6 I did not include listening as a component of Turkey's public diplomacy due to the very limited amount of public opinion polling and public diplomacy evaluations. However, Turkey's network of state institutions in the Middle East, Balkans and Central Asia are performing better in taking cultural variables into consideration before designing public diplomacy initiatives.

References

Anadolu Agency. n.d. "History." Accessed August 23, 2020. https://www.aa.com.tr/en/p/history.

Aras, Bulent and Zulkarnain Mohammed. 2019. "The Turkish Government Scholarship as a Soft Power Tool." *Turkish Studies* 20, no. 3: 421–441. https://doi.org/10.1080/14683849.2018.1502042.

Arkan, Zeynep and Muge Kinacioglu. 2016. "Enabling Ambitious Activism: Davutoglu's Vision of a New Foreign Policy Identity for Turkey." *Turkish Studies* 17, no. 3: 381–405. https://doi.org/10.1080/14683849.2016.1185943.

Atli, Altay. 2011. "Businessmen as Diplomats: The Role of Business Associations in Turkey's Foreign Economic Policy." *Insight Turkey* 13, no. 1: 109–128.

Cevik, B. Senem. 2015. "The Benefactor: NGOs and Humanitarian Aid." In *Turkey's Public Diplomacy*, edited by B. Senem Cevik and Philip Seib, 121–152. New York, Basingstoke: Palgrave Macmillan.

Cevik, Senem and Efe Sevin. 2017. "A Quest for Turkey's Soft Power: Turkey and the Syrian Refugee Crisis." *Journal of Communication Management* 21, no: 4: 399–410.

Cull, Nicholas J. 2019. *Public Diplomacy: Foundations for Global Engagement in the Digital Age*. Cambridge, UK and Medford, MA: Polity.

Czerep, Jedrzej. 2019. "Turkey's Soft Power Crisis in Africa." The Polish Institute of International Affairs No 3 (173). https://www.pism.pl/file/74517028-14f5-4734-be9f-b294dcf4071f.

Davutoglu, Ahmet. 2012. "Principles of Turkish Foreign Policy and Regional Political Structuring." International Policy and Leadership Institute. SAM Vision Papers No 3. Ankara: Republic of Turkey MFA Center for Strategic Research. http://www.mfa.gov.tr/site_media/html/bakanmakale_tepev.pdf.

Davutoglu, Ahmet. 2013. "Turkey's Humanitarian Diplomacy: Objectives, Challenges and Prospects." *Nationalities Papers: The Journal of Nationalism and Ethnicity* 41, no. 6: 865–870. https://doi.org/10.1080/00905992.2013.857299.

Donelli, Federico and Ariel Gonzalez Levaggi. 2016. "Becoming Global Actor: The Turkish Agenda for the Global South." *Rising Powers Quarterly* 1, no. 2: 93–115.

Eyrice Tepeciklioglu, Elem, Ali Onur Tepeciklioglu and Betul Aydogan Unal. 2018. "Turkey's Public Diplomacy Initiatives in Sub-Saharan Africa." *Ege Academic Review* 18, no. 4: 605–618. doi:10.21121/eab.2018442990.

Eyrice Tepeciklioglu, Elem, M. Evren Tok, Syed Abul Basher. 2017. "Turkish and BRICS Engagement in Africa." *Journal of Sustainable Development Law and Policy* 8, no. 2: 48–66.

Ipek, Volkan. 2014. "The 2011 Landing of Turkey on Somalia: The State to People Aspect of Turkish Foreign Policy Towards Sub-Saharan Africa." *European Scientific Journal*, 412–428. https://doi.org/10.19044/esj.2014.v10n10p%25p

Kirisci, Kemal. 2011. "Turkey's Demonstrative Effect and the Transformation of the Middle East." *Insight Turkey* 13, no. 2: 33–55.

Murinson, Alexander. 2006. "The Strategic Depth Doctrine of Turkish Foreign Policy." *Middle Eastern Studies* 42, no. 6: 945–964. https://doi.org/10.1080/00263200600923526.

Ozturk, Ahmet Erdi. 2017. "Delectation or Hegemony: Turkey's Religious Actors in South Eastern Europe and Central Asia." *Euxeinox* 23: 15–24.

Ozkan, Behlul. 2014. "Turkey, Davutoglu and the Idea of Pan-Islamism" *Survival* 56 no. 4: 119–140. https://doi.org/10.1080/00396338.2014.941570.

Ozkan, Mehmet. 2011. "Turkey's 'New' Engagements in Africa and Asia: Scope, Content and Implications." *Perceptions* 16, no. 3: 115–137.

Parlar Dal, Emel and Samiratou Dipama. 2020. "Assessing the Turkish 'Trading State' in Sub-Saharan Africa." In *Turkey's Political Economy in the 21st Century*, edited by Emel Parlar Dal, 239–270. New York, Basingstoke: Palgrave Macmillan.

Powers, Shawn M. and Youmans William. 2012. "A New Purpose for International Broadcasting: Subsidizing Deliberative Technologies in Non-Transitioning States." *Journal of Public Deliberation* 8, no. 1, Article 13: 1–14.

Sancar, Gaye Asli. 2015. Turkey's Public Diplomacy: Its Actors, Stakeholders, and Tools. In *Turkey's Public Diplomacy*, edited by B. Senem Cevik and Philip Seib, 13–42. New York and Basingstoke: Palgrave Macmillan.

Selcuk, Orcun. 2013. "Turkish Airlines: Turkey's Soft Power Tool in the Middle East." *Akademik Ortadogu* 7, no. 2: 175–199.

Sevin, Efe. 2017. *Public Diplomacy and the Implementation of Foreign Policy in the U.S., Sweden and Turkey*. New York and Basingstoke: Palgrave Macmillan.

Shinn, David Hamilton. 2015. "Turkey's Engagement in Sub-Saharan Africa: Shifting Alliances and Strategic Diversification." *Chatham House*, 1–20. https://www.chathamhouse.org/sites/default/files/field/field_document/20150909TurkeySubSaharanAfricaShinn.pdf.

TRT World. n.d. "About Us." Accessed May 1, 2020. https://www.trtworld.com/about.

Turkiye Maarif Foundation. n.d. "TMF in the World." Accessed April 25, 2020. https://turkiyemaarif.org/page/42-tmf-worldwide-16.

Turkiye Scholarships. n.d. "Burs Programlari." Accessed April 25, 2020. https://www.ytb.gov.tr/en/international-students/turkey-scholarships.

Wheeler, Thomas. 2011. "Ankara to Africa: Turkey's Outreach since 2005." *South African Journal of International Affairs* 18, no. 1: 43–62.

Yunus Emre Institute. n.d. "About." Accessed April 25, 2020. http://www.yee.org.tr/en.

10 Turkey's development assistance in Africa in the 2000s

Hybrid humanitarianism in the post-liberal era

Gonca Oğuz Gök

Introduction

Africa has always been at the center of various actors' humanitarian efforts, including states, International Organizations (IOs) and Non-Governmental Organizations (NGOs) throughout its history. Foreign aid was earlier considered to be a strict flow of money and resources from the industrialized democratic Western states conceptualized as North to developing or underdeveloped states of the South in Africa. Since the 2000s, humanitarian efforts have been transforming as Western norms of market liberalism and democracy are in sharp decline. The weakening of liberal democracy is closely associated with major global shifts in the world order since the global financial crisis of 2008. The rising economic power of states from the Global South, such as China, India and Brazil, coincided with a period in which Western states' economic prosperity, financial resources and normative appeal have been in relative decline (Onis 2017). The popular ideas of post-Cold War neoliberal peace and multilateralism seem to be rapidly deteriorating while authoritarianism and populism is on the rise in almost all parts of the world.

Within the context of these structural transformations, the aid landscape has changed in the African continent with the rise of emerging powers from Asia and Latin America who are also becoming significant providers of foreign aid, especially in the 2000s (Tjønneland 2015). South–South cooperation has already become a new alternative model to the established North–South development cooperation in Africa (Sodenberg 2010). As Michael Barnett (2011) asserts, humanitarian efforts have become a "status symbol" for emerging powers in global politics. In this regard, Africa has become the main target of rising donors, searching for more substantial roles in global governance (Abdenur and Da Fonseca 2013). Accordingly, Official Development Assistance (ODA) levels have increasingly been used as a cooperative denominator for power and wealth as well as a status for states looking for more significant roles beyond their borders.[1] These emerging powers insist their aid is distinct in principle and practice from more traditional Western donors (Weiss and Abdenur 2014). Onis and Kutlay

(2020) define this new post-liberal area as the "age of hybridity," in which no overriding set of development paradigms or policies predominantly shape global governance.

Among other emerging powers, Turkey's rise is noteworthy. Turkish foreign policymakers also began to voice their willingness to actively engage in humanitarianism in different regions of the world during the 2000s, most notably in Africa. Accordingly, one of the defining aspects of Turkish foreign policy has become the increased role of development cooperation programs evidenced by an expanding international aid budget towards the continent. Ankara, increasingly labeled as a "donor country" with its ODA gradually reaching US$8.07 billion in 2018 ranked first in humanitarian aid, followed by the USA with US$6.68 billion, Germany with US$2.98 billion and the UK with US$2.52 billion whereas the EU ranked fifth with US$2.25 billion (Development Initiatives 2019).

Against this background, this chapter will critically engage with the rise of humanitarianism in Turkish foreign policy in the 2000s regarding its development cooperation activities towards Africa. Drawing on Michael Barnett's classification of "liberal humanitarianism," the paper will question how Turkey's development cooperation activities towards Africa in the 2000s fit into or diverge from the framework of liberal humanitarianism (Barnett 2011). In order to better engage with this question, the first part briefly summarizes the historical background of Turkey's humanitarianism towards Africa within Barnett's framework of the "ages of humanitarianism" (Barnett 2011). The second part will precisely focus on Turkey's development cooperation activities in Africa in the 2000s with specific reference to the nexus between government agencies and other humanitarian NGOs (HNGOs) in constructing Turkey's "donor state" identity. The third part will compare and contrast Turkey's development cooperation activities with those of traditional donors such as the EU and rising donors such as BRICS in order to depict any similarities as well as differences in Turkey's humanitarianism in the 2000s.

The paper argues that in terms of humanitarianism, one can talk about a new "post-liberal era" in the making shaped by systemic shifts in the last two decades, especially in the 2010s. Turkey's development cooperation activities in Africa could best be described as "hybrid humanitarianism" in the sense that it encompasses the aims, means and ends of both liberal humanitarianism and rising powers' emerging humanitarian efforts, yet also differs from both of them by its attempt to offer an alternative "Turkish aid model." Turkey's humanitarianism in Africa crosscuts political motives with humanitarian aims and is constructed upon civil society and state networks as well as the domestic and foreign policy nexus. Building on and departing from Barnett's widely acknowledged classification of the "ages of humanitarianism" (see Table 10.1), the paper attempts to provide a framework called "hybrid humanitarianism" in the new post-liberal era of the 2010s exemplified by the Turkish case towards Africa.

Framing Turkey's humanitarianism vis-à-vis Africa in the historical context

Humanitarianism is widely defined as "the impartial, independent, and neutral provision of relief to those in immediate danger of harm" (Barnett 2009). Barnett (2011) classifies the historical evolution as well as the transformation of humanitarianism in three phases, which he categorizes as "the ages of humanitarianism": (1) imperial humanitarianism (1800–1945), (2) neo-humanitarianism (1945–1990s), (3) liberal humanitarianism (post-Cold War era).

Turkey's relations with the African continent date back centuries. During the "imperial era" of humanitarianism, the Ottomans had good relations with the continent and, in fact, actively worked to "prevent the spread of colonialism" to Africa (Hazar 2017; see Chapter 2 by Palabiyik). With the Turkish Republic's establishment in 1923, there was not much manifestation of a humanitarian role towards Africa. Security and economic issues were at stake, and Ankara struggled hard to develop, secure and legitimize the new Turkish Republic both at home and abroad.

In the era of "neo-humanitarianism," which corresponds to the post-WWII era, security issues continued to be at stake. Economically, Turkey was defined as a developing country and development aid receiver. ODA to Turkey through the Marshall Plan helped it to lay the foundation for its economic development in the 1950s. Although Turkey transformed into a multiparty regime after 1945, its democratization was interrupted several times with no less than three military coups. However, with its willingness, Ankara became a part of the UN-led human rights regime and joined the European human rights regime by ratifying the European Convention on

Table 10.1 Ages of humanitarianism vis-à-vis Africa

	Ages	*Humanitarian efforts*
Imperial humanitarianism	1800–1945	Colonization, civilizing discourse, intervention, patriarchal.
Neo-humanitarianism	1945–1990	Growing role of IOs, UN, decolonization human rights regimes, NGOs, development project.
Liberal Humanitarianism	1990–2010	Humanitarianism transformed, intense NGOs–state nexus, governance, professionalization, and politicization of aid, humanitarian intervention and r2p.
Post-Liberal Humanitarianism	2010–	Declining democracy, rising authoritarianism, South–South cooperation, status competition over ODA, clash of development norms, hybrid humanitarianism.

Source: Drawing on Barnett's (2011) Classification of "Ages of Humanitarianism," this table is revised, adapted and structured by the author.

Human Rights and Fundamental Freedoms in 1954 (Turkmen 2007). In Africa, when the decolonization process accelerated in the 1960s, Turkey's relations with the continent remained limited. There was no manifestation of an adopted humanitarian role, mostly due to the above-mentioned domestic instabilities and security concerns of the Cold-War era (Ozkan 2012). Turkey's growing involvement in Africa can be traced back to its first-aid package to the Sahel countries in 1985, under the Turgut Ozal government. Bolstering Turkey's economic strength by integrating it into the world economy and using aid as a powerful instrument to enhance trade and soft power were among Prime Minister Ozal's foreign policy priorities. Accordingly, a comprehensive aid package of US$10 million was implemented in 1985 to develop Sahel countries' institutional capacity, namely Gambia, Guinea, Guinea Bissau, Mauritania, Senegal, and Somali, and Sudan (Birtek 1996). Therefore, Ankara initiated its ODA program under the Ozal government, yet remained an aid receiver state (Oguz Gok and Parlar Dal 2016).

The exact inclusion of a humanitarian agenda, as well as development efforts in Turkish foreign policy, corresponds mainly to the post-Cold War era. In the 1990s, defined as the age of "liberal humanitarianism," several internal reforms and external pressures led to a growing humanitarian agenda in Turkey's foreign policy (Oguz Gok 2020). An important landmark event that affected an extended humanitarian agenda was the declaration of Turkey's official candidacy for EU membership in 1999. To fulfill the membership commitments, the Turkish parliament adopted in 2001 one of the most comprehensive packages of constitutional amendments, including human rights (Aras and Akpinar 2015). Furthermore, by the early 1990s, Turkish leaders began to realize that development assistance efforts would be more effectively administered through the establishment of an official state-sponsored agency. Accordingly, in 1992, the Turkish Cooperation and Coordination Agency (TIKA) was established. However, during this period, Turkish ODA was restricted to providing development assistance based on technical support for the infrastructure of newly independent states of Turkic countries in Central Asia and the Caucasus (Fidan and Nurdun 2008).

Turkey's humanitarianism vis-à-vis Africa in the 1990s was highly dependent upon the use of "military means." Turkey deployed significant military forces to the peacekeeping missions in a diverse range of countries affected by humanitarian crises. Turkey was part of the United Nations Peacekeeping Operations in Somalia under the command of General Cevik Bir during 1993 (Hirsch and Oakley 1995). However, political instability due to fragile coalition governments and recurring economic crises prevented Turkey again from adopting an effective humanitarian role throughout the 1990s. The rise of "humanitarianism" in foreign policy in general and intensifying development cooperation towards Africa precisely corresponds to the 2000s.

Understanding humanitarianism in Turkish foreign policy towards Africa in the 2000s

During the first decade of the 2000s, humanitarianism has become one of the most preferred concepts in Turkish foreign policy. Compared to the 1990s, Turkey's humanitarianism has shifted dramatically from military missions to humanitarian aid and development assistance efforts (Oguz Gok and Parlar Dal 2016). Turkey has increasingly begun to channel its resources for global development efforts in countries affected by conflicts and natural disasters. In 2018, Ankara allocated humanitarian aid that surpasses much more prosperous and larger economies, including the USA, China and the EU (Cihangir-Tetik and Muftuler-Bac 2020). Ankara expanded its role as one of the most influential humanitarian aid donors among non-OECD-DAC countries (Guo 2020). As documented by Humanitarian Assistance Reports, Ankara continued to be labeled among the top three most generous countries concerning its GDP between 2013–2019 (Development Initiatives 2013–2019). Turkey's commitment to international development assistance efforts is evidenced by its participation in the United Nations Development Program (UNDP), South–South cooperation (SSC) and its initiatives with Least Developed Countries throughout the 2000s. Turkey is also defined as an "emerging donor country" by the World Food Program (Oguz Gok and Parlar Dal 2016).

One should note here that Turkey's growing humanitarian role in general and development assistance towards Africa has explicitly been shaped by various "systemic" and "domestic" developments in the 2000s as well as "ideational" and "material" factors. In this regard, taking the advantage of systemic and domestic developments, Ankara's development assistance efforts aimed at creating and promoting a benign "humanitarian actor" identity both at home and abroad.

First, "systemic shifts" at the international level created a favorable environment for Turkish foreign policymakers for linking the country's foreign policy framework to the new trends and approaches in international relations in the early 2000s. Accordingly, Turkey witnessed a foreign policy change accompanied by a renewed emphasis on foreign policy instruments like mediation, trade, humanitarian and development aid in the first decade of the 2000s (Oguz Gok and Parlar Dal 2016). Among others, aid has been one of the vigorous foreign policy elements and a "niche area" in Turkey's overall foreign policy and its Africa policy in particular in the 2000s (Korkmaz and Zengin 2020). In parallel with this, foreign policy decision makers adopted a discourse which identifies Turkey as a humanitarian, morally driven state. Accordingly, "humanitarian diplomacy" was set as the new objective of Turkish foreign policy (Davutoglu 2013).

Second, the increasing humanitarianism in Turkish foreign policy was made possible due to favorable "domestic democratic" and "economic" developments in the first decade of the 2000s. Since 1999, when Turkey was attributed official candidate status to the EU, it has implemented a series of reforms on civil liberties and democracy regarding many issue areas. Turkey's economic growth in this period also provided favorable domestic conditions to adopt a humanitarian role. In the early 2000s, Turkey rapidly recovered from the 2001 financial crisis's adverse effects and reached a steady growth rate in its economic performance. In "material" terms, the country also survived the 2008 global economic crisis with minimum damage. These "domestic factors" created a favorable environment for the adoption of development assistance as one of the state's key foreign policy tools (Oguz Gok and Parlar Dal 2016).

Turkey's humanitarianism in Africa gained momentum, especially after the Somalian drought crisis in 2011. Turkish government organizations, businesses and NGOs have provided significant amounts of humanitarian and development aid following the then Turkish Prime Minister Recep Tayyip Erdogan's visit to Mogadishu in August 2011. It was a significant event since it was the first visit to Mogadishu by a head of state from outside Africa in almost 20 years. Accordingly, Turkey became the first non-African country to appoint a new ambassador to Somalia in more than two decades, located at an embassy in Mogadishu. In 2011, Somalia became the fourth-highest recipient of Turkey's development assistance, behind Pakistan, Syria and Afghanistan and ranked first in Turkey's ODA in 2012. However, Turkey's humanitarianism in Somalia is not only limited to ODA. Turkish aid allocation for specific sectors between 2005 and 2017 demonstrates a significant role for "humanitarian aid" in foreign aid (Cihangir-Tetik and Muftuler-Bac 2020). As Eyrice Tepeciklioglu (2019) puts it, Somalia has been particularly striking in Turkey's humanitarian efforts towards Africa between 2011–2018, since Ankara's humanitarian and development aid amounted to a total of US$745 million dollars to Somalia.

According to the most recent TIKA Development Cooperation Report of 2019, Turkish development assistance reached US$9,927.5 million in total; including US$8,797.7 million for official flows carried out by public institutions, US$1,129.8 million for private flows, and US$8,612.4 million for official flows composed of official development assistance. The US$8,423.7 million for official development assistance composed of bilateral ODA illustrates the weight of bilateral flows in Turkey's aid. Among the bilateral ODA, US$7,331 million official humanitarian assistance also demonstrates the priority given to humanitarian assistance. Turkey stands out with over US$1 billion of the private sector and US$826.5 million NGO assistance from official assistance (TIKA 2019). Therefore, according to the TIKA 2018 Development Cooperation Report, various actors such as state institutions, NGOs and private sector partners have been active in Turkey's humanitarian efforts, which are delivered through mostly bilateral channels encompassing predominantly humanitarian aid, among others.

Africa's share in Turkey's bilateral development assistance increased to US $134.8 million in 2018 compared to –US$296,6 million USD in 2017, demonstrating a tremendous increase. Among the Least Developed Countries benefiting from Turkey's bilateral assistance, Somalia ranked second with US$31.8 million following Afghanistan with US$38.2 million in 2018 (TIKA Development Assistance Report 2019). In this regard, Africa in general and Somalia specifically continues to be a remarkable case demonstrating Turkey's growing humanitarianism in the 2000s, which corresponds to a network of various state and non-state actors and crosscutting humanitarian, ideational and material motivations and means.

State–civil society nexus in Turkey's humanitarianism towards Africa

In parallel with what Barnett (2011) classifies as liberal humanitarianism, Turkey's development assistance activism in Africa corresponds to a network of multiple crosscutting actors that encompasses the "nexus between state and non-state actors" help to display Turkey as "donor state."

First, the government's official contribution is substantial, considering a remarkable increase in capabilities of the governmental humanitarian assistance organizations in both budget and functionality in the 2000s. State institutions such as the TIKA, the Housing Development Administration of Turkey (TOKI), and Disaster and Emergency Management Presidency (AFAD) are highly involved in the process of delivering assistance to Africa. Besides, several ministries, including the Ministry of Foreign Affairs, the Ministry of Interior, and the Ministry of Health and Education, have been active in humanitarian efforts (Cevik, Sevin and Baybars-Hawks 2018). The Ministry of Education provides scholarships to African students and supports educational institutions abroad. The Turkish government launched the Turkiye Scholarships Program in 2012 and has provided a substantial number of scholarships to African students at all levels. There are currently 5,437 students in higher education and 116 visiting professors/research assistants from African countries (MFA n.d.). The growing role of TIKA has been tremendous as the AKP government transformed TIKA into a more global aid agency and turned it into a dominant player after in the 2000s in Africa (Altunisik 2019). The number of TIKA's coordination offices increased to 61 in 2018, as compared to 12 offices in 2002 (Eyrice Tepeciklioglu 2019). TIKA assists in the coordination of initiatives, such as the "Africa Agricultural Development Program," the "Africa Health Program" and the "Africa Vocational Training Program," among many others (Murphy and Sazak 2012).

As a niche area, the "health sector" is among the top areas in the government's humanitarian efforts to African countries. Ankara has signed health cooperation agreements with around 20 African countries. TIKA built the Turkish-Sudanese Research and Training Hospital in Nyala. In Somalia, Turkey has built and equipped the biggest hospital in Mogadishu. The Educational Hospital in Juba (South Sudan) and the Black Lion Hospital in Addis Ababa (Ethiopia) are among the health institutions to which the

Turkish Ministry of Health has made significant contributions (MFA n.d.). Most recently, Turkey sent medical and humanitarian aid to more than ten countries, including South Africa, Niger, Chad and Burkina Faso, to treat the Covid-19 pandemic.

In addition to these institutions, the Turkish Red Crescent (KIZILAY) and the Directorate of Religious Affairs (Diyanet) have also become key actors in the government assistance efforts (Cevik, Sevin and Baybars-Hawks 2018). For instance, the first involvement of the Diyanet in Somalia was solely in the form of direct humanitarian aid. However, it has shifted the focus of its projects to its core purpose, such as education, religious services and bringing students to theology faculties for religious studies in Turkey (Ozkan 2014). Diyanet has delivered US$111.6 million aid to the African continent since its foundation in 1975. Diyanet also provided scholarships to 1,003 students from Africa (TDV 2019). KIZILAY also provides voluntary health service with its field hospital in Sudan and drug store in Chad in Africa. In recent pandemic crises, KIZILAY sent medical supplies to African countries.[2]

Second, non-government public diplomacy has also become an essential part of Turkish foreign policy in line with the "total performance" approach meaning inclusiveness in the foreign policy agenda of non-state actors like NGOs, business circles, think tanks and public intellectual figures (Donelli 2015). Especially after 2011, HNGOs have become visible with their growing involvement, professionalization and expertise in the field (Guo 2020). A common aspect of Turkish HNGOs across the African continent is that a majority have religious backgrounds, such as the Humanitarian Relief Foundation (IHH), *Cansuyu, Yeryuzu Doktorları* (Doctors Worldwide) and *Deniz Feneri* (Lighthouse Association). Before TIKA began to operate in Africa, the activities of Turkish HNGOs were predominantly ad hoc, single-country emergency aid campaigns, supplying food and clothing mostly at times of crises (Ipek and Biltekin 2013) Such a campaign evolved into more sustainable development assistance in the form of construction and infrastructure projects. Turkish NGOs carry out different development projects such as school construction, capacity building training programs, distributing the livestock to locals, and even establishing radio stations for educational purposes. Turkish NGOs also play a humanitarian role, which includes assistance programs such as disaster assistance, medical assistance and food assistance. For instance, the IHH's activities increased in Africa in many sectors as the number of countries to be assisted increased as well from 10 to 30, with more than 60 construction projects. Since 2007, the IHH has also introduced a foreign student program, especially for African students (Dag 2018).

The nexus between government-based institutions and HNGOs in the field has been a defining aspect of Turkey's humanitarianism in Africa. These HNGOs frequently cooperate with state officials and provide logistical support. The Turkish government uses their expertise in host countries and collaborates with them in delivering aid. These HNGOs also often express national pride by carrying the Turkish flag in distant geographies and conflict zones (Aras and Akpinar 2015). The presence of Turkish HNGOs in some instances precedes that of embassies, and so became a source of information about local conditions in Africa. For instance, the former head of Yeryuzu Doktorları, Dr. C. Kani Torun, after serving in Somalia for many years, became Turkey's first ambassador after the country reopened its embassy in Mogadishu in 2011 (Celik and Iseri 2016). Not only the state, but NGOs also benefit from this nexus in the sense that party affiliation provides more political leverage to non-state actors. For instance, the Human Rights Platform, of which IHH is a member, has signed a contract with AFAD, the Turkish Embassy in Chad and the Chadian Ministry of Health to discuss aid projects (IHH 2014).

The government–NGO nexus could also be traced to Turkey's humanitarianism via the health sector as a niche area. Turkish doctors took part in many health campaigns organized by HNGOs in cooperation with the Ministry of Health and TIKA between 2007 and 2010. Over 280,000 Africans have undergone health screening. For instance, the "Africa Cataract Project" has been implemented in four countries (Niger, Somalia, Ethiopia and Sudan), collaborating with a Turkish HNGO—IHH—and a total of 21,600 patients was operated on in 2018 (MFA n.d.) One should note here that "clientelism" also provides economic benefits to HNGOs and businesses. For instance, the Port of Mogadishu was constructed by conservative Albayrak Insaat and the Mogadishu airport by Cengiz Insaat. The support base of patrons linked with the conservative Independent Industrialists' and Businessmen's Association (MUSIAD) and the Turkish Confederation of Businessmen and Industrialists (TUSKON) indicates a visible connection between these businesses and humanitarian assistance (Cevik, Sevin and Baybars-Hawks 2018).

Domestic and foreign policy nexus in Turkey's humanitarianism

Turkey's humanitarianism discourse in general and foreign aid policies, in particular, has increasingly been used to achieve various foreign policy goals in the 2000s. The first fundamental priority of Turkish development assistance is declared as "the implementation of projects and activities that comply with Turkish foreign policy" (Cihangir-Tetik and Muftuler-Bac 2020). Echoing the "world is bigger than five" rhetoric, Turkey's growing involvement in humanitarianism in Africa could also be explained in terms of Turkey's quest for a more significant global governance status among established and rising donors in Africa. Turkey's previous campaign for a non-permanent UN Security Council seat for the 2009–2010 period also precipitated a wave of Turkish aid activism. It was accompanied by the opening of embassies and the financing of projects to secure several votes for Turkey during its successful bid for a UN Security Council seat. The support of African countries, with their 54 UN members—representing the biggest regional block in the organization—was vitally important for Turkey's UNSC nomination (Oguz Gok and Parlar Dal 2016).

Despite much rhetoric on humanitarian issues, Turkey's humanitarianism has also been driven by the need to diversify "economic relations" in a new global political economy (Ozkan 2012). Data reveals that Turkey's development aid to Somalia has contributed to bilateral economic ties between the two states. Turkey's exports to Somalia have increased dramatically since 2011, from US$4.8 million in 2010 to US$39.5 million in 2011, reaching US $181.5 million in 2018 (Devecioglu 2019). Recent research findings on established donors compared to rising donors like Turkey suggest that trade partnership is ultimately a more important factor than political affinity in determining aid, which is valid for both OECD-DAC members and Turkey (Zengin and Korkmaz 2019). In this regard, trade recipients who import Turkish goods at even an average level are expected to receive significantly more aid (Kavakli 2018). Turkish aid to Africa has been regarded as an opportunity for Turkish firms. In this regard, Turkey's aid structure indicates interconnectedness between Islamic institutions by way of political discourse, which serves the interests of the state, government, NGOs and other stakeholders (Cevik, Sevin and Baybars-Hawks 2018).

Accordingly, Turkey's humanitarianism demonstrates the nexus between state and civil society in "constructing and legitimizing the new state identity." Drawing highly upon Ottoman history, Ankara aimed at articulating a uniquely Turkish moral mission in global affairs, and thus promoting the aid initiatives at home and abroad has become a nation branding which positions the country as a "donor state." Some of the key components of aid manifested in political rhetoric such as "aid as a moral duty," "defending the interests of all aggrieved nations" and "aid as Turkey's manifest destiny" all highlight Turkish leaders' intention to draw historical connections with the generous Ottoman image (Cevik, Sevin and Baybars-Hawks 2018). In their quantitative study, Zengin and Korkmaz (2019) conclude that recipients of aid with an Ottoman past attract more Turkish foreign aid than countries without Ottoman pasts. In another recent quantitative study, Mehmetcik and Pekel (2019) found that the percentage of Muslims living in the recipient country is a significant variable for determining Turkish assistance. However, these findings should be interpreted cautiously as a significant number of Muslim majorities in recipient countries are struggling with severe humanitarian crises to varying degrees.

One should also note here that AKP rulers not only referred to this "altruistic identity" (Cevik, Sevin and Baybars-Hawks 2018) at the international level, but also frequently used it in "domestic politics" to legitimize and consolidate its power among its electorate as well as to enhance the party's humanitarian, historical and religious visions in the eyes of its domestic constituency (Zengin and Korkmaz 2019). Therefore, although Turkey moves with the discourse of "One Africa," political, economic and ideological motivations have also been decisive in Turkey's humanitarianism towards Africa (Eyrice Tepeciklioglu 2019).

Turkey's "hybrid humanitarianism" in the post-liberal era

Turkey's humanitarianism in general and development cooperation activities in Africa could best be explained in the light of systemic changes in the 2000s' post-liberal world. The embeddedness of political/economic motives within humanitarian aims has become a characteristic of Turkish "hybrid humanitarianism." This characteristic distinguishes Turkey from both emerging and traditional donors, whose aid efforts have been largely motivated by development-based or politics-based ends, respectively (Zengin and Korkmaz 2019). Turkish development assistance is constructed upon a "non-imperial benign" state image, with a "win–win" strategy and operational procedures built upon direct contact with local populations in the field.

It is liberal in the sense that it fits into Barnett's framework of liberal humanitarianism. It is highly politicized encompassing the means of state–civil society nexus as well as a shared agenda with institutionalized efforts of HNGOs in Africa. Compared to emerging donors, Turkey is part of the traditional Western development and cooperation system as a founding member of the OECD and has been engaged in accession negotiations with the EU since 2005. Although Ankara did not join the OECD's Development Assistance Committee (DAC), it voluntarily reports to DAC. Furthermore, as Cihangir-Tetik and Muftuler-Bac (2020) found in their comparative study, Turkish humanitarian aid complements the EU's development goals.

Although traditional Western donors such as the EU emphasize democracy and the rule of law as political conditions for aid, absence of political conditions for delivering aid makes Turkey similar to other emerging powers such as BRICS. The use of historical and religious rhetoric by Turkish rulers and NGOs has served to legitimize Turkey's presence in Africa as a "benign" actor that can function as an alternative role model. One of the crucial dimensions of Turkey's humanitarianism is that Ankara defined itself as the opposite of traditional donors like the EU and the US. For instance, Langan (2017) argues that AKP leaders have constructed the concept of "virtuous power Turkey" in contrast to a European "other." Turkish humanitarianism in Africa is legitimized as a more trustworthy partner than the EU (Langan 2017). Turkish leaders also frequently refer to identifications like "clean state" in their dealings with African countries. President Erdogan uses "Africa belongs to Africans" and "win–win" rhetoric while defining Turkey's "uniqueness" as compared to Western history and the approach to African aid throughout the 2000s.[3]

As compared to traditional Western donors, rising powers like BRICS prioritize economic ties, trade relations and security interests, rather than democratic ideals. In fact, rising donors in Africa, most notably China, also do not have any political conditionality compared to traditional donors and place emphasis on the sovereignty of aid recipient countries. Nevertheless, in practice, they seek comparative advantages and long-term economic gains. For instance, rising powers mostly carry out development projects in exchange for access to rights to natural resources, mining or the purchase of their goods and services. For example, concessional aid or grants such as "loans-for-oil" underscores an essential component of China's aid policy. Moreover, BRICS' policies focus on the import and control of Africa's natural resources through developing market opportunities with significant investments in Africa's energy and mining sectors (Tepeciklioglu, Tok and Basher 2017).

Like rising donors, Ankara does not have any political conditionality. However, this "unconditionality" should not be understood as being independent from any economic or political considerations. Turkey's focus on trade in the 2000s made it more similar to OECD-DAC donors in economic aid (Kavakli 2018). On the other hand, Turkey's humanitarian and development aid is delivered mostly without any conditions. There is no manifestation of initiatives regarding Ankara's long-term interest in Africa's vast natural resources (Tepeciklioglu, Tok and Basher 2017). One crucial difference is also the weight of Turkey's state–civil society nexus on humanitarianism as compared to rising powers like BRICS. While BRICS' economic gains constitute the primacy over non-governmental and civil forms of engagement, Turkey's humanitarianism is heavily constructed upon substantial state–civil society nexus. The growing importance of religious identity in humanitarian aid allocation and state–civil society nexus have distinguished Turkey from many of the other donors (Kavakli 2018). Federico Donelli (2015) defines Turkey as a "hybrid non-traditional actor" as it combines a traditional political-stability perspective (US, UE) with an economic-trade perspective of emerging powers (China, India, Brazil). Therefore, Turkey is argued to have a more balanced perspective regarding economic and humanitarian concerns (Tepeciklioglu, Tok and Basher 2017).

One important denominator of Turkey's hybrid humanitarianism compared to rising donors such as BRICS is its strong emphasis on "bilateral means." BRICS' resort to mostly global multilateral channels with an emphasis on South–South cooperation is also opposed to Turkey's bilateral humanitarian diplomacy efforts with the increasing role of Turkish NGOs (Tepeciklioglu, Tok and Basher 2017). Turkish aid contribution to multilateral institutions initially decreased from 2005 to 2011 while its bilateral aid increased drastically (Cihangir-Tetik and Muftuler-Bac 2020). This increase might result from a desire to enhance Turkey's visibility in humanitarian and development assistance as a niche area or develop deeper bilateral relations with African states. Decreasing belief regarding the efficiency of multilateral mechanisms might have predicted a wave of bilateral aid in the 2010s (Zengin and Korkmaz 2019). Turkey's aid has been faster so far on the ground compared to the slow delivery of multilateral institutions like the UN (Eyrice Tepeciklioglu 2019).

Turkey's humanitarianism is also different from both traditional and rising donors as Turkish TIKA and NGOs offices are in Mogadishu while most of the other actors are outside. For instance, in Somalia, Turkish NGOs coordinated with Somalian authorities and collaborated with local partners. Therefore, it increases Turkish aid's reliability and makes it faster and more adaptable to change. In this regard, direct contact with local populations without having the burden of an imperial past have all argued to help increase Turkey's credibility and reliability in development efforts (Ozerdem 2019).

On the other hand, Ankara's humanitarian efforts have been criticized on the grounds of not having a long-term vision, lack of genuine knowledge regarding the internal dynamics of the region, and lack of proper coordination with regional and multilateral organizations, and local and international NGOs in the field. Turkey's increasing strategic, political and economic involvement have made it more difficult to reconcile the humanitarian interests of the recipients with Turkey's interests (Akpinar 2013). Emergency humanitarian aid provided in conjunction with civil society organizations has been an integral part of Turkish humanitarian aid to African countries. However, Turkey's potential to create long-term effects in targeted states' socio-economic structure continues to be a big question mark. Therefore, although there is a tremendous quantitative increase in Turkish aid, the qualitative contributions have not been fully endorsed (Eyrice Tepeciklioglu 2019). In this regard, once assistance is decided upon, there seems to be no effective mechanism for monitoring and evaluating its impact (Altunisik 2014). The provision of Turkish arms in sub-Saharan Africa more widely is also deemed questionable in terms of normative credentials (Langan 2017). Despite all, considering Turkey is a relative latecomer to the Africa development cooperation field, it has played crucial roles in constructing a "hybrid model" in the continent.

Conclusion

Turkey's humanitarianism in Africa has been strongly influenced by the systemic shifts of the "post-liberal era" in the 2000s. In an era of clash of norms, Turkey's development assistance activities could best be conceptualized as "hybrid humanitarianism" encompassing the norms and instruments of both traditional and emerging donors.

Ankara's humanitarian initiative towards Africa seems to evolve into a more comprehensive policy. It encompasses emergency aid funding, development projects, opening schools, taking a leading role in shaping state-building agenda involving opening military facility bases, mediating peace talks[4] as well as taking part in exploring oil in Somalia's[5] seas upon invitation. This expanded agenda in Africa has already put Turkey's humanitarianism into a more complicated and multidimensional one.

Evidence suggests that Ankara has been enthusiastically exercising a rising donor role and has been quite successful in terms of constructing humanitarianism as a "niche area" in its foreign policy throughout the 2000s. However, whether it will construct a credible and durable humanitarian power role in Africa will depend on its domestic economic and political conditions as well as its robust, durable and consistent normative approach to international affairs.

Overall, this study aimed to understand how Turkey's development cooperation activities towards Africa fit into Barnet's (2011) classification of the "liberal humanitarianism." The paper concludes that, "domestic and foreign policy nexus" and "civil society and state networks" have been defining characteristics of Turkey's "hybrid humanitarianism" towards Africa in the last two decades. Ankara's development cooperation activities also crosscut various political and economic motives with humanitarian aims. This eclecticism of various economic, political and humanitarian aims is the main element of Turkey's hybrid humanitarianism in the 2000s which encompasses the norms and instruments of both traditional and emerging donors. Yet, Ankara's quest for constituting Turkey-specific norms, instruments of development assistance as well as concrete achievements on the ground has neither been negative, nor positive, but rather incomplete.

Notes

1 OECD defines Official Development Assistance as: "Government aid designed to promote the economic development and welfare of developing countries. Loans and credits for military purposes are excluded. Aid may be provided bilaterally, from donor to recipient, or channeled through a multilateral development agency such as the United Nations or the World Bank. Aid includes grants, 'soft' loans (where the grant element is at least 25% of the total), and the provision of technical assistance." The OECD maintains a list of developing countries and territories; only aid to these countries counts as ODA. See https://data.oecd.org/oda/net-oda.htm (accessed May 18, 2020).
2 https://www.aa.com.tr/en/africa/turkish-medical-aid-arrives-in-sudan-amid-covid-19/1878242.
3 See for instance https://www.tccb.gov.tr/konusmalar/362/75311/25-mayis-afrika-gunu-konusmasi.
4 https://www.horndiplomat.com/2019/11/06/turkey-offers-mediating-role-in-the-talks-between-somalia-and-somaliland-fm-mevlut-cavusoglu/.
5 https://www.dw.com/en/turkey-sets-its-sights-on-the-horn-of-africa/a-52111261.

References

Abdenur, Adriana Erthal and João Moura Estevão Marques Da Fonseca. 2013. "The North's Growing Role in South-South Cooperation: Keeping the Foothold." *Third World Quarterly* 34, no. 8: 1475–1491.

Akpinar, Pinar. 2013. "Turkey's Peacebuilding in Somalia: The Limits of Humanitarian Diplomacy." *Turkish Studies* 14, no. 4: 735–757.

Altunisik Meliha. 2014. "Turkey as an 'Emerging Donor' and the Arab Uprisings." *Mediterranean Politics* 19, no. 3: 333–350. https://doi.org/10.1080/13629395.2014.959761.

Altunisik, Meliha. 2019. "Turkey's Humanitarian Diplomacy: The AKP Model." CMI Brief. https://www.cmi.no/publications/6973-turkeys-humanitarian-diplomacy-the-akp-model.

Aras, Bulent and Pinar Akpinar. 2015. "The Role of Humanitarian NGOs in Turkey's Peacebuilding." *International Peacekeeping* 22, no. 3: 230–247. https://doi.org/10.1080/13533312.2015.1033374.

Barnett, Michael. 2009. "Evolution Without Progress? Humanitarianism in a World of Hurt." *International Organization* 63: 621–663. https://doi.org/10.1017/S0020818309990087.

Barnett, Michael. 2011. *Empire of Humanity*. Ithaca: Cornell University Press.

Birtek, Nuri. 1996. "*Turkiye'nin Dis Yardimlari ve Yonetimi.*" Expert Thesis. State Planning Organization of Turkey.

Celik, Nihat and Emre Iseri. 2016. "Islamically Oriented Humanitarian NGOs in Turkey: AKP Foreign Policy Parallelism." *Turkish Studies* 17, no. 3: 429–448.

Cevik, Senem B., Efe Sevin, and Banu Baybars-Hawks. 2018. "State–Civil Society Partnerships in International Aid and Public Diplomacy: The Case of Turkey and Somalia." In *Communicating National Image through Development and Diplomacy*, edited by James Pamment and Karin Gwinn Wilkins, 169–192. Cham: Springer.

Cihangir-Tetik, Damla and Meltem Muftuler-Bac. 2020. "A Comparison of Development Assistance Policies: Turkey and the European Union in Sectoral and Humanitarian Aid." *Journal of European Integration*. doi:10.1080/07036337.2020.1734587.

Dag, Ahmet Emin. 2018. "The Role of Turkish NGOs in Southern Africa," INSAMER. https://insamer.com/en/the-role-of-turkish-ngos-in-southern-africa_1185.html.

Davutoglu, Ahmet. 2013. "Turkey's Humanitarian Diplomacy: Objectives, Challenges, and Prospects." *Nationalism Papers: Journal of Nationalism and Ethnicity* 41, no. 6: 865–870.

Devecioglu, Hakan. 2019. "Turkey's Humanitarian Diplomacy in Somalia: From Past to Present." *Daily Sabah*, October 16, 2019. https://www.dailysabah.com/op-ed/2019/10/16/turkeys-humanitarian-diplomacy-in-somalia-from-past-to-present.

Development Initiatives. 2013–2019. "Global Humanitarian Assistance Reports 2013 to 2019." https://devinit.org/resources/global-humanitarian-assistance-report-2020/.

Development Initiatives. 2019. "Global Humanitarian Assistance Report." http://devinit.org/wp-content/uploads/2019/09/GHA-report-2019.pdf.

Donelli, Federico. 2015. "Turkey's Presence in Somalia: A Humanitarian Approach." In *The Depth of Turkish Geopolitics in the AKP's Foreign Policy: From Europe to an Extended Neighbourhood*, edited by Alessia Chiriatti, Emidio Diodato, Salih Dogan, Federico Donelli and Bahri Yilmaz, 35–51. Perugia: Università per Stranieri Perugia.

Eyrice Tepeciklioglu, Elem, 2019. *Turk Dis Politikasinda Afrika: Temel Dinamikler, Fırsatlar ve Engeller*. Istanbul: Nobel.

Eyrice Tepeciklioglu, Elem, M. Evren Tok and Syed Abul Basher. 2017. "Turkish and BRICS Engagement in Africa: Between Humanitarian and Economic Interests." MPRA Paper. https://mpra.ub.uni-muenchen.de/77549/.

Fidan, Hakan and Rahman Nurdun. 2008. "Turkey's Role in the Global Development Assistance Community: The Case of TIKA." *Journal of Southern Europe and the Balkans* 10, no. 1, 93–111.

Guo, Xiaoli. 2020. "Turkey's International Humanitarian Assistance during the AKP Era: Key Actors, Concepts and Motivations." *Asian Journal of Middle Eastern and Islamic Studies* 14, no. 1: 121–140.

Hazar, Numan. 2017. *Turkiye-Afrika İliskileri*. Ankara: Akcag Yayınevi.
Hirsch, John L. and Robert B. Oakley. 1995. *Somalia and Operation Restore Hope: Reflections on Peacemaking and Peacekeeping*. Washington, DC: United States Institute of Peace.
IHH. 2014. "Turkiye Orta Afrika'ya Umut Tasidi." https://www.ihh.org.tr/haber/tur kiye-orta-afrikaya-umut-tasidi-2378.
Ipek, Volkan and Gonca Biltekin. 2013. "Turkey's Foreign Policy Implementation in Sub-Saharan Africa: A Post-International Approach." *New Perspectives on Turkey* 49: 121–156.
Kavakli, Kerim Can. 2018. "Domestic Politics and the Motives of Emerging Donors: Evidence from Turkish Foreign Aid." *Political Research Quarterly* 71, no. 3: 614–627.
Korkmaz, Abdurrahman and Huseyin Zengin. 2020. "The Political Economy of Turkish Foreign Aid." In *Turkey's Political Economy in the 21st Century*, edited by Emel Parlar Dal, 133–162. Cham: Palgrave MacMillan.
Langan, Mark. 2017. "Virtuous Power Turkey in Sub-Saharan Africa: The Neo-Ottoman' Challenge to the European Union." *Third World Quarterly* 38, no. 6: 1399–1414.
Mehmetcik, Hakan and Sercan Pekel. 2019. "The Determinants of Turkish Foreign Aid: An Empirical Analysis." In *Turkey's Political Economy in the 21st Century*, edited by Emel Parlar Dal, 195–213. Cham: Palgrave MacMillian.
MFA (Turkish Ministry of Foreign Affairs). n.d. "Turkey Afrika Relations." Accessed March 24, 2020. http://www.mfa.gov.tr/turkey-africa-relations.en.mfa.
Murphy Teri and Onur Sazak. 2012. "Turkey's Civilian Capacity in Post-Conflict Reconstruction." Istanbul Policy Center-Sabancı University. https://research.saba nciuniv.edu/21550/1/IPM-Turkish-CivCap.pdf.
Oguz Gok, Gonca. 2020. "'Humanitarianism' Transformed? Analyzing the Role of Transnational Humanitarian NGOs in Turkish Foreign Policy Toward the Middle East in the 2000s." In *A Transnational Account of Turkish Foreign Policy*, edited by Hazal Pabuccular and Deniz Kuru, 227–258. Cham: Palgrave Macmillian.
Oguz Gok, Gonca and Emel Parlar Dal. 2016. "Understanding Turkey's Emerging 'Civilian' Foreign Policy Role in the 2000s through Development Cooperation in the Africa Region." *Perceptions* 21, no. 3–4: 67–100.
Onis, Ziya. 2017. "The Age of Anxiety: The Crisis of Liberal Democracy in a Post-Hegemonic Global Order." *The International Spectator* 53, no. 3: 18–35. https://doi.org/10.1080/03932729.2017.1325133.
Onis, Ziya and M. Kutlay. 2020. "The New Age of Hybridity and Clash of Norms: China, BRICS, and Challenges of Global Governance in a Postliberal International Order." *Alternatives*. DOI: https://doi.org/10.1177/0304375420921086.
Ozerdem, Alparslan. 2019. "Turkey as an Emerging Global Humanitarian and Peacebuilding Actor." In *The Routledge Handbook of Turkish Politics*, edited by Alparslan Ozerdem and Mathew Whiting, 470–480. London and New York: Routledge.
Ozkan Mehmet. 2012. "A New Actor or Passer-By? The Political Economy of Turkey's Engagement with Africa." *Journal of Balkan and Near Eastern Studies* 14, no. 1: 113–133.
Ozkan, Mehmet. 2014. "Turkey's Involvement in Somalia: Assessment of a State-Building in Progress," SETA, Foundation for Political, Economic and Social Research. Accessed March 17, 2020. http://file.setav.org/Files/Pdf/20141021155302_41_somali_eng-web.pdf.

Sodenberg, Marie. 2010. "Challenges or Complements for the West: Is there an 'Asian' Model of Aid Emerging?" In *Challenging the Aid Paradigm Western Currents and Asian Alternatives*, edited by Sörensen, Jens Stilhoff, 107–137. Basingstoke: Palgrave Macmillian.

TDV. 2019. "TDV'den Afrika ulkelerine 111.6 milyon dolarlik yardim." https://tdv.org/tr-TR/tdvden-afrika-ulkelerine-111-6-milyon-dolarlik-yardim/.

TIKA. 2019. "Development Assistance Report of 2019." https://www.tika.gov.tr/upload/2020/02/kyk%202018/TurkiyeKalkinma2018ENGWeb.pdf.

Tjønneland, Elling N. 2015. "African Development: What Role do Rising Powers Play?" Norwegian Peacebuilding Resource Center Report. https://www.files.ethz.ch/isn/187491/fa8aeed1b5911794106c324bf90d0e09.pdf.

Turkmen, Fusun. 2007. "Turkey's Participation in Regional and Global Human Rights Regimes." In *Human Rights in Turkey*, edited by Zehra F. Kabasakal Arat, 149–261. Philadelphia: University of Pennsylvania Press.

Weiss, Thomas G. and Adriana Erthal Abdenur. 2014. "Introduction: Emerging Powers and the UN – What Kind of Development Partnership?" *Third World Quarterly*, 35, no.10: 1749–1758. doi:10.1080/01436597.2014.971583.

Zengin, Huseyin and Abdurrahman Korkmaz. 2019. "Determinants of Turkey's Foreign Aid Behavior." *New Perspectives on Turkey* 60: 109–135.

11 Turkey's religious diplomacy in Africa

Elem Eyrice Tepeciklioğlu

Introduction

Religion has increasingly become a useful foreign policy tool for nations in the pursuit of their political goals. The application of religious/faith diplomacy in the conduct of foreign policy is nothing new. Yet, religion was assumed to be obsolete in the post-Westphalian world order, and its importance in the lives of publics have been recognized only in the 1970s and 1980s. It is now admitted that religion has a significant influence not only in public life but also in the diplomacy of states. It acts as an ideological tool to justify political power at home but it also serves as a legitimizing source for the purposes of foreign policy.

There are various reasons why states conduct religious diplomacy in their relations with other countries and regions. It is a valuable asset of soft power that can promote the acceptance of a country's foreign policy while also conveying a particular message to targeted societies and influencing their opinions and policy preferences. The use of religious symbols or ideas can also improve a country's image in the eyes of other people and help the country to raise its profile among those nations.

Turkey, governed by an Islamically-oriented political party since the early 2000s, has been increasingly deploying religion as a form of soft power in order to satisfy its foreign policy ambitions in different regions. Turkey's religious diplomacy efforts have accelerated during the JDP (Justice and Development Party) government that assumes the leadership of the Muslim world and advocates a moderate blend of Islam. This is exceptional and interesting given the role religion played in Turkey's foreign policy implementation was minimal until the JDP's coming to power in 2002.

The previous involvement of religion in the foreign policymaking process started in the early 1970s with the use of Turkey's Presidency of Religious Affairs (hereinafter Diyanet), Turkey's top religious body, to reach Turkish communities abroad. Prior to this period, Diyanet's role was limited to the domestic sphere and it had almost no administrative capability beyond Turkey's borders. At the beginning of the 1970s, Diyanet started to offer religious services to Turkish immigrants in European countries as part of government policy. During the 1980s, the military government started to use the organization to promote official Turkish Islam to migrant communities in order to prevent the spread of radical beliefs among those communities (Ozturk and Sozeri 2018, 5–6; Tol 2019). Under Turgut Ozal's prime ministry, Diyanet established a Foreign Affairs department in 1983 (Lepeska 2015) while in 1999, it opened an interfaith dialogue branch (Yilmaz and Barry 2020, 4). This increasing involvement of Diyanet in Turkish foreign policy helped to build the country a new international profile. The overseas activities of Turkish faith-based non-governmental organizations (NGOs), on the other hand, were very limited due to bureaucratic restrictions.

Most of the legal limitations on NGOs were abolished under the first term of the JDP government. This enabled the religiously motivated NGOs to enhance their activities abroad. During the same period, Diyanet also enhanced its international presence and emerged as a significant foreign policy instrument of the incumbent government. Turkey's state-level religious diplomacy efforts are now mostly implemented by Diyanet, and its proxy organization, Turkiye Diyanet Vakfi (TDV), established in 1975 in order to support Diyanet's activities. The Turkish Cooperation and Coordination Agency (TIKA) also helps to spread Turkey's religious presence in different geographies including Africa. Together with Diyanet and TIKA, Turkish faith-based NGOs contribute to Turkey's (religious) soft power. In Africa, their activities mostly concentrate on those countries that are predominantly Muslim or have a significant Muslim minority. They often act in harmony with public institutions in a way to complement Turkey's Africa policy.

The Gulen movement, a former ally of the JDP government, also acted as an important (religious) diplomacy actor and once contributed to Turkey's (religious) soft power in Africa. This was before cooperation between these former allies was shattered first in December 2013 and then after the 2016 coup attempt, attributed by the government to what is now called, the Fethullahci Teror Orgutu (FETO).[1] Defined as "an Islamic transnational religious and social organization" (Donelli 2019, 67), following the teachings of Islamic cleric, Fethullah Gulen, the activities of the movement were not limited to Turkey with its affiliated international humanitarian organizations, schools and business associations playing a central role in opening up to Africa. Religious proximity initially played an important role in the movement's engagement across the continent. For example, the majority of Gulen-associated schools were opened in African countries with significant Muslim populations with the few exceptions including South Africa and Angola. Ankara enjoyed the benefits of the movement's activities that helped to strengthen Turkey's presence in the region. Yet, following the recent split between the two, the government has been calling African countries to shut down all activities affiliated with the movement (Donelli 2019, 73). On the other hand, the vacancies left by the movement were filled by conservative Islamist groups that also have close connections with the JDP (Ozturk 2019, 92).

The religious diplomacy efforts, conducted either by state or non-state actors, aim at furthering Ankara's foreign policy objectives. Experts note that as a rising power, Turkey's religious initiatives are part of a broader strategy to have a larger influence in world politics (Mandaville and Hamid 2018, 22). It is expected to serve its rising power aspirations as well as its religious leadership claims. In its rivalry with other regional countries for the religious (Sunni) leadership including Saudi Arabia, United Arab Emirates (UAE) and Egypt that has long-established ties especially with the Horn of Africa, Turkey promotes its own religious brand and advertises its brand of Islam as being more tolerant and less extreme (Tol 2019).[2] Taking Turkey as an emerging power that had integrated religion into its broader soft power strategies across Africa, Mandaville and Hamid (2018, 24) further note that:

> where Turkey is seeking to expand its broader partnerships (particularly on the economic front) in Muslim countries or in nations with a significant or influential Muslim minority, adding a religious dimension to its diplomacy allows Ankara to establish a baseline of cultural proximity and affinity—and a basis for further partnership.

As Turkey recognized religion's potential to enhance its influence in Africa (Frohlich 2019), it started to use religious soft power also in advancing its political, economic and geostrategic interests in Africa. Although religion has now become an integral part of Turkey's Africa policy, the literature on Turkey's religious diplomacy efforts in Africa is conspicuously limited.[3] This chapter essentially aims at contributing to the expanding literature on Turkey–Africa relations through the integration of the religious dimension. It argues that countries that have predominantly Muslim populations cover more of Turkish religious initiatives in the continent. Moreover, religious and cultural similarity play an important role in the distribution of Turkish aid delivered both by public institutions and religiously motivated Turkish NGOs. The chapter further notes that the importance of religious factor in Turkish foreign policy is growing and the application of religious diplomacy in Africa is not separable from the general course of Turkish foreign policy. After briefly presenting the relationship between religion and diplomacy, this chapter then proceeds to analyze the evolving role of religion in formulating Turkish foreign policy. As the religious dimension is essential to comprehend Turkey's overall Africa strategy, the further focus of this chapter is Turkey's religious activities in the continent.

Religion and diplomacy

The secular thought in social sciences postulated that religion was excluded from politics with the emergence of the modern system of nation states in the seventeenth century. Taking religion as irrelevant in the modern secular era and defining their disciplinary boundaries in secular terms, scholars have not featured it as an important influence in human affairs and politics (Philpott 2001, 9; Stempel 2000, 1). Most scholars put the blame on the secularization theory for this neglect (Sandal and Fox 2013, 2). The key proposition of this secular account was that modernity inevitably led to the decline of religion (Berger 1967, Martin 1978; Wilson 1966).[4] It was not until the late 1970s that this very idea of secularization "theory" was challenged and scholars began to place more attention on religion in the study of international affairs.

It was mostly the third wave of democratization that witnessed democratic transitions all around the world and led many scholars to question the basic claims of the rationalist argument (Alasuutari 2004, 150). Other important regional and international incidents that brought religion from the "Westphalian Exile" (Hatzopoulos and Petito 2003) back to world politics and led to its revival in scholarly debates include the Iranian Revolution, the September 11 attacks, the rise of religious fundamentalism on the world stage, ethno-religious conflicts in different parts of the world and the successes of religious political parties (Hatzopoulos and Petito 2003).

Scholars have eventually accepted that the world is often shaped by religion (Danan 2013, 181) and, so attempted to integrate it into their analysis of international relations. Even the influential socialist, Peter Berger, one of the foremost proponents of the secularization theory, later acknowledged the importance of religion in understanding the various aspects of international affairs. Concluding that secularization theory was essentially mistaken, Berger further noted in his widely quoted study that:

> The point of this little story is that the assumption that we live in a secularized world is false: The world today, with some exceptions attended to below, is as furiously religious as it ever was, and in some places more so than ever.
>
> (1996/97, 3)

This global "resurgence" of religion has transformed our understanding of international relations in different ways (Thomas 2005) with its widespread employment in politics being acknowledged in political and academic circles. As Seib puts it, one cannot ignore the role of faith in an increasingly religious world. As he further notes, the success of a country's soft power depends on the inclusion of cultural elements such as religion in the planning of public diplomacy (2013, 7).

Religious diplomacy is now an important element in building the soft power of particular countries. It can be roughly defined as the use of religion in foreign policy. It is

> the whole set of mechanisms for state cooperation with religious associations in the pursuit of pragmatically defined national interest, use of the international activity of religious institutions, ideas and religious

symbols (appropriately interpreted to comply with current political aims) and so on.

(Curanović 2012, 7)

Wellman argues that we should distinguish between two broad categories of analysis in analyzing diplomatic practices around religion. The first category (religion and diplomacy) refers to the practice of track-one diplomacy among nation-state actors while the second category (faith-based diplomacy) generally refers to the practice of diplomacy on the part of track-two actors involving religiously motivated NGOs or religious figures. Yet, he also acknowledges that "in practice they often do not operate discretely" (2016, 577).

The convergence of the activities of public institutions and civil society organizations in the application of religious practices in foreign policy is now highly visible in the Turkish context. This is the consequence of multiple processes that took place in the country's political life and made it almost impossible to make predictions on Turkish foreign policy without considering the influence of religion. As will be discussed in more detail, the instrumentalization of religion by the political elites as well as the overseas religious activities of Turkish NGOs accelerated during the JDP administration. Under JDP rule, track-one diplomacy is mostly applied by Diyanet, TDV and TIKA while several civil society organizations and religious groups are involved in track-two diplomacy.

The evolving role of religion in Turkish foreign policy

In order to understand Turkey's use of religion in foreign affairs, we should start with Diyanet, "the representative of official Islam" that underwent a major transformation under subsequent JDP governments (Ozturk 2016, 2019). Diyanet was founded shortly after the establishment of the Turkish Republic with the aim to regulate Islamic services, to enlighten society on religion and to manage the places of worship (Gozaydin 2008, 216). The newly established republic also abolished the caliphate, closed the religious courts and madrasas (Islamic religious schools) and banned religious orders in an effort to protect the secular character of the republic. By establishing a state institution responsible for managing religious affairs and regulating Islamic faith and practice, it also aimed at limiting the power of religion and bringing it under tight state control. Serving as an important means to reinforce state ideology, Diyanet's duties and international presence significantly expanded first in the early 1980s, and then under the JDP governments (Adanali 2008, 228; Ozturk 2016, 619–620).

As discussed above, Diyanet's initial involvement in the application of foreign policy started with the 1970s following labor migration from Turkey to European countries. In order to spread its own interpretation of Islamic knowledge among Turkish communities, Diyanet established organizations such as the Turkish Islamic Cultural Federation while it was also represented by the counsellors of religious services attached to Turkish embassies (Gozaydin 2010, 2–3). In the aftermath of the 1980 coup d'état, the military started to instrumentalize the organization to counter leftist/communist ideologies taken as a serious threat to their survival. This period also saw the emergence of Turkish–Islamic synthesis (TIS), a mixture of Turkish nationalism and Sunni Islam, supported by military rule. Diyanet took the responsibility to promote Turkish Islam abroad through TIS especially in those countries with large Turkish diasporas and sent imams to different regions in an effort to propagate Sunni Islam among those communities (Ozturk 2016, 619–626; Ozturk and Sozeri 2018, 628–630; Yilmaz and Barry 2020, 2–4).

Following the independence of former Soviet territories in the early 1990s, Diyanet started to provide religious services to Muslim communities in the Balkans, Caucasia and Central Asia. Since the mid-1990s, it has been organizing regular meetings of the Eurasian Islamic Council (EIC) with the participation of religious leaders from Eurasia and the Balkans. Diyanet has also hosted the annual summit of Balkan Muslim Leaders since 2007. These forums promote cooperation among the Muslim spiritual boards and provide a space where the issues of Islamic practice are discussed. Diyanet extended its assistance in other areas including the organization of the pilgrimage, the training of local imams and construction or restoration of mosques and Islamic schools (Demirtas 2015, 134; Gozaydin 2010, 7; Ozkan 2014, 231–234). TIKA has also been embarking on symbolic projects including the restoration of Ottoman-era mosques in addition to its conventional non-religious projects such as capacity building, health care and agriculture (Oktem 2012, 38). With regards to the Balkans, Oktem states that: "construction also seems to be a significant act of symbolic re-appropriation of Ottoman material heritage and an affirmative statement of the role of Turkey as protector of the Muslim communities of the Balkans" (2012, 39). Turkey's religious outreach was also complemented by faith-based organizations, most notably, the Gulen network that helped to enhance Turkey's regional presence (Oktem 2012, 31–32).

Turkey's religious activities initially targeted those countries where Turkey has religious, cultural and historical similarities or ties through Ottoman legacy (Mandaville and Hamid 2018, 23–24). Diyanet's religious services, however, also reached distant geographies including Latin America and Africa. For example, Diyanet hosted a Summit of Latin American Muslim Religious Leaders in Istanbul in late 2014, with the participation of 40 countries. The discussions at the meeting largely revolved around the problems of Latin American Muslims and possible areas of cooperation (Ozkan 2014, 228).

The role religion plays in the formulation and exercise of Turkish foreign policy accelerated under JDP rule. Accordingly, religion has become a key foreign policy instrument to enhance Turkey's influence in countries from

Latin America to Africa (Tol 2019). Shortly after the JDP assumed power, a Turkish national, Ekmeleddin Ihsanoglu was elected to the position of Secretary General of the Organization of Islamic Cooperation (OIC) in 2004. This is important considering that Turkey's relations with Islamic states including its Middle Eastern neighbors were long defined by neglect. Turkey even hesitated to join the organization when it was established in 1969 because it was thought that this would contradict its "Western-oriented secular modernization process" (Oguzlu 2007, 90).

Diyanet's sphere of influence was also enhanced during the same period while the JDP increased the size and budget of the organization (Yilmaz and Barry 2020, 7). Diyanet's budget has expanded more than fourfold since 2006 (Beck 2019). Having now a larger budget than half of the state ministries including the Ministry of Foreign Affairs and the Ministry of Interior, its share of government spending has also increased by about a third while its staff has more than doubled. Diyanet's administrative capacity also increased during JDP rule (Lepeska 2015; T24 2019). This period also saw Diyanet's transformation into a state apparatus responsible for implementing and supporting the government's policy discourses and practice (Ozturk 2016).

In addition to Diyanet's larger role in foreign policymaking, the increasing interaction between the state and Turkish faith-based organizations has also increased with JDP rule, which similarly illustrates religion's expanding role in Turkish foreign policy. Prior to this period, the foreign aid activities of those Islamically-oriented humanitarian NGOs were limited because of mistrust towards those NGOs coupled with bureaucratic restrictions (Celik and Iseri 2016, 435). They have flourished following the first term of the JDP government that has not only encouraged their aid activities abroad but also eased most of the legal limitations on these NGOs and allowed them to collect more donations (Tol 2019; Turhan and Bahcecik 2020, 2–5). This was mostly made possible by Law No. 5253 on Associations (published in the Official Gazette on November 23, 2004) that regulated their finances and activities abroad. For example, Article 5 of the law allows them to be involved in foreign aid activities and cooperate with their international counterparts while Article 21 states: "associations may receive aid from persons, institutions and organizations at abroad."[5] In order to further enhance cooperation between the state and NGOs, the Presidential Decree No: 1 dated July 10, 2018 stipulated the establishment of a special administrative unit, namely, the Cooperation Coordination Office, within TIKA (Turhan and Bahcecik 2020, 6–7).

Many of those organizations have close contacts with senior officials in the party (Tol 2019) while it is very common to see people in important positions in public institutions that have an NGO background. An important factor contributing to their position and providing an advantage vis-à-vis government bodies is their earlier presence in crisis regions and close relations with local populations. It is a reciprocal process where the government benefits from their knowledge and network while NGOs increase their ability to shape the country's humanitarian agenda. Some of those civil society organizations were already involved in humanitarian aid activities in African countries before Turkey's Africa policy began in the late 1990s (Turhan and Bahcecik 2020, 8–13). Although they initiate their aid activities in countries with non-Muslim populations as well, they focus their attention mostly on Muslim-majority countries. Their religious identity motivates the aid activities and they see themselves as contributing to Turkish foreign policy and Turkey's soft power (Celik and Iseri 2016, 436). This explains the "parallelism" between the discourse and practice of those aid agencies and the application of foreign policy (Celik and Iseri 2016, 430).

Turkey's religious diplomacy in Africa

Religion is a distinctive feature of Turkey's Africa policy while providing legitimacy to its activities in the continent (Ozkan 2013, 45). Turkey's state-level religious activities in Africa are mostly applied by Diyanet in cooperation with TDV. Together, they have delivered an estimated US$111.6 million in humanitarian aid to African countries in the last 44 years (TDV 2019). Having counsellor offices and attachés in 15 African countries (Tokat, Ozturk and Mercan 2019), Diyanet and TDV finance theological education in Africa, build mosques and implement aid campaigns especially during the holy months of Ramadan and Eid Al-Adha. They train imams from African countries, open Quran learning centers, translate the Quran professionally, print Quran and other religious publications in local languages and deliver copies of those publications to Muslim local communities. The Diyanet has so far issued Quran translations in nine (African) languages and distributed the translations in 24 African countries (Ozturk and Tokat 2019; TDV 2019; Tokat, Ozturk and Mercan 2019).

Diyanet aims at influencing Africa's Muslim population especially through its increasing aid campaigns. The organization pays special attention to qurban (sacrifice) organizations in African countries. Diyanet's "qurban by proxy" program, started in 2018, aims at particularly intense conflict-ridden African countries including Chad, Sudan, South Sudan, Niger, Mali, Central African Republic and Burundi. For example, Diyanet was able to collect 19.5 million Turkish liras in donations for its Mali campaign launched in 2012 following the humanitarian crisis in the country (TDV 2020a). Another US $4 million was raised as part of Diyanet's Sudan campaign in 2019 (TDV 2020c) in the aftermath of the flood disaster that caused extensive damage in many parts of the country.

Diyanet's sister-city project also aims to increase cooperation with Muslim communities and to help those communities preserve their religious identities. The project started after the collapse of the Soviet Union in the early 1990s in order to meet various needs of citizens in Turkic Republics and was called "bond of brotherhood." It later became "Sister City Project" in the second half of the 2000s. The project includes sister cities in various African capitals as well. For example, Cankaya district in Ankara has become sister cities with Djibouti City, Amasya's Merzifon district has become sister cities with Dakar in Senegal, and Izmir's Buca district has become sister cities with Maputo in Mozambique (Diyanet 2017).

Diyanet also organizes meetings that bring together religious leaders from different African countries. Although Turkey refrained from hosting religious meetings and being a participant in those events (Ozkan 2013, 48), they are now being held on a regular basis. The first African Muslim Religious Leaders Summit took place in Istanbul in 2006. It was attended by representatives from 19 African countries while the second summit, organized in 2011, was attended by religious authorities from 42 countries. The third summit was organized in 2019 with the participation of 112 Muslim leaders such as ministers, presidents of religious affairs, head muftis, and academicians from 51 countries. The parties agreed to increase their cooperation and communication especially in religious education in Africa (Diyanet 2019). Officials argue that such meetings help to promote Turkish culture and history in addition to the Turkish way of understanding Islam (Ozturk and Tokat 2019) and to expand Turkey's political and economic relations with African countries (Tokat, Ozturk and Mercan 2019).

Following the first summit, TDV started to provide scholarships for Muslim students from African countries to study religion at high schools and at university theology faculties across Turkey. The Foundation has two different scholarship programs: International Imam Hatip High School Scholarship Program and International Islamic Sciences Scholarship Program both aim "to contribute Islamic education of the Muslim communities ... and to build cultural bridges between Turkey and related societies" (TDV n.d.). Those who receive religious education in Turkey are from 111 different countries while a total of 15,531 students study in those schools at high school, undergraduate and graduate levels (TDV 2020b, 4). The number of African students that apply for Diyanet's funds reached 1,000 in 2019 (TDV 2019). TDV also restored the Sheikh Sufi Imam Hatip High School in Somalia's capital, Mogadishu that currently hosts 500 students (Awel 2018).

The most visible soft power initiative of Diyanet is the construction of Ottoman-style (mega-)mosques or restoration of existing mosques and madrasas. Turkey's mosque-building program is taken as part of its grand strategy to place the country at the center of the Islamic world (Jones 2015) and to extend its prestige and power in the global scene (*The Economist* 2016). The mosque being built by Diyanet in the Albanian capital, Tirana, will be the largest in the Balkans while the US$100-million Muslim center in Maryland including a large mosque and a cultural center is said to be the biggest Islamic campus in the Western hemisphere (Beck 2019). Among the other mega-mosques is the Central Mosque of Imam Sarakhsi in Kyrgyzstan's capital, Bishkek, the largest in Central Asia and the Accra Mosque in Ghana, the largest in West Africa. TDV built East Africa's biggest mosque, Abdulhamid Han II Mosque, in the capital city of Djibouti, a small but strategically important African country of less than a million people (Getachew 2018).[6] The Nizamiye Mosque built by the TDV in South Africa is the largest in the Southern hemisphere. Turkey has also been involved in the renovation of the Mosque of Islamic Solidarity in Somalia's capital, Mogadishu, the largest mosque in the Horn of Africa while it has also helped to renovate mosques in South Africa. Turkish mosques are scattered among different African countries including Burkina Faso, Mali and Chad (Frohlich 2019).[7]

In the delivery of humanitarian aid, Diyanet works mostly in cooperation with the Turkish Red Crescent (Kizilay), Disaster and Emergency Management Presidency (AFAD), TIKA and other Turkish charities. Launching various projects some of which are religious in nature (Kayaoglu 2016, 19) and helping to develop relations with grassroots Muslim organizations (Oktem 2012, 37), TIKA is also involved in Turkey's track-one diplomacy. It promotes Turkey's religious influence especially in former Ottoman territories by renovating Ottoman-era buildings and constructing and restoring mosques, tombs and other religious buildings. TIKA was assigned to conduct Turkey's restoration efforts abroad with the Prime Ministry Circular issued in 2008. More than 50 mosques have been restored in the last five years as part of TIKA's mosque restoration projects. The reported aim is to protect the cultural heritage in countries that were once part of the Ottoman Empire (TIKA 2019a). Being responsible for the distribution of the country's development assistance, TIKA also implements several development cooperation projects in African countries through its program coordination offices (PCOs).

TIKA has PCOs in 24 African countries which correspond to approximately 40 percent of the total PCOs. Bryant and Hatay (2013, 2) noted that most of those coordination offices are located in countries with significant Muslim populations and that Turkish aid investment also focuses mostly on the Muslim countries of North and sub-Saharan Africa including Somalia, Sudan, Libya and Djibouti. Against these critiques, that TIKA gives priority to countries with high Muslim populations, Erdogan said that "We do not only help countries with a Muslim population, we also send assistance to suffering and aggrieved non-Muslim countries and we will continue to do so" (TIKA 2018). Yet, the location of TIKA's PCOs in Africa indicates that only six are in countries without sizeable Muslim populations.[8]

The aid delivered by the Turkish HNGOs (humanitarian non-governmental organizations) also focuses mostly on Muslim-populated areas although they do claim not to discriminate against aid recipients because of their religion or belief. This is justified by referring to their religious obligations (the idea of ummah) to fellow Muslim brothers. The perception that Muslim communities suffer more but receive less aid than other communities also plays a role in their motivations (Aras 2018, 6). Providing significant amounts of humanitarian assistance and emergency relief especially in former Ottoman territories, Turkish faith-based NGOs also serve as agents of public diplomacy (Cevik 2014).

Various studies discuss the connection between Turkish foreign policy and the complementary activities of faith-based NGOs. For example, Aras and Akpinar (2015, 240) note that:

> the work of the HNGOs intersects with national foreign policy objectives. Humanitarian activity has increased in the geographies of Turkey's foreign policy activism. In some cases, HNGO activities in Africa and Asia actually precede Turkey's official reach, leading rather than following this foreign policy activism.

Celik and Iseri (2016, 437) also reiterate: "Members of the NGOs praise Turkey's foreign policy activism, its opening in Africa ... They regard Turkey as a rising power and responsible for the Muslim World." A recent study by Zengin and Korkmaz (2019) revealed that religious/cultural affinity, historical affiliations and Ottoman past are the major determinants of Turkey's foreign aid behavior. Another study also noted that Turkey's humanitarian decisions are affected by cultural and religious proximities with the local populations, in contrast to Western donors (Thiessen and Ozerdem 2019). An NGO official working in Somalia reportedly noted that the fact that Turkey is a predominantly Muslim country provides it an important advantage. Another humanitarian leader said: "religious affinity allowed and required Turkish actors to expand their influence beyond the conventional – funding the restoration of mosques, facilitating imam exchanges to Turkey and working closely with Turkey's Ministry of Islamic Affairs to issue scholarships for Somali students to study religion in Turkey" (Thiessen and Ozerdem 2019, 1987).

There are various humanitarian NGOs operating in different African countries, most of them religiously-motivated.[9] As noted in TIKA reports, those NGOs with which TIKA cooperates in initiating aid activities include *Insan Hak ve Hurriyetleri Insani Yardim Vakfi* (Humanitarian Relief Organization: IHH), *Dosteller* (Friendly Nations), *Besir* Foundation, *Cansuyu* (Life Water) Society of Aid and Solidarity, *Deniz Feneri* (Lighthouse) Association, *Dost Eli* (Friend's Hand) Society of Aid and Solidarity, Sadakatashi Society, *Yardımeli* (Helping Hands) Society, Society of Doctors of Earth, *Yeryuzu Doktorlari* (Doctors Worldwide Turkey), Aziz Mahmut Hudayi Foundation, *Hayrat* Humanitarian Assistance Foundation and Hasene International. Most are members of the Union of NGOs of the Islamic World.[10] The latest TIKA report on Turkey's development assistance reveals that NGO assistance reached US$826.5 million in 2018 (2019b, 10). Their aid projects cover different sectors including education, health, emergency and humanitarian aid, water and sanitation, social infrastructures, capacity building and agricultural development. Yet, they largely focus on drilling water wells in different African countries reasoning that an important difficulty in the region is the lack of access to safe water. In 2018, 2,400 wells were drilled by these NGOs, of which 369 were in Chad, 193 in Somalia, 120 in Mali, 74 in Tanzania, 72 in Kenya, 72 in Ethiopia, 64 in Burkina Faso, 60 in Guinea, 58 in Cameroon, 50 in Zimbabwe and 50 in Niger (which corresponds to half of these water drills; TIKA 2019b, 121). Similar to Diyanet and TIKA, they are also involved in the construction and renovation of religious buildings, initiate qurban campaigns (such as the distribution of meat and food packages) and increase their activities significantly especially on religious holidays to show their solidarity with fellow Muslims in African countries (Ozkan and Akgun 2010, 541).

Among the many NGOs, taking the lead in Africa is the IHH, established in 1992. Experts note that Turkish leaders have included IHH projects in the agenda of their meetings (Ozkan and Akgun 2010, 541) and that the IHH has even "paved the way for the acceleration of Turkey–Africa relations, exemplifying the converging interests between state and civil society" (Ozkan and Akgun 2010: 539). Advertising itself as "the first NGO in the Islamic world that carries out humanitarian diplomacy," the IHH was also the first Turkish NGO in Turkey to launch a nationwide campaign for Africa (2006 Africa Emergency Aid Campaign) and to initiate the biggest healthcare campaign in Africa with its cataract project (IHH n.d.).

Among those Islamically-oriented NGOs focusing mostly on the health sector, *Yeryuzu Doktorlari* aims at being the leading NGO in healthcare aid. It has initiated health projects in different African countries including Chad, Cameroon, Kenya, Niger, Somalia, Sudan, Tanzania and Uganda. This involves providing emergency treatment services examination, medication and consumables support, maternity services and surgery. The *Deniz Feneri* Association has its own cataract project that covers the costs of cataract operations of Africans. With its water wells Project, it also has 905 water wells opened in 11 African countries affected by recurrent water shortages. The Association also builds masjids in African countries including Benin, Ghana, Somalia and Ethiopia reasoning; "along with clean water, food, health and education services in Africa, one of the biggest needs is the place of worship." It conducts a special campaign, "The Quran is the Best Gift" and distributes the Quran to Africans "who try to learn their religion under very difficult conditions" (Deniz Feneri Association 2018).

Several Islamic NGOs also work in the field of education including *Hasene* International, the Nile Foundation, *Cansuyu* Foundation, DUNYEV, *Deniz Feneri* Foundation, *Yardımeli* and *Besir* Foundation, open schools and other educational centers in different African countries and provide scholarships and training for African students and religious personnel. In Somalia alone, Turkish NGOs built 11 educational buildings and provided 1,000 scholarships for Somalian students (Aras and Akpinar 2015, 236–246).

Before the split between the government and Gulen movement, the latter invested heavily in education and has been opening schools in sub-Saharan Africa since the late 1990s. However, the movement is also known for its humanitarian work including the distribution of qurban donations. According to Ali Erbas, the President of Diyanet, the Gulen movement is utilizing the qurban organizations in a way to exploit the religious sensitivities of people "by including the names of the Prophet and the great figures of Islam in their exploitative activities" (Diyanet 2018). Gulen-affiliated aid agencies also establish hospitals, clinics and orphanages across the continent. For example, *Kimse Yok mu* Solidarity and Aid Association (KYM), the main aid channel of the movement, was once very active in Africa through its humanitarian work since the second half of the 2000s. KYM distributed approximately US$17.5 million of assistance to 43 African countries in 2013 (Donelli 2019, 74). It was closed down by a government decree following the 2016 coup attempt together with more than 2,000 Gulen-linked establishments including private education institutions, associations and dormitories operating across Turkey (Senen and Gunerigok 2016). The political fallout between the government and the movement can potentially undermine Turkey's humanitarian and religious involvement in the continent.

Conclusion

Turkish foreign policy under the JDP government witnessed the increasing use of religion. This chapter, essentially, attempted to analyze how Turkey has incorporated religion into its broader foreign policy conduct with a special focus on the religious component in Turkey's Africa policy. Religion serves as a key element in Ankara's quest for a greater international influence and a legitimizing tool for its regional leadership claims. This religious dimension also distinguishes Turkey's engagement in Africa from many of the rising players. While religion played a significant role in expanding Turkey's influence in Africa, especially in Muslim-majority countries, it also has inherent vulnerabilities.

Despite the official rhetoric emphasizing how Turkey's religious outreach activities are welcomed by the recipients, some African countries may view Turkey's efforts with suspicion and even interpret the pronouncements of government officials against the Gulen movement's religious activities as interference in their domestic politics. So, Turkey's religious diplomacy can produce varied results. The increasing reference to religious ties and Islamic solidarity might contribute to Turkey's appeal in African countries with large Muslim populations but such narratives also have the potential to jeopardize Turkey's relations with non-Muslim majority countries in SSA, if they are not carefully managed (Eyrice Tepeciklioglu 2019, 14). What is more, the recent rift between the government and the faith based-Gulen movement might complicate Turkey–Africa relations especially in the NGO sphere.

Notes

1 Chapter 9 by Cevik provides details on the government–Gulen conflict and its repercussions on foreign policy.

2 As Ahmed (2020) states: "The reversion of the Hagia Sophia to a mosque, a role it fulfilled for almost five hundred years, is the latest development as Erdogan reasserts Turkey's status as a regional power ... the 300-year struggle for the leadership of Sunni Islam appears to be edging back in Turkey's favor, with the Hagia Sophia move being the latest projection of Ankara's soft power."
3 Mehmet Ozkan's 2013- and 2014-dated publications (noted in the reference list) are the only exceptions in this regard. While the former is a brief analysis of six pages focusing on both religious and socio-political elements visible in Turkey's Africa policy, the latter has a separate section for Turkey's religious diplomacy efforts in Africa along with other sections on Latin America, the Balkans and Eurasia.
4 Although there were many advocates of this rationalist approach that undermined the role of religion in international relations, the most influential sociologists of religion that are accepted to have developed the secularization theory during the 1960s and 1970s were Berger, Martin and Wilson. It was mostly the works of Durkheim and Weber that laid the foundation for the secularization theor(ies).
5 See the English translation of the law at: Laws Turkey. n.d. "5253 Law on Associations." Accessed October12, 2020. http://www.lawsturkey.com/law/law-on-associations-5253.
6 Turkey also has plans to build grand mosques in Latin American countries of Cuba and Venezuela. The former is a communist state inhabited by a predominantly Catholic population and only a few thousand Muslims. When Turkish President Erdogan visited the country in 2015, he proposed the construction of the first mosque in the Cuban capital, Havana (Butler 2015).
7 For a detailed list of Turkish mosques abroad, see the webpage of TDV at: TDV n.d. "Camiler" (Mosques). Accessed September 22, 2020. https://tdv.org/tr-TR/faaliyetlerimiz/camiler/.
8 The list includes those countries having a Muslim population ratio below 20 percent.
9 There are also non-religious NGOs (i.e. Sen de Gel) implementing aid activities in Africa but they are limited in number while some recently-founded NGOs including Association of the Friends of Africa (TADD) and Afrika İnsani Dernegi (Africa Human Association), focus their activities solely on Africa.
10 The headquarters of the organization is in Istanbul, Turkey. See The Union of NGOs of the Islamic World n.d. "About." Accessed October 10, 2020. https://www.idsb.org/en/kurumsal/about.

References

Adanali, Ahmet Hadi. 2008. "The Presidency of Religious Affairs and the Principle of Secularism in Turkey." *The Muslim World* 98, no. 2–3: 228–241. https://doi.org/10.1111/j.1478-1913.2008.00221.x.

Ahmed, Omar. 2020. "Turkey may have Reclaimed the Leadership of Sunni Islam from Saudi Arabia." *Middle East Monitor*. July 30, 2020. https://www.middleeastmonitor.com/20200730-turkey-may-have-reclaimed-the-leadership-of-sunni-islam-from-saudi-arabia/.

Alasuutari, Pertti. 2004. *Social Theory & Human Reality*. London, Thousand Oaks and New Delhi: Sage Publications.

Aras, Bulent. 2018. "Medical Humanitarianism of Turkey's NGOS: A 'Turkish Way'?" *Alternatives: Global, Local, Political* 42, no. 4: 1–12. https://doi.org/10.1177%2F0304375418754404.

Aras, Bulent and Pinar Akpinar. 2015. "The Role of Humanitarian NGOs in Turkey's Peacebuilding." *International Peacekeeping* 22, no. 3: 230–247. DOI https://doi.org/10.1080/13533312.2015.1033374.

Awel, Munira Abdelmenan. 2018. "Somalia: Turkish Foundation's School Hosts 500 Students." Anadolu Agency. January 30, 2018. https://www.aa.com.tr/en/africa/somalia-turkish-foundations-school-hosts-500-students/1047638.

Beck, John. 2019. "Turkey's Global Soft-Power Push is Built on Mosques." *The Atlantic*, June 1, 2019. https://www.theatlantic.com/international/archive/2019/06/turkey-builds-mosques-abroad-global-soft-power/590449/.

Berger, Peter L. 1967. *The Sacred Canopy*. Garden City, NY: Doubleday.

Berger, Peter L. 1996/97. "Secularism in Retreat." *The National Interest* 46: 3–12.

Bryant, Rebecca and Mete Hatay. 2013. "Soft Politics and Hard Choices: An Assessment of Turkey's New Regional Diplomacy." Peace Research Institute Oslo (PRIO) PCC Report 2. https://www.prio.org/utility/DownloadFile.ashx?id=439&type=publicationfile.

Butler, Daren. 2015. "Turkey's Erdogan Proposes Building Mosque in Cuba." Reuters. February 12, 2015. https://www.reuters.com/article/us-turkey-cuba-mosque-idUSKBN0LG1E220150212.

Celik, Emre and Emre Iseri. 2016. "Islamically Oriented Humanitarian NGOs in Turkey: AKP Foreign Policy Parallelism." *Turkish Studies* 17, no. 3: 429–448. https://doi.org/10.1080/14683849.2016.1204917.

Cevik, Senem. 2014. "The Rise of NGOs: Islamic Faith Diplomacy." CPD Blog, USC Center on Public Diplomacy. May 27, 2014. https://uscpublicdiplomacy.org/blog/rise-ngos-islamic-faith-diplomacy.

Curanović, Alicja. 2012. "The Religious Diplomacy of the Russian Federation." Ifri - Russia/NIS Center, Paris. https://www.ifri.org/sites/default/files/atoms/files/ifrirnr12curanovicreligiousdiplomacyjune2012.pdf.

Danan, Liora. 2013. "Shaping the Narrative of Religious Freedom." In *Religion and Public Diplomacy*, edited by Philip Seib, 181–213. New York, NY: Palgrave Macmillan.

Demirtas, Birgul. 2015. "Turkish Foreign Policy Towards the Balkans: A Europeanised Foreign Policy in a De-Europeanised National Context?" *Journal of Balkan and Near Eastern Studies* 17, no. 2: 123–140. https://doi.org/10.1080/19448953.2014.994283.

Deniz Feneri Association. 2018. "Masjid Project." https://www.denizfeneri.org.tr/en/bagis/masjid-project_1841/.

Diyanet. 2017. "208 Sister Cities in 93 Countries." https://www.diyanet.gov.tr/en-US/Institutional/Detail/9978/208-sister-cities-in-93-countries.

Diyanet. 2018. "Introductory Meeting for the 'Qurban' (Sacrifice) by Proxy Program 2018." https://www.diyanet.gov.tr/en-US/Content/PrintDetail/11758.

Diyanet. 2019. "3rd African Summit of Muslim Religious Leaders Ends with the Final Declaration to be Read." https://diyanet.gov.tr/en-US/Content/PrintDetail/26049.

Donelli, Federico. 2019. "The Gulen Movement in Africa: From Turkish Transnational Asset to Anti-State Lobby." *Israel Journal of Foreign Affairs* 13: 67–80. https://doi.org/10.1080/23739770.2019.1632588.

Eyrice Tepeciklioglu, Elem. 2019. "Turkey-Africa Relations in 2018: Two Decades after Turkey's Opening to Africa.", *Africa Yearbook 2018*, Wilson Center Africa Program.

Frohlich, Silja. 2019. "Mosques in Africa: A Test of Strength in the Middle East." *Deutsche Welle*. December 18, 2019. https://www.dw.com/en/mosques-in-africa-a-test-of-strength-in-the-middle-east/a-51717439.

Getachew, Addis. 2018. "Turkey to Inaugurate Largest Mosque in Djibouti in Feb." Anadolu Agency. December 7, 2018. https://www.aa.com.tr/en/africa/turkey-to-inaugurate-largest-mosque-in-djibouti-in-feb/1332035.

Gozaydin, Istar B. 2008. "Diyanet and Politics." *The Muslim World* 98, no. 2–3: 216–227. https://doi.org/10.1111/j.1478-1913.2008.00220.x.

Gozaydin, Istar B. 2010. "*Religion as Soft Power in the International Relations of Turkey.*" Paper presented at International Political Science Association. Sao Paulo, February 2010. http://www.psa.ac.uk/Proceedings.

Hatzopoulos, Pavlos and Fabio Petito, eds. 2003. *Religion in International Relations: The Return from Exile.* Palgrave Macmillan.

IHH. n.d. "Our History." Accessed May 19, 2020. https://www.ihh.org.tr/en/history.

Jones, Dorian. 2015. "Does Turkey Aspire to the Leadership of the Islamic World?" Qantara.de, March 13, 2015. https://en.qantara.de/content/turkeys-mosque-building-programme-does-turkey-aspire-to-the-leadership-of-the-islamic-world.

Kayaoglu, Turhan. 2016. "Getting Turkey Back on Track to Democracy, Human Rights, and Religious Freedom." *The Review of Faith & International Affairs* 14, no. 2: 14–22. https://doi.org/10.1080/15570274.2016.1184447.

Lepeska, David. 2015. "Turkey Casts the Diyanet: Ankara's Religious Directorate Takes Off." *Foreign Affairs.* May 17, 2015. https://www.foreignaffairs.com/articles/turkey/2015-05-17/turkey-casts-diyanet.

Mandaville, Peter and Shadi Hamid. 2018. "Islam as Statecraft: How Governments use Religion in Foreign Policy." Foreign Policy at Brookings. https://www.brookings.edu/wp-content/uploads/2018/11/FP_20181116_islam_as_statecraft.pdf.

Martin, David. 1978. *A General Theory of Secularization.* Oxford: Basil Blackwell.

Oguzlu, Tarik. 2007. "Soft Power in Turkish Foreign Policy." *Australian Journal of International Affairs* 61, no. 1: 81–97. https://doi.org/10.1080/10357710601142518.

Oktem, Kerem. 2012. "Global Diyanet and Multiple Networks: Turkey's New Presence in the Balkans." *Journal of Muslims in Europe* 1: 27–58. https://doi.org/10.1163/221179512X644042.

Ozkan, Mehmet. 2013. "Turkey's Religious and Socio-Political Depth in Africa." *LSE IDEAS Special Report 16*: 45–50. https://www.lse.ac.uk/ideas/Assets/Documents/reports/LSE-IDEAS-Emerging-Powers-in-Africa.pdf.

Ozkan, Mehmet. 2014. "Turkey's Religious Diplomacy." *The Arab World Geographer* 17, no. 3: 223–237.

Ozkan, Mehmet and Birol Akgun. 2010. "Turkey's Opening to Africa." *The Journal of Modern African Studies* 48, no. 4: 525–546. https://doi.org/10.1017/S0022278X10000595.

Ozturk, Ahmet Erdi. 2016. "Turkey's Diyanet under AKP Rule: From Protector to Imposer of State Ideology?" *Southeast European and Black Sea Studies.* 16, no. 4: 619–635. https://doi.org/10.1080/14683857.2016.1233663.

Ozturk, Ahmet Erdi. 2019. "An Alternative Reading of Religion and Authoritarianism: The New Logic between Religion and State in the AKP's New Turkey." *Southeast European and Black Sea Studies* 19, no. 1: 79–98. https://doi.org/10.1080/14683857.2019.1576370.

Ozturk, Ahmet Erdi and Semiha Sozeri. 2018. "Diyanet as a Turkish Foreign Policy Tool: Evidence from the Netherlands and Bulgaria." *Politics and Religion* 11: 624–648. https://doi.org/10.1017/S175504831700075X.

Ozturk, Mehmet and Faruk Tokat. 2019. "Turkey's Activities 'Wholeheartedly' Welcomed in Africa." Anadolu Agency. October 20, 2019. https://www.aa.com.tr/en/africa/turkey-s-activities-wholeheartedly-welcomed-in-africa/1619913.

Philpott, David. 2001. *Revolutions in Sovereignty: How Ideas Shaped Modern International Relations*. Princeton and Oxford: Princeton University Press.

Sandal, Nukhet A. and Jonathan Fox. 2013. *Religion in International Relations Theory Interactions and Possibilities*. London and New York: Routledge.

Seib, Peter. 2013. "Introduction." In *Religion and Public Diplomacy*, edited by Philip Seib, 1–7. New York, NY: Palgrave Macmillan.

Senen, Tutku and Servet Gunerigok. 2016. "Turkey Shuts Down over 2,000 Gulen-Linked Institutions." Anadolu Agency. July 23, 2016. ttps://www.aa.com.tr/en/todays-headlines/turkey-shuts-down-over-2-000-gulen-linked-institutions-/613991.

Stempel, John D. 2000. "Faith and Diplomacy in the International System." The Patterson School of Diplomacy and International Commerce. http://www.uky.edu/~stempel/pdf/FaithDip&Int_syst_2_00.pdf.

T24. 2019. "Diyanet'in 2020 butcesi sekiz bakanligi geride birakti, butcenin 125 milyon lirasi derneklere aktarilacak." October 24, 2019. https://t24.com.tr/haber/diyanet-in-2020-butcesi-sekiz-bakanligi-geride-birakti-butcenin-125-milyon-lirasi-derneklere-aktarilacak,845137.

TDV. 2019. "TDV'den Afrika ulkelerine 111.6 milyon dolarlik yardim." https://tdv.org/tr-TR/tdvden-afrika-ulkelerine-111-6-milyon-dolarlik-yardim/.

TDV. 2020a. "Afrika." https://bagis.tdv.org/Pages/DonationDetail.aspx?dsc=3006&dc=3000#/0.

TDV. 2020b. "International Imam Hatip High School Scholarship Program / Application Guide." https://diyanetburslari.tdv.org/wp-content/uploads/2020/01/lise_klavuz_tumdiller_ Sayfa_026.jpg.

TDV. 2020c. "Kriz Bolgeleri." https://tdv.org/tr-TR/faaliyetlerimiz/kriz-bolgeleri/.

TDV. n.d. "Diyanet Scholarships." Accessed August 12, 2020. https://diyanetburslari.tdv.org/en/.

The Economist. 2016. "Turkey's Religious Diplomacy: Mosqued Objectives." January 21, 2016. https://www.economist.com/europe/2016/01/21/mosqued-objectives.

The Union of NGOs of the Islamic World. n.d. "About." Accessed October 10, 2020. https://www.idsb.org/en/kurumsal/about.

Thiessen, Chuck and Alpaslan Ozerdem. 2019. "Turkey in Somalia: Challenging North/Western Interventionism?" *Third World Quarterly* 40, no. 11: 1976–1995. https://doi.org/10.1080/01436597.2019.1619074.

Thomas, Scott M. 2005. *The Global Resurgence of Religion and the Transformation of International Relations: The Struggle for the Soul of the Twenty-First Century*. New York, NY: Palgrave Macmillan.

TIKA. 2018. "President Erdogan Welcomed TIKA Coordinators." https://www.tika.gov.tr/en/news/president_erdogan_welcomed_tika_coordinators-43472.

TIKA. 2019a. "TIKA has Restored more than 50 Mosques in the Past 5 Years." https://www.tika.gov.tr/en/news/tika_has_restored_more_than_50_mosques_in_the_past_5_years-53824.

TIKA. 2019b. "Turkish Development Assistance Report." https://www.tika.gov.tr/upload/2020/02/kyk%202018/TurkiyeKalkinma2018ENG.pdf.

Tokat, Faruk, Mehmet Ozturk and Ahmet Furkan Mercan. 2019. "Afrika'daki dini kuruluslar arasinda birligin tesisi icin calisiyoruz." Anadolu Agency. October 20, 2019. https://www.aa.com.tr/tr/turkiye/afrikadaki-dini-kuruluslar-arasinda-birligin-tesisi-icin-calisiyoruz/1620047.

Tol, Gonul. 2019. "Turkey's Bid for Religious Leadership: How the AKP Uses Islamic Soft Power." *Foreign Affairs*. January 10, 2019. https://www.foreignaffairs.com/articles/turkey/2019-01-10/turkeys-bid-religious-leadership.

Turhan, Yunus and Serif Onur Bahcecik. 2020. "The Agency of Faith Based NGOs in Turkish Humanitarian Aid Policy and Practice." *Turkish Studies*. https://doi.org/10.1080/14683849.2020.1756786.

Wellman, David Joseph. 2016. "Religion and Diplomacy." In *The Sage Handbook of Diplomacy*, edited by Costas M. Constantinou, Pauline Kerr and Paul Sharp, 577–590. Los Angeles: Sage.

Wilson, Brian R. 1966. *Religion in Secular Society*. Harmondsworth, Middlesex, UK: Penguin Books, Ltd.

Yilmaz, Ihsan and James Barry. 2020. "Instrumentalizing Islam in a 'Secular' State: Turkey's Diyanet and Interfaith Dialogue." *Journal of Balkan and Near Eastern Studies* 22, no.1: 1–16. https://doi.org/10.1080/19448953.2018.1506301.

Zengin, Huseyin and Abdurrahman Korkmaz. 2019. "Determinants of Turkey's Foreign Aid Behavior." *New Perspectives of Turkey* 60: 109–135. https://doi.org/10.1017/npt.2019.1.

12 Turkish Airlines as a source of soft power in Africa

Orçun Selçuk

Introduction

As the main theme of the book suggests, Turkey aspires to be a rising power in global politics, which manifests itself in the country's developing diplomatic, commercial and humanitarian engagement with its immediate neighborhood as well as more distant geographies. In line with this theme, this chapter considers Turkish Airlines a soft power tool that complements Turkey's rising power status and nation branding through its operations in Africa. Building on my previous work on the subject (Selcuk 2012, 2013), in this chapter, I argue that the Justice and Development Party (AKP) governments have successfully utilized Turkey's national airline company as a foreign policy tool to support their rising power ambitions in Africa. As Turkish Airlines has dramatically increased its number of flight destinations from 4 to 58, it has facilitated the physical movement of people as well as goods across national boundaries. In parallel with the growing number of flight destinations, Turkish Airlines has also increased its humanitarian and cultural engagement with African audiences, which helps to boost Turkey's image as a benign country, and most importantly, perceptions of a rising power in the continent.

To evaluate Turkey's rising power status (Parlar Dal 2016), Turkish Airlines' increasing presence in the African continent strengthens its claim to be a leading country with the ability to play a more active role on the world stage. As Turkey opens new embassies in African countries and Turkish Airlines inaugurates new flight destinations in coordination with diplomatic engagement, its claim to be an active player becomes more credible and convincing. Materially speaking, as the Turkish economy is growing, Turkish Airlines facilitates commercial relations with the continent and incentivizes businesspeople on both sides to increase the volume of trade and foreign direct investment. It is striking that the inaugural flights to African countries always include the representatives of Turkish companies, who are willing to explore new markets and diversify their global portfolio. From an ideational perspective, Turkish Airlines' involvement in cultural and humanitarian activities boosts Turkey's attempts to be perceived as a rising power among

Muslim populations in countries such as Somalia, Nigeria, Senegal and Ethiopia. Overall, through these concerted mechanisms, the AKP governments use Turkish Airlines as a contributor to Turkey's rising power status.

To further scrutinize how Turkish Airlines contributes to Turkey's rising power status in Africa, the chapter is organized as follows. The next section provides a broad overview of the relationship between national airlines and foreign policy. The second section reviews Turkish Airlines' historical role in the context of Turkish foreign policy. The third section describes the evolution of Turkish Airlines under the AKP governments into a soft power tool amid rising power ambitions and nation branding. Building on this theoretical and historical background, the fourth section outlines Turkish Airlines' role in Africa. In conclusion, the chapter restates the main findings of the chapter.

National airlines and foreign policy: A global view

Since the early years of the aviation industry, political factors have influenced the operations of airline companies. At the very outset, airlines utilize runways, airports and airspace of sovereign states, and they are subject to a set of regulations like any other enterprise that operates inside an internationally recognized territory. From the perspective of states, the development of national airlines is not only a profit-oriented business but also has ramifications for domestic and international politics. At the domestic level, airlines facilitate the nation-building process through delivering mail and cargo, allowing citizens to travel within the country, providing employment and backing up defense capability in case of an emergency (Thornton 1971; Rhoades 2002; Shaw 2004). At the international level, the establishment of a national airline boosts a country's status, prestige and self-confidence. Since national airlines carry the flag of their country around the globe, they are often viewed as a symbol of status and national strength (O'Connor 1971; Hanlon 1996; Thrulow and Aiello 2007). Accordingly, if a national airline goes bankrupt, is involved in a fatal accident, or even loses a passenger's baggage, it could potentially lead to negative attitudes towards its country of origin as well. On the flip side, if a national airline is thriving and its passengers enjoy their interactions with the flight crew, in-flight meal and whole travel experience, it should have a positive contribution to the perception of a country and its global image. This phenomenon is also known as the inverse country-of-origin effect, when brands like IKEA, Red Bull and Skype enhance the image of Sweden, Austria and Estonia respectively (White 2012). Thus, national airline companies could also be conceptualized in this manner.

Before delving into the historical relationship between Turkish Airlines and politics, it is important to identify a list of airline companies with a clear mission of serving their country's domestic and foreign policy tools. To start with the historical cases, Pan American World Airways represented

American national interest in the Western hemisphere and around the world. At the height of its operations, the unofficial flag carrier of the United States effectively coordinated with the State Department and acted like "the savior and the protector of the American way of life" (Durepos, Mills and Mills 2008, 123). In a similar fashion, the British Empire used Imperial Airways to assert its sovereignty in distant territories and fulfill a feeling of unity in the Commonwealth. To achieve those objectives, an overwhelming majority of flight destinations in the 1930s belonged to the routes of the empire (Pirle 2004). Another imperial power, France has also used its national airline company to sustain its cultural influence over its former colonies in West Africa, the Caribbean, and elsewhere (Golder 1997).

Among national flag carriers in Asia, Malaysian Airlines contributed to the nation-building process through its flights to distant parts of the country. For a city-state like Singapore, having a top-ranked national airline company served as a tool of nation branding (Raguraman 1997). A similar framework applies to Qatar Airways, Emirates Airlines and Etihad Airways, which are global brand ambassadors of small but powerful petrostates in the Persian Gulf (Peterson 2006). During the Cold War, Yugoslav Airlines (JAT) aimed to project power to its citizens at home and promote the country's status as one of the leading members of the non-aligned movement. In line with Yugoslavian foreign policy objectives, JAT inaugurated flights to other non-aligned states in Africa, Asia and the Middle East (Subotić 2018). In the same period, newly independent African countries established a multi-national airline company called Air Afrique, which promoted the ideals of Pan-Africanism and regional integration (Amankwah-Amoah and Debrah 2014).

Turkish Airlines and Turkish foreign policy

Akin to the above-mentioned airline companies, Turkish Airlines has always had a political dimension that is essentially tied to Turkey's foreign policy goals, orientations and ambitions. When Turkish Airlines was established in 1933, the Republican elite saw it as a symbol of national prestige and a proof of the country finally catching up with modernity and civilization (Albayrak 1983). From a foreign policy standpoint, it is important to note that one of the five airplanes in the Turkish Airlines fleet at that time was given by the Soviet Union to mark the Turkish Republic's tenth anniversary (Nergiz 2008). Considering the close relations between the two governments at that time, this development is anything but surprising. Based on a similar logic, following the Second World War, as Turkey perceived the Soviet Union as a threat instead of a friend, Turkish Airlines started to develop closer ties with the United States and its Western allies. In the early years of the Cold War, Turkey's increasing anti-Soviet and pro-Western foreign policy manifested itself with the purchase of American and British aircraft and the inauguration of the first international flight to Athens as a symbol of Turkish–Greek friendship (Albayrak 1983). In the 1950s, Turkish Airlines sold 6.5 percent of its shares to British Overseas Airways Corporation as an indication of partnership with another NATO member (Turk Hava Yollari 2009).

In the 1960s, the Cyprus conflict and the Cuban Missile Crisis shook the foundations of Turkey's pro-Western foreign policy. As Turkey was disappointed with the foreign policies of the United States and its Western allies, it looked for alternatives and pursued closer relations with Eastern Bloc countries in the Balkans. In line with this shift in Turkish foreign policy, between 1965 and 1967, Turkish Airlines added Belgrade (Yugoslavia), Sofia (Bulgaria) and Budapest (Romania) to its flight route. It also sent a delegation to the Soviet Union to negotiate a possible purchase of aircraft, which was primarily a political act (Albayrak 1983; Kline 2002; Nergiz 2008). Following the Labor Recruitment Agreement, in the 1970s, Turkish Airlines established a series of flight routes in West Germany to meet the increasing demand from Turkish workers. After Turkey's military intervention to the island in 1974, Turkish Airlines partnered with the Turkish Cypriot community and established Cyprus Turkish Airlines. Even though the Turkish Cypriots lacked international recognition, this symbolic move aimed to convey a feeling of independence and prestige for Northern Cyprus. In the anti-imperialist mood of the era, the Minister of Finance also nationalized the British shares of Turkish Airlines in 1977 (Nergiz 2008). In the late 1970s, amid developing relations with the countries in the region, Turkish Airlines also increased its presence in the Middle East with the inauguration of Baghdad (Iraq), Tehran (Iran), Dhahran (Saudi Arabia), Kuwait and Jeddah (Saudi Arabia) routes (Albayrak 1983). Overall, the developments in Turkish foreign policy incentivized the national airline company to increase its involvement in Turkey's neighborhood.

In 1983, Turkish Airlines celebrated its 50th anniversary, which was also the year Turgut Ozal became the prime minister of Turkey. During the Ozal era, Turkish Airlines developed a new vision in line with the government's attempts to open up the economy to the rest of the world. As part of Turkey's opening to the rising East Asian markets, Turkish Airlines started to fly to Singapore, Mumbai (India) and Tokyo (Japan; Turk Hava Yollari 2009). Besides new route openings, just before the inception of the Iran–Iraq War, Prime Minister Ozal authorized an operation that rescued 215 Japanese citizens from Tehran. In 2015, this heroic gesture became a subject of the movie *"125 Years Memory,"* which tells a story of Japanese–Turkish friendship over time. The movie, of which Turkish Airlines and the Minister of Culture and Tourism were among the sponsors, connects the tragic sinking of an Ottoman frigate off the Japanese coast with the rescue of the Japanese citizens from Iran by Turkey's national flag carrier. Indeed, the Consul General of Japan in Istanbul, Hisao Hishimaki, refers to the Turkish–Japanese production as evidence of a historical bond between the two countries (Consulate General of Japan in Istanbul 2018).

Another international development that occurred under Ozal was the end of the Cold War in 1989. Only 18 days after the collapse of the Berlin Wall, Turkish Airlines started its flights to Moscow. According to the CEO of Turkish Airlines, Cem Kozlu, Ozal had already instructed him to consider flying to the Soviet Union, which would facilitate Turkey's engagement with Turkish speaking populations in Central Asia. In fact, as the Soviet Union was disintegrating, Turkey saw this as an opportunity to connect with the Turkic people. Parallel to this vision, in 1991, soon after Ozal's visit to the Soviet Union, Turkish Airlines started to operate flights to Baku (Azerbaijan). The following two years, it added Almaty (Kazakhstan), Tashkent (Uzbekistan) and Ashgabat (Turkmenistan) to its flight destinations (Kozlu 2009). Thanks to these new flight routes, Azerbaijan and the Central Asian Republics had an alternative hub to connect with the rest of the world.

The rise of Turkish Airlines under the JDP

In the post-Cold War era, another critical juncture for Turkish Airlines was the 2002 parliamentary elections, which ended a decade of unstable coalition governments. Once the AKP came to power, the government appointed new board members to Turkish Airlines. During my interview with Candan Karlitekin, who was appointed as the President of Turkish Airlines Board of Directors, he confirmed that Recep Tayyip Erdogan, Abdullah Gul and Ahmet Davutoglu set up a vision for Turkish Airlines in line with the AKP's foreign policy orientation (Karlitekin 2011). Similar to Ozal, then Prime Minister Erdogan envisaged Turkish Airlines as a foreign policy tool to facilitate Turkey's openings to the Middle East, Africa, the Black Sea region and the Balkans.

In the preface of the book prepared for Turkish Airlines' 75th anniversary, the prime minister described its role as a flag carrier of Turkey's road to modernization and a symbol of multilateral foreign policy. From an economic standpoint, Erdogan also underlined Turkish Airlines' potential to boost tourism and contribute to the country's growth and development. In the same book, the CEO of Turkish Airlines, Temel Kotil, described Turkish Airlines as the largest brand of Turkey in the world with its goal to be a major player in the global aviation industry. Kotil also drew an analogy likening Turkish Airlines to the Turkish national football team as both represent the Turkish flag at the international level (Turk Hava Yollari 2009).

In the early years of the AKP governments, similar to other instances in the history of Turkish Airlines, foreign policy considerations influenced the purchase of 36 aircraft from the European producer Airbus. As Turkey was aspiring to start accession negotiations with the European Union, the purchase of Airbus aircraft over the American company Boeing seemed to have a political dimension. During my interview with Karlitekin, who put his signature on the deal as the President of Turkish Airlines Board of Directors, he insisted that the decision was based on rational economic calculations, but, at the public level, it was presented as if political motives were the primary reason (Karlitekin 2011). As an indication of political considerations, Prime Minister Erdogan, French President Jacques Chirac and German Chancellor Gerard Schroder were present at the signing ceremony of the Airbus–Turkish Airlines deal in 2004.

From an economic standpoint, another development that occurred under the AKP's first parliamentary term (2002–2007) was the waves of privatization that reduced the state's share in Turkish Airlines to 49 percent and ended its status as a public entity. As a result of this change, the Prime Ministry Inspection Board no longer audited Turkish Airlines. Even though the majority of its shares were privately owned, the Turkish state, as the largest shareholder, remained dominant over the management of its national flag carrier. Overall, the influence of the Turkish government did not disappear but changed its format (Cicekci 2006). Since 2006, the share structure of Turkish Airlines has remained the same, which allows the Turkish government to influence the decision-making process including route openings and aircraft purchases. It also facilitates Turkish Airlines' coordination with other state agencies such as the Ministry of Foreign Affairs, Turkish Cooperation and Coordination Agency (TIKA), Turkish Radio and Television (TRT), Disaster and Emergency Management Presidency (AFAD), Yunus Emre Institute, Maarif Foundation, and Directorate of Religious Affairs to implement Turkish foreign policy objectives around the world. In this new era, Turkish Airlines not only reacted to foreign policy developments but also took an active and explicit role amid rising power ambitions.

Under the AKP governments, between 2004 and 2019, Turkish Airlines experienced continuous growth in terms of the number of passengers, transfer passengers and flight destinations (Turkish Airlines 2019; Sabah 2020). In 2004, Turkish Airlines carried a total of 11.9 million passengers. In 2010, this number reached 29 million. In 2018, the total number of passengers reached 75.1 million. In 2019, there was a slight decline to 74.2 million (Figure 12.1). The regional distribution of Turkish Airlines passengers in 2019 in scheduled flights (Figure 12.2) is as follows: Middle East (6.3 million), Europe (23.7 million), Far East (5.9 million), North America (2.4 million), Africa (3.6 million), Latin America (477 thousand) and Domestic (30.2 million). In 2019, Turkish Airlines also carried the following amount of cargo (Figure 12.3) for each region: Middle East (164.6 thousand), Europe (451.3 thousand), Far East (471.3 thousand), North America (142.6 thousand), Africa (127.3 thousand), Latin America (35.4 thousand) and Domestic (70.6 thousand). When we analyze both data points at the same time (Figure 12.4), Far East (79.8 thousand), Latin America (72.9 thousand) and North America (59.3 thousand) have the highest amount of cargo per million passengers.

In the last 15 years, in line with Turkish Airlines' growth strategy, the number of transfer passengers rose from a million in 2004 to 5 million in 2010, and 24.6 million in 2019. In 2019, one out of three Turkish Airlines passengers were transit passengers, which experienced a 5.4 percent increase

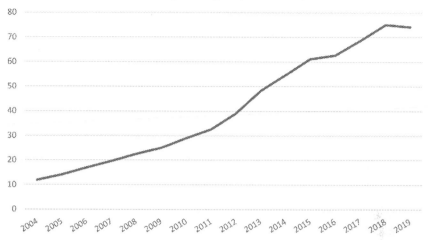

Figure 12.1 Turkish Airlines' number of passengers (2004–2019)
Source: Turkish Airlines, https://www.turkishairlines.com/en-us/press-room/about-us/turkish-airlines-in-numbers/.

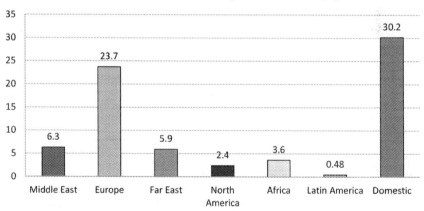

Figure 12.2 Turkish Airlines' number of passengers by region in 2019
Source: *Sabah*, https://www.sabah.com.tr/ekonomi/2020/01/10/2019da-742-milyon-yolcu-thy-ile-uctu-transit-yolcu-sayisi-245-milyona-yukseldi.

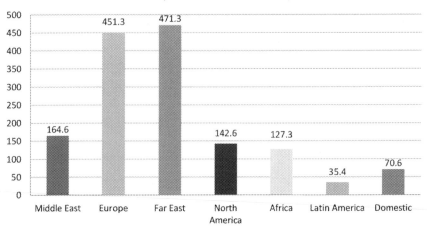

Figure 12.3 Amount of cargo carried by Turkish Airlines by region in 2019
Source: *Sabah*, https://www.sabah.com.tr/ekonomi/2020/01/10/2019da-742-milyon-yolcu-thy-ile-uctu-transit-yolcu-sayisi-245-milyona-yukseldi.

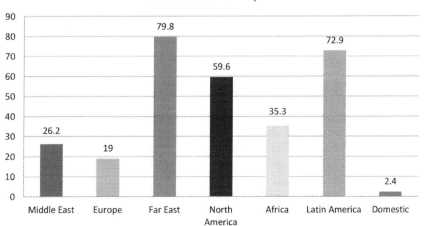

Figure 12.4 Amount of cargo carried by Turkish Airlines per million passengers in 2019
Source: *Sabah*, https://www.sabah.com.tr/ekonomi/2020/01/10/2019da-742-milyon-yolcu-thy-ile-uctu-transit-yolcu-sayisi-245-milyona-yukseldi.

compared to the previous year (Sabah 2020). Until the inauguration of Istanbul Airport (IGA) in April 2019, Turkish Airlines used Istanbul Ataturk Airport (IST) as its main hub, which had contributed to Turkey's centrality especially in the eyes of transit passengers. For example, a Nigerian student who studies at the University of Chicago would first take the Lagos–Istanbul flight and then transfer to Chicago, which promotes Istanbul and Turkey's centrality to connect with the rest of the world. Similarly, a Ukrainian businessperson from Lviv could easily travel to Buenos Aires through a connecting flight in Istanbul, which boosts Turkey's position in the context of globalized commercial relations. Aware of this potential, Turkish Airlines offers connecting international passengers whose layover is between 6 and 24 hours a free sightseeing tour of Istanbul. In the Touristanbul, transit passengers get to see "the most significant historical sights of a city that has hosted major civilizations of the world" including the Dolmabahce Palace, Galata Tower, Golden Horn and Walls of Constantine (Turkish Airlines 2020a). Turkish Airlines also provides free hotel accommodation for business and economy class passengers for layovers of more than nine and twelve hours respectively (Turkish Airlines 2020b).

Turkish Airlines' continuous increase in its number of passengers and the amount of cargo is a direct result of its new flight destinations in the Middle East, Europe, the Far East, North America, Africa, Latin America and inside Turkey. In 2010, Turkish Airlines joined the ranks of the world's top ten airlines in terms of the number of flight destinations, which had reached a total number of 174 (42 domestic and 132 international). By the end of the decade, Turkish Airlines had almost doubled its number of flight destinations. Within Turkey, it flies to 50 cities and 52 airports. Internationally, Turkish Airlines flies to 124 countries, 263 cities and 264 airports. Out of 264 international airports, 116 are in Europe. Turkish Airlines also flies to 58 destinations in Africa. Table 12.1 shows a regional breakdown of Turkish Airlines flight destinations.

Table 12.1 Turkish Airlines flight destinations by region

	Country	*City*	*Airport*
Turkey	1	50	52
Europe	43	115	116
Far East	22	38	38
Middle East	13	35	35
Africa	38	58	58
N. America	2	11	11
L. America	6	6	6
Total	125	313	316

Source: Turkish Airlines, https://www.turkishairlines.com/en-us/press-room/about-us/turkish-airlines-in-numbers/.

Based on these numbers, Turkish Airlines leads all airline companies in terms of the number of countries it flies to. As the next section elaborates further, Turkish Airlines' growing number of flight destinations is a result of Turkish foreign policy's openings to not only its immediate neighborhood but also to countries in sub-Saharan Africa and even Latin America. In the latter region, it is striking that Turkish Airlines inaugurated flights to Caracas in 2016 when major airline companies such as Lufthansa, Alitalia and Avianca were canceling the route due to the political and financial crisis. Without the developing relations between Turkey and Venezuela (Oner 2020), the Caracas route would be hard to understand or justify on purely economic terms.

Last but not least, Turkish Airlines boosts Turkey's image through awards, sponsorships and humanitarian missions. In the last 15 years, Turkish Airlines won Best Airline in Europe, Best Airline in Southern Europe, World's Best Economy Class Onboard Catering Award, and Best Credit Card Program among other prestigious honors (Turkish Airlines 2020c). To promote its name through sports, Turkish Airlines sponsored clubs such as FC Barcelona and Manchester United, famous athletes such as Kobe Bryant and Leonel Messi as well as events such as EuroLeague and The Super Bowl (Kansu and Mamuti 2013; Turkish Airlines 2020d). Moreover, Turkish Airlines participated in humanitarian relief efforts during the Arab Spring in Libya, famine in Somalia and the coronavirus crisis in China. As the next section further elaborates, Turkish Airlines has become an effective soft power tool that acts in coordination with Turkey's foreign policy objectives to become an influential player in world politics. In that sense, Turkish Airlines' involvement in Africa is far from being an isolated incident. Rather, it is a reflection of the general trend especially in the last 15 years under the AKP governments led by Abdullah Gul, Ahmet Davutoglu, Binali Yıldırım and Recep Tayyip Erdogan.

Turkish Airlines as a soft power tool in Africa

As other chapters of the book elaborate, until the adoption of the Africa Action Plan in 1998, Turkey's relations with the African continent were mainly limited to countries in North Africa such as Egypt, Libya, Morocco and Algeria. Since the adoption of a new plan, Turkey has actively engaged not only with North Africa but also with sub-Saharan African countries. Especially, under the successive AKP governments, Turkey has gradually increased its engagement with Africa on diplomatic, commercial, touristic, humanitarian and cultural levels (Hazar 2003; Ozkan and Akgun 2010; Dahir 2019). In this section of the chapter, I describe the role of Turkish Airlines in the context of Turkey's foreign policy opening to Africa on multiple levels. Therefore, I argue that Turkish Airlines, as Turkey's national flag carrier, is a soft power tool that closely coordinates with the Ministry of Foreign Affairs, TİKA, TRT, AFAD, Yunus Emre Institute, Maarif

Foundation, and Directorate of Religious Affairs. Thanks to its increasing presence in the continent, Turkish Airlines complements the work of other foreign policy instruments and helps Turkey achieve its material and ideational goals in Africa. In that sense, Turkish Airlines strengthens Turkey's claim to be a rising power in Africa and beyond.

From the standpoint of liberal international relations theory, Turkish Airlines fits Joseph Nye's definition of soft power tool since it contributes to winning the hearts and minds of foreign publics (Nye 2004, 2008). As Turkey's national flag carrier, Turkish Airlines promotes the country's name all around the world. Its increasing number of flight destinations also raises the global profile of Istanbul, as millions of transit passengers use the Istanbul (formerly IST) Airport (IGA) as a hub. Besides geographical centrality, Turkish Airlines also boosts tourism, people-to-people contact and business activity across international borders. Through its sponsorship deals, Turkish Airlines makes Turkey more attractive in the eyes of foreign audiences (Selcuk 2012, 2013; Anaz and Akman 2017).

Under the soft power framework, Turkish Airlines contributes to Turkey's nation branding and rising power ambitions. As Turkey aspires to become an active player in world politics, the AKP governments use it especially when Turkish diplomats and businesspeople open up to new geographies, regions and countries. Among foreign audiences with no or little knowledge of the country and its people, Turkish Airlines enhances Turkey's perceptions and complements its foreign policy strategies. In their public statements, Turkish Airlines and government officials acknowledge the company's role to promote Turkey's image, culture, attraction, visibility and centrality at the international level. In the early 2010s, then Foreign Minister Ahmet Davutoglu used to highlight Turkish Airlines' role to facilitate his proactive foreign policy doctrine based on employing rhythmic diplomacy, zero problems with neighbors or making Turkey a central country. Along with similar themes, in a 2018 speech, Davutoglu's successor, Mevlut Cavusoglu underlined the importance of soft power in today's world and listed Turkish Airlines as one of Turkey's assets (Hurriyet Daily News 2018). Similarly, from the perspective of foreign audiences, a Kenyan social scientist, Liz Ng'ang'a, recognizes Turkish Airlines as a source of soft power in the African context (Ng'ang'a 2018).

In 2019, Turkish Airlines flew to 38 countries and 58 cities on the African continent. Fifteen years ago, Turkish Airlines only flew to four destinations: Cairo (Egypt), Algiers (Algeria), Tunis (Tunisia) and Tripoli (Libya). In the second half of the 2000s, Turkish Airlines added Casablanca (Morocco), Addis Ababa (Ethiopia), Khartoum (Sudan), Lagos (Nigeria), Cape Town (South Africa), Johannesburg (South Africa), Nairobi (Kenya), Dakar (Senegal), Benghazi (Libya) and Dar es Salaam (Tanzania) to its flight route. In the 2010s, Turkish Airlines continued to add more flight destinations, especially in sub-Saharan Africa. In one of the most recent flight destinations, a Turkish Airlines official described the Port Harcourt–Istanbul route as a

228 Selçuk

cultural bridge between Turkey and Nigeria (Taskiran 2019). In a similar vein, Foreign Minister Cavusoglu acknowledged the political will behind the opening of the Banjul (The Gambia) and said the following: "Upon the orders of President Recep Tayyip Erdogan, Turkish Airlines flies to Banjul twice a week and this number will increase to three on May 1" (Zontur 2019).

From a diplomatic point of view, the inauguration of Turkish Airlines flights tends to follow the opening of new embassies and consulates as well as official visits by Turkish presidents, prime ministers and foreign ministers with a delegation of businesspeople. Since his trip to Ethiopia in 2005, during his tenure as prime minister, Erdogan has traveled to 28 African countries in 50 visits (TRT World 2020). During his presidency, Abdullah Gul also visited several African countries to develop diplomatic and business ties with the continent. In his 2011 visit to Ghana, Gul acknowledged the role of Turkish Airlines to reduce the distances and create opportunities on both sides (Abdullah Gul Official Website 2011). Parallel to this high-level diplomatic engagement, today, Turkey has 42 embassies and three consulate-generals in 42 African countries. Except for Angola, Burundi, Botswana, Equatorial Guinea, Namibia, South Sudan and Zimbabwe, Turkish Airlines flies to all countries where Turkey has diplomatic representation. In the Republic of Congo and Uganda, instead of flying into the capital cities, Turkish Airlines flies to Pointe-Noire and Entebbe respectively. Furthermore, Turkish Airlines flies to Seychelles, Mauritius and Moroni (Comoros) even though Turkey does not have an embassy or a consulate-general in these countries (Table 12.2).

Table 12.2 Turkey's diplomatic representation in Africa and Turkish Airlines flights

Country	Diplomatic representation	Turkish Airlines flight
Algeria	Algiers (Embassy)	Yes
Angola	Luanda (Embassy)	No
Benin	Cotonou (Embassy)	Yes
Botswana	Gaborone (Embassy)	No
Burkina Faso	Ouagadougou (Embassy)	Yes
Burundi	Bujumbura (Embassy)	No
Cameroon	Yaoundé (Embassy)	Yes
Chad	N'Djamena (Embassy)	Yes
Republic of the Congo	Brazzaville (Embassy)	Yes
DR Congo	Kinshasa (Embassy)	Yes
Djibouti	Djibouti (Embassy)	Yes
Egypt	Cairo (Embassy)	Yes
	Alexandria (Consulate–General)	Yes
Equatorial Guinea	Malabo (Embassy)	No

Turkish Airlines as a source of soft power 229

Country	Diplomatic representation	Turkish Airlines flight
Eritrea	Asmara (Embassy)	Yes
Ethiopia	Addis Ababa (Embassy)	Yes
Gabon	Libreville (Embassy)	Yes
The Gambia	Banjul (Embassy)	Yes
Ghana	Accra (Embassy)	Yes
Guinea	Conakry (Embassy)	Yes
Ivory Coast	Abidjan (Embassy)	Yes
Kenya	Nairobi (Embassy)	Yes
Libya	Tripoli (Embassy)	Yes
	Misurata (Consulate–General)	Yes
Madagascar	Antananarivo (Embassy)	Yes
Mali	Bamako (Embassy)	Yes
Mauritania	Nouakchott (Embassy)	Yes
Morocco	Rabat (Embassy)	Yes
Mozambique	Maputo (Embassy)	Yes
Namibia	Windhoek (Embassy)	No
Niger	Niamey (Embassy)	Yes
Nigeria	Abuja (Embassy)	Yes
Rwanda	Kigali (Embassy)	Yes
Senegal	Dakar (Embassy)	Yes
Sierra Leone	Freetown (Embassy)	Yes
Somalia	Mogadishu (Embassy)	Yes
	Hargeisa (Consulate-General)	No
South Africa	Pretoria (Embassy)	Yes
South Sudan	Juba (Embassy)	No
Sudan	Khartoum (Embassy)	Yes
Tanzania	Dar es Salaam (Embassy)	Yes
Tunisia	Tunis (Embassy)	Yes
Uganda	Kampala (Embassy)	Yes
Zambia	Lusaka (Embassy)	Yes
Zimbabwe	Harare (Embassy)	No

Sources: Author's compilation from the Ministry of Foreign Affairs and Turkish Airlines websites.

In summary, there is a significant relationship between the establishment of a Turkish embassy, official visits and the inauguration of Turkish Airlines flights in Africa. In countries such as Ethiopia and Sudan, Turkish Airlines inaugurated new flight destinations to Addis Ababa and Khartoum following official visits. In others such as Tanzania and Uganda, the flights predated the opening of the embassy. Regardless of the direction of the causal arrow, there is overt coordination between the AKP governments and Turkish Airlines when it comes to the company's involvement in Africa.

In addition to complementing Turkey's diplomatic presence in Africa, the inauguration of new flight destinations in the continent aims to facilitate the movement of goods and people. During the initial stages of Turkey's opening to Africa, then President Abdullah Gul attended several business councils in the region to help businesspeople establish commercial relations. With that goal in mind, the government expected Turkish diplomats to promote bilateral trade and investment. In the early years of the AKP period, the government worked closely with the Gulen Movement to establish and develop commercial relations especially in sub-Saharan Africa (Donelli 2019). For example, in 2006, the Gulenist business organization (TUSKON) organized the Turkey–Africa Foreign Trade Bridge with the participation of 500 African businesspeople from 35 countries and 1,000 businesspeople from Turkey. Until 2011, TUSKON organized 11 of those meetings with the participation of businesspeople on both sides (Gunay 2011). In 2010, the African Union Commissioner of Trade, Elizabeth Tankeo praised the efforts of the Turkish business community and specifically TUSKON to develop commercial activities in the continent, which is evidence of positive reception of Turkey's rising power status by third parties (Sungu 2010; Figure 12.5).

Since the deterioration of relations between the AKP and the Gulen Movement, the primary role of TUSKON has been replaced by other business associations including the Foreign Economic Relations Board (DEIK), Independent Industrialists' and Businessmen's Association (MUSIAD), and the Turkish Industry and Business Association (TUSIAD) (Parlar Dal and Dipama 2020). Therefore, when Turkish Airlines inaugurates a new route today, the representatives of the above-mentioned organizations are often

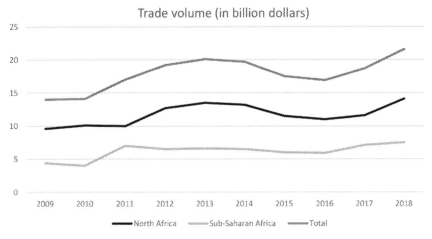

Figure 12.5 Turkey–Africa trade volume (2009–2018)
Source: Turkish Statistical Institute, https://www.tuik.gov.tr/en/.

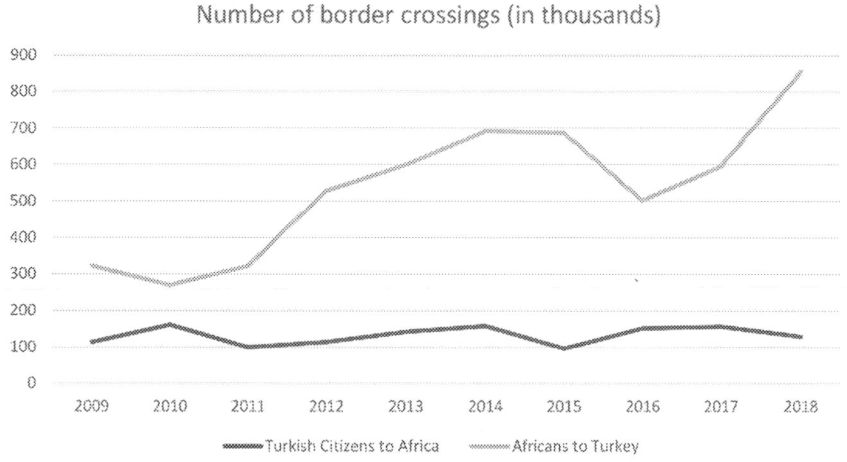

Number of border crossings (in thousands)

Figure 12.6 Turkey–Africa border crossings (2009–2018)
Source: Turkish Statistical Institute, https://www.tuik.gov.tr/en/.

present at the official ceremony instead of members of TUSKON, who are associated with the criminalized "Fetullahist Terrorist Organization" (FETO). In this context, the surprise departure of Turkish Airlines CEO, Temel Kotil, months after the 2016 coup attempt is often linked to his close ties with the Gulen Movement (Kidik 2016; Figure 12.6).

To analyze Turkey's trade volume with Africa, between 2009 and 2018, Turkey's volume of imports to North Africa increased from 2.2 billion dollars to 4.6 billion dollars. In sub-Saharan Africa, the same number increased from 1.7 to 2.5 billion dollars. During the same period, Turkey's exports to North Africa increased from 7.4 to 9.5 billion dollars. In sub-Saharan Africa, exports increased from 2.7 to 5 billion dollars. Overall, in the last decade, Turkey's trade volume with the entire African continent increased from 14 to 21.6 billion dollars (see Figure 12.5). Compared to 2001, when the total trade volume was only 4.3 billion dollars, there has been a 400 percent increase, which is positively correlated with Turkish Airlines' increasing number of flights and cargo operations in Africa. However, it is also important to emphasize that Turkey's trade with countries in sub-Saharan Africa has been nearly flat for the last ten years. In terms of the number of border crossings, in 2018, 129,000 Turkish citizens traveled to Africa as opposed to 113,000 in 2009. The numbers are more dramatic when it comes to the number of African citizens visiting Turkey, which increased from 322,000 in 2009 to 856,000 in 2018 (see Figure 12.6). To summarize, the increasing number of Turkish Airlines flights have boosted people-to-people contact, especially when we look at the rise in the number of Africans who visit Turkey.

Besides the diplomatic and commercial aspects of Turkish Airlines' engagement in the continent, the national airline company's humanitarian engagement further strengthens its potential as a soft power tool in Africa.

Turkish Airlines' involvement in Somalia is a primary example of humanitarianism in coordination with other foreign policy instruments. In response to the famine and drought in Somalia, in 2011, the Turkish government initiated a campaign to raise funds as well as awareness. In the absence of scheduled flights, Turkish Airlines collaborated with TIKA, the Turkish Red Crescent Society, Diyanet and AFAD and transported humanitarian aid to Somalia by its cargo planes. During its flights between August 23 and September 4, 2011, Turkish Airlines personnel and passengers raised nearly a million Turkish liras to contribute to humanitarian relief in Somalia. Turkish Airlines also brought 14 Somali children to Turkey for medical treatment (Haberturk 2011).

Following the first wave of humanitarian aid, a year after Prime Minister Erdogan's first visit to the country, in March 2012, Turkish Airlines inaugurated its scheduled flights to the Somali capital, Mogadishu. This decision had symbolic importance as Turkish Airlines became the first major commercial airline to land in the city for more than 20 years. As an indication of its symbolic importance, the President of Somalia, the United Nations officials, and ambassadors were present in the airport to welcome the first Turkish Airlines flight from Istanbul to Mogadishu. In the official ceremony, the Somali Foreign Minister Abdullahi Haji welcomed the development as it would connect the Somali diaspora with the homeland as well as promote peace and development (BBC 2012). Similarly, the Turkish Foreign Minister Ahmet Davutoglu acknowledged the presence of political motives behind the decision to start Turkish Airlines flights to Somalia. He argued that the new route would increase Turkey's visibility in the continent and facilitate the rebuilding of the war-torn country (Zaman 2012).

In 2017, Turkish Airlines participated in another wave of humanitarian aid, which started as a result of the popular hashtag #TurkishAirlinesHelpSomalia to address the ongoing famine in Somalia. The hashtag was initially shared by a Vine and Snapchat celebrity, Jerome Jarre, who posted a video to raise awareness of the humanitarian crisis and call Turkish Airlines for action. Shortly, other celebrities including Ben Stiller and Colin Kaepernick shared the hashtag and supported the initiative. In response to the growing social media campaign, Turkish Airlines gladly agreed to carry humanitarian aid to alleviate the famine in Somalia. During the social media campaign, which reached more than one billion people, in three days, #LoveArmyforSomalia raised over 1.5 million dollars with 55,000 supporters in 125 countries. As a result, Turkish Airlines delivered 60 tons of food to address the famine in Somalia (Skylife 2017). Turkish Airlines' involvement in this humanitarian campaign once again illustrated its soft power potential to win the hearts and minds of not only Somalis who live in difficult life conditions but also a broader community of human rights activists in the West.

Other than Somalia, Turkish Airlines has taken part in several other humanitarian and cultural projects in the African continent. In its 2007 annual report, Turkish Airlines refers to an agreement with the Turkish Red Crescent to support its activities in Africa (Turkish Airlines 2007). In 2011, during the early stages of the Libyan Civil War, the Turkish government launched a rescue operation by sea and air. In that context, Turkish Airlines successfully evacuated Turkish citizens as well as foreigners from the conflict-ridden country (Bloomberg 2011). In 2016, Turkish Airlines sponsored cataract surgeries of more than a thousand Ethiopian citizens (Getachew and Aktas 2018). In the region, Turkish Airlines also collaborated with TIKA and TRT to renovate schools, radio stations, orphanages and places of worship. Under the Africa Experience Sharing Preparation Program, Turkish Airlines sponsored Turkish students to engage in developmental and humanitarian aid in the continent (Mehmet 2017). Finally, to promote cultural exchange, Turkish Airlines provided plane tickets to the African recipients of scholarships to study in Turkey (Farah and Barack 2019). Through these humanitarian practices, Turkish Airlines has boosted Turkey's perception in the continent as a rising but also a benign power, who is willing to use its resources to help the people in need.

Conclusion

In this chapter, I have demonstrated Turkish Airlines' growing involvement in the African continent in line with Turkey's foreign policy objectives. From a theoretical standpoint, the chapter argues that Turkish Airlines is one of Turkey's soft power tools in Africa to achieve material and ideational goals. Amid Turkey's rising power ambitions, in the African continent, Turkish Airlines not only increases its number of flight destinations but also contributes to the establishment of commercial, humanitarian and cultural relationships. Hence, Turkish Airlines works closely with other foreign policy institutions that help Turkey's rise. Overall, Turkish Airlines contributes to Turkey's prestige, centrality and visibility, hence its soft power in the eyes of African audiences.

Another main finding of the chapter is that Turkish Airlines' involvement in the African continent is far from being unique. Historically, foreign policy considerations have always affected Turkish Airlines' air routes, aircraft purchases and other commercial strategies. Similar to other national airlines, since its establishment in 1933, Turkish Airlines has been a symbol of Turkey's prestige, modernity and standard of civilization. Under the AKP period, Turkish Airlines' use as a foreign policy tool has only been more pronounced and overt. As an ambitious rising power, Turkey has successfully used Turkish Airlines to complement its foreign policy openings not only in Africa but also in the Middle East, Eurasia and Latin America. Given the high degree of state involvement in decision making, as long as the AKP and President Erdogan remain in power, Turkish Airlines will be a relevant actor when scholars, policymakers and analysts discuss Turkish foreign policy, specifically its increasing engagement in Africa. In the upcoming years, the economic crisis associated with the COVID-19 pandemic may potentially undermine Turkish Airlines' ability to continue its scheduled flights to African countries and project Turkey's soft power in the continent.

References

Abdullah Gul Official Website. 2011. "Turkiye'nin Afrika Acilimi: Gana ve Gabon'a Cumhurbaskani Duzeyinde Ilk Ziyaret." March 26, 2011. http://www.abdullahgul.gen.tr/haberler/170/79301/turkiyenin-afrika-acilimi-gana-ve-gabona-cumhurbaskani-duzeyinde-ilk-ziyaret.html.

Albayrak, I. 1983. *Dunden Bugune Turk Hava Yolları 1933–1983*. Istanbul: Cem Ofset.

Amankwah-Amoah, J. and Y.A. Debrah. 2014. "Air Afrique: The Demise of a Continental Icon." *Business History* 56, no. 4: 517–546. https://doi.org/10.1080/00076791.2013.809523.

Anaz, N. and E. Akman. 2017. "Turkey's Soft Power Capacity: Geopolitics of Aviation and the Turkish Airlines." *The Arab World Geographer* 20, no. 4: 303–316. https://doi.org/10.5555/1480-6800.20.4.303.

BBC. 2012. "Somalia: Turkish Airlines Begins Flights to Mogadishu." March 6, 2012. https://www.bbc.com/news/world-africa-17269620#TWEET94279.

Bloomberg. 2011. "Libya Evacuation Largest in Turkish History, Davutoglu Says." February 23, 2011. https://www.bloomberg.com/news/articles/2011-02-23/turkey-mounts-biggest-evacuation-in-its-history-to-rescue-5-000-from-libya.

Cicekci, S. 2006. *Hava Taşımacılığının Ozelleştirilmesi ve Türk Hava Yolları Ornegi*. Master's Thesis, Marmara University.

Consulate General of Japan in Istanbul. 2018. October. Accessed April 15, 2020. https://www.istanbul.tr.emb-japan.go.jp/files/000419250.pdf.

Dahir, A.H. 2019. Reconsidering Turkish Foreign Policy towards Sub-Saharan Africa: Rationale and Mechanisms. TRT World Research Center.

Donelli, F. 2019. "The Gulen Movement in Africa: From Turkish Transnational Asset to Anti-State Lobby." *Israel Journal of Foreign Affairs* 13, no.1: 67–80. https://doi.org/10.1080/23739770.2019.1632588.

Durepos, G., Mills, J. H. and Mills, A. J. 2008. "Flights of Fancy: Myth, Monopoly and the Making of Pan American Airways." *Journal of Management History* 14, no. 2: 116–127. https://doi.org/10.1108/17511340810860249.

Farah, A.O. and C.O. Barack. 2019. "The Quest for Turkish Scholarships: African Students, Transformation and Hopefulness." *African Journal of Science, Technology, Innovation and Development* 11, no. 7: 883–892. https://doi.org/10.1080/20421338.2019.1592329.

Getachew, A. and T. Aktas. Anadolu Ajansi, October 24, 2018. https://www.aa.com.tr/en/africa/turkish-surgeons-restore-sight-to-420-ethiopians/1291288.

Golder, M.R. 1997. *The Changing Nature of French Dirigisme: The Case Study of Air France*. Master's Thesis, Oxford University.

Gunay, M. 2011. "Turkey-Africa Relations." Speech given April 14, 2011 at Chatham House, London. Transcript. https://www.chathamhouse.org/sites/default/files/public/Meetings/Meeting%20Transcripts/140411gunay.pdf.

Haberturk. 2011. "THY'den seferberlik!" October 4, 2011. https://www.haberturk.com/ekonomi/airport/haber/676022-thyden-seferberlik.

Hanlon, J.P. 1996. *Global Airlines: Competition in a Transnational Industry*. Oxford: Butterworth-Heinemann.

Hazar, N. 2003. *Kureselleşme Surecinde Afrika ve Turkiye-Afrika İlişkileri*. Ankara: Yeni Medya Hizmetleri.

Kansu, A.S. and A. Mamuti. 2013. "The Use of Celebrity Endorsement as Marketing Communication Strategy by Turkish Airlines." *International Journal of Academic*

Research in Business and Social Sciences 3, no. 12: 676–683. https://doi.org/10.6007/IJARBSS/v3-i12/484.

Karlitekin, C. Interview by Orçun Selçuk. 2011. (December 21).

Kidik, A. 2016. "Vay be Temel...." *Airport Haber*, October 24, 2016. https://www.airporthaber.com/kose-yazilari/vay-be-temel.html.

Kline, S. 2002. *A Chronicle of Turkish Aviation*. Istanbul: Havas.

Kozlu, C. 2009. *Bulutların Uzerine Tirmanirken: THY, Bir Donusumun Oykusu*. Istanbul: Remzi Kitapevi.

Mehmet, F.H. 2017. "Turkish Students to Take Part in African Aid Projects." Anadolu Ajansi, August 3, 2017. https://www.aa.com.tr/en/africa/turkish-students-to-take-part-in-african-aid-projects-/875896.

Nergiz, A. 2008. *Türkiye'de Sivil Havacılığın Gelişimi ve THY*. Master's Thesis, Marmara University.

Ng'ang'a, L. 2018. "Turkey's Growing Soft Power in Africa." *Daily Sabah*, May 11, 2018. https://www.dailysabah.com/op-ed/2018/05/11/turkeys-growing-soft-power-in-africa.

Nye, J.S. 2004. *Soft Power: The Means to Success in World Politics*. New York: Public Affairs.

Nye, J.S. 2008. "Public Diplomacy and Soft Power." *The ANNALS of the American Academy of Political and Social Science* 616, no. 1: 94–109. https://doi.org/10.1177%2F0002716207311699.

O'Connor, W.E. 1971. *Economic Regulation of the World's Airlines*. New York: Praeger Publishers.

Oner, I. 2020. *Turkey and Venezuela: An Alliance of Convenience*. Washington DC: Wilson Center.

Ozkan, M. and B. Akgun. 2010. "Turkey's Opening to Africa." *Journal of Modern African Studies* 48, no. 4: 525–546. https://doi.org/10.1017/S0022278X10000595.

Parlar Dal, E. 2016. "Conceptualising and Testing the 'Emerging Regional Power' of Turkey in the Shifting International Order." *Third World Quarterly* 37, no. 8: 1425–1453. https://doi.org/10.1080/01436597.2016.1142367.

Parlar Dal, E. and S. Dipama. 2020. "Assessing the Turkish 'Trading State' in Sub-Saharan Africa." In *Turkey's Political Economy in the 21st Century*, edited by Emel Parlar Dal, 239–270. Cham: Palgrave Macmillan.

Peterson, J.E. 2006. "Qatar and the World: Branding for a Microstate." *The Middle East Journal* 60, no. 4: 732–748.

Pirle, G. 2004. "Passenger Traffic in the 1930s on British Imperial Air Routes: Refinement and Revision." *Journal of Transport History* 25, no. 1: 63–83. https://doi.org/10.7227%2FTJTH.25.1.4.

Raguraman, K. 1997. "Airlines as Instruments for Nation Building and National Identity: Case Study of Malaysia and Singapore." *Journal of Transport Geography* 5, no. 4: 239–256. https://doi.org/10.1016/S0966-6923(97)21–25.

Rhoades, D.L. 2002. "Liberalization of International Air Transportation Markets: The Effect of Terrorism on Market Trends." *Journal of Transportation Management* 13, no. 2: 45–58. https://doi.org/10.22237/jotm/1030838700.

Sabah. 2020. "THY 2019'da 74,2 milyon yolcu tasidi!" January 10, 2020. https://www.sabah.com.tr/ekonomi/2020/01/10/2019da-742-milyon-yolcu-thy-ile-uctu-transit-yolcu-sayisi-245-milyona-yukseldi.

Segell, G. 2019. "Neo-Colonialism in Africa and the Cases of Turkey and Iran." *Insight on Africa* 11, no. 2: 184–199. https://doi.org/10.1177%2F0975087819845197.

Selcuk, O. 2012. *Turkish Airlines as a Soft Power Tool in the Context of Turkish Foreign Policy.* Master's Thesis, Bogaziçi University.

Selcuk, O. 2013. "Turkish Airlines: Turkey's Soft Power Tool in the Middle East." *Akademik Ortadogu* 7, no. 2: 175–199.

Shaw, S. 2004. *Airline Marketing and Management.* Aldershot: Ashgate.

Skylife. 2017. "#TurkishAirlinesHelpSomalia." April 2017. https://www.skylife.com/en/2017-04/-turkishairlineshelpsomalia.

Subotić, J. 2018. "JAT-More Than Flying: Constructing Yugoslav Identity in the Air." *East European Politics and Societies and Cultures* 32, no. 4: 671–692. https://doi.org/10.1177%2F0888325417740628.

Sungu, Y. 2010. "Artik gucsuz bir Turkiye kimsenin isine gelmiyor." *Yeni Safak*, June 20, 2010. https://www.yenisafak.com/yazarlar/yasarsungu/artik-gucsuz-bir-turkiye-kimsenin-iine-gelmiyor-22833.

Taskiran, I. 2019. "THY Afrika'da 56. destinasyonunu ucus agina ekledi." Anadolu Ajansı, June 25, 2019. https://www.aa.com.tr/tr/dunya/thy-afrikada-56-destinasyonunu-ucus-agina-ekledi/1515362.

Thornton, R.L. 1971. "Government and Airlines." *International Organization* 25, no. 3: 541–553.

Thrulow, C. and G. Aiello. 2007. "National Pride, Global Capital: A Social Semiotic Analysis of Transnational Visual Branding in the Airline Industry." *Visual Communication* 6, no. 3: 305–344. https://doi.org/10.1177/1470357207081002.

TRT World. 2020. "What makes Erdogan's Africa tour so significant?" January 27, 2020. https://www.trtworld.com/africa/what-makes-erdogan-s-africa-tour-so-significant-33263.

Turk Hava Yollari. 2009. *"75. Yılında Türk Hava Yolları."* Istanbul: Elma Bilgisayar ve Basim.

Turkish Airlines. 2007. "Annual Report 2007." https://investor.turkishairlines.com/documents/ThyInvestorRelations/download/yillik_raporlar/faaliyetraporu2007_en.pdf.

Turkish Airlines. 2019. "In Numbers." December 5, 2019. https://www.turkishairlines.com/en-us/press-room/about-us/turkish-airlines-in-numbers/.

Turkish Airlines. 2020a. "Touristanbul." https://www.turkishairlines.com/en-us/flights/fly-different/touristanbul/tour-schedule/.

Turkish Airlines. 2020b. "Great Accommodation with Connecting Turkish Airlines flights." https://www.turkishairlines.com/en-int/flights/hotel-service/.

Turkish Airlines. 2020c. "Awards." https://www.turkishairlines.com/en-int/press-room/awards/.

Turkish Airlines. 2020d. "Our Sponsorships." https://www.turkishairlines.com/en-us/press-room/sponsorships/.

White, C.L. 2012. "Brands and National Image: An Exploration of Inverse Country-of-Origin Effect." *Place Branding and Public Diplomacy* 8: 110–118. https://doi.org/10.1057/pb.2012.6.

Zaman. 2012. *February* 23. Accessed February 23, 2012.

Zontur, E.C. 2019. "Turkey, Gambia should increase trade volume to $40M: FM." Anadolu Ajansı. April 18, 2019. https://www.aa.com.tr/en/africa/turkey-gambia-should-increase-trade-volume-to-40m-fm/1457050.

13 Turkey's diplomatic charm offensive in sub-Saharan Africa

Is Ankara winning the hearts and minds of Africans?

Alexis Habiyaremye

Introduction

With its mostly young and dynamic population of 1.25 billion people, Africa is expected to offer the world's most attractive growth opportunities for business and investments in the next two to three decades (Gunay 2011; Ayuk 2020). To take advantage of geopolitical and business gains offered by Africa's growth potential, Turkey has metamorphosed its relations with African countries from marginal interest during the Cold War to an unprecedented intensification and expansion initiated towards the turn of the century (Ozkan and Akgun 2010; Rudincova 2014).[1] Ankara's foreign policy pivot to Africa was born out of the growing realization (both in the country's ruling political elite and the business sector) that Turkey needed to develop multiple ties and engage with non-traditional partners as the best strategy to secure its post-Cold War economic and security interests (Davutoglu 2008; Ozkan 2012).[2] Expanding relations with Africa, especially with sub-Saharan Africa has therefore been one of the key tenets of the ruling Adalet ve Kalkınma Partisi's (Justice and Development Party, JDP) foreign policy since it assumed power in 2002 (Ayuk 2020; Vrey 2020).

Because of the advantages offered by its geographical and cultural proximity to Africa, Turkey chose to chart its way between the US big stick approach (US AFRICOM to coerce Africans) and the Chinese carrot (Belt and Road Initiative to entice them) by deploying a multi-stakeholder diplomacy involving state and non-state actors working jointly to win Africa's hearts and minds and secure access to their strategic resources and diplomatic support in global forums (Siradag 2015; Baba 2018). The long-term success of Turkey's engagement in Africa is therefore largely dependent on its ability to shape positive perceptions among African population, business communities and policymakers. How do Africans view Turkey's growing influence and its diplomatic approach to carving its own sphere of influence between old colonial Western and new Eastern partners of the continent? To answer this question, this study explores how Turkey's approach to engaging African countries has succeeded in shaping positive attitudes towards a new partner who had long remained at the margins for the most part of the colonial and the Cold War periods.

To secure its place in this expanding lucrative market amidst sharpened global rivalry between the world biggest economic powerhouses, Turkey has sought to position itself as a reliable and efficient partner to African countries in need of infrastructure investments and technology for their economic take off (Akca 2019; Ayuk 2020). Inspired by the geopolitical conceptions of his ruling party's strategists, Erdogan's government deployed what Vertin (2019) calls the "schools and mosque" diplomacy by stressing Islamic solidarity and cultural affinity (especially in 19 majority-Muslim countries in sub-Saharan Africa) as an effective approach to seduce them into a partnership unburdened by past colonial domination (Akca 2019; Habiyaremye and Oguzlu 2014).[3] The JDP's new foreign policy doctrine based on Davutoglu's *"strategic depth"* conceptualization (which underlies the repositioning towards Africa and the Middle East), has been criticized as a sign of Ankara's neo-Ottoman ambitions to take Turkey closer to the status of global power (Koundouno 2020; Akca 2019; The World 2020; Daloglu 2013). The ruling JDP elites have dismissed the hegemonic connotations of neo-Ottomanism, preferring to put the emphasis on the past anticolonial alliance between the Ottomans and African countries as well as the humanitarian nature of its current civilian and military interventions in the area (Daloglu 2013; Ozkan and Akgun 2010; Rudincova 2014; Siradag 2015). The architects of current Turkish foreign policy have presented its neo-Ottoman identity as a new "virtuous power" in global politics, motivated by benevolence and solidarity in the Global South as opposed to Western neo-colonialism (Ozkan and Akgun 2010; Langan 2016; Akca 2019).

To achieve this strategic goal of winning hearts and minds, the JDP government has deployed a multi-stakeholder approach based on five main pillars: (1) expansion of diplomatic representation, (2) geopolitical involvement in peace and security matters in Africa,[4] (3) official development aid and humanitarian relief through civil society organizations, (4) Turkey–Africa trade and investment bridges though allied private business and contractors (Melvin 2019; Ozkan and Akgun 2010; Rossiter and Cannon 2019; Eyrice Tepeciklioglu 2017; Vertin 2019), (5) Turkish education and cultural exchange through Turkish schools active in target countries and scholarships offered to African students to attend Turkish universities. Whereas diplomatic ties facilitate the intensification of government-to-government official communication, participation in peacekeeping missions can be interpreted as a display of Turkey's interest and commitment to peace and security in Africa. Turkey's growing influence in Africa and in African institutions such as the African Development Bank (AfDB) was conceived as a means to secure diplomatic support for its own emergence as a regional power that can be used as a bargaining chip in negotiations with the European Union and other Western partners (Langan 2016).[5] Peacekeeping is used as a bridge to access trade with African countries (see, e.g. Satana 2012) while involvement in security in the Horn of Africa serves to build a strong influence to counter the diplomatic forays of its regional rivals (see Vertin 2019). But, from the constructivist point of view, it is mainly through official development cooperation and humanitarian assistance that Ankara's goodwill towards Africa touches the lives of ordinary Africans and produces the intended developmental outcomes as well as the concomitant soft power (Siradag 2015). Trade and investment bridges represent the expectation of actual flows of goods, capital and technological knowledge necessary to push economic convergence and generate the desired win–win outcomes. Schools and scholarships, for their part, contribute to the effort by bridging the mutual knowledge gap, breaking the language and cultural barriers and forming the next generation of leaders who can take the cooperation to higher levels because of increased cognateness.

This study attempted to probe how ordinary Africans have appraised the convergence between the practices of the five pillars of Turkey's pivot to Africa policy with their respective countries' developmental interests and aspirations. It explores how these different pillars of Turkish pivot to Africa policy have contributed to winning the hearts and minds of Africans with the aim to secure a long-term development partnership congruent with the official policy objectives of creating win–win outcomes beneficial to both Turkey and African countries. Through key informant interviews with government officials, academics, civil society members and sector actors familiar with any aspect of Turkish engagement in Africa, the study attempts to gauge the extent of trust building between Turkey and Africa as perceived by Africans. A survey was also administered to respondents based in four out of the five regional subdivisions of the continent to gauge the degree of trust towards Turkish institutions through which the engagement with Africa is shaped. The observed trust scores are presumed to provide an approximate glance into the way the various instruments of Turkish engagement in Africa are winning the hearts and minds of ordinary Africans. Trust measures are a basic indicator of the cooperative behavior (Fukuyama 1996, 26–27), which portends long-term sustainability of the engagement relations. In this chapter, awareness and trust scores obtained from interviews and field survey are analyzed to generate insights into Turkey's ongoing battle of hearts and minds in Africa. Our findings suggest that Turkey's pivot to Africa seems to have succeeded in laying a solid foundation for long-term relations but will require a further strengthening of mutual trust and knowledge sharing in order to generate the desired win–win outcomes.

The chapter proceeds as follows: the second section gives an overview of the deployment of the five pillars of Ankara's pivot to Africa policy. The third section outlines the methodology followed to explore the dynamics of Turkey's attempts to win hearts and minds in the Maghreb and in sub-Saharan Africa. The fourth section presents the findings while the fifth section concludes and points to some emerging issues of global importance for Africa and Turkey.

The five pillars of Turkish pivot to Africa policy

Turkey's modern Africa policy that emerged at the very end of the twentieth century was driven by two main considerations: the need to diversify its economic relations in order to reduce its dependence on European countries and Russia in a post-Cold War geopolitical context and the necessity of a shift from its Western-centric foreign policy to a more multidimensional diplomacy commensurate with its ambitions of a regional power in global politics (Ozkan 2012; Habiyaremye and Oguzlu 2013; Austvik and Rzayeva 2016). According to Eyrice Tepeciklioglu (2017), this shift was contemplated after Turkish membership of the European Union had been rejected at the Luxemburg Summit of December 1997, while Turkey's ambition to create a Turkish union with newly independent republics of Central Asia (with which it shares language and cultural affinities) had also failed to gain the expected traction (see also Ozkan and Akgun 2010; Langan 2016). The increasingly powerful Turkish industrial bourgeoisie (the so-called Anatolian Tigers) also played an important role in calling for a foreign policy reorientation, with Africa as a focus, because of the associated growth potential (Eyrice Tepeciklioglu 2017). These considerations were converted into concrete strategy in 1998 by Ismail Cem who became an influential advocate of Turkish multidimensional foreign policy. Since relations with North Africa had seemed quite natural in the conception of Turkish foreign policy even during the Cold War period, the pivot in foreign policy towards Africa was essentially a pivot towards sub-Saharan Africa.

The implementation strategy of this new policy entailed therefore the opening of new embassies in sub-Saharan African countries, which could help develop economic and political contacts with Africa. On the diplomatic level, the charm offensive of the new Africa policy has produced substantive successes. Turkey was declared a strategic partner with the status of observer by the African Union in 2008 and obtained the support of the 50 African countries in its successful bid to become a non-permanent member of the UN Security Council over the 2009–2010 period (Tepebas 2015). Turkish diplomatic representation on the continent expanded rapidly, whereby the number of embassies went from 12 in 2003 to 42 and 26 commercial consulates in 2018 (Ministry of Foreign Affairs, Republic of Turkey 2020; Duz 2019). As a powerful instrument in that approach, national flag carrier Turkish Airlines (THY) has established the most extensive air connection network of any non-African airline on the African continent (Akca 2019; Vertin 2019).[6]

On the geopolitical level, Turkish engagement in Somalia to train the country's military personnel represented perhaps the strongest signal of the value that Ankara attaches to its emerging role as serious player in global geopolitics (Rossiter and Cannon 2019). The strategic location of Somalia along overly sensitive oil shipment routes going through the Gulf of Aden to the Suez Canal has made the Horn of Africa an attractive position to all foreign powers seeking to assert their geopolitical interests in that region. In addition to its involvement in Somalia, Turkey has increased its geopolitical position in the Red Sea region through the signing of a 99-year lease to redevelop the Sudanese island of Suakin as a tourism hub. Turkey's move to develop Suakin island is perceived as a significant move in the rivalry opposing its ideological adversaries Saudi Arabia and the UAE, who also wish to expand their influence in the Horn of Africa through the so-called "paycheck diplomacy" (Vertin 2019). Since the beginning of January 2020, Turkey has also deployed its combat and support forces to Libya to help stabilize the country. This unprecedented deployment of troops in a combat zone has catapulted Turkey into a new dimension of external power projection.

Turkish police and military forces have also provided a small but active contributor to seven out of nine UN peacekeeping missions in Africa, namely the joint African Union/UN Mission in Darfur (UNAMID), the UN Mission in the Democratic Republic of Congo (MONUSCO), the UN Mission in Côte d'Ivoire (ONUCI), the UN Mission in Liberia (UNMIL), the UN Mission in Sudan (UNMIS), the UN mission in Mali (MINUSMA), the UN Assistance Mission in Somalia (UNSOM) and the UN Mission in the Central African Republic (MINUSCA), in addition to the above-mentioned military intervention in Somalia and Libya (Rudincova 2014).[7]

In terms of development cooperation and humanitarian aid, Turkish humanitarian NGOs have also substantially increased their activity on the continent as another pillar of the new multidimensional foreign policy (Siradag 2015). As an important implementation agent of Turkey's development aid to Africa, the (official) Turkish Cooperation and Coordination Agency (*Turk Isbirligi ve Koordinasyon Ajansi Baskanligi*, TIKA) currently operates on the continent through 23 program coordination offices to provide development assistance and humanitarian aid to corresponding African countries (Siradag 2015; Presidency of the Republic of Turkey 2020). By the year 2014, Turkey was disbursing USD 3.3 billion to Africa based on development cooperation projects and had become the third-largest donor in the world (*Daily Sabah* 2019).

In tandem with the diplomatic expansion, the now dissolved Turkish Confederation of Businessmen and Industrialists (*Turkiye Isadamlari ve Sanayciler Konfederasyonu*, TUSKON) and Independent Industrialists and Businessmen's Association (*Mustakil Sanayici ve Isadamları Dernegi*, MUSIAD) were busy on the business front organizing the Turkey–Africa Trade Bridge (Gunay 2011; Eyrice Tepeciklioglu 2017).[8] In 2019, the trade volume between Turkey and the African continent amounted to USD 26 billion while cumulative bilateral trade volume over the period 2009 to 2018 had reached USD 179 billion. Despite all its praiseworthy achievements, however, Turkey's pivot to Africa is still confronted with important hurdles in its efforts to boost bilateral trade. The growth potential is very high, yet the trade figures are still low in comparison to what the Turkish government had targeted (Presidency of the Republic of Turkey 2020).

Finally, education forms another key pillar of Turkish strategy of one mosque one school approach used to establish close connections with African countries (Tepebas 2015; Habiyaremye and Oguzlu 2014; Vertin 2019). Together with the education that is offered to African students who receive scholarships to study at Turkish universities, Turkish schools providing education in Africa contribute to breaking the cultural and language barriers between the partner countries by ensuring that a growing number of Africans can speak the Turkish language and develop an understanding of the Turkish culture. They have earned a considerable measure of trust among Africans, not only because of the good quality of the education provided, but also because they managed to build positive relationships with government officials in the countries where they operate (Yazar 2010; Samuel 2014). Turkish universities have also become an attractive destination for African students (Duz 2019). Fethullah Gulen's movement had the largest network of Turkish schools operating throughout the world (also in Africa) before clashing with the Erdogan government because of Gulen's suspected role in the failed coup against Erdogan in July 2016. After branding the movement a terrorist organization, the Turkish government has been putting pressure on various African countries to close the Gulen-affiliated schools (Akca 2019; Lepeska 2018; Petesch 2018).

Probing African views on the implications of expanding Turkey–Africa ties

Trust as an indicator of social capital for managing change

Turkey's new foreign policy creators have predicated Ankara's engagement in Africa on the virtuous nature of its neo-Ottoman approach as a benevolent new actor motivated by the value of South–South solidarity in contrast to the unequal exchange that continues to characterize Africa's relations to its old colonial powers (Langan 2019). Notwithstanding the tangible achievement that Turkish humanitarian organizations and official cooperation projects have exhibited so far, there have been numerous reasons to be cautious about the purported difference between Turkey and other foreign powers expanding their influence in Africa (Akca 2019; Langan 2016). To win the hearts and minds of Africans, Turkey's engagement in Africa will have to enlist, not just the nod of the African political elites, but also the trust of ordinary people and civil society organizations. Fukuyama (1996, 26–27) defines trust as "the expectation that arises within a community of regular, honest, and cooperative behavior, based on commonly shared norms, on the part of other members of that community." Trust is therefore essential in social interactions, thus also in international relations, because it is the cement that holds together the foundation of cooperative behavior.

To explore the perceptions of ordinary Africans on Turkish engagement in Africa, the study therefore sought to understand the degree of mutual trust that underpins the expanding relationship and how it is perceived by ordinary Africans who might have come in contact with one or multiple actors or institutions involved in Turkey's increasing influence in Africa. The importance of measuring the trust dimension of Turkey's engagement in Africa is underscored by the connection between trust and the local social capital upon which the effective management of the expected transformative change is dependent. Social capital is indeed a capability that arises from the prevalence of trust in a society or in certain parts of it, as highlighted by Fukuyama (1996, 26–27). Trust is a key component of the structural and cognitive dimensions of social capital measures (Acquaah et al. 2014), which strengthens positive interdependence by influencing people's preferences and by facilitating the exchange of information (Bouma et al. 2008). It enables interaction partners to lower transaction costs by eliminating the necessity of written contracts. The trust inventory in a community is therefore an important indicator of social capital and can be used as a predictor of that community's capacity to interact with external actors (Fukuyama 1996, 27). Without understanding the dimensions and directions of trust of Turkey's policy instruments by African populations, the success of its penetration in the African socio-economic landscape becomes difficult to predict (Liu et al. 2018).

Defining the dimensions of perceptions

Subjective assessment of win–win outcomes

In order to gain the necessary insights into the ways in which Africans assess the observable outcomes of Turkey–Africa engagement over the period 2005 to the present, a semi-structured interview questionnaire was designed to capture the assessment of key practices and outcomes of current engagement by key informants active in academic research, in government functions, in the business sector and in civil society organizations based in a sample of African countries where the multiple pillars of the new Turkish foreign policy have been deployed. The general intention of the interviews was to garner reliable assessment of the potential of current Turkey–Africa cooperation practices and policy instruments to generate the purported win–win outcomes as evoked in the official policy discourse. Interviews specifically targeted the win–win outcomes of the following five dimensions associated with the various instruments of Turkish foreign policy in Africa: (1) geopolitical positioning and military interventions, (2) the congruence of political and diplomatic interest between Turkey and Africa, (3) access to African markets and natural resources by Turkish entities, (4) Turkish trade and investment practices in Africa, (5) education and cultural affinities. These dimensions were chosen on the basis of their frequency in the stated policy objectives (and related outcomes) by researchers as important factors/instruments of Turkish foreign policy in Africa (Ozkan and Akgun 2010; Siradag 2015;

Wheeler 2011; Langan 2016; Habiyaremye and Oguzlu 2014; Eyrice Tepeciklioglu 2017; Akca 2019)

Survey of trust perceptions

The study also strived to map the distribution of trust intensity with respect to various actors and institutions involved in the growing Turkish engagement in Africa by administering a survey questionnaire that captured subjective perceptions of the dynamics of this engagement along with a series of identified policy objectives and several dimensions of trust. The objective of this exercise was to link the likelihood of popular support for Turkey–Africa relations to the scores of trust capital captured through the survey questionnaire. Respondents were asked to rate their trust towards Turkish state representatives, military personnel involved in peacekeeping operations, Turkish schools of their respective localities, humanitarian organizations, official cooperation agency, the private sector and Turkish tourists visiting their countries on a number of objectives representing win–win benefits of the mutual engagement. The objectives on which trust perception was surveyed relate to the following six aspects: (1) advancement of common geopolitical interests, (2) help and support in case of need, (3) technology sharing and learning opportunities, (4) quality of products and services supplied by Turkish trade partners, (5) sourcing of reliable information and (6) long-term sustainability of the mutual cooperation.

Responses were rated using the following Likert-scale levels: 1 = not at all, 2 = I trust somewhat, 3 = I trust quite well, 4 = I trust strongly, 5 = I trust absolutely.

Sampling and data collection approach

The data collection process was organized on the basis of a multilayered sampling aimed at maximum representation of the target population. Five countries representing four out of the five regional subdivisions of the African continent were targeted: Morocco and Sudan in North Africa, Cameroon in Central Africa, Kenya in East Africa and South Africa in Southern Africa. These countries were randomly selected in a layered sampling intended to cover all five regional subdivisions of the continent. Owing to time limitation and logistical difficulties resulting from the current Covid-19 pandemic restrictions, it was unfortunately not possible to arrange interviews in any of the West African countries. For the survey on trust capital, the aim was to reach groups of 100 to 120 participants in each of the five countries, preferably gender balanced and covering the three age categories: young = 18–30, middle-aged = 31–45, and mature = 46 and above. The response group in each country had to include, whenever possible, people who work for the government as well as those who work in private businesses and members of civil society organizations. For people working in the private sector, the targeting strived to include as far as possible those who work for Turkish companies or companies doing businesses with Turkish firms, either domestically or through imports and/or exports. With such balanced sampling within each country, the main demographic characteristics of age, gender and occupation status were covered by our respondents, so that bias could be reduced. The same logistic limitations prevented us from organizing large-scale surveys on big samples with more variations in demographic characteristics, which would have been more representative of the underlying population.

Final data collection

The data collection consisted of semi-structured interviews with key informants through telephone and administering the short survey on subjective assessment of trust towards Turkish entities and institutions among a sample of local community members in the selected countries. In total, 12 telephonic interviews were conducted with respondents based in South Africa (four), Kenya (three), Sudan (two) and Cameroon (three). In terms of their activities, respondents include three academics, five government officials and four businesspeople involved in trade or contracting with Turkish companies.

Data collection in these countries was made possible by the active support mobilized through a network of connected alumni from *Afrotalya*, the Association of former African Students based in Antalya. The questionnaire was distributed through personal connections of the different alumni. While the survey had targeted 130 people in each country, the number of respondents remained limited (Morocco = 37; Sudan = 29; Cameroon = 41, Kenya = 36; South Africa = 47). While the study design strived for a random selection of respondents to avoid the bias of subjective selection, the data collection constraints have reduced our sample to a convenience sample based on the availability of respondents through the mailing as the optimal means of communication during the lockdown period. The collected responses are therefore not intended to be interpreted as representative of the general level of trust in the country. They rather serve as an approximate barometer of some of the prevailing perceptions of Turkish growing presence in Africa.

Interpreting African perspectives on Turkey–Africa relations

The perceptions conveyed by political scientists and international relations commentators suggest that African perspectives on relations with Turkey are characterized by a mixture of hopeful expectations and confusion about the real intentions of Turkey in Africa (Ozkan 2012). Whereas Turkey has set up think tanks and committed resources on research to analyze Africa and generate the necessary insights to guide its Africa policy formulation, African countries are yet to have a good understanding of Turkey, its culture, its history and its post-Cold War identity as a central country with multi-dimensional interests. The information collected on respondents from five countries covering four sub-regions has been compiled and analyzed to assess the nature of attitudes, perceptions and influences that could enhance or hinder the success of the growing interconnection between Turkey and Africa.

Assessment of engagement instruments and outcomes

Geopolitical positioning and military interventions

The important role that Africa plays in Turkish geopolitical considerations of its strategic depth has been increasingly visible over this past decade, especially since the country's military involvement in Somalia, Sudan and Libya. One of our key informants sees the intensification of Turkish military presence in the Horn of Africa as directly linked to the strategic location of Somalia and Suakin Island on the main shipment routes of Persian Gulf oil to the Mediterranean. By so doing, Turkey seems to have joined the fray of numerous foreign powers seeking to assert their geopolitical interests in that crucial region for energy security.

Independent deployment of troops in the Libyan conflict zone is viewed by African diplomats and scholars as a clear signal of Turkey's assertiveness in assuming an autonomous geopolitical role in its proximate zone of influence in Africa. According to one of our African respondents, Turkey's geopolitical positioning in Africa should be interpreted as a corollary of Davutoglu's (2001) doctrine which permeated into JDPs ruling elites. Some of our other respondents believe that Turkey may be intending to use Libya as a testing opportunity for the strength of its military power as an instrument of foreign policy with the corresponding potential to market its military industry products in Africa. Others think that the intervention in North Africa is connected to the regional dynamics of rivalry related to maritime claims of sovereignty over energy deposits in the eastern Mediterranean (see, e.g. Morel 2020). The success of this operation will be defining for the future of foreign policy instrumentarium available to Ankara.

The congruence of political and diplomatic interests between Turkey and Africa

When Turkish president Abdullah Gul said the Republic of Turkey would be the spokesman of Africa at the UN during his 2009 visit to East Africa, it was understood to imply that Turkey would seek a convergence of political and diplomatic interests with Africa, so that national and international issues of importance to Africa would also be important to Turkey. Turkey's military base in Mogadishu and its involvement in the training of military forces in the Horn of Africa is perceived by one of our respondents as the clearest indication of Ankara's vision of its engagement in a long-term role. This means that Turkey is trying to tie its strategic interests to the long-term political stability of the area. Another respondent points out the imbalance between Turkey and its African partner countries in diplomatic and political dealings. Taken individually, none of the African countries can match Turkey's economic and political strength. This creates a considerable skewness in the conduct of such engagements, which gives Turkey a bargaining advantage that it gladly makes use of. The forced closure of Gulen-affiliated schools in more than 30 African countries is perhaps one of the most visible manifestations of such imbalances. Dealings with Pretoria are relatively less skewed because of the key technological advances that South Africa enjoys in some sectors, especially in the military industry.

Access to African markets and natural resources by Turkish entities

Turkey has insisted that its approach to cooperation with African countries would be based on shared values unlike other foreign actors primarily interested in African resources (Langan 2016; Akca 2019). Official numbers show a relatively low level of involvement of Turkish companies in the energy sector in Africa, but the interactions are expected to intensify as Turkey's growing energy demand continues to outstrip its own generation capacity. Two of our respondents agree that Turkey's eagerness to expand Turkish Airlines' network to resource-rich countries in Africa should be seen more as a means of developing the necessary network to facilitate the sourcing of strategic materials that are critical to Turkish industries. A key informant sees no reason for Turkey to be shy about its ambitions to access African resources, since other emerging powers engaged in Africa are openly competing for them. The country's growing industries require raw materials and energy input. Ankara could advantageously leverage its geographical and cultural proximity with Africa to secure its place in the strategic resource arena. Respondents feel that Turkish companies active in the resource sector will be tempted to imitate their Western counterparts and engage in secret deals that drain African resources without any accountability. A large portion of the natural resource market in Africa is indeed shrouded in much secrecy, especially through the strong connection to private ownership of most mineral deposits by Western companies registered in tax havens (see, e.g. Habiyaremye 2020).

Turkish trade and investment practices in Africa

In its dealings with African countries, Turkey presents itself as a comparatively more advanced economy with a skilled labor force, technological know-how and international market experiences that it can use to grow mutual trade and investments. Turkish construction companies play an important role in trade and investment in Africa because of their good reputation for quality and efficiency. This is exemplified by the impressively rapid construction of the Kigali Arena, a 10,000-seat indoor stadium successfully completed in less than eight months. Africans have generally responded enthusiastically to the prospects of the nascent collaboration with Turkish contractors active in their economies. Turkish firms and contractors are perceived as contributing to transforming the continent and raising living standards. They are viewed favorably for hiring locals in their projects, in contrast to Chinese entrepreneurs who prefer to import workers from their home base. Our respondents active in the construction industry raised some concerns about delays and cost overspending among some Turkish contractors, especially those active in the energy sector. The negative perception of individual behaviors of bad performers may damage the reputation of other construction companies and jeopardize their growth potential on the continent. Turkish products enjoy a good reputation among African consumers for their good price–quality ratio. Some of the respondents deplore the unavailability of their preferred Turkish products and specialties on the local market. The demand for Turkish building materials is also growing as result of clear demonstration effects that emerge wherever Turkish entrepreneurs have shown their building skills. The potential for growth remains therefore large for Turkish agro–food industries and the construction market.

Education and humanitarian assistance

Our respondents generally viewed Turkish schools as playing a very positive role in the relationship between Turkey and their country of implantation because of the high quality of the education they provided. Before their closure for the suspected role in the failed coup of July 2016, they were also highly appreciated because of their contribution to breaking the cultural and language barriers between Turkey and its African partners. The closure of these schools at the behest of Ankara has left numerous families stranded, without an alternative school for their children to attend in the interim (Akca 2019; Lepeska 2018; Petesch 2018). It was experienced as a significant loss for many parents, not simply because of the education quality but also the opportunity they offered to their graduates to pursue higher education in connected private universities in Turkey.

Trust capital of African public towards institutional agents of Turkish engagement in Africa

Persuasion rather than coercion is a more sustainable indicator of the ability of leaders to mobilize their followers in order to achieve the intended objectives. Trust also reflects the convergence of interest between partners and is therefore likely to represent lasting influences instead of temporary interactions. In order to get a picture of the trust map towards Turkish institutions and agents, the analysis grouped the trust survey scores from the five countries into two subdivisions corresponding to the conceptual categorization of

Africa by the Turkish political elite and society in general: the scores for Morocco and Sudan were combined to represent North Africa, while the scores for Cameroon, Kenya and South Africa were aggregated to stand for sub-Saharan Africa. The scores represent the perceived extent to which each component is likely to persuade Africans to support their operations with the understanding that supporting those operations will also act in their own interest.

Table 13.1 displays the trust scores for each of the identified pillars of Turkey's pivot to Africa policy for North Africa while Table 13.2 reports the corresponding scores for sub-Saharan Africa. Turkish humanitarian organizations and Turkish schools appear to score systematically higher than any other pillar, even though the differences are not strongly significant. For the advancement of common geopolitical interests, help in case of need, as well as sharing technology and learning opportunities, African respondents seem to trust Turkish government representatives (and even tourists) slightly more than they trust private businesses and investors (average scores of trust at the level: "Quite well" for the former versus "somewhat" for the latter). This may relate to the fact that businesses and contractors interact with local residents primarily through for-profit transactions and may be perceived as being motivated by the pursuit of their own interests. The level of trust for the quality of products/service supplied as well as for provision of reliable information reaches an average of "quite well." Importantly, the trust score for technology sharing and learning opportunities by private businesses remains at the moderate level "somewhat," implying that respondents are not quite sure whether Turkish private enterprises active in Africa offer sources of technologies that can be adopted by their African counterparts. In contrast, Turkish schools and humanitarian organizations score relatively higher on the learning opportunities they offer.

Much like their counterparts in North Africa, humanitarian organizations and Turkish schools operating in sub-Saharan African countries received the highest trust scores among respondents. Turkish businesses and investors score an adequate level of trust on the quality of their products and provision of reliable information. In contrast, their score is only moderate on the other account. Government institutions and their representatives enjoy a robust level of trust on almost all accounts.

These score averages imply that the primary Turkish institution in which local populations put their trust are the humanitarian organizations active in their regions, followed by Turkish schools implanted in their cities. Even though those humanitarian organizations do not hold authority to make political decisions, they enjoy significant influence among the people and may be a valuable channel for advancing mutual interests. Their crucial role in helping fight the burden of diseases, such as cataract cecity that would otherwise go untreated, is perceived with gratitude and can therefore be a source of considerable soft power. Likewise, schools are the primary channels

Table 13.1 North Africa trust scores for key Turkish foreign policy pillars

Trust domain Institution	Advancing mutual geo-political interests	Help and support in case of need	Sharing technology and learning opportunities	Quality of products or service	Source of reliable information	Sustainability of cooperation
Turkish government and diplomats	2.71	3.28	2.87	3.45	2.88	3.14
Turkish military/peacekeeping operations	2.57	2.93	2.12	2.73	2.82	2.17
Turkish humanitarian organizations	3.42	4.33	4.25	4.19	4.55	4.46
Turkish schools in Africa	3.19	3.34	3.47	3.55	3.23	3.31
Turkish businesspeople and investors	2.50	2.72	2.71	3.36	3.14	2.81
Turkish tourists coming here	3.24	3.47	3.51	2.94	2.84	3.49

Trust level by score: 1 = not at all, 2 = somewhat, 3 = quite well, 4 = strongly, 5 = absolutely

Table 13.2 Sub-Saharan Africa trust scores for key Turkish foreign policy pillars

Trust domain Institution	Advancing mutual political interests	Help and support in case of need	Sharing technology and learning opportunities	Quality of products or service	Source of reliable information	Sustainability of cooperation
Turkish government and diplomats	2.71	3.08	2.91	3.33	3.22	3.08
Turkish military/peacekeeping operations	2.69	2.75	2.62	2.73	2.91	2.65
Turkish humanitarian organizations	3.32	4.70	4.32	4.26	4.35	4.40
Turkish schools in Africa	3.05	3.30	3.06	3.18	3.28	3.31
Turkish businesspeople and investors	2.32	2.15	2.26	3.24	3.13	2.25
Turkish tourists coming here	3.05	3.08	3.02	2.94	2.97	3.05

Trust level by score: 1 = not at all, 2 = somewhat, 3 = quite well, 4 = strongly, 5 = absolutely

of cultural exchange between Turkey and African countries as it is through their learning facilities that the language barrier can be broken to make the cultural exchange smoother. Their proven capacity to make connections with the local circles of influence gives them additional room to maneuver for continuity and growth in the countries where they operate. Parents and communities in general hope that the new *Maarif* Foundation will be able to reopen the schools and maintain the quality and the reputation that they had already built.[9]

Conclusion

Turkey's growing involvement in Africa has been driven by a shift in its foreign policy orientation as a result of its quest for strategic depth in the post-Cold War configuration. Its approach towards relations with hitherto unknown sub-Saharan Africa has been presented as that of virtuous power motivated by values of solidarity and South–South cooperation to achieve mutual beneficial outcomes in multiple areas of common interests. The rapid expansion of diplomatic representations throughout Africa signaled the corresponding growth in diplomatic influence while wide coverage of Turkish airlines' flight network on the continent laid the foundation for growth in trade and investments. The actual trade flows between Africa and Turkey are still below the anticipated levels, but the potential for growth is underscored by the growing trust for Turkish institutions and investors by ordinary Africans. Trust in various institutional agents of Turkey's foreign policy engagement in Africa is characterized by a strong confidence in the work of Turkish humanitarian organizations active in Africa as well as an adequate trust for Turkish state representatives in Africa. The quality of Turkish products and services marketed in Africa also receives adequate recognition. Importantly, trust in the ability and willingness of Turkish private sector operators to advance mutual interests by sharing technology is only moderate. Turkish visitors who come to African countries also contribute to conveying a positive image of Turkey–Africa cooperation potential. By providing recognizable quality education, Turkish schools have equally played an important role in nurturing mutual trust between Turkey and its African partner countries where they were established. Given the value attached to those schools throughout Africa in bridging the cultural gap, the Turkish government should consider finding an accelerated way of restarting them as one of the main pillars of its quest for the realization of mutually beneficial outcomes in the domain of technology transfer and learning opportunities.[10]

On the question of whether Turkish engagement in Africa is winning the battle for hearts and minds by generating mutually beneficial outcomes, the trust scores bring to light that some areas still need improvement. This study identified five main objectives for Turkey's pivot to Africa: (1) Gaining diplomatic support for its role as a regional power and using it as leverage in

EU negotiations, (2) Countering the influence of its regional rivals (Egypt and Saudi Arabia), (3) access to African markets and natural resources, (4) constructivist approach to building soft power in South–South cooperation and (5) strengthening cultural bridges based on perceived affinities with African countries.

On the first two objectives, Turkey seems to have obtained the support and trust it needs from the African political elite as evidenced by its recognition as a strategic partner of the AU as well as the quasi-unanimous support for its UNSC candidacy back in 2009. The trust built during humanitarian assistance, especially in Darfur and Somalia, has enabled Turkey to build the type of influence it needed to outflank its regional rivals in the Horn of Africa (hence the Suakin Island agreement and the large military base in Somalia). It also helped build the kind of soft power to open the region for Turkish goods and cultural products. The market access objective has been slower, but it is growing and can only be reasonably assessed in the long run. For the soft power in other parts of Africa, the trust scores reflect perceptions rather than genuine understanding because of limited knowledge among ordinary Africans about Turkey's geopolitical motives. However, whether Turkey can leverage it in its negotiations with its Western rivals is a totally different matter. As for the cultural bridge, religious congruence facilitates trust building in majority Muslim countries, but more efforts will be needed to close the gap with non-Muslim countries, and this is where the role of Turkish schools and scholarships become crucial. *Maarif* will have to match or exceed its predecessor in terms of quality and trust building with local communities.

The low trust score for technology sharing by Turkish private enterprises implies that more efforts are necessary both on the side of African enterprises and on the side of their Turkish partners to increase learning incentives and enhance collaboration in research and innovation. The similarity in trust scores between North Africa and sub-Saharan Africa imply that similar efforts will be required to improve trust, but trust building will have to adapt to local culture and institutions. African countries will however not attain the full benefits of cooperation without investing in adequate knowledge generation about Turkey's internal as well as external policy dynamics. Whereas Turkey has set up think tanks to generate sufficient knowledge about Africa in order to guide its engagement efforts, African countries are yet to develop a similar understanding of Turkish internal political dynamics, its foreign policy motivations, its geopolitical intentions and ultimately the sustainability of its African partnership. Growing exchanges between Turkey and Africa will hopefully contribute to reducing the mutual knowledge gaps. Finally, the presence of competitors from other emerging economies vying for a piece of the African pie implies that Turkey will have to leverage the efficiency advantage offered by its geographical proximity and the quality of its products in order to carve its own Africa niche with a long-term growth potential.

Notes

1. From the establishment of the republic in Turkey all the way through the Cold War, the government has consistently followed a foreign policy predicament inspired by Kemal Ataturk's vision of Turkey's insertion in the West, seen as the modern civilized world.
2. In Davutoglu's (2008) view, Ankara's foreign policy and security interests are maximized when the country follows a multifaceted approach because Turkey has multiple regional identities.
3. This is an approach based on forging close ties through cooperation in education, cultural and religious solidarity.
4. Mainly through participation in peacekeeping operations, military interventions and bilateral security cooperation agreements in Libya and in the Horn of Africa.
5. Participation in the AfDB was also motivated by the prospect of opening the opportunity to Turkish companies in the bidding for contracts financed by that bank.
6. As of 2019, Turkish Airlines had 58 airline destinations in 38 countries across the continent (Presidency of the Republic of Turkey 2020).
7. Turkey's troop contributions were mostly symbolic with small units of police personnel. There are currently (July 2020) 22 Turkish police personnel participating in UNMISS, 19 in UNAMID, three in MONUSCO and one expert in UNSOM, according to UN sources. Turkey has also participated in the US-led Combined Force 151 which has carried out antipiracy patrols off the coast of Somalia since 2009 (Vertin 2019).
8. TUSKON was forced to dissolve in the wake of the failed attempt to overthrow Erdogan's government in July 2016, because of its suspected close connections to Fethullah Gulen's movement which controlled many business organizations around the world. Gulen is suspected to have been involved in masterminding the failed July 2016 coup.
9. As of July 2020, the Maarif Foundation reportedly operates 146 schools in Africa, many of them being the former Gulen-affiliated schools. https://turkiyemaarif.org/page/553-maarif-in-the-world-16.
10. With the pressure to close Gulen-affiliated schools, the Turkish president promised to replace them by a new school network run by the Maarif Foundation, which was established in 2016 with the purpose of taking over these schools and offering alternative school programs. Only a handful of students from the closed schools in Africa chose to go to the new Maarif Foundation-run schools. The majority was forced to look for other schools because they did not trust the new foundation to guarantee their desired quality of education.

References

Acquaah, M., K. Amoako-Gyampah, B. Gray and N.Q. Nyathi. 2014. "Measuring and Valuing Social Capital: A Systematic Review." Network for Business Sustainability South Africa. https://static1.squarespace.com/static/5d5156083138fd000193c11a/t/5f2f7af40c19916a42632eb2/1596947240444/NBS-SA-Social-Capital-SR.pdf.

Akca, Asya. 2019. "Neo-Ottomanism: Turkey's Foreign Policy Approach to Africa." *New Perspectives in Foreign Policy* 17: 3–8. https://www.csis.org/neo-ottomanism-turkeys-foreign-policy-approach-africa.

Austvik, Ole Gunnar and Gulmira Rzayeva. 2016. "Turkey in the Geopolitics of Natural Gas." *M-RCBG Associate Working Paper Series* 66: 9–16.

Ayuk, N.J. 2020. "Turkish Construction Companies Help to Move Africa Forward." *Africa Business Magazine*, March 15, 2020. https://africanbusinessmagazine.com/opinion/turkish-construction-companies-help-to-move-africa-forward/.

Baba, Gurol. 2018. "Turkey's Multistakeholder Diplomacy: From a Middle Power Angle." In *Middle Powers in Global Governance: The Rise of Turkey*, edited by Emel Parlar Dal, 75–96. Cham: Palgrave Macmillan.

Bouma, Jetske, Erwin Bulte and Daan Van Soest. 2008. "Trust and Cooperation: Social Capital and Community Resource Management." *Journal of Environmental Economics and Management* 56, no. 2: 155–166.

Daily Sabah. 2019. "Turkey Emphasizes Cooperation, Solidarity with African Countries." May 27, 2019. www.dailysabah.com/diplomacy/2019/05/27/turkey-emphasizes-cooperation-solidarity-with-african-countries.

Daloglu, Tulin. 2013. "Davutoglu Invokes Ottomanism as New Mideast Order." *Al-Monitor*, March 10, 2013. https://web.archive.org/web/20140717193008/http://www.al-monitor.com/pulse/originals/2013/03/turkey-davutologu-ottoman-new-order-mideast.html.

Davutoglu, Ahmet. 2001. *Stratejik Derinlik: Türkiye'nin uluslararası konumu*. Istanbul: Kure Yayinlari.

Davutoglu, Ahmet. 2008. "Turkey's Foreign Policy Vision: An Assessment of 2007." *Insight Turkey* 10, no 1: 77–96. https://www.jstor.org/stable/i26328777.

Duz, Zehra Nur. 2019. "Number of Turkish Embassies in Africa Rises from 12 to 42." Anadolu Agency, October 10, 2019. https://www.aa.com.tr/en/africa/-number-of-turkish-embassies-in-africa-rises-from-12-to-42/1619429.

Eyrice Tepeciklioglu, Elem. 2017. "Economic Relations between Turkey and Africa: Challenges and Prospects." *Journal of Sustainable Development Law and Policy* 8, no. 1: 1–33. https://doi.org/10.4314/jsdlp.v8i1.2.

Fukuyama, Francis. 1996. *Trust: Social Virtues and the Creation of Prosperity*. Harmondsworth: Penguin.

Gunay, Mustafa. 2011. "Turkey-Africa Relations." Speech given April 14, 2011 at Chatham House, London. Transcript. https://www.chathamhouse.org/sites/default/files/public/Meetings/Meeting%20Transcripts/140411gunay.pdf.

Habiyaremye, Alexis. 2020. "Natural Resource Abundance: A Hidden Drag on Africa's Development?" In *The Palgrave Handbook of African Political Economy*, edited by Samuel Oloruntoba and Toyin Falola, 699–723. Cham: Palgrave Macmillan. https://doi.org/10.1007/978-3-030-38922-2_38.

Habiyaremye, Alexis and Tarik Oguzlu. 2014. "Engagement with Africa: Making Sense of Turkey's Approach in the Context of East–West Geostrategic Rivalry." *Uluslararasi Iliskiler* 11, no. 41: 65–85. https://www.jstor.org/stable/43926533.

Koundouno, Tamba Francois. 2020. "Turkey's Hegemonic Bet: Neo-Ottomanism with Pan-Islamist Face." *Morocco World News*, January 7, 2020. https://www.moroccoworldnews.com/2020/01/290627/turkey-hegemony-neo-ottomanism-pan-islamism/.

Langan, Mark. 2016. "Virtuous Power Turkey in Sub-Saharan Africa: The "Neo-Ottoman" Challenge to the European Union." *Third World Quarterly* 38, no. 6: 1399–1414. https://doi.org/10.1080/01436597.2016.1229569.

Lepeska, David. 2018. "Turkey's Global Grab for Gulen Schools." *Haval News*, November 18, 2018. https://ahvalnews.com/Gülen-movement/turkeys-global-grab-Gülen-schools.

Liu, James H., Petar Milojev, Homero Gil de Zúñiga and Robert Jiqi Zhang. 2018. "The Global Trust Inventory as a "Proxy Measure" for Social Capital: Measurement and Impact in 11 Democratic Societies." *Journal of Cross-Cultural Psychology* 49, no. 5: 789–810. https://doi.org/10.1177/0022022118766619.

Melvin, N. 2019. "The Foreign Military Presence in the Horn of Africa Region." SIPRI Background Paper. https://sipri.org/sites/default/files/2019-04/sipribp1904.pdf.

Ministry of Foreign Affairs, Republic of Turkey. 2020. "Turkey-Africa Relations." http://www.mfa.gov.tr/turkey-africa-relations.en.mfa.

Morel, Jean Michel. 2020. "Why is Turkey Sending Forces to Libya? The Answer is Gas." *Middle East Eye*, January 20, 2020. https://www.middleeasteye.net/opinion/turkey-sends-forces-libya-play-natural-gas.

Ozkan, Mehmet. 2012. "A New Actor or Passer-By? The Political Economy of Turkey's Engagement with Africa." *Journal of Balkan and Near Eastern Studies* 14: 113–133. https://doi.org/10.1080/19448953.2012.656968.

Ozkan, Mehmet and Birol Akgun. 2010. "Turkey's Opening to Africa." *Journal of Modern African Studies* 48, no. 4: 525–546. https://doi.org/10.1017/S0022278X10000595.

Petesch, Charles. 2018. "Senegal Closes schools Linked to Turkish Cleric in Exile." Associated Press, March 18, 2018. https://apnews.com/a482d24970784efbb3e3a232936d1ddb.

Presidency of the Republic of Turkey. 2020. "We will Increase our Trade Volume with African countries to $50 billion." https://www.tccb.gov.tr/en/news/542/116415/-we-will-increase-our-trade-volume-with-african-countries-to-50-billion-#:~:text=Noting%20that%20the%20total%20trade,as%20far%20as%20%242%20billion.

Rossiter, Ash and Brendon Cannon. 2019. "Re-examining the 'Base': The Political and Security Dimensions of Turkey's Military Presence in Somalia." *Insight Turkey* 21, no. 1: 167–188. https://www.jstor.org/stable/26776053.

Rudincova, Katerina. 2014. "New Player on the Scene: Turkish Engagement in Africa." *Bulletin of Geography. Socio–Economic Series* 25: 197–213. https://doi.org/10.2478/bog-2014-0039.

Samuel, Michael. 2014. "The Other and I: Turkish Teachers in South Africa." *Education as Change* 18, no. 1: 9–20. https://doi.org/10.1080/16823206.2013.847019.

Satana, Nil. 2012. "Peacekeping Contributor Profile: Turkey." http://www.providingforpeacekeeping.org/2014/04/03/contributor-profile-turkey/.

Siradag, Abdurrahim. 2015. "Benevolence or Selfishness: Understanding the Increasing Role of Turkish NGOs and Civil Society in Africa." *Insight on Africa* 7, no. 1: 1–20. https://doi.org/10.1177/0975087814554066.

Tepebas, Ufuk. 2015. "Turkey in Africa: Achievements and Challenges." *Dis Politika* 42, no. 1: 47–70.

The World. 2020. "Is Turkey Seeking a Neo-Ottoman Empire?" January 2, 2020. https://www.pri.org/stories/2020-01-02/turkey-seeking-neo-ottoman-empire.

Vertin, Z. 2019. "Turkey and the New Scramble for Africa: Ottoman Designs or Unfounded Fears?" Brookings Report, May 19, 2019. https://www.brookings.edu/research/turkey-and-the-new-scramble-for-africa-ottoman-designs-or-unfounded-fears/.

Vrey, François. 2020. "Turkey in Africa: What a Small but Growing Interest Portends." *The Intercept*, February 5, 2020. https://theconversation.com/turkey-in-africa-what-a-small-but-growing-interest-portends-130643.

Wheeler, Tom. 2011. "Ankara to Africa: Turkey's Outreach since 2005." *South African Journal of International Affairs* 18, no. 1: 43–62. https://doi.org/10.1080/10220461.2011.564426.

Yazar, Isa. 2010. "Every Minister I Met in Africa Asked for More Schools." https://hizmetnews.com/237/every-minister-i-met-in-africa-asked-for-more-schools/#.Xw2xKSgzZPY.

Conclusion

Turkey: Just another emerging power in Africa?

Elem Eyrice Tepeciklioğlu and Ali Onur Tepeciklioğlu

The Third Turkey–Africa Summit, scheduled to be held in Istanbul, Turkey in 2019 was postponed and set to be organized in April 2020. It is accepted by some commentators as a result of Turkey's deteriorating relations with Egypt, which held the chairmanship of the African Union in 2019 (e.g. see Kucuk 2020). The summit is postponed once again to 2021 while no official reason is announced by the Turkish authorities. The decision appears to be related to the Covid-19 outbreak that led to the cancellation or postponement of many global events. It is yet to be seen whether the outbreak will further affect Turkey's links with Africa, a region that now occupies an important place in Turkish foreign policy. The summit coordinator, Ambassador Can Incesu (n.d.) noted that the third summit would review the progress made on the partnership with Africa following the second summit and provide policy frameworks for Turkey's cooperation with the continent for the upcoming five-year period. The implications of the pandemic on Turkey–Africa relations will most likely be another focus.

Turkey has engaged in coronavirus diplomacy with Africa at a time when its international prestige was at a low point (Ozhisarciklioglu quoted in Pitel 2020). Turkey's Covid-19 donation diplomacy clearly demonstrates its increasing ambitions to have a larger influence in regional and global affairs. In early August 2020, Turkish President Recep Tayyip Erdogan announced that the number of countries to which Turkey sent medical aid to support their fight against the virus exceeded 150 (Bulut 2020). The list includes the United Kingdom (UK), the United States of America (USA), China and Israel while medical supplies were also provided to various African countries. With the Third Turkey–Africa Summit postponed, Africa has become an important scene for Turkey's Covid-19 diplomacy. Turkish assistance is welcomed in the continent with vulnerable populations facing infectious disease outbreaks, weak health care systems and poor economies. While there are concerns that the global pandemic could have a more devastating impact in Africa, it also has the potential to transform the Turkey–Africa relationship.

The trajectory of Turkey's African engagement depends on its ability to maintain those relations at a time when the economy has been hit hard by the effects of the outbreak. As the increasing number of new cases requires additional resources to control the pandemic at home, the resulting economic decline could lead to a lesser engagement with Africa albeit not a complete withdrawal from the continent. The ongoing pandemic has highlighted the vulnerability of the Turkish economy while experts expect that economic stagnation could last a long time. Coupled with a near public health crisis, the current financial crisis may well limit Turkey's involvement in the continent. Together with other foreign policy concerns and challenges, the potential financial crisis might further reduce the importance of Africa in foreign policy. Even if the economy recovers in the post-Covid period, policymakers are preoccupied with more immediate foreign policy priorities at the time of writing. They include Turkey's involvement in the Libyan and Syrian conflicts, the various humanitarian and security challenges along its Syrian border, outstanding issues in the Eastern Mediterranean, relations with Greece over the Aegean Sea as well the downgrade of relations with its traditional partners including the USA, the turbulent relations with Russia and the slowing down of the European Union (EU) membership process. Turkey's future relations with Africa cannot be fully appreciated without a proper analysis of recent foreign policy challenges.

Implementing foreign policy in a volatile period

In its search to redefine its place in world affairs, Turkey puts a lot of effort into playing a more active role in different regions but faces fierce challenges. The main setback in foreign policy remains with its longtime ally, the USA, on issues over the extradition of Turkish cleric, Fethullah Gulen, different foreign policy attitudes towards the Assad regime in Syria (i.e. Turkish operations in Syria, the reluctance of the USA to intervene in the country and its military assistance for the YPG—People's Protection Units, an extension of the PKK—Kurdistan Worker's Party, defined both by the USA and Turkey as a terrorist organization) and Turkey's decision to buy Russia's S-400s, an anti-aircraft missile system.

The latter also destabilized relations with NATO (North Atlantic Treaty Organization), which resulted in Turkey's removal from the F-35 joint strike fighter program by the USA in July 2019 (Hernandez 2020). Tensions on the issue could have broad implications for Turkey's role in NATO (Zanotti and Thomas 2020). Despite concerns that Turkey's possession of the Russian air defense system would pose security risks to the wider F-35 program and create a rift in the NATO alliance, Turkey countered that the S-400s would not be integrated to NATO systems (Bilginsoy 2018; Hernandez 2020). Turkish officials also stress that the Turkish decision to purchase the S-400 missile defense system came after the American government refused to sell the Patriot missile defense system to Turkey (TRT World 2020). This is not the first time the two NATO members have had disagreements on foreign policy issues but they have remained allies (Ward 2019). As observed by

Bilginsoy (2018), Turkey "may be engaged in a balancing act, tactically turning to Russia as ties with the United States further deteriorate."

However, relations with Russia, traditionally characterized by mutual distrust, suspicion and political crisis, have also been tense. Supporting rival factions in both Libya and Syria, the two countries have conflicting interests and diverging agendas in the Eastern Mediterranean despite working together to reach political resolution and reconcile their interests in both cases. In Libya, Turkey supports the UN-recognized Government of National Accord (GNA) while Russia backs Khalifa Haftar's Libyan National Army (LNA). Both Turkey and Russia provide military and logistical support to these opposing sides. Other issues related to their maritime agenda (i.e. accessing energy resources in the Eastern Mediterranean and Russia's historical quest to gain access to warm water ports; Borshchevskaya 2020), the quest for a larger military reach in the region and economic imperatives motivate their active engagement in the Libyan conflict. The latter is especially important as both countries seek to secure contracts for their companies in order to compensate for the billions they invested in Gaddafi's Libya before the civil war interrupted their operations. Libya is also an important client of Russian arms sales (Borshchevskaya 2020) but the military cooperation agreement signed between Turkey and the GNA in 2019 allows Turkey to sell weapons, vehicles and other military equipment to the GNA upon the request of the latter. The region has been on the agenda of various other regional and international players (Inat, Ataman and Duran 2020). Yet, having the longest coastline in the Eastern Mediterranean, Turkey does not define itself as an external power as Libya lies in its wider neighborhood.

The discovery of hydrocarbon reserves in the region intensified the competition over access to the energy resources among the regional and outside players. While Turkey pursues assertive policies as it feels threatened by the Greek and Egyptian rapprochement, Turkey's presence in the country is also viewed by some regional countries—most notably, by Egypt, which entered into an agreement with Greece in August 2020, designating an exclusive economic zone in the Eastern Mediterranean—as a long-term security concern (Ahmad 2020). Tensions between Turkey and its neighbors are coupled with the establishment of the Eastern Mediterranean Gas Forum in Cairo, Egypt, on 22 September 2020. The signatories of the agreement, the governments of Egypt, Israel, Jordan, Italy, Greece and the Republic of Cyprus aim at contesting Turkey's regional intentions (Shokri 2020). Turkey, on the other hand, stresses that the member countries of the forum aim at leaving Turkey out of the energy equation in the region but that it will continue to claim its legitimate rights under international law (Zorlu 2020). Apart from Egypt, relations with other Arab states including the United Arab Emirates (UAE) and Saudi Arabia are also at odds on many fronts (Zanotti and Thomas 2020), one example being competition over the leadership of the Muslim World.

Syria is another conflict zone where Turkey has been deeply involved since the outbreak of the civil war in 2011. As the deepening crisis in Syria has triggered regional instability, it has quickly emerged as a national security priority for Turkey (MFA n.d.). The national interests and the security agenda of Turkey and Russia, backing rival conflicting groups in the country, have also collided from the very outset of the conflict (Mammadov 2020). Russia is inclined to keep the Assad regime while Turkey assists the opposition groups in northern Syria and finds itself parting not only with Russia but also with Iran and the USA (Handy 2018). Ataman and Ozdemir (2018, 13) present six factors that explain Turkey's military assertiveness in the country: "Managing the humanitarian crisis, materializing the fall of the Assad regime, aiding the opposition forces, waging a proxy war with Iran, eliminating the threat of Daesh, and preventing the PYD/YPG from creating an area of dominance." The political turmoil in Syria and the resulting refugee crisis continue to challenge Turkey in various areas.

As Syria's civil war displaced a significant part of the Syrian population, Turkey has become an important destination for the refugee influx, together with neighboring Lebanon (Myers 2016). According to UNHCR (United Nations Refugee Agency) data (2019, 1), Turkey hosts the world's largest refugee population, with nearly four million Syrian refugees. The integration of these refugees requires enormous human and material resources. The official statistics estimate that Turkey has alone spent US$37 billion for Syrian refugees over the course of eight years (Kamu Bulteni 2019). The migration deal Turkey signed with the EU in 2016 stipulated that €6 billion was to be granted to Turkey to address the needs of refugees and improve their living standards. Turkey's EU accession process was also to be revitalized (Pacaci Elitok 2019, 3). On the other hand, the deal aimed to discourage the flow of irregular migration through the Aegean Sea (Mehmet 2019). However, Ankara expects greater support from the EU while complaining that the organization was too slow to disburse the funds it pledged to address the needs of refugees and fulfill its side of the deal (i.e. visa liberalization for Turkish citizens; Mandiraci 2020; Mehmet 2019). Disagreements over the Syrian crisis also strain Turkey's relations with the EU, which have already been in a slow phase. Observers hold that tensions in other areas including Turkey's involvement in the Libyan crisis and the intensifying dispute in the Eastern Mediterranean over gas reserves especially with Greece and the Republic of Cyprus could endanger the start of talks with the EU (Pitel and Foy 2020).

Surrounded by different conflict zones and regional uncertainties, complicated challenges in Turkey's wider neighborhood aggravate its security concerns, which could in turn adversely affect its foreign relations. Turkey's overloaded foreign policy agenda in recent years has already shifted the country's priorities from more distant regions to its immediate vicinity. However, Africa stands as the cornerstone of Turkey's global ambitions. As Turkish foreign policy passes through a volatile period, its Africa policy is probably the only area where it has not faced serious challenges. This does not necessarily mean that Turkey's engagement in Africa is free of problems or controversies. For example, one of the biggest challenges in Turkey's involvement in Africa remains the recent rift with the Gulen movement and the earlier presence of the Gulen network in the region.

In building its African engagement largely on humanitarian aid and the economy, the Turkish government has supported and benefited, at least until recently, from the activities of the civil society elements affiliated with the Gulen movement. The movement ran various humanitarian assistance organizations, including *Kimse Yok Mu* (KYM, Is Anybody There) and business associations such as TUSKON (the Confederation of Businessmen and Industrialists of Turkey), a business confederation that has been instrumental in increasing trade links with African countries. Above all, it is especially active in education and has been opening schools in sub-Saharan Africa (SSA), which has been appreciated in government circles for enhancing Turkey's international profile.

For a time, the government viewed these civil society elements as one of the main components of Turkey's soft power in Africa. More recently, however, they are defined by Ankara as being part of a "parallel structure" that has infiltrated state institutions. The Gulen-linked institutions within Turkish borders were closed down by a government decree after the failed coup on 15 July 2016. The Turkish government believes that Gulen followers were behind the failed coup. So, the movement was declared a terrorist group after the coup attempt. Turkey requested the support of African leaders for the closure of schools run by the Gulen network and their transfer to Turkish Maarif Foundation (TMV). Yet, the movement still has a well-established network of supporters around the world including some African countries.

The smallest or politically and/or economically weakest African countries that are more dependent on Turkish foreign aid are likely to follow Turkey's demand to close down those schools and other establishments with ties to Gulenists, so as not to jeopardize relations with Turkey (Angey 2018). For example, the schools associated with the Gulen network in Somalia and Niger that receive susbtantial amounts of Turkish aid, were transferred to the TMV two days after the thwarted coup attempt. Conversely, some of the regional powers such as Nigeria, South Africa, Angola and Kenya are reluctant to comply with Turkey's recommendations and close down Gulen-associated schools, which attract the children of local businesspersons and bureaucrats (Angey 2018). A Nigerian official is even quoted as saying that it is a domestic matter that requires domestic measures (Jalloh 2016).[1]

Obviously, the internal rift between the Turkish government and the Gulen movement having a vast network in the region will likely have serious repercussions on Turkey's Africa policy. As Donelli (2019, 77) puts it:

> The Gulen movement's lobbying efforts in Africa have the potential to damage or even reverse Turkey's gains on that continent. Indeed, the consequences of the domestic political warfare between Ankara and the

movement may partly affect Turkey's humanitarian efforts and public diplomacy, compromising its reputation in the region.

Accordingly, any policy to counter the movement's influence requires cautious moves. Ankara expects the cooperation of African countries against Gulen activities but a policy of pressuring could undermine the overall progress realized in Turkey's relationship with Africa and endanger the attainments of the last years (Donelli 2019, 78). Moreover, it will challenge Turkey's non-interference policy.

Turkey's struggle with the Gulen movement might not only limit its contemporary presence in Africa but it will potentially have serious impacts on its wider foreign policy agenda that is already constrained by a series of difficult domestic and international problems. The country's rise was mostly associated with its economic growth, democratic success and an independent and assertive foreign policy. However, the sources of power that once created advantages in Turkey's foreign policy are now in turmoil.

Another disadvantage that could potentially hinder Turkey's efforts in Africa appears to be the deteriorating economic conditions. Economic performance was impressive during most of the 2000s. While most of the major economies faced recession in 2008/2009, Turkey recovered well from the global economic crisis (Eghbal 2009; The World Bank 2020). However, the current macroeconomic indicators tell otherwise as the Turkish economy is struggling with high unemployment rates, double-digit inflation and huge foreign debt. The Turkish currency also hit a series of record lows against the US dollar and Euro despite the efforts of the Turkish Central Bank to stabilize the lira (Hessler 2020; Sezer Bilen 2020). The economic outlook is uncertain giving the economy is forecast to contract by 4% in 2020 and the lira to fall further (Hessler 2020; The World Bank 2020). While some observers (e.g. Ulgen 2020) hold that a failing economy is not a constraint on Turkey's assertive and hard power-based foreign policy, the last decade has indicated that the country's success in its foreign policy objectives largely depends on its economic performance.

Coupled with the persistent economic problems and the ongoing tensions in foreign policy during the pandemic, there are concerns over the growing authoritarian politics of the Justice and Development Party (JDP) government. While Turkey's economic performance was seen as promising in the first two terms of the JDP government, its democratization efforts were also applauded by many observers. With its democratic credentials and the secular character of the regime, it was even promoted as a model for the regional countries (Ozpek 2020). As the party consolidated its power at home, the last decade saw the country's transformation into a "populist authoritarian regime" (Ozpek 2020). The democratic reversal was accelerated first following the 15 July 2016 failed coup and then with the constitutional amendment on 16 April 2017 that extended the powers of the president and abolished the decades-old parliamentary system (Cook 2016; Yilmaz and Turner 2019).

This authoriatarian turn and the accompanying democratic backsliding had certain repercussions beyond the domestic sphere and shattered Turkey's image as a model for its wider neighborhood. Africa remains, however, as a region that offers important opportunities for Turkish foreign policymakers. The overriding question, here, is whether Ankara could bear the costs of its rising power aspirations in Africa.

An outsider, a latecomer or a returner?

At a time when Turkey is dealing with various internal issues and foreign policy challenges, Africa provides a space where it can play the role of a new humanitarian and benign power and leverage its global influence. Despite the many complexities, Turkey has managed to enhance its involvement in Africa and become an increasingly visible yet re-emerging player in the continent. The relevant chapters in this volume have mostly concluded that it is not a stranger, outsider or a newcomer in Africa. Given its Ottoman heritage, Turkey's engagement in Africa can best be described as a "return" to the region rather than an "arrival."

The Ottoman past gives Turkey the upper hand particularly in former Ottoman territories, while this historical legacy puts it in a unique position compared to most of Africa's external partners. More importantly, this heritage does not carry the burden of a troublesome colonial past or Atlantic slave trade, unlike a number of EU countries or the USA (Eyrice Tepeciklioglu 2020). Relying on this Ottoman legacy and its old ties with the region, Turkey strives to expand its presence in the former peripheral provinces in North Africa while at the same time establishing new friendships in the SSA.

Notwithstanding the Ottoman Empire's earlier presence in the continent, Turkey's reappearance in Africa came only after a century-long absence and neglect. This book has attempted to analyze Turkey's recently revived partnership with Africa. It started with the theoretical, historical and political analysis of Turkey–Africa relations and discussed the main features of its diplomatic, political, economic, cultural and military relations that have developed with African countries in recent times. The historical overview of Turkey's Africa relationship has enabled the reader to have an understanding of the Ottoman Empire's direct and indirect rule in North Africa and Ottoman perceptions of African territories, as well as the Ottoman Empire's reactions to European colonialism in the nineteenth century and the legacy of Ottoman rule in Africa in contemporary Turkish foreign policy discourse. The historical analysis of Turkey–Africa relations also detailed the main motives and strategies of Turkey's Africa policy within its wider foreign policy agenda. It revealed that the key feature in Turkey's engagement in Africa is rooted in its desire to have a higher profile in global affairs. As the theoretical part argued, Turkey's growing involvement in Africa can be better explained by its rising power ambitions. Drawing upon the rising powers literature, the theoretical chapter discussed the various ways rising powers engage with Africa and focused on the peculiarities of Turkey's Africa relationship. That said, other factors underlying Turkey's Africa strategy include the quest to diversify foreign policy allies and trade partners. Turkey's ambitions beyond its immediate neighborhood also explain its increasing engagement with the Global South. The first part of the book finally elaborated the South–South dimension in Turkey's Africa policy and explored the similarities between the Turkish approach and South–South cooperation.

As competition from the emerging countries intensified, Turkey established a strong presence in Africa through the effective use of different soft power instruments. The soft power tools and strategies Turkey deploys in Africa are a means of securing economic deals with African countries while trade and aid linkages facilitate its military expansion. The second part of the book focused on Turkey's economic and military relations with African countries. On the economic front, Turkey views Africa as a region with many opportunities for its business community. As discussed in more detail, business circles have been instrumental in Ankara's opening to new regions including Africa. This part started with a discussion of Turkey–Africa relations from a political economy perspective and argued that the country's liberal structuring, started in the early 1980s, led to the emergence of a new bourgeoisie fueling the need for new markets. Trade links with Africa are explored in a separate chapter through an assessment of the relationship between Turkey's new identity building process and its economic relations with African countries. It located Turkey as a rising power as well, which has used trade as an instrument of foreign policy and status enhancing. However, Africa is more than an alternative investment destination or a market for Turkish products. In addition to the economic aims of Ankara's Africa policy, Turkey has also enhanced its military deployment in the region.

Ankara tries not to be a part of the conflicts in African countries and refrains from resorting to hard power in the region, with Libya being an exception. Instead, it relies on soft power tools in expanding its presence in the continent. Its military involvement in Africa was confined to its participation (mostly with a limited number of personnel) in United Nations (UN) peacekeeping operations across the continent, such as in Somalia. A Turkish general, Cevik Bir was the force commander of UNOSOM II (United Nations Operation in Somalia) in 1993 and Turkish naval forces assumed the command of the Combined Task Force (2009–2010), established to conduct counter piracy operations off the coast of Somalia. Yet, its military strategy towards Africa is more recent amidst the increasingly rising number of foreign military bases across the continent. Despite its recent arrival, Turkey has been instrumental in reforming the Somalian army and it has managed to have a significant sphere of influence in the country.

The second part also explored the military dimension of Turkey's Africa policy in more detail and argued that it does not have a clear military strategy in the continent. In other words, Turkey's military engagement in Africa is not one of the defining characteristics of its policy towards the region. It also noted that Turkey's military and security interactions with Africa exhibit different features in North Africa and SSA. The last chapter of this part focused on Ankara's discursive constructions towards its contribution to UN peacekeeping operations (UNPKO) with selected cases from Africa. This overview allowed us to elaborate how Turkey benefits from its meager participation in the UNPKO in order to create a narrative that distinguishes its peacekeeping efforts from other external players.

The third part of the book focused on Turkey's soft power investment that aims at serving the dual functions of enhancing Turkey's presence and wiping out the Gulen movement's influence in the region. One major focus has been Turkey's engagement in public diplomacy, which emerged as a vital component of Turkey's Africa policy. Public institutions such as Yunus Emre Institute, Presidency for Turks Abroad and Related Communities, Maarif Foundation and Anadolu Agency engage in Turkey's public diplomacy in collaboration with relevant state ministries. The third part discovered that Turkey's public diplomacy in Africa is linked to state-based cultural, educational and broadcasting initiatives that promote and advance Turkey's foreign policy goals. It also elaborated the potential as well as the limits of Turkey's public diplomacy engagement in the continent. As more countries with global ambitions are turning to aid initiatives in order to boost recognition for their respective countries, Turkey also enhanced its humanitarian involvement in the region. This part noted that Turkey's engagement in the humanitarian domain suggests an alternative approach from other emerging powers in Africa. Here, the official narrative reflects Turkey as a state with no colonial ambitions that follows policies entirely different from that of its Western counterparts. As Turkish humanitarian assistance is provided by public institutions, business groups and NGOs, the nexus between government agencies and civil society institutions in Turkey's humanitarian assistance efforts has been another focus of this part.

As the religious element has become increasingly visible in Turkey's humanitarian activities, this part of the book also highlighted that Turkish aid going to Africa is agreed bilaterally and is concentrated mostly on the countries with significant Muslim populations. Turkey benefits from its Ottoman heritage and religious identity when approaching those African countries. Broadly speaking, the Turkish Presidency of Religious Affairs (Diyanet) and Turkish Cooperation and Coordination Agency (TIKA) have emerged as the key players in the application of Turkey's religious diplomacy. However, recent years have also seen Turkish Islamic NGOs play a growing role in Turkey's aid landscape. Religion is now not separable from the general course of Turkish foreign policy while this religious dimension differentiates Turkey's efforts from most of the emerging powers in Africa. As another strategy adopted by Turkey to support its rising power aspirations in Africa, the book focused on Turkey's aviation diplomacy. It noted that Turkish Airlines, Turkey's national airline company, has always been a part of government strategy to raise Turkey's image and attraction abroad. Yet, its use as a foreign policy tool has been more overt under JDP rule thanks to the apparent politically motivated decisions in introducing new routes. The launch of new flight destinations in Africa contributes to cultivate solid relationships with African nations while also complementing the extension of Ankara's diplomatic presence.

Officials often enjoy highlighting Turkey's good intentions when approaching African countries. As Turkey seeks to present itself as an alternative power willing to cooperate with its African counterparts on an equal basis, it has been steadily raising its profile in the continent especially over the past decade. However, African reactions to Turkey may be varied and far more complex than one might anticipate. Turkey's Ottoman legacy, increasing focus on relations with Africa's big powers, its ideological motivations and close cooperation with countries having significant Muslim populations all account for this variation. The book therefore included a chapter on African perceptions towards Turkey's foreign policy in the region and the major strategies Turkey has deployed to win the hearts and minds of African people.

The individual chapters noted that Turkey's increasing involvement in Africa is characterized by its pursuit of status in the international system and its assertive foreign policy. They referred to the rising powers literature in explaining Turkey's involvement in Africa while offering new theoretical insights individually. Additionally, those chapters explored whether Turkey's Africa strategy differs from the other rising powers and if its engagements with the region will make it a major player in the region. They further discussed the major challenges that could hinder the future of Turkey–Africa relations.

A new competitor?

Turkey is competing with both traditional donors and emerging actors for a role in Africa. While it is questionable whether it has the ability to contest other players, its growing African involvement will potentially exacerbate competition in the continent. However, in most cases, Ankara's Africa strategy does not aim at countering other players. In other words, it does not want to secure a position for itself in the continent at the expense of others. Yet, its intervention in the region over the last years increases the bargaining power of African countries and diminishes their dependency on the more established powers in the region, these being Western donors and China. While Turkey offers an alternative to African nations, in return it expects Africa's support.

Turkey distinguishes its African policy from that of other external actors especially with a heavy focus on its non-colonial past and Ottoman legacy. Many of those players also benefit from such carefully crafted discourses in their relationship with Africa. For example, Chinese and Russian resources highlight their support for numerous African national liberation movements; Indonesia seeks to revive the "Bandung Spirit" and Brazil refers to the historical relations with Africa linked to slavery along with African descendants that now form the majority of the Brazilian population. Neither Turkey's rhetoric nor its practice differ fundamentally from the rest of Africa's external partners. Moreover, Turkey's African outreach shares similar characteristics with that of other rising powers including an emphasis on the use of soft power instruments, increasing trade relations and cooperation in different sectors. In this sense, Turkey is not different from the other players in the region.

With the militarization of its foreign policy, Turkey has increasingly relied on the use of hard power and has involved itself directly in regional conflicts (Ulgen 2020). Yet, its Africa strategy is underpinned by the use of soft power assets where its national interests are not directly at stake, such as the case in Libya. It simply means that Turkey does not have a holistic approach towards the region despite the official rhetoric which emphasizes otherwise. Turkey's policies towards North Africa and SSA are driven by different motivations. In North Africa, located in its immediate vicinity, Turkey has more developed relations and defines itself with the Ottoman legacy with an aim to revive old ties. On the other hand, it has demonstrated that it would not hesitate to intervene in regional conflicts when its national security interests are at stake.

Conversely, it avoids intervening in internal conflicts in SSA and does not want to be interpreted as pursuing hard power-based policies in the region. Turkey's military and security cooperation with Somalia does not reveal otherwise, but instead, its leading role in reconstruction of the war-torn country, provides it an advantage over other rising powers. In addition to the establishment of a military facility that trains Somali soldiers, Turkey assumed the role of a neutral mediator between Somalia and Somaliland, provided technical cooperation, supported local governance structures and capacity building and deployed Turkish experts in important sectors including water, sanitation, health, agriculture and technology. As security is a major concern for many African countries, the high visibility and comprehensive nature of Turkey's peacebuilding efforts in the country is a valuable asset. Turkey's comparative advantage in comparison to other emerging countries is also visible in the education sector. While Turkey still struggles to take over the Gulen movement's role in Africa, Turkey's Maarif Foundation could assume the control of schools in most African countries.

On the economic side, Turkish companies significantly expanded their operations and investments in Africa. On the other hand, Turkish aid activities both initiated and facilitated trade relations with African countries. For example, two Turkish companies, namely, Favori LLC and Albayrak Group, assumed control of Mogadishu's airport and seaport operations. As Turkey strengthened commercial relations with its African partners, its business activities have not faced serious criticism from them; however, it is also true that Turkey lags behind the other rising powers in terms of economic performance. The current economic indicators unveil that it lacks the economic might to compete with Africa's more established partners. While Ankara has much to offer to African countries in terms of security cooperation and development assistance, it has less to offer in the form of economic development. Yet again, it is also worth noting that Turkey, in its engagement in Africa, including its trade links, humanitarian assistance, educational activities and peacebuilding efforts mostly concentrates on countries with Muslim-majority populations.

As noted, one of the most distinctive aspects of Turkey's Africa policy is the increasing use of religion in legitimizing its foreign policy agenda in the region. Mosque building is arguably the most visible of those religious initiatives but its religious outreach in the continent goes beyond such symbolic moves and covers aid initiatives as well. However, Turkey's religious diplomacy efforts might slow down and its aid preferences (i.e. Turkish aid recipient countries) might radically alter in the case of a change of government. Such a drastic change will most likely change the investor group that formed the incumbent JDP's electoral and economic support base. So, this will have a huge impact on the course of Turkey's African involvement albeit not totally. Moreover, domestic political factors might lead to a redefinition of foreign policy priorities if the new government does not place the same emphasis on Turkey's Ottoman past and religious kinship. With the pandemic creating new challenges for Turkey's Africa policy, it is too early to speculate whether Turkey's African initiative could continue to contribute to its rising power ambitions. Nevertheless, next year's Turkey–Africa Summit, a very important venue to instrumentalize the Turkey–Africa partnership, will more clearly identify Turkey's priorities in Africa.

Note

1 In 2015, Shinn noted that among the 96 Gulen-affiliated schools in SSA countries, Nigeria has the most with 17 schools (and the only Gulen-associated university in Africa, the Nigerian Turkish Nile University), followed by Ethiopia, Kenya, Mali, Senegal, South Africa and Tanzania all having six or more schools.

References

Ahmad, Talmiz. 2020. "Libyan Cease-Fire may Reconcile Turkish-Russian Interests." *Arab News*. August 24, 2020. https://www.arabnews.com/node/1723901.

Angey, Gabrielle. 2018. "The Gulen Movement and the Transfer of a Political Conflict from Turkey to Senegal." *Politics, Religion & Ideology* 19, no. 1: 53–68. https://doi.org/10.1080/21567689.2018.14532.

Ataman, Muhittin and Cagatay Ozdemir. 2018. "Turkey's Syria Policy: Constant Objectives, Shifting Priorities." *Turkish Journal of Middle Eastern Studies* 5, no. 2: 13–35. https://doi.org/10.26513/tocd.466046.

Bilginsoy, Zeynep. 2018. "In Familiar Dance, Turkey Warms to Russia as US ties unravel." The Associated Press (AP), August 27, 2018. https://apnews.com/article/02efd2ebf4a8430c96c496d0aa1cb63f.

Borshchevskaya, Anna. 2020. "Russia's Growing Interests in Libya." The Washington Institute. https://www.washingtoninstitute.org/policy-analysis/view/russias-growing-interests-in-libya.

Bulut, Firdevs. 2020. "'Turkey has sent Medical Aid to 150 Countries': President." Anadolu Agency, August 9, 2020. https://www.aa.com.tr/en/health/turkey-has-sent-medical-aid-to-150-countries-president/1936658.

Cook, Steven A. "How Erdogan made Turkey Authoritarian Again." *The Atlantic*, July 21, 2016. https://www.theatlantic.com/international/archive/2016/07/how-erdogan-made-turkey-authoritarian-again/492374/.

Donelli, Federico. 2019. "The Gulen Movement in Africa: From Turkish Transnational Asset to Anti-State Lobby." *Israel Journal of Foreign Affairs* 13, no. 1: 67–80. https://doi.org/10.1080/23739770.2019.1632588.

Eghbal, Media. 2009. "The Global Financial Crisis: Recession Bites into Western Europe." *Euromonitor International*, December 1, 2009. https://blog.euromonitor.com/the-global-financial-crisis-recession-bites-into-western-europe/.

Eyrice Tepeciklioglu, Elem. 2020. "Turkey's African Engagement: A Critical Analysis." In *Eurasia Goes to Africa*, 47–59. European Policy Centre and Friedrich Ebert Stiftung.

Handy, Nathaniel. 2018. "The Misak-i Milli and the Expanding Turkish Sphere of Influence in the Middle East." *Platform Peace & Justice*. http://www.platformpj.org/the-misak-i-milli-and-the-expanding-turkish-sphere-of-influence-in-the-middle-east/.

Hernandez, Michael. 2020. "US Air Force officially buying Turkey's F-35." Anadolu Agency, July 21, 2020. https://www.aa.com.tr/en/americas/us-air-force-officially-buying-turkeys-f-35/1917806.

Hessler, Uwe. 2020. "Why the Turkish Lira is in Free Fall." Deutsche Welle, August 17, 2020. https://www.dw.com/en/erdogans-credit-binge-fuels-lira-depreciation/a-54524078.

Inat, Kemal, Muhittin Ataman and Burhanettin Duran, eds. 2020. *Eastern Mediterranean and Turkey's Rights*. Ankara: SETA Publications.

Incesu, Can. n.d. "Towards the 3rd Turkey-Africa Partnership Summit." *Business Diplomacy*. Accessed October 2, 2020. https://businessdiplomacy.net/towards-the-3rd-turkey-africa-partnership-summit/.

Jalloh, Abu-Bakarr. 2016. "Erdogan's Bid to Close Gulen Schools in Africa Opposed." Deutsche Welle, August 12, 2016. https://www.dw.com/en/erdogans-bid-to-close-gulen-schools-in-africa-opposed/a-19470391.

Kamu Bulteni. 2019. "Cumhurbaskani Erdogan: Suriyeliler icin 37 Milyar Dolar Harcadik." June 29, 2019. https://www.kamubulteni.com/turkiye/cumhurbaskani-erdogan-suriyeliler-icin-37-milyar-dolar-harcadik-h11496.html.

Kucuk, Yusuf Kenan. 2020. "Turkey-Africa Relations: Setbacks amidst Advances." Africa Up Close, February 21, 2020. https://africaupclose.wilsoncenter.org/turkey-africa-relations-setbacks-amidst-advances/.

Mammadov, Rauf. 2020. "Russia and Turkey on Collision Course in Libya's Conflict." The New Arab, August 4, 2020. https://english.alaraby.co.uk/english/indepth/2020/8/4/russia-and-turkey-on-collision-course-in-libyas-conflict.

Mandiraci, Berkay. 2020. "Sharing the Burden: Revisiting the EU-Turkey Migration Deal." International Crisis Group. https://www.crisisgroup.org/europe-central-asia/western-europemediterranean/turkey/sharing-burden-revisiting-eu-turkey-migration-deal.

Mehmet, Fatih Hafiz. 2019. "EU: Sum Paid for Refugees in Turkey must be Clarified." Anadolu Agency, September 9, 2019. https://www.aa.com.tr/en/europe/eu-sum-paid-for-refugees-in-turkey-must-be-clarified/1578213.

Myers, Caysie N. 2016. "Turkey's Role in the Refugee Crisis." Turkish Heritage Organization. https://www.turkheritage.org/en/publications/factsheets/humanitarian-aid/turkeys-role-in-the-refugee-crisis-2493.

Ozpek, Burak Bilgehan. 2020. "Can Turkish-American Relations be Restored?" LSE (blog), March 25, 2020. https://blogs.lse.ac.uk/mec/2020/03/25/can-turkish-american-relations-be-restored/.

Pacaci Elitok, Secil. 2019. "Three Years on: An Evaluation of the EU-Turkey Refugee Deal." MiereKoc Working Papers. https://mirekoc.ku.edu.tr/wp-content/uploads/2019/04/Mirekoc_Elitok_2019_Report_ThreeYearsOn-AnEvaluationOfTheEU-TurkeyRefugeeDeal.pdf.

Pitel, Laura. 2020. "What is Behind Erdogan's Coronavirus Diplomacy?" *Financial Times*, April 30, 2020. https://www.ft.com/content/8602c2da-f1d0-4a78-b848-4c8bf8b9e311.

Pitel, Laura and Henry Foy. "Erdogan says Europe Must Back Turkey in Syria to end Refugee Crisis." *Financial Times*, March 4, 2020. https://www.ft.com/content/0ca9ee32-5e07-11ea-b0ab-339c2307bcd4.

Sezer Bilen, Seda. 2020. "Turkey's Strategic Play in Libya to Help Reap Economic Gains." Deutsche Welle, July 3, 2020. https://www.dw.com/en/turkeys-strategic-play-in-libya-to-help-reap-economic-gains/a-54037623.

Shinn, David. 2015. "Turkey's Engagement in Sub-Saharan Africa: Shifting Alliances and Strategic Diversification." Chatham House Research Paper.

Shokri, Omid. 2020. "Energy Resources and the New Great Game in the Eastern Mediterranean." The Jamestown Foundation, October 1, 2020. https://jamestown.org/program/energy-resources-and-the-new-great-game-in-the-eastern-mediterranean/.

The World Bank. 2020. "Turkey: Overview." https://www.worldbank.org/en/country/turkey/overview.

TRT World. 2020. "Turkey Ready to Address F-35 Issue with US." July 29, 2020. https://www.trtworld.com/turkey/turkey-ready-to-address-f-35-issue-with-us-38485.

Turkish Ministry of Foreign Affairs (MFA). n.d. "Relations Between Turkey-Syria." Accessed October 12, 2020. http://www.mfa.gov.tr/relations-between-turkey%E2%80%93syria.en.mfa.

Ulgen, Sinan. "A Weak Economy Won't Stop Turkey's Activist Foreign Policy." Foreign Policy, October 6, 2020. https://foreignpolicy.com/2020/10/06/a-weak-economy-wont-stop-turkeys-activist-foreign-policy/.

UNHCR. 2019. "Turkey Fact Sheet." https://reliefweb.int/sites/reliefweb.int/files/resources/UNHCR-Turkey-One-Pager-Fact-Sheet-Oct2019.pdf.

Ward, Alex. 2019. "How America's Relationship with Turkey Fell Apart." Vox, April 11, 2019. https://www.vox.com/world/2019/4/11/18292070/usa-turkey-trump-erdogan-s400.

Yilmaz, Zafer and Bryan S. Turner. 2019. "Turkey's Deepening Authoritarianism and the Fall of Electoral Democracy." *British Journal of Middle Eastern Studies* 4, no. 5: 691–698. https://doi.org/10.1080/13530194.2019.1642662.

Zanotti, Jim and Clayton Thomas. 2020. "Turkey: Background and U.S. Relations in Brief." Congressional Research Service. https://fas.org/sgp/crs/mideast/R44000.pdf.

Zorlu, Faruk. 2020. "Eastern Mediterranean Gas Forum 'far from reality'." Anadolu Agency, January 1, 2020. https://www.aa.com.tr/en/turkey/eastern-mediterranean-gas-forum-far-from-reality-/1705346.

Index

Addis Ababa 57, 139, **177**, 188, 227, 229
AFAD 70, 188, 190, 208, 222, 226, 232
African Development Bank (ADB) 65, 238
African Union (AU) 65, 68, 97, 149, 230, 240–241, 258
Anatolian tigers 5, 28, 95, 120, 168
Ankara consensus 76, 80–81, 83–84, 86
Arab spring 52, 98, 103, 131, 145, 155, 226
armored vehicles 131–132, 137–138
Aselsan 128, 130

Bandung: Conference 58, 77; spirit 267
bilateral trade 5, 112, 122, 241
BRICS 21, 79

Cairo 57, 131, 171–172, 176–177, 227–228, 259
covid-19 189, 244, 257–258.
civilization 30, 45–51, 219, 225, 251
colonial(ism): anti- 2, 86; expansion 1, 38, 42, 45, 49, non- 1, 25, 28, 266; past- 28, 112, 263, 266; rule 1, 42–43, 48–49, 57; Western 7, 25, 50, 85, 238
Cyprus issue 2, 19, 31, 60, 61, 64, 127, 153–154, 220
China 1–3, 9, 20, 22–23, 56, 69–70, 75, 78, 81, 83, 119–120, 122–123, 132, 146–147, 167, 175, 183, 186, 192–193, 226, 257, 266

Darfur 68, 135, 148, 153, 241, 253
Davutoglu, Ahmet 26, 50–51, 84, 133, 153, 155, 168–169, 178, 186, 221, 226–227, 232, 237–238, 246

development: aid 21, 24, 27–28, 31, 78, 81, 83, 184, 186–187, 238, 241; cooperation 7, 11–12, 75–76, 79–80, 86, 182–183, 185, 187, 192, 195, 208, 241
Diyanet 11, 28, 70, 189, 199–200, 203–211, 232, 265
Djibouti 51, 63, **66–67**, 121, *175*, 207–208, **228**
drones 129, 131–132, 137–138

East Africa 97, 207, 244, 246
Eastern Mediterranean 40, 52, 129, 131–132, 246, 258–260
Egypt 10, 38–43, 46, 51, 58–59, 62, 67–68, 97, 115, **117–118**, 121, 129, 130–131, 133, 138, 171, 173, 176, 201, 226–227, **228**, 253, 257, 259
Emerging power 1, 7, 19, 24, 25, 70, 76–79, 83–84, 120, 122, 124, 168–169, 182–183, 192–193, 201, 247, 257, 265
energy 5, 246, 259; input 247; plant 97; resources 23, 28, 259; sector 247–248; security 5, 78, 246
Equatorial Guinea 66, **67**, 228
Erdogan, Recep Tayyip 4–5, 29–30, 51–52, 65–68, 84–85, 112, 128, 130–132, 134, 137, 169, 174, 178, 187, 192, 208, 221–222, 226, 228, 232–233, 238, 242, 257
Ethiopia 57, 61, **65–67**, 68, 97, 132, 146, 172, **175**, 188, 190, 210, 218, 227–229, 233
European Union (EU) 102–103, 114,147–148, 153–156, 183–184, 186–187, 192, 204, 221, 238, 240, 258, 260
External partners 8, 111, 120, 263

Index

foreign policy activism 31, 101, 111, 209
France 59–60, 137, 219.
free trade agreement (FTA) 68, 97, 121–124
French 38, 41–43, 48–49, 59–60, 176, 222
Front de Libération Nationale (FLN) 59

geopolitical 3–4, 39, 52, 238, 240–241, 243, 246, 249, 253
geostrategic 4, 6, 57, 111, 201
global North 84
global South 8, 75–76, 79, 81, 86–87, 146, 182, 238, 264
Government of National Accord (GNA) 69, 131–132, 259
group of 77 (G77) 77
Gul, Abdullah 6, **67**, 68–69, 112, 221, 226, 228, 230, 246
Gulen, Fethullah 200, 242, 258; affiliated schools 169, 173–174, 247; affiliated organizations 211, 230; movement (network) 11, 13, 70, 97, 168–172, 174, 176 178, 200, 204, 210, 231, 242, 261–262, 265, 267; as terrorist organization (FETO) 176, 200, 231;
Gulf of Aden 153, 240

hard power 9, 10, 98, 129, 133, 134, 262, 264, 267
Havelsan 128, 130
Horn of Africa 1, 10, 70, 133–135, 201, 208, 239–241, 246, 253
humanitarian: actor 120, 169, 186; aid and assistance 7, 12, 20, 25, 27, 56, 64, 85, 112–113, 119–120, 169, 183, 186–187, 189–190, 192–194,206, 208–209, 232, 239, 241, 248, 253, 261, 265, 268; campaign 151, 232; crisis 82, 206, 232, 260; engagement 12, 85, 217, 231; diplomacy 27, 85, 186, 193, 210; intervention 79, **184**; NGOs 11, 183, 205, 209, 241; power 11, 195

International Monetary Fund (IMF) 21–22, 85, 94, 123
Islamic identity 1, 85, 112
Islamic solidarity 208, 211

Kenya 61, **66–67**, 69, 132, 172, **177**, 210, 227, **229**, 244–245, 249, 261
Kizilay/KIZILAY (Turkish Red Crescent) 70, 189, 208, 232

Liberia 66, 68, 135, 241
Libya 47, 52, 56, **67**, 68–69, 71, 87, 115, **117–118**, 121, 129–132, 138, 153, 173, **177**, 208, 226–227, **229**, 233, 241, 246, 259, 264, 267, -n crisis/conflict 10, 13, 69, 246, 259–260; -n civil war 31–233
Libyan National Army (LNA) 69

Maarif Foundation 10, 70, 169–170, 174–175, 222, 226, 252–253, 261, 265, 267
mediation 5, 82, 111, 145, 186
military: bases/facilities 9–10, 127, 133, 138, 194, 246, 253, 264, 267; capability/capacity/power 21, 23, 31, 95, 129, 134, 246; equipment 68–69, 128, 133, 137, 259; strategy 10, 127, 264; operation 98, 148, 153
Mogadishu *see* Somalia
Morocco 60, 67–68, 97, 115, **117–118**, 121, 171, 173, 226, 227, **229**, 244–245, 249
multilateral(-ism) 21–23, 77, 84, 144, 159, 182, 193–194, 221
MUSIAD 63, 98, 101–102, 121, 168, 190, 230, 241
Muslim countries 85, 201, 206, 208, 211, 238, 253

nation branding 191, 217–219, 227
neo-colonialism 112, 154, 238
neo-Ottomanism 50–51, 84, 86, 156, 238, 242
New International Economic Order (NIEO) 77
Nigeria 42, 58, 61, 63, **66–67**, 97, 136–137, 172–173, **177**, 218, 225, 227–228, **229**, 261
Non-Aligned Movement (NAM) 58, 77, 85
national security 10, 57, 127, 129–130, 133–134, 260, 267
national interest 19, 21, 71, 78, 202, 219, 260, 267

official development assistance (ODA) 75, 182–185, 187
Organization of Economic Cooperation and Development (OECD) 24, 80, 83, 186, 191–193
Organization of Islamic Cooperation (OIC) 83, 205
Ottoman Empire 1, 7, 19, 38–39, 41–43, 47, 51–52, 57, 86, 114, 119, 208, 263

Index

peacebuilding 7, 10, 21, 24–25, 29, 31, 81, 152, 267–268
peacekeeping: efforts 10, 265; missions 65, 68, 135, 185, 238, 241 operations 10, 135, 144, 148, 157, 185, 244, **250–251**, 264–265
piracy 41, 135, 264
proactive foreign policy 147, 156, 167, 227
public diplomacy: actors 178; efforts 10–11, 168, 170, 177; initiatives 12, 168, 178; toolkit 167–168, 177

Red Sea 40–41, 134
religious diplomacy 20, 27, 199–202, 206, 211, 265, 268
Roketsan 128, 130

slave trade 26, 39, 41, 50, 53, 263
slavery 52, 85, 267
soft power: instruments and tools 8, 10, 56, 109, 185, 217–218, 226–227, 231, 233, 264, 267; investment 5, 10, 265; religious 199–202; sources 25, 217, 227, 249
Somalia 9–10, 29–31, 61–62, **66–67**, 68–69, 81–83, 132–134, 136–138, 146, 148–153, 155, 157, 168–169, 171, 173, **175–177**, 185, 187–191, 194, 207–210, 218, 226, **229**, 232, 240–241, 246, 253, 261, 264, 267
South Africa 20, 23, 38, 44, 48, 65, **66–67**, 68, 93, 97, 104, 115, **117**, 121–122, 132, 146, 171–172, **177**, 189, 200, 208, 227, **229**, 244–245, 247, 249, 261
South-South Cooperation (SSC) 8, 25, 29, 76–84, 86, 186
state-building 9, 29, 82
strategic depth 168, 170, 238, 246, 252
Suakin 9, 40, 133–134, 241, 246, 253
Sub-Saharan Africa (SSA) 5, 41, 65–66, 82–83, 85, 93, 97, 110, 115, 123, 127, 129–133, 137–138, 167, 194, 208, 210, 226–227, 230–231, 237–238, 249, 252, 261

Tunisia 38–43, 45, 47–48, 60, 97, 115, **116**, 121, 129, 131–132, 138, 171, 227, **229**
Turkish Aerospace Industries (TAI) 128–131
Turkish Armed Forces (TAF) 69, 127, 130, 134–135, 148
Turkish Cooperation and Coordination Agency (TIKA) 11, 28, 63, 70, 82, 132, 185, 187–190, 194, 200, 203–205, 208–210, 232–233, 241, 265
Turkish Radio and Television (TRT) 148, 169–170, 176–177, 222, 226, 228, 233, 258
Turkiye Diyanet Vakfi (Turkish Diyanet Foundation: TDV) *see* Diyanet
TUSIAD 5, 99, 101–103, 121, 230
TUSKON 97–98, 101–102, 168–169, 190, 230–231, 241, 261

United Nations Conference on Trade and Development (UNCTAD) 77
United Nations General Assembly (UNGA) 60–61, 77
United Nations Security Council (UNSC) 6, 21–22, 30, 65–66, 81, 85, 146–147, 149–150, 190, 240

Virtuous power 192, 238, 252

Washington consensus 95
West Africa 97, 132, 135–136, 207, 219, 244
World Bank 21–22, 85, 94, 262

YEE (Yunus Emre Enstitusu/Institute) 10, 69, 168, 170–172, 222, 226, 265
YTB (Presidency For Turks Abroad and Related Communities) 10, 69, 168, 170, 173, 265

Printed in the United States
by Baker & Taylor Publisher Services